# New Jersey

WESTHOLME STATE MILITARY HISTORY SERIES

# New Jersey
## A Military History

### The Third State of the Union

## Joseph G. Bilby

WESTHOLME
Yardley

Westholme Publishing, LLC
904 Edgewood Road
Yardley, Pennsylvania 19067
Visit our Web site at www.westholmepublishing.com


ISBN: 978-1-59416-277-0

Printed in the United States of America

# Contents

This book is dedicated to the memory of my beloved wife, Patricia Ann Ziegler Bilby, to my children, Katherine, Margaret, and John and their spouses, Eric, Jarrett, and Carol, and their children, Anna, Angelica, and Joseph, as well as to the memory of Jerseymen Sergeant John Ziegler, US Army Air Force, 1942–1945, his wife, Frances Whelan, and Private first class Samuel Bilby, US Army artillery, 1943–1946, and his wife Margaret Geoghegan, and all who came before.

# List of Maps

# Introduction

The military history of New Jersey, from New Netherland's struggles with the Lenape through colonial wars of empire to twenty-first century conflicts in Iraq and Afghanistan, is far more extensive and significant than most of the state's modern residents realize, and although a brief history of the state's military affairs was published by the New Jersey Historical Commission in 1991, it was, by intent and definition, not a detailed account.

New Jersey justly earned the title "Crossroads of the Revolution" as a major combat theater in the War for Independence, and made a significant contribution to the Union victory in the Civil War as well. The state's frontier position on the Atlantic Coast brought war to the home front in 1812, 1918, and 1942. New Jersey was also the site of Bergen County's Camp Merritt, which processed most of the American soldiers who went overseas in World War I, Fort Dix, a major training base, and Fort Monmouth, a significant center for military technology development in the twentieth century.

Over the centuries, New Jersey transitioned from an agricultural state into a major industrial one, and the nation's periodic conflicts accelerated that transition. During the Civil War the state was a major manufacturing center for railroad engines, uniforms, and leather goods, and the first workable submarine, sold to the Navy in 1900, was developed in New Jersey. In World War I, New Jersey produced more munitions than any other state. World War II added ships, aircraft, and parachutes to the list as the Garden State became a vital gear in the engine of the "Arsenal of Democracy."

Over more than 350 years as a colony and state, hundreds of thousands of New Jersey residents have served in regular armed forces, militia, and National Guard units or in direct support of those organizations. New Jerseyans in the military included Sergeant William Mc-Crackan of Somerset County, a 1757 prisoner of war who ended up in France, General "Scotch Willie" Maxwell of Sussex County, an unappreciated Revolutionary War master tactician, First Sergeant George Ashby of Allentown, of Company H, 45th United States Colored Infantry, the state's last surviving Civil War veteran, Clara Maas of Newark, a nurse who sacrificed her life in the effort to eradicate Yellow Fever, Captain William J. Reddan, who led his company into hell during the Meuse-Argonne offensive in 1918, and Medal of Honor winner John Basilone, whose sense of duty and honor led him to return to combat and death.

This book is an attempt to tell the long, diverse, and sometimes complicated story of New Jersey's citizens and their significant and continuing role in their country's defense.

# 1. New Jersey's Native People and Early European Contact

Before the coming of the Europeans, the Lenape, New Jersey's Native American people, were inhabitants of the larger homeland of Lenapehoking, a territory covering portions of several modern states, including New York, Maryland, Pennsylvania, and Delaware as well as New Jersey. The Lenape were members of the Munsee (north) and Unami (central and south) language subgroups. As far as modern archeologists can estimate, they and their forebears had been residents of Lenapehoking for up to 12,000 years. Along with practicing a subsistence level agriculture producing corn, beans, and squash, the Lenape hunted game, including white-tailed deer, elk, and even bison, as well as birds and small mammals. They also foraged for nuts and berries and fished in inlets, bays, and rivers. Shellfish, high on the Lenape list of favorite foods, were eaten fresh or dried and were, in addition, a source of tools made from their shells. Clam shells were also the components of a money-like product called wampum, as well as personal jewelry. Middens, consisting of large piles of oyster shells, have been discovered at many sites along the New Jersey coast, from Raritan Bay to Cape May,

and survived as evidence of industrious Indian shell fishermen for many years, until European colonists and their descendants began to use them as construction and road paving material. Other middens were buried during twentieth-century building projects.[1]

The original meaning of the word "Lenape," which has slight variant pronunciations in Munsee and Unami, has been variously interpreted and disputed over the years. Late Seton Hall University archeologist Herbert Kraft, the leading expert on New Jersey's Indians, wrote that it might have several meanings, including "real person," or "men of the same nation." The Lenape were not a "nation" in the European sense of the word, but an aggregation of small bands of connected families with a similar language, although Unami and Munsee speakers were not necessarily completely intelligible to each other. A third dialect among the Lenape, Unalachtigo, an offshoot of Unami used by Lenape in northeast Pennsylvania, was apparently not easily accessible to the other two. Lenape political structure was basic and decentralized. Each band had a nominal male (and rarely, a female) "chief," or

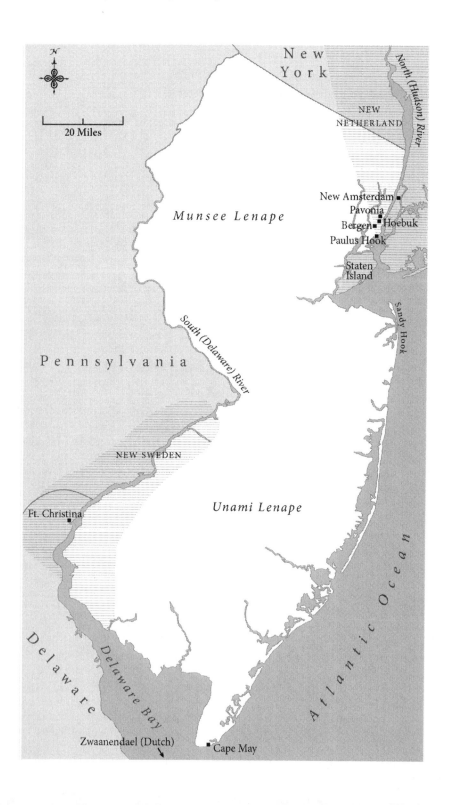

Lenape artifacts, including tools, projectile points, and pottery shards discovered in Jackson Township, New Jersey, in the 1940s.

*sakima* of matrilineal descent, but the position carried no special privilege, and decisions—usually limited to mediating civil disputes—were subject to consensus approval by an informal council of elders.[2]

Contrary to the romantic beliefs of some modern Americans, ecological exploitation was far from unknown among Native Americans prior to the advent of the Europeans, and New Jersey's Lenape, like other Indians, had no comprehensive concept of maintaining the balance of nature or practicing conservation in the current sense. They exploited what they could in order to survive, and their methods included setting fires to drive game and clear land for planting. Due to the small indigenous population of Lenapehoking, however, environmental damage was very limited and healed fairly rapidly. In many cases, albeit unknown to those who set them, the aftermath of forest fires actually had a beneficial effect on both plant life and animals. Likewise, the limited number of warriors available, coupled with local feuds—Lenape in central New Jersey, for example, reputedly detested those living on Manhattan Island—between bands, and an unsophisticated political structure unable to marshal large armies, severely limited overall Lenape war-making capability. Because of this, rais-

ing significant military organizations and engaging in large scale combat involving heavy casualties and widespread destruction were impossible. One European observer noted that "it is a great fight where seven or eight is slain." This does not mean that inter-band violence did not occur, as evidenced by the discovery, in 1895, of a Staten Island burial in which the deceased was apparently shot by thirty-three arrows, but it was limited in scope. Kraft reported that "very few" excavated Lenape burials "show evidence of warfare or death through violence." We have no written or even traditional anecdotal record of just what these conflicts were about, but squabbles over hunting and fishing territories, or personal enmity based on some sort of grudge, can be assumed.[3]

At the time of European contact, the chief Lenape weapon was the "self-bow," which, although similar in length, contrasted unfavorably in power with the English longbow, as well as the composite or laminate bow used by other Native Americans. Hand-to-hand combat weapons included war clubs of various types. A ball headed club, probably Lenape, from the New Sweden colony along the Delaware River, survives in Skokloster Castle in Sweden. Arrowheads and knives were chipped from flint at the time of first contact between natives and

Europeans. Lenape tactics were simple, and limited to ambushes and surprise raids on rival groups. The Lenape code required that killings in war or personal feuds be avenged, but the continual spiral of violence that this belief suggests could be, and usually was, short-circuited by negotiations and payments to relatives of the deceased. Interestingly, in these settlements, the lives of women were apparently accounted more important than those of men. These Lenape concepts of war and peace, as well as property ownership, would change dramatically with the arrival of Europeans in Lenapehoking.[4]

### FIRST EUROPEAN CONTACT

The first known European to sail along the present New Jersey shore was Giovanni de Verrazano, an Italian employed by King Francis I of France with orders to find a passage through America to East Asia. In the spring of 1524, Verrazano reached the coast of today's North Carolina, and then headed north, vainly seeking the nonexistent passage. As the Native Americans along the shore of Lenapehoking observed Verrazano's ship, *La Dauphine*, glide by, it is doubtful that they remotely anticipated what was in store for them and their descendants over the next two centuries. One thing that can be said for sure, however, is that they were not afraid of the Europeans. When *La Dauphine* rounded Sandy Hook into Raritan Bay, which Verrazano called Santa Margarita, large numbers of Lenape rushed down to the shore with great excitement, launching canoes to get a closer look at the white men. Prevailing winds prevented a landing, however, postponing a face-to-face meeting between Lenape and Europeans. There is no existing evidence of any closer en-

Portrait of a Native American from Virginia by Wenceslaus Hollar, 1645. While exploring both sides of Delaware Bay, the Dutch encountered Indians from a variety of tribes.

counters between the two cultures for the rest of the sixteenth century, although one or more are certainly possible, even probable, considering that a number of European fishermen and explorers sailed into American waters over those years.[5]

The next verifiable contact between the Lenape and Europeans in what is now New Jersey occurred when Henry Hudson, an Englishman exploring on behalf of the Dutch, entered Raritan Bay in 1609. The Dutch had created an independent state from what had been an obscure province of Spain and became the Netherlands, a rising maritime power in the seventeenth century world. Hudson, yet another explorer seeking the elusive "Northwest Passage" to East Asia, became the first European to make documented contact with the Lenape of present-day New Jersey. As in 1524, the Indians demonstrated no fear of their visitors, but on this occasion what began as a series of seemingly innocuous trading opportunities ended badly. The lack of trust, cultural insensitivity, bullying, and outright theft that Hudson's men displayed during a number of forays into Raritan and New York Bays resulted in several deadly incidents, including one in which a sailor was killed when hit in the throat by a flint-tipped arrow, and another in which eight or ten Lenape were blown out of the water and several canoes sunk by small arms and cannon fire from Hudson's ship, the *Half Moon*. The unfortunate fatality, one John Colman, was reportedly buried on Sandy Hook, the first recorded European combat casualty suffered in today's New Jersey. Likewise, the unnamed Lenape sprayed with fire from Hudson's ship were the first New Jerseyans documented as combat casualties. Hudson had more luck trading farther up the river that today bears his name, where he swapped some metal hatchets and hoes, whiskey and wine for beaver pelts, corn, and tobacco.[6]

## NEW NETHERLAND

Although Hudson's expedition was deemed a failure since he did not discover a northwest passage, the Englishman's initial success in trading trinkets and liquor for valuable furs with the natives inspired Dutch merchants to follow in his wake. Their voyages produced more detailed maps of the New Jersey coastline, particularly from Raritan Bay north into the North (today's Hudson) River. In addition to maps, these traders created a culture of chaotic cutthroat business practices, which led the directors of the Netherlands States General, in

an attempt to establish some sort of order, to charter the United New Netherland Company. The States General allowed the company to stake a trading monopoly claim to mid-Atlantic North America, which gained the name New Netherland. In contrast to those who established English colonies to the north and south, the New Netherland Company was more interested in creating fur trading posts than permanent colonial settlements. Among the company's more lasting sites was one established in 1614 at today's Albany, New York, in order to do business with the Mohawks, a tribe of the powerful and politically sophisticated Iroquois Confederacy who had displaced the Mahicans in the area, and "Fort Manhattes," an earthwork defensive position located on Manhattan Island. The Dutch may also have built a blockhouse on the site of today's Jersey City in the same year. New Netherland, thinly populated throughout its brief history, extended at one time or another over parts of the current states of Connecticut, New York, New Jersey, Pennsylvania, Delaware, and Maryland. The New Netherland Company presence in the modern state of New Jersey was limited to a few fur trading stations across the river from Manhattan and along the lower Delaware River, where the Dutch came in contact with English and Swedish traders on the same mission. The outposts established as part of these early mercantile efforts were subsequently abandoned with the expiration of the company's monopoly in 1618 and its disbandment in 1621, but they were later rebuilt in the 1630s.[7]

## DUTCH WEST INDIA COMPANY

A return to trade wars following the end of the New Netherland Company's control of the fur franchise led the States General to charter a successor monopoly, the Dutch West India Company, which proved a more enduring organization. Along with reestablishing some of the earlier trading posts, in 1624 the West India Company founded genuine settlements on Manhattan Island, including the colony's capital, New Amsterdam, and at Fort Orange (Albany), as well as along the Connecticut River to the north, and south on the Delaware River at the site of today's Burlington, New Jersey. The settlements were intended to provide support and supplies to the trading posts. Many of the New Netherland settlers were not, strictly speaking, entirely "Dutch" as the ethnic term is understood today. The first contingent were Walloons, a French-speaking minority from what is now Belgium, who were later supplemented by refugee French Protestant Huguenots and other disparate groups fleeing religious wars and persecution in Europe. As an incentive to settlement, the West India Company promised free transportation and land to anyone who would agree to reside in New Netherland for at least six years. The settlers were expected to practice the Calvinist "Reformed" religion and perform work for the company, including building fortifications and serving in a military capacity against other Europeans or natives when called on, although the latter duty and any specific military training to fulfill it were not defined. Following their six-year obligation, settlers were free to sell their property and return to Europe or remain in the colony. Due to the company's settler recruiting demographics, New Netherland became an extremely diverse place. By one account, in 1643 there were eighteen different languages in use in New Amsterdam.[8]

As New Netherland began to assume a degree of permanence, especially in the environs of Manhattan, the West India Company made efforts to expand the production of enough locally produced food to make its North American colony totally self-sufficient. The original settlers' subsistence agricultural practices were not enough to feed a growing population so the company granted "patroonships," or large plots of land along the North River up to Fort Orange to wealthy merchants, who were, in turn, obligated to establish farming estates on the grants. Patroon Michiel Reyniersz Pauw received such a grant across the river from New Amsterdam in 1630, with his land stretching from modern Staten Island to Hoboken. Although Pauw never left the Netherlands, his agent, Cornelius Van Vorst, established a farm or "bouwerie," in Pavonia, within the boundaries of today's Jersey City, apparently on Harsimus Cove. Other homesteads were established on Paulus Hook, the closest point to New Amsterdam across the river. Pavonia was the first permanent European settlement in modern day New Jersey. Van Vorst hedged his bets, locating at a strategic spot where Lenape fur traders crossed the river to New Amsterdam, thus adding trading to his agricultural efforts.[9]

Few settlers followed Van Vorst across the North River, and Pavonia reverted to the West India Company's control, although the pioneering Dutchman remained on his own bouwerie until his death in 1683. The company rented some land to commuting farmers from New Amsterdam and leased bouweries to some permanent settlers who moved across the river to combine farming with fur trading. Pavonia, the first substantial European settlement in modern-day

New Jersey, grew slowly until a tragic turn of events dramatically reversed the process. Although initial Dutch relations with the Lenape had been cordial, increased settlement amplified tensions, as European domestic animals wandered through Indian fields rooting up maize and bean crops. Lenape dogs harassed the trespassing pigs and cattle, and trade cheating by the Dutch and petty theft by the Indians escalated. Given the attitude of the otherwise tolerant Dutch toward Native Americans—that they were "savage and wild" and must give way to a superior European civilization—war was perhaps inevitable, but it was New Netherland director general Willem Kieft who dramatically accelerated the downward spiral in relations following his arrival at New Amsterdam in 1637.[10]

Early in his tenure, Kieft ordered an attack on a band of Raritan Lenape for allegedly stealing pigs on Staten Island, a crime of which they proved innocent. He subsequently levied a tax on local Native Americans and threatened to attack them if it was not paid. All of these activities may well have been part of a program to foment a large scale conflict which Kieft apparently had no doubt he would win. The final act in his provocation program occurred over the winter of 1642–1643. A battered band of Wiechquaeskeck Lenape, their village north of Manhattan destroyed by an attack perpetrated by either Mohawk or Mahican Indians armed with firearms most likely supplied by the English or Dutch, fled to New Amsterdam and then crossed the North River to the vicinity of Pavonia, where they sought refuge with the local Hackensack band. (The Dutch were very reluctant to supply the Native Americans of Lenapehoking with guns, although they freely sold them to the

Mohawks who brought furs to Fort Orange up the river.)

On February 23, 1643, Kieft, over the protest of some of the influential citizens of New Amsterdam, ordered his soldiers to conduct an unprovoked surprise night attack on the Hackensack village and massacre its inhabitants, while simultaneously conducting a raid on an Indian band camped at Corlaer's Hook on the East River. David Pieterz de Vries, a Dutchman who had opposed Kieft's policies and observed the Pavonia attack from New Amsterdam, recalled: "I heard a great shrieking . . . and I looked over to Pavonia. Saw nothing but firing, and heard the shrieks of the savages murdered in their sleep." Kieft's troops indiscriminately killed men, women, and children. Some of the latter, according to De Vries, were "hacked to pieces in the presence of the parents, and the pieces thrown into the fire and in the water. " De Vries wrote that some soldiers brought human heads back across the river as trophies. Another colonist described the events as "a disgrace to our nation." A recent writer has concluded that De Vries, who was dedicated to getting Kieft removed from office, "may have exaggerated the horrors," but concedes that it was indeed a disgraceful affair, with, as in most wars, unforeseen consequences accruing to those who initiated it.[11]

## NEW NETHERLAND COMPANY SOLDIERS

The New Netherland Company "army" that Kieft fielded against the local native population was a rather rag-tag organization. The colony's first "regular" troops, known as "sea soldiers" due to their assignment to posts in faraway colonies, were one-year contract employees of the West India Company. Around fifty of them arrived in New Amsterdam in 1633 to take up residence at the town's fort, which had been enhanced by a blockhouse and wooden palisade. Two thirds of these soldiers were apparently homeless Germans who drifted into the Netherlands seeking work, although some were English, French, or Scandinavian. They were described as "men picked up with no special regard for character, experience or ability," and commanded by "commercial and military adventurers." On arrival in Amsterdam these migrants were given food and shelter by innkeepers known as *zielverkopers* or "sellers of souls" who, when either the East or West India Company put out a call for soldiers or sailors, produced them. A recruit was enlisted as either a common soldier for eight or nine guilders a month or an *adelborst*, or "cadet," a junior noncommissioned officer rank, at ten guilders a month (by 1644 soldiers were paid thirteen guilders and cadets fifteen guilders a month) and received a two-month advance on his salary, paid to his host for room and board. Some *zielverkopers* attached the men's future salaries as well.[12]

The Company soldiers were not issued uniforms. Officers were authorized to wear orange sashes to denote their rank, although one source believes that these insignias were only worn on special occasions. Since they were discharged at the end of their one-year commitment and allowed to take up land as settlers, the training these men received appears to have been minimal and the attention they paid to their military duties was probably not as assiduous as it could have been. Despite its lackluster garrison, usually between forty and fifty men, the New Amsterdam fort gradually expanded, however, with eventual dimen-

sions of 250 by 300 feet, enclosing a barracks and guardhouse, under Kieft's predecessor Wouter Ban Twiller, whose home was also erected within the walls. The command structure of the garrison is uncertain, but appears to have been limited to company grade officers. There were no staff officer positions and only one gunner for the fort's cannon, which would apparently be manned, in an emergency, by the infantry under his instruction. Seven other small, even more loosely organized garrisons were established at intermittently occupied forts throughout the colony, including along the South (Delaware) River in today's New Jersey, although thinly settled Pavonia was never granted a fort. At its height, in 1664, the garrison of all the Dutch New Netherland posts numbered between 250 and 300 men, 180 of them in New Amsterdam. Kieft's maximum available force of full time soldiers two decades earlier was significantly smaller.[13]

Detailed documentation on the nature of the arms supplied the "sea soldiers" is lacking, but they apparently were issued both muskets and swords, as evidenced by the descriptions of the wounds inflicted on the Pavonia casualties. It appears that muskets using the matchlock ignition system, in which the gun was fired by squeezing a bar or trigger that lowered a length of glowing potassium nitrate soaked "match cord" into a pan of priming powder to ignite the main charge, were the most common firearms among the early settlers of New Netherland in 1624, although more modern wheel lock and flintlock ignition system guns were present among privately owned arms brought by later colonists. The matchlock survived in Europe as an inexpensive weapon to equip large armies to the end of the seventeenth century, but the firearm of choice for individual colonists, who had significantly different small arms requirements than their European cousins, became the wheel lock or flintlock, the latter also known as a "firelock." These systems, using pyrites or flint to create sparks to ignite the main charge rather than a glowing match cord, were, when properly handled, less susceptible to the vagaries of weather than the matchlock and could be more rapidly reloaded.[14]

Harold Peterson, an authority on American colonial small arms and artillery, notes, however, that "the Dutch leaders, unlike those in the English colonies, clung tenaciously to the older forms [matchlocks] for military use," at least through the 1650s. Peterson reports that by 1655 the New Amsterdam government, in a request to the West India Company for more troops, requested that half be armed with wheel locks and the other half with flintlocks; a year later the colony asked that a fort garrison be armed half with matchlocks and half with wheel or flint lock weapons. This arms ratio seems to have been a Dutch policy, as the 150-man force Peter Stuyvesant mustered in 1656 to capture the Swedish settlements on the Delaware River was armed with a similar mix of flint and match. Ironically the same officials requested that the personal arms of all new civilian settlers be restricted to matchlocks, apparently out of fear that they might trade or lose more modern arms through theft to the local Lenape. These restrictions did not affect a lively Dutch gun trade with the Iroquois through Fort Orange, however, where flintlocks were readily exchanged for furs. By 1650, many Lenape, acting as middlemen in the fur trade, secured "firelocks and hatchets," and quickly learned how to use them. According to one account: "They are exceedingly fond

A Dutch soldier prepares to fire his matchlock musket.

of guns, sparing no expense for them; and they are [so] skillful in the use of them that they surpass many Christians."[15]

The West India Company apparently intended its inadequate little army to be supplemented by militiamen, or at least armed citizens. In a prelude to the Second Amendment to the United States Constitution, all immigrants entering New Netherland were required to bring personally owned firearms with them, but the colony seems to have survived without a formal militia. In 1640, the declared *Freedoms and Exemptions* formally required "all colonists, both free men and servants" to defend the colony. Kieft's increasingly aggressive and provocative attitude towards the Lenape, however, led to fear of Indian retaliation that resulted in the passage of a formal militia law by the New Amsterdam Council, obligating all residents of the town to provide themselves with arms and muster at a particular location in case they were needed for an emergency. There is no indication that this legislation produced an effective military organization, nor any evidence that the law had any force across the North River in today's New Jersey.[16]

KIEFT'S WAR

David De Vries had led a force of 100 men, presumably militiamen, against the Raritans following the swine killing incident of 1640. By his account the men were more an armed mob "that wished to kill and plunder" than a military organization. De Vries appears to have had little control over his men and learned afterward that some of them "tortured the [Raritan] chief's brother in his private parts with a piece of split wood." As Kieft's massacre led to all-out war with the Lenape, the necessity of a more disciplined backup force to the "sea soldiers" became apparent. The "Burgher Guard" or "Burgher Militia," that grew out of the 1640 law was an organization of substantial citizens, drawn from the ranks of merchants and other tradesmen in New Amsterdam, who were expected to provide their own arms and serve under the command of trade guild leaders acting as officers. The Burgher Guard at Albany apparently preferred to contract out defense to Iroquois mercenaries. This organization did not, needless to say, guarantee military efficiency or competence on the part of its members. A lesser force, the *shutterji*, or citizens' militia, was composed of men further down the social scale and was considered, at least on paper, as a backup for the Burgher Guard. As Native Americans

sought revenge for the Pavonia massacre, what passed for a military organization in New Netherland, however, collapsed.[17]

Neither the regular troops nor militia were able to handle the retribution visited by the Lenape in what came to be called "Kieft's War," which was criticized by much of the New Netherland population as much on rational grounds as moral ones. Dramatically outnumbered by the Indians, most settlers living outside the walls of Fort Amsterdam did not look forward to an Indian war. Likewise, Dutch fur traders who would be cut off from their sources were not enthusiastic supporters of Kieft's ethnic cleansing campaign. Although the colony's government continued to placate the powerful Mohawks, that policy had little benefit for settlers living on Manhattan Island and Pavonia. The worst came to pass. The Lenape, in keeping with their traditional organization patterns, did not form a large army, but disparate bands, realizing that they were in an unavoidable struggle to preserve Lenapehoking, united in an unprecedented series of attacks on New Netherland.[18]

Pavonia was lightly settled—a 1639 map reveals only eight houses and no fortifications—and the Dutch settlers there, who appear to have been poorly armed and/or militarily unorganized, were killed or fled to New Amsterdam, where they eked out an existence as impoverished refugees as escalating violence left New Netherland only a tiny toehold on the west bank of the North River. The war spread rapidly across the colony in the opening act in an off and on again struggle that would endure through 1664. Word of Kieft's treacherous attack traveled rapidly along the Lenape grapevine, and Aert Theunisen, trading along the Navesink River to the south, was killed by local Indians seeking

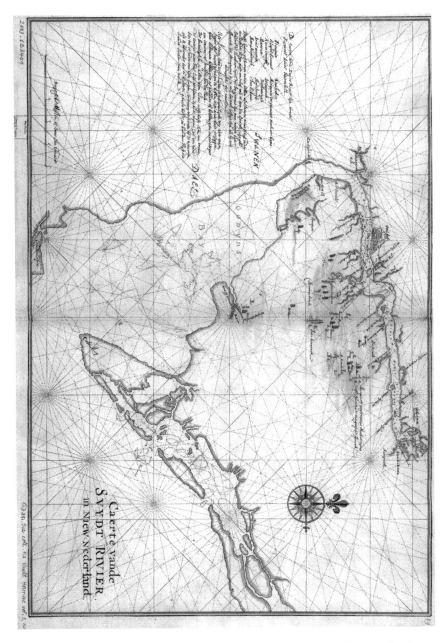

A circa 1639 Dutch map of New Netherlands and Delaware Bay showing the short-lived colony of Zwaanendael that was located near modern Lewes, Delaware, across the bay from New Jersey.

revenge for the massacre of their brothers to the north. As many as 1,500 warriors from various bands descended on Manhattan Island, killing a number of settlers and driving the others behind the walls of New Amsterdam. Many fled the colony altogether.[19]

The inept Kieft quickly realized he had bitten off far more than he could chew, and turned to professional Indian fighters from outside New Netherland. He had previously encouraged the spillover population of New England to settle in areas claimed by the Dutch, including Long Island and parts of today's Connecticut; some English settlers, among them Protestant religious refugees from the strictures of Massachusetts Puritanism, had even ended up in New Amsterdam itself. A nominal oath to the Netherland States General was the only requirement for admission to the colony. One of these settlers was prominent religious dissenter Anne Hutchinson, who, exiled from the Massachusetts Bay Colony along with much of her family, settled in one of the governor's "buffer zones" and lost her life to Indian raiders due to Kieft's blundering.[20]

Kieft decided to make use of the English as potential emergency allies, and contracted with Connecticut captain John Underhill, who raised a 120-man force among English settlers on Long Island. The ruthless Underhill had combat command experience in the bloody Pequot War, and had made Indian massacres his trademark. He and his mercenaries surrounded a Lenape village in current Westchester County, New York, and proceeded to slaughter virtually all of the 180 inhabitants. Underhill's men set dwellings afire and tossed those who tried to escape back into the flames in a reenactment of the 1637 Missistuk (Mystic) Connecticut massacre perpetrated upon the Pequot in which the captain had been a major participant. Underhill provided the war-making expertise the Dutch lacked, and turned the military situation around. Both sides agreed to an uneasy truce in August 1645, but in the wake of his disastrous policies, combined with complaints about his dictatorial actions by prominent citizens of New Amsterdam, Kieft was recalled to the Netherlands to explain his actions. He died in 1647 in a shipwreck on the way home.[21]

## PETER STUYVESANT

Kieft was replaced by the more efficient, if similarly dictatorial, Peter Stuyvesant. Under Stuyvesant's administration Dutch settlements in the area of modern Hudson County slowly began to expand again, and new communities were established at Communipaw and Paulus Hook. Stuyvesant, with more military experience than Kieft, attempted to muster the militia and inspect both troops and arms. The governor discovered to his dismay that there were not even enough arms available to supply the Burgher Guard, much less a common militia. Stuyvesant ordered firearms issued from Fort Amsterdam, but, a year later, mustered the Guard without their weapons, as he was apparently apprehensive that an unhappy armed citizenry might attempt to overthrow his rule. As a result of citizen complaints to the Company, armed Burgher Guard musters resumed, but muskets were numbered and stamped with the West India Company mark, ostensibly to trace any illegally sold to Indians. When a Burgher Guard captain who had traveled to the Netherlands to testify against Stuyvesant's iron rule returned with one hundred Company issued muskets for

Peter Stuyvesant (1610–1672), the last director-general of the colony of New Netherland.

his men in 1650, Stuyvesant seized them and allegedly sold some to the Indians himself. Thus began the twisted tale of "gun control" in New York and New Jersey, a perennially failed effort to allegedly keep firearms out of the hands of certain people deemed unreliable by the authorities. Subsequent Indian "troubles" and conflict with English settlers on Long Island and in Connecticut, including the recently employed belligerent Captain Underhill, resulted in the Burgher Guard finally being called out to fill a military role in 1653, although no combat occurred.[22]

NEW SWEDEN

While the Dutch were engaged in colony building in stops and starts along the banks of the North River, the Swedes, albeit with largely Dutch financing, began to establish rival settlements along the South River. Beginning in 1638, "New Sweden," established, like New Netherland, as a private trading enterprise

under the leadership of former New Netherland director Peter Minuet, grew into a web of scattered trading posts in the present-day states of New Jersey, Pennsylvania, and Delaware. As entrepreneurship faltered, then failed, the Swedish government took over the colony in 1642, but never invested enough capital or manpower to establish a serious American foothold. Many of the settlers in New Sweden were actually ethnic Finns, who are credited with introducing the log cabin to America.

New Sweden's initial settlement at Fort Christina (now Wilmington, Delaware) gradually expanded under Governor Johan Prinz to include outposts near the present locations of Philadelphia and Salem, New Jersey. These posts were garrisoned by a small number of soldiers in Swedish government service supported by a militia which was apparently as disorganized and ineffective as its Dutch counterpart to the north, if not more so. The garrison of Fort Elfsborg was actually driven out by mosquitoes. When Peter Stuyvesant took advantage of Swedish inattention due to a war in Europe in 1655 to attack the Swedes, he easily conquered the colony. The vast majority of the settlers remained, but now as New Netherlanders.

When Stuyvesant sailed south with his sea soldiers the Burgher Guard was called up to temporarily replace the New Amsterdam garrison. Unfortunately, another Indian war broke out across the North River from Manhattan, and most of the Dutch were swept back to New Amsterdam again, leaving all their villages and bouweries, save Communipaw, in ashes. Subsequent reoccupation of the west shore was more carefully controlled. Following an Indian treaty in 1658, new and returning settlers were formally licensed, ordered to build fortified villages, and required to have at least one man capable of bearing arms in each farmstead. The first new village established was Bergen, and this time it was here to stay.[23]

In an attempt to further professionalize the part-time soldiers of the Burgher Guard, the West India Company issued them flags, "partisans, halberds and drums" in 1658. In 1659 the New Amsterdam Guard, which also functioned as a night patrol police force intended to sweep up drunks, consisted of three small companies. Governor Stuyvesant called for volunteers from the guard to mount an offensive campaign against some disaffected Indians, with mixed success. The state of the guard's discipline is questionable, as the extant record indicates a disinterest by members in night patrols. Fines established for citizen soldiers who fired their muskets at flags, windows, gables, weather vanes, and signs suggest basic discipline was a problem. Some guardsmen apparently took part time soldiering seriously, however, as an account of a unit holding a target shooting match exists.[24]

## THE END OF DUTCH NORTH AMERICA

Unlike Bergen, a solid and permanent settlement in today's New Jersey, Dutch North America soon became a thing of the past. The English Civil War and its aftermath, including the execution of King Charles I and the subsequent dic-

tatorship of Oliver Cromwell, ended with the coronation of Charles's son as Charles II in 1660. In 1664, King Charles granted New Netherland to his brother James, Duke of York, based on the premise that John Cabot, a Venetian explorer working for England, had sailed nearby in 1498. Since the Dutch were not likely to agree with the king's award, the duke dispatched a fleet to New Amsterdam to enforce his will. Despite the belligerence of Stuyvesant, who wanted to fight, New Amsterdam, its defenses against a European invader in shambles, quickly capitulated to the British under James's governor Colonel Richard Nicolls on September 29, 1664, and the colony was renamed New York.

Although he recognized existing Dutch settlements, Nicolls wasted no time in granting land in the territory across the North River to Englishmen. In April 1665 the governor, acting in the duke's name, awarded the Navesink patent to a group of Long Island Quakers and Baptists. Navesink, which gained its name from the Lenape living there, was a roughly triangle-shaped parcel. Its base stretched from Sandy Hook to the mouth of the Raritan River, then twenty-five miles up the Raritan. The border then angled roughly southeast to Barnegat Bay, and back up the coast to Sandy Hook. The grantees agreed to settle one hundred families on the land and erect fortifications for their defense.[25]

# 2. New Jersey Under English Rule, 1664–1775

Richard Nicolls stressed that his first land grant in New Jersey, part of which became the townships of Middletown and Shrewsbury, had to be formally purchased from the local Lenape. In fact, the new governor was doing no more than validating a March 1664 agreement between the Long Islanders and Navesink chief Popamora. Payment included wampum, shirts, coats, guns, tobacco, wine, gunpowder, and lead. Although some local Navesink apparently moved inland after the deal, one account notes that at the time of the purchase "few Indians were permanent residents of the actual shore and its immediately contiguous area." As noted in the previous chapter, this was not necessarily the case, although European-borne disease could well have reduced the local population significantly in the years between initial European contact and 1664. At least some Lenape remained in close contact with the settlers for a period of time. A decade later, Richard Hartshorne of Middletown wrote that one could "buy as much of Fish from an *Indian* for a pound and a half of [gun] Powder as will serve 6 or 8 men; deer are also very plenty in this Province; we can buy a fat buck of the *Indians* much bigger than the *English* deer for a pound and a half of Powder or Lead." A few Navesink were still hunting game and trapping fur bearers to sell to white settlers in Monmouth County as late as 1715.[1]

The bloodless British conquest opened up the land between the North and South Rivers, which, prior to 1664, had few European settlers other than the Dutch foothold in Pavonia and environs and the Swedish settlements along the Delaware that Peter Stuyvesant had conquered in 1655. Robert Treat, leader of a band of Connecticut Puritans seeking a place to plant a pure theocracy, had negotiated unsuccessfully for a land purchase with Stuyvesant prior to the English conquest of New Netherland, and quickly responded to Nicolls's offers of land. Treat's party settled what would become Newark. Other English towns sprouted up across eastern New Jersey, including Elizabethtown and Woodbridge, settled by Long Islanders and New Englanders and even a party from Barbados, while Dutch settlers from New Amsterdam crossed the river to expand Bergen and soon spread southwards.[2]

## EAST AND WEST JERSEY

Nicolls, upon learning that the Duke of York had transferred the colony's ownership to two of his cronies, Lord John Berkeley and Sir George Carteret, resigned as governor and was replaced by Philip Carteret, a 26-year-old distant cousin of Sir George. The young governor's tenure proved controversial, as he undid Nicolls's land grants, maintaining that New Jersey was essentially private property to be dispensed as the new proprietors thought proper. Lord Berkeley, hard up for cash, sold his thinly populated western half of the colony to Quaker proprietors in 1676, and in the aftermath New Jersey was divided into East and West New Jersey, also known as "the Jerseys," along a diagonal line extending from Little Egg Harbor to the upper Delaware River, which reduced Carteret's governance to East Jersey. The Quaker domination of West Jersey, which included much of the colony's southern section, would have a significant cultural effect, lasting, many say, to the present day. Quaker proprietors bought East Jersey as well from George Carteret's widow in 1680, and then, discovering it was populated by Puritans, Baptists, and other denominations, quickly sold it off to Scottish investors. The residents of East Jersey claimed that both sales were essentially illegal, since they had been granted the land by Nicolls and paid the Lenape for it. The dispute set the stage for generations of political and judicial wrangling.[3]

## DECLINE OF THE NATIVE POPULATION

Despite land ownership confusion, European settlers began to stream into the Jerseys, displacing most of the remaining natives within a few decades. Monmouth County's Navesink Lenape, who had traded with the Dutch and English for a number of years, had seen no permanent settlers in their territory until the arrival of the Long Islanders in 1665. Indian understanding of land sales and their impact on traditional rights to hunt, fish, and forage conflicted with the new inhabitants' European concept of property ownership, and led to problems. Angered and confused at being shut out of much of their traditional hunting territory, some Indians began to kill domestic stock and appropriate other material goods. Richard Hartshorne, annoyed by Lenape hunting, fishing, and cutting trees to make dugout canoes on Sandy Hook, which he believed he owned in the English sense, eventually purchased final rights from them, specifying that henceforth "no Indian or Indians, shall or hath pretense to lands or timber or liberty, privilege, or not pretense whatsoever" on his property. Although there was friction between the English and the Lenape in New Jersey, it never erupted into open warfare as had occurred with the Dutch some years before. The major reason was most likely the rapidly declining population and potential power of New Jersey's Native Americans.[4]

It is unclear how large New Jersey's Native American population actually was at the time Europeans initially appeared off the coast. Estimates range all over the lot, from 2,400 to 7,000 to 12,000 to a high of 50,000; those tending toward the middle numbers seem more probable. Whatever the number was, it would never get any higher. One estimate is that by 1700 "probably less than six thousand" Indians remained, while another posits that there were only 1,500 Lenape left in the colony as early as 1669, with a full third of those living within the boundaries of modern Monmouth

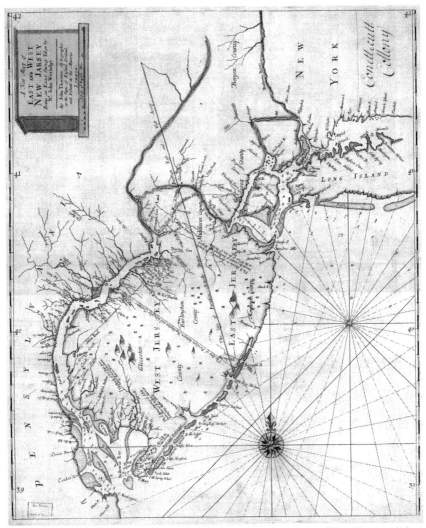

"A new mapp of East and West New Jarsey: being an exact survey," by John Worlidge and John Thorton, London, 1706.

County, then lightly populated by Europeans. Estimates of the total white population of East and West Jersey in that period range from 16,000 to 20,000. In the first four decades of the eighteenth century the already wobbly decentralized Lenape nation, inundated by English settlers, collapsed dramatically. Casualties suffered in the wars with the Dutch were vastly exceeded by those inflicted by deadly European-borne illnesses, most notably smallpox, but also measles and forms of viral infections, which periodically swept through the Lenape people and, by one estimate, killed half of them.[5]

In addition to suffering from decimating diseases, New Jersey's Native Americans were also increasingly elbowed aside and confined to a steadily shrinking homeland by a continuing wave of settlement following the 1664 English conquest. There seemed no place in the rapidly evolving social and land tenure structure for the time honored lifestyles of the surviving Lenape. Some Indians attempted to cling to their old customs, while others tried to assimilate to a rapidly changing world, but all became dependent on trade goods, from iron tools and guns to cooking pots, blankets, and clothing. Even before 1700, Lenape traditional culture began a rapid decline. One small Unami band living near Trenton "eked out a mendicant existence on the shabby fringes of the white settlements, simultaneously dependent on and resented by the whites." As the eighteenth century progressed, many Lenape, anxious to preserve what remained of their identity, migrated west of the Delaware River.[6]

## MILITIA ESTABLISHED

Although the Lenape were no longer a threat, the "concessions and agreements" initially awarded the English colonists of New Jersey by Lords Berkeley and Carteret to authorize a government gave them the right to "constitute trained bands and companies" and wage defensive or offensive war under the authorization of the governor or a "commander in chief" appointed by the governor. What sort of military organization, if any, resulted from this initial authorization is unknown, as legislation to create an actual militia was not enacted until the General Assembly first met in No-

vember 1668. The Assembly authorized the establishment of a militia and required all men between the ages of sixteen and sixty to muster for "at least four days in the year." There were supposed to be two days of training in spring and two in fall, with ten days between each training day. Needless to say, such a schedule did not make for a cutting edge military organization. In order to maintain at least minimal seriousness, the Assembly prohibited the sale of liquor to militiamen during drills. There is evidence that the rapid passing of the frontier and limited danger from Indian raids save along the upper reaches of the Delaware led to a haphazard militia organization in the colony. What militia spirit there was lay largely in East Jersey, since pacifist Quakers predominated in West Jersey. Mark Lender aptly notes that "no colonial governor of New Jersey ever formed an effective fighting force from the formal militia structure."[7]

## THE DUTCH RETURN

Despite the establishment of a more formal militia structure than the Dutch, the defenses of the new colonies of New York and New Jersey against European powers remained almost as decrepit as those of the old New Netherland. War broke out again in Europe in 1672, with France and England allied against Holland. Although the Dutch fared poorly in land operations, the war at sea went much better for them. In August 1673 a Dutch fleet appeared off Manhattan and landed 600 soldiers to besiege New York's Fort James, which was held by an 80-man garrison. Surrender was swift, and New York became, not New Netherland again, but New Orange, after William of Orange, the Dutch Stadholder, or chief executive. New Jersey towns quickly sent delegations to New Orange to surrender; most individual English settlers quickly took an oath of allegiance to their apparent new overlords and the militia made no attempt to defend New Jersey at all. Although the Dutch briefly reestablished the old Burgher Militia, the new order proved ephemeral. A February 1674 treaty ending the war transferred the colonies back to England, and control was formally relinquished in July. There were apparently no consequences for those who had switched loyalties, although the turnover from the Dutch to the English king, rather than English proprietors, complicated already murky legal questions regarding property ownership. Quit-rents demanded of settlers by absentee landlords led to rioting and political strife, culminating in the establishment of a unified royal colony with a governor appointed by the British crown in 1702.[8]

## MILITIA AND THE QUAKERS

Under the law of 1668, ordinary militiamen could avoid service by paying a fine in lieu of showing up for drill, and members of certain professions, from ministers to captains of ships of a certain size and government officials, were exempt from duty. According to the Assembly the militiaman was obligated to provide his own weapon, "a good and sufficient firelock" (matchlocks were finally out of the picture), a pound of powder, and "24 bullets fitted to the gun," as well as tools for cleaning and maintaining his musket. Militiamen were allowed freedom as to how to prepare and carry their ammunition, either as paper cartridges in a cartridge box or with powder charges carried separately from balls in a "bandoleer" of wooden bottles, or a powder horn. Periodic militia laws essentially re-

stating the points of the initial legislation were passed in 1679, 1682, and 1693. Militia service was designed to be limited and chiefly defensive. In 1698 the Assembly declared that no "free man shall be compelled, enforced, pressed or arrayed" to leave his township for military service save to repel an invasion or "by Special Act of the General Assembly." New Jersey's large Quaker population, principally in West Jersey, lobbied for exemption from militia duty due to their religion's pacifist doctrine, and the West Jersey proprietors were more than willing to grant those exemptions. In 1683, after a number of legislative battles, Quakers were officially exempted from duty in East Jersey without requirement to pay a fine or provide a substitute, which weakened the force both in actuality and morale, and left no effective militia in West Jersey when the entire colony came under royal control in 1702.[9]

## LORD CORNBURY

The first royal governor, Edward Hyde, better known by his title of Lord Cornbury, was also governor of New York. Hyde received a hefty salary from that colony, and expected the same compensation from a reluctant New Jersey. The governor, portrayed as a transvestite by his opponents, was a grifter of monumental proportions, and the resulting feud between his supporters—enlisted through a considerable patronage-dispensing political machine—and other New Jerseyans, particularly the Quakers, intensified throughout his tenure. In an act of revenge against the Quakers, Cornbury's adherents in the Assembly rammed through a law that required every male of military age, regardless of religious affiliation, to purchase a musket and drill four times a year, removing the religious exemption and thus restoring the fine for missing drill to Quakers.[10]

Although ordinarily no Jerseyman could be ordered out of his colony or even neighborhood for military service without authorization from the Assembly, volunteers could be solicited from the militia for units intended to serve beyond the colony's borders—and, in a declared emergency, militiamen could be drafted for such service. As the colonial wars for empire heated up in the eighteenth century, volunteer units to assist British regular troops were called for with regularity. Despite its weakness, the very existence of the English militia, a more organized and better armed force than was ever mustered by the Dutch and Swedes, established the concept that citizens owed their society military duty in time of war and provided, in addition to an emergency defense force, a somewhat trained recruiting base for longer service units. Although the colony would never become the scene of major fighting, wars between the English and the French and Spanish became a regular occurrence, and New Jerseyans served outside the colony with increasing frequency as the century passed. Although most records of the period are lost, there is evidence that New Jersey volunteer troops were stationed in Albany as early as 1693, during what was known as King William's War (1688–1698).[11]

QUEEN ANNE'S WAR, WAR OF JENKINS'S EAR, KING GEORGE'S WAR

During the drawn-out inconclusive struggle known as "Queen Anne's War" (1702–1713), conflict came home to the Jersey coast when sailors from a French privateer off Sandy Hook landed at "the Neversinks" and plundered several homes before withdrawing in June 1702. Other French privateers appeared off the coast and captured trading vessels in succeeding years, and English privateers commissioned out of New York pursued enemy merchantmen as well. Privateering, or freelance naval warfare against an enemy's merchant fleet, was a form of legalized piracy, and far more profitable for those engaged than serving as soldiers or militiamen. In addition to naval efforts, the colony raised £3,000 in 1709 to support military operations on land and recruited 200 volunteers to aid a British fleet in the capture of Canada. In the event, the fleet never arrived, but Governor Robert Hunter raised £5,000 more and another 200 volunteers, who were ordered to march to Albany as part of a new campaign to capture Montreal. A British naval force that was supposed to cooperate in this effort was badly damaged by storms while attempting to enter the Saint Lawrence River and sailed back to England, and the Jerseymen returned home without engaging in combat.[12]

The "War of Jenkins' Ear" (1739–1749) began as a conflict with Spain over naval and trading issues, ostensibly when a British sea captain, Robert Jenkins, had his ear sliced off by a Spanish sailor's cutlass in an incident off the coast of South America. In 1742 the conflict merged into the War of the Austrian Succession in Europe, which brought France to Spain's assistance in a larger struggle referred to as "King George's War" in America.

New Jersey's initial response to hostilities was to commission privateers to prey on Spanish shipping, but in late 1740 the British government enlisted volunteers from the militia of several colonies, among them New Jersey, and organized these troops into "provincial" units that joined a British army in Jamaica under Admiral Edward Vernon. The New Jersey Assembly appropriated £2,000 to support the expedition, and an unspecified number of Jerseymen boarded ships at Perth Amboy to sail to the Caribbean. Vernon attacked Cartagena in New Grenada (modern Colombia) in 1741, but the expedition ended in disaster. Not only did the British fail to make headway against strong Spanish defenses and an able commander, but much of Vernon's army, apparently including most of the Jerseyans, died as combat casualties or of yellow fever.[13]

In 1745, the New Jersey Assembly appropriated £2,000 to fund a force that successfully captured the French fortress of Louisburg on Cape Breton Island. The British campaign plan for 1746 included an invasion of Canada, and men were recruited in New Jersey to fill the ranks of a provincial regiment to support that effort. These soldiers, save perhaps the officers, were not recruited from among the colony's elite. They included "freemen and well affected Indians," who were given "relief from small debts and pardon from minor crimes." Indentured servants and even slaves could enlist in the unit without their masters' permission, suggesting that it was a racially integrated organization. Each volunteer received a £6 bounty and was promised in addition "all bounties, plunder and advantages" of regular British army soldiers. The regiment's companies sailed from Newark and Perth Amboy and up the Hudson to Albany under the command of Colonel Peter Schuyler, a wealthy and prominent New Jerseyan. Promised British reinforcements never arrived, however, and the Jerseymen spent thirteen months at Albany and Saratoga. The Assembly had subscribed

£10,000 to maintain the regiment, expecting reimbursement from the Crown, but that did not eventuate and quartermaster services apparently collapsed. Complaints of lack of food, clothing, pay, and even weapons made their way back to New Jersey. One private, Alexander Miles, complained in November 1746 that the soldiers were issued "stinking beef," and that the regiment's muskets were "so rusted and rotten so as not to be the value of old iron" and that cutlasses or short swords issued "would bend and stand bent like lead." He laid the blame at the feet of private contractors into whose hands, for a five percent commission, the Assembly had placed the supply services of the regiment.[14]

The Assembly refused to appropriate more money for the soldiers serving its cause, so that, in addition to their other miseries, the volunteers were not paid. In April 1747 all these issues came to a head in a mutiny, in which the Jerseymen threatened to desert and take whatever public property they could, including weapons, with them. Colonel Schuyler sympathized with his men and instead of suppressing the mutiny with force, paid them out of his own pocket, gaining the enmity of New York governor George Clinton, who was concerned that other unpaid provincial troops would now mutiny, and, unaccountably, believed that not paying soldiers kept them from deserting. With the end of the war in 1748, the understandably surly Jerseyans returned home, without seeing a shot fired in anger.[15]

## THE FRENCH AND INDIAN WAR

There would be one more climactic colonial contest, and New Jerseyans would see considerable action, gaining in the process an iconic nickname for its soldiers that would remain down to modern times. The conflict, known as the Seven Years War in Europe and the French and Indian War in the colonies, began with a frontier encounter between George Washington's Virginia provincial regiment and French forces in 1754. When New Jersey governor Jonathan Belcher initially requested funding for the war effort, the colony's Assemblymen claimed they could not afford to appropriate funds without a convoluted loan from the British Privy Council to secure an issue of "bills of credit," and then adjourned. After Washington's defeat at Fort Necessity in July, however, the Assembly appropriated £500 to provide provisions for British regular army troops marching through the colony. Subsequently, under increased pressure, the legislators voted to issue £15,000 in bills of credit to help cover the military expenses of the newly named British commander-in-chief in America, General Edward Braddock. Bills of credit were essentially IOUs that circulated as paper money for a five-year period, after which they were supposed to be redeemed by actual money. They had been issued as appropriations in the cash-short colony since 1709, but were always a source of controversy. Included in the amount was funding to provide "Pay, Cloathing, and Subsistence of 500 men," again including Lenape Indian residents of the colony, to be organized into a provincial volunteer regiment. Command was awarded to the closest individual New Jersey had to a professional soldier, the aging Colonel Schuyler. Despite disasters like Cartagena and the dismal Albany experience in the recent past, recruits in search of adventure or perhaps the £1 bounty offered quickly filled the ranks. A Trenton correspondent wrote that "the Country Fellows [en]list like mad."[16]

Each recruit was authorized issue of "one good sheepswool blanket, a good lapel coat of coarse cloth, a felt hat, two check shirts, two pair of Osnaberg [muslin] trousers, a pair of shoes and a pair of stockings . . . a good firelock, a good cutlass sword or bayonet, a cartouche box and a hatchet." A tent was issued to every five men and the regiment as a whole was supplied with "fifteen barrels of pork, forty-five hundred weight of lead [for casting bullets] and other necessaries." Once the ranks were filled, the New Jersey regiment left the colony for Albany.[17]

By summer, in the aftermath of General Braddock's disastrous defeat on the Monongahela in Pennsylvania, refugees from French and Indian frontier raids began to cross the Delaware into New Jersey, unsettling the residents of the northwestern part of the colony. Despite this, the Assembly, denied its loan from the Crown, initially refused to cooperate with Belcher's request for another war appropriation, then granted him half the £70,000 in bills of credit he requested. In the autumn of 1755, Indians attacked the Moravian mission at Gnadenhutten, Pennsylvania, and threatened the Delaware River frontier, sparking desperate calls for assistance that forced the Assembly to issue another £10,000 in bills of credit to construct blockhouses and fund military operations. In November, Governor Belcher ordered the militia to muster for inspection and called some militiamen to temporary active duty on the Sussex county frontier. Several hundred Sussex citizen-soldiers under Colonel John Anderson crossed the river to campaign alongside their Pennsylvania counterparts, but the brief expedition failed to intercept the raiders. By December, the Assembly was vainly calling for the return of the provincial regiment to defend the northwest border.[18]

LAST LENAPE LAND CLAIMS

In April 1756, Indians, some of them no doubt descendants of Lenape refugees from New Jersey, raided Paulins Kill, and the sixty families living there fled to Amwell. By June the colony was recruiting a full time "Frontier Guard" unit to be paid two shillings a day to man blockhouses and patrol along the Delaware River. The Frontier Guards were to supply their own clothing, equipment and weapons, including a "good and sufficient musket." Governor Belcher claimed that the Lenape had "violated their treaties," and were "Enemies, Rebels and Traitors to his most sacred Majesty," and then proposed bounties for Indians, dead or alive. Belcher's proclamation would not have applied to the colony's remaining resident Native American population, some of whom were actually serving in the ranks of the New Jersey provincial regiment, however. A conference held at Crosswicks between the few resident New Jersey Indians and the colony's government was held in January 1756 and resulted in an agreement with the remaining Lenape. Anxious not to be identified with some of their trans-Delaware kinsmen who were at that time actively siding with the French, the New Jersey resident Indians agreed with the governor's proposals that they relinquish any land claims. Some resettled at the Brotherton reservation in Burlington County (today's Indian Mills), established in 1758, while others continued to live in small out of the way communities.[19]

Discoveries at the Burr-Haines archeological dig at the Brotherton site provide a rare look at the life of mid-

eighteenth century New Jersey Native Americans. Cuff links and pins found at the site indicate that the Lenape wore European-style clothing. Other evidence, however, suggests a lifestyle that made use of ancient technologies, including stone tools, along with European metal knives and spoons and lead shot. Animal bones uncovered indicated a diet of wild game, supplemented by pigs, but not sheep, cattle, or chickens. The colonial era method of raising pigs by letting them roam the woods until slaughter time, which had originally caused much strife between the Lenape and the Dutch, probably fit in better with attempts at holding on to part of a traditional hunting and foraging lifestyle by the late eighteenth century.[20]

NEW JERSEY SOLDIERS ALONG THE FRONTIER

While border troubles simmered, the New Jersey regiment joined volunteer soldiers from New York and New England at Albany under Sir William Johnson as part of an expedition initially intended to capture Crown Point on Lake Champlain. Half of the Jerseymen, under Colonel Schuyler, were, however, diverted to Oswego, on Lake Ontario, where they built and garrisoned one of three forts. In August 1756 the French commander in Canada, Major General Louis-Joseph de Montcalm, captured the Oswego forts and the Jerseyans serving there, including Colonel Schuyler. Lord Loudon, then overall commander in America, called for more assistance from the colonies, including 1,000 more men from New Jersey; the reluctant Assembly called instead for 500 volunteers in 1757. It appears that any recruits raised, including Sergeant William McCrackan of Somerset County, who had prior service in a British mounted unit, were used to replace losses sustained by the New Jersey regiment already in the field. Colonel John Parker replaced Schuyler, now a prisoner in Montreal, in command. The rebuilt regiment camped at Fort William Henry, established at Lake George on General Johnson's orders following an inconclusive September 1755 battle nearby. The fort itself only had room for a garrison of 500 men, so most of the provincial troops were housed in an adjacent entrenched camp.[21]

On July 21, 1757, Fort William Henry commander lieutenant colonel George Monro ordered Colonel Parker to take a 350-man force of New Jersey and New York troops up Lake George by boat on a reconnaissance-in-force to determine the location of General Montcalm's French army, which was advancing south from Fort Carillon on Lake Champlain. The expedition rowed to Sabbath Day Point, where it was ambushed by a force of French and Indians who opened fire from shore, then encircled Parker's men with canoes. The provincials panicked, losing 160 men killed or drowned and many of the remainder captured, while the French lost one man wounded. It was reported that Ottawa warriors subsequently dined on at least one unfortunate Jerseyan. Parker, who managed to escape with one hundred survivors, later transferred to the Royal American regiment and died of a fever during an expedition to Havana. Fort William Henry and its adjacent camp, with 301 Jerseyans in the garrison, was besieged by the French on August 3 and fell five days later. An Indian attack on the surrendered and paroled British and provincial soldiers marching to Fort Edward afterwards resulted in additional New Jersey casualties, including Sergeant McCrackan, who was carried off to Canada

by Indians. By the terms of the capitulation and subsequent parole, the Fort William Henry garrison, including 239 Jerseymen who survived Sabbath Day Point, the siege, and the massacre, were forbidden to bear arms against the French for an eighteen-month period. McCrackan ended up, however, along with some of the Oswego prisoners, in France. He was eventually exchanged but then became stranded in Ireland through 1763, until he earned enough money to pay for his passage home. Perhaps the disasters proved all too much for Governor Belcher, who, ailing for some time, died on August 31. The governor was temporarily succeeded in office by Senior Councilor John Reading, an elderly man who served as acting governor until a newly appointed Crown official arrived.[22]

## THE "JERSEY BLUES"

As 1757 waned, New Jersey began to recover from its multiple disasters. Colonel Schuyler was paroled by the French that summer and, after a hearty welcome home to his estate, "Petersborough," on the Passaic River outside Newark, including "bonfires, illuminations, cannonading, and health drinking," set about arranging a permanent exchange for himself and other prisoners. Unfortunately, there was no one in British custody to exchange for him and in June 1758, he returned to French captivity until he was officially traded for a captured French officer of equal rank in November. In his absence, the colony raised a new regiment to replace the unit destroyed at Oswego and Fort William Henry. Recruits, at least some of whom may have been survivors of the initial regiment, were provided with "a cloth pair of breeches, a white shirt, a check

The "Old Barracks" in Trenton was built in 1759 to house regular British soldiers during the French and Indian War. It housed British and Hessian soldiers at the time of the Battle of Trenton, and later housed wounded Continental soldiers during the latter part of the American Revolution. The Old Barracks is the only French and Indian War building still standing in New Jersey.

shirt, two pair of shoes, two pair of stockings, one pair of ticken breeches, a hat, blanket, canteen and hatchet for each recruit, under a bounty of £12." The significant bounty, compared with the £1 previously offered, was intended to head off a draft from the militia requested by General James Abercrombie, who had succeeded Lord Loudon in the American command. The new soldiers would also be paid £1.13s.6d a month and "a dollar to drink his Majesty's Health" on enlistment. The men of the revived regiment, which left for Albany under the command of Colonel John Johnson in May, were the first Jerseymen who could accurately be called "Jersey Blues," a nickname that would stick to New Jersey soldiers ever after. They were dressed in "Uniform blue, faced with red, grey stockings and Buckskin Breeches." One account has the regimental coat tailored "after the Highland manner" or cut

short. Although another source maintains that the nickname was used as early as 1747, the first documented record is in a letter dated June 1759. In addition to raising new troops, the Assembly voted to build barracks in Elizabeth, Perth Amboy, New Brunswick, Trenton, and Burlington to house British regular army soldiers rather than quarter them in private homes. The Trenton barracks alone survives to this day, the only remaining French and Indian War barracks in the United States.[23]

In September 1757, Lord Loudon called on the colony to muster another unit, a 100-man company of rangers to serve in New York. There is no evidence that these men were enlisted due to any special frontier skill sets they might have had, and they were apparently recruited in Perth Amboy. Although no specific uniform was specified, the Assembly provided the rangers with "one good

Blanket, a half thick Under-Jacket, a kersey lapell'd Jacket, Buckskin Breeches, two check Shirts, two pair of Shoes, and two pair of Stockings, a Leather cap and a Hatchet." John Magee, a deserter, was reportedly wearing "A Grey lapell'd Waistcoat, and an under green Jacket, a Leather Cap, and Buckskin Breeches" issued by New Jersey. Unlike militiamen, the rangers were not required to bring their personal weapons to the war, and the Assembly requested that these soldiers be armed by the British. The rangers were stationed in Stone Arabia, New York, through April 1758, when they were discharged. It appears that ten men died in ranger service, although it is not known whether they were casualties of combat or disease.[24]

The "Blues" were engaged in yet another colonial military disaster in July 1758, when the British army under General Abercrombie bungled an attempt to capture Fort Carillon on Lake Champlain. Although Abercrombie's army of 16,000 men, including the Jersey provincials, vastly outnumbered the French under General Montcalm, a series of British frontal assaults on a French defensive line in advance of the fort proved disastrous. Fortunately for the Jerseymen, they did not participate in the major thrust of the attacks, although they still lost Lieutenant-Colonel Thomas Shaw of Burlington, who had survived the Fort William Henry debacle, along with ten other men killed and 44 wounded. In the wake of his defeat, Abercrombie was replaced by General Jeffrey Amherst, and with a new war leader in London, William Pitt, who had ascended to the office of prime minister in 1757, the tide began to turn in favor of the British, as they subsequently captured Louisbourg and Forts Frontenac and Duquesne. A detachment of Jersey

Blues was part of the force that captured Frontenac.[25]

## FINAL INDIAN SKIRMISHES

A new royal governor, Francis Bernard, arrived in New Jersey in June 1758 as the frontier war along the Delaware once again erupted in a series of raids that killed several local citizens. The militia was mobilized to support the full time paid soldiers of the 250 man Frontier Guard. Sergeant John Van Tile and a "private Titsort" were awarded silver medals featuring "an Indian prostrate at the Feet of the said Van Tile and Lad aforesaid" for their service in repulsing raiders. Raiding along the Delaware ended following a conference at Easton, Pennsylvania, in October 1758, when the governors of New Jersey and Pennsylvania concluded a treaty with representatives of most of the Native American nations engaged in war with the British. The Lenape west of the Delaware River were granted a thousand Spanish dollars to relinquish any claims they might have to land within the colony of New Jersey.[26]

By 1759 there were an estimated 300 Christian Lenape still living in New Jersey, 200 of them on the colony's three-thousand-acre Indian reservation at Brotherton. One source cites a total of only 200 Lenape living on the state's entire coastal plain by 1775. The remaining Brotherton Indians, fewer than 100 in number, left for New Stockbridge in New York in 1801, effectively ending the Lenape presence in the state, although scattered individuals and small family groups apparently remained here and there, primarily in the southern counties, as others intermarried with the black and white populations. In 1832, the New Jersey legislature paid $2,000 to forty Lenape then living with the Stockbridge

Indians near Green Bay, Wisconsin, in a final settlement for "the right of fishing in all the rivers and bays south of the Raritan and of hunting in all unenclosed lands." In 1970, there were 4,706 Native Americans residing in the state; none counted as full blooded Lenape. Most modern Lenape live in Oklahoma.[27]

## NEW JERSEY VOLUNTEERS

With successive British victories in Canada and the Champlain Valley, the New Jersey Assembly called for 1,000 militiamen to volunteer for active duty under the now exchanged Colonel Schuyler, with recruiting offices opened in Salem, Gloucester, Burlington, Bordentown, and Newton. In succeeding years New Jersey raised more volunteers to serve in New York and Canada, and the Assembly voted money to equip and

pay them. New Jersey volunteers were part of the British force that attacked Havana in 1762. In all, one scholar estimates that as many as 3,000 men served in provincial forces of one kind or another or in the British regular army (which regularly enlisted colonists in its ranks) between 1755 and 1763, "a level of participation requiring the enlistment of every fourth free male between the ages of sixteen and forty-five who was not a Quaker." When the war ended in 1763, with British dominance in North America assured, it would seem that the future of the Royal Colony of New Jersey, tucked within that empire, and with its ramshackle militia replaced with wartime trained and experienced officers and enlisted men, would be secure. Perhaps—but not for long.[28]

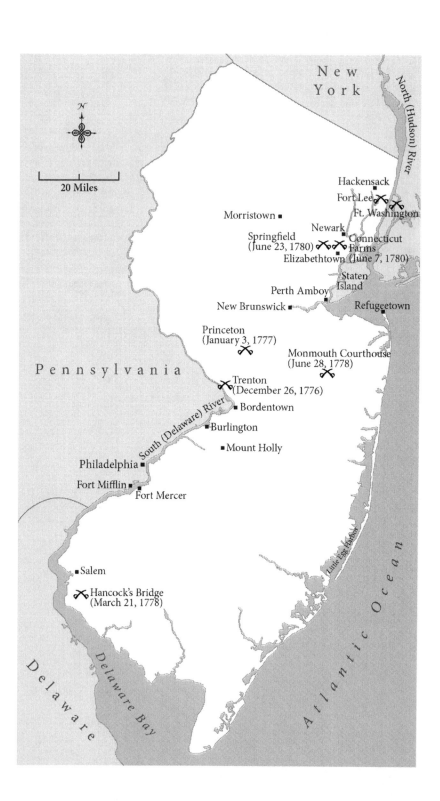

New
York

North (Hudson) River

20 Miles

Hackensack

Fort Lee

Ft. Washington

Morristown

Newark

Springfield
(June 23, 1780)

Connecticut
Farms

Elizabethtown (June 7, 1780)

Staten
Island

Perth Amboy

New Brunswick

Refugeetown

Princeton
(January 3, 1777)

Monmouth Courthouse
(June 28, 1778)

Pennsylvania

Trenton
(December 26, 1776)

South (Delaware) River

Bordentown

Burlington

Mount Holly

Philadelphia

Fort Mifflin

Fort Mercer

Salem

Hancock's Bridge
(March 21, 1778)

Little Egg Harbor

Delaware

Delaware Bay

Delaware

Atlantic Ocean

# 3. New Jersey and the American Revolution, 1775–1777: The Opening Struggle

Historians have characterized the majority of New Jersey's people as somewhat reluctant revolutionaries as the 1770s unfolded. William Franklin, Benjamin's son and the last royal governor, was a popular and clever politician who continued to contest the growing tide of revolution in the colonies even after Lexington and Concord; his efforts abetted by a seemingly ambivalent population. There had been a "Tea Party" in Greenwich, down by Delaware Bay, on December 22, 1774, with local protestors dressed as Indians in imitation of the Boston incident of the previous year, but the breadth and depth of such feelings at the outbreak of hostilities is difficult to determine.

Religion and politics were entwined in New Jersey. Following the opening shots of the Revolution, fired in April 1775, most Quakers remained loyal to the king or adopted a precarious neutrality. Other denominations, including the Dutch Reformed Church, split into pro- and anti-war factions. The Presbyterians, along with Baptists, were strongly opposed to Governor Franklin's prewar effort to declare the Anglican Church the colony's official religion, and so were firmly in the

Patriot camp. There were other determinants of loyalty to one side or the other, including a continuing fiscal conflict with the home country on the issuance of bills of credit, or paper money, by the Assembly.[1]

Following the fighting at Lexington and Concord, New Jersey Loyalists sought a low profile as Patriot forces seized political control through local Committees of Safety and established a Provincial Congress. Governor Franklin tried to convince his old Colonial Assembly to establish a committee for reconciliation with the king, while instructing the colony's delegates to the Continental Congress to vote against any proposals for independence. The internal struggle ended with Franklin's arrest in January 1776. Initially held at his official residence in Perth Amboy, and then his Burlington estate, Franklin was transported to Connecticut, arriving, ironically, on July 4, and was held there as a prisoner of war until exchanged in October 1778. On returning to British controlled New York City, the governor plotted revenge on New Jersey's Patriots, initially as an organizer of the "Refugee Club," and subsequently as president of the board of directors of the Associated Loyalists, an organization that raised paramilitary forces and sponsored raids that ravaged the state until the end of the war.[2]

## NEW JERSEY'S MINUTE MEN

In June 1775, the New Jersey Provincial Congress had bypassed Franklin, initiating a "plan for regulating the militia of the Colony." The law revived the old militia ordinances that had fallen into disuse, required a census of males between the ages of 16 and 50 capable of bearing arms and ordered townships to form them into companies, select officers and noncommissioned officers, and dictate times and places for training. Those who missed drill or refused to bear arms, including Quakers, were subject to fines. The law also provided for the creation of companies of "Minute Men" who were expected to drill every evening, be ready to march at a minute's notice, and serve four month tours of active duty. Captain Frederick Frelinghuysen's Minute Man company from Somerset County's Millstone Township "wore long smock frocks, broadbrimmed black hats and leggings; their own firelocks were on their shoulders, 22 cartridges in their cartouch boxes; the worm, priming wire and 12 flints in their pockets and a pound of powder and three pounds of bullets at their homes." By November, Philip Vickers Fithian of Cohansey, a young Presbyterian minister who enlisted as a militia chaplain, reported "Drums & Fifes rattling—Military Language in every Mouth" in southwestern New Jersey.[3]

Minute Man companies could be rallied in short order through the use of signal fires lit on "signal stations" atop prominent hills. In Morris County there

Asher R. Hart served in the 1st Hunterdon County Militia Regiment. He represents the typical New Jersey Revolutionary War militiaman.

were stations on "Pigeon Hill," in today's Denville, and Beacon Hill in Summit. The stations were the site of log towers "built in the form of a pyramid with loose brush filling in the spaces between the logs and topped with 'a stout sapling.'" These companies were integrated into the regular militia as the war progressed.[4]

## NEW JERSEY'S CONTINENTAL SOLDIERS

In October 1775 the New Jersey Provincial Congress, acting on the request of the Continental Congress, authorized the raising of two eight-company battalions of Continental or regular army soldiers for one year of service. The companies were to be composed of sixty-eight privates, four corporals, four sergeants, one ensign, and one lieutenant, with a captain commanding each. Recruits were paid five dollars a month and, in lieu of a bounty, issued "a felt hat, a pair of yarn stockings, and a pair of shoes: the men to find their own arms." The Continental Congress promised to furnish each recruit with "a hunting shirt, not exceeding the value of one dollar and one-third of a dollar, and a blanket, provided these can be procured."[5]

In line with the old colonial divisions, one battalion was raised in East Jersey and the other in West Jersey. The First, or East Jersey, battalion was recruited at Elizabethtown and Perth Amboy with men from Middlesex, Morris, Somerset, Monmouth, Essex, and Bergen counties in the ranks. The men of the Second, or West Jersey, battalion were from Gloucester, Hunterdon, Burlington, Salem, and Sussex counties and mustered into service at Trenton and Burlington. Recruiting was brisk, and officers found no trouble filling the ranks.[6]

On November 10, the six companies of both battalions that had been recruited to that date were sent to garrison a fort in the Hudson River highlands. Subsequent recruits were transferred to barracks in New York City on November 27 and formed into companies there. All the companies of both battalions were reunited in New York in December, where they were formally mustered into Continental service for one year.

In the waning months of 1775, General Thomas Gage, the British commander in America, remained bottled up in Boston following the fights at Lexing-

ton, Concord, and Bunker Hill, and the subsequent siege mounted by the New England militia. General William Howe replaced Gage in November, and evacuated Boston by ship to Halifax, Nova Scotia, when a growing American army under General George Washington seized strategic high ground and emplaced heavy artillery to dominate the city. By June the British commander, his original force bolstered by reinforcements, including paid German auxiliaries on their way from England with a fleet under the command of his brother Admiral Richard Howe, resumed the offensive. Howe's target was New York City, a choke point between the middle and southern colonies and New England.

In January 1776 three companies of New Jersey Continentals were ordered to join some of the colony's Minute Men under Colonel Nathaniel Heard of the Middlesex County militia "for duty in arresting tories and disaffected persons in Queens County, New York." The remaining men of the First and Second Battalions were stationed in Perth Amboy and Elizabethtown. A Third New Jersey battalion was authorized in January 1776 and recruited at Elizabethtown between February and May. In the latter month all the New Jersey Continentals were ordered north to join an expedition headed for an invasion of Canada. The First and Second Battalions engaged in combat with the enemy at Three Rivers, Canada, on June 8, and then withdrew south to Fort Ticonderoga. The Third Battalion was diverted to duty chasing Loyalists and guarding against Indian attacks in the vicinity of Johnstown and German Flats. With the state's regular regiments far away to the north, New Jersey had to rely on militiamen for its local defense needs, which would become critical in the summer and fall of 1776.[7]

## NEW JERSEY "STATE TROOPS"

Since Continentals, the American equivalent of a regular army, could be ordered wherever Congress wished, New Jersey lawmakers decided to raise another class of soldiers, or "levies" also known as "state troops" for defined periods of time, from three to twelve months of service. Although Colonel Heard's men could be considered such a unit, the first definitively authorized "state troops"—volunteers from the militia classified somewhere between militiamen and Continentals—were the members of the Eastern Company of Artillery, under Captain Frederick Frelinghuysen, and the Western Company of Artillery, under Captain Samuel Hugg. In December 1776, the Eastern Company joined the Continental army. Infantry and artillery units of state troops would be formed for various periods of service in the coming years, and they formed a significant segment of the state's military for the remainder of the war.[8]

George Washington was well aware that New York was the probable British target for 1776 and ordered General Charles Lee to the city to supervise its defense. Although Lee, a former British officer, would gain lasting fame through failure on the Monmouth battlefield in 1778, he was undeniably an experienced soldier and a fairly astute one. Lee's accurate analysis of New York City as a poor potential defensive position was not encouraging. With British command of the sea, Manhattan Island, surrounded by navigable water, was extremely vulnerable. Before he was transferred to bolster the defenses of Charleston, Lee attempted to make the best of a bad situation and ordered the Americans in New York to begin digging defensive trenches at likely landing spots

around Manhattan. Washington directly assumed responsibility for the defense of New York in April 1776, and by the time Howe arrived off Sandy Hook on June 25, the American general had mustered more than 20,000 soldiers for the defense of the city, although most were inexperienced militiamen, including men from New Jersey. In June the Continental Congress had asked the Provincial Congress for 3,300 men in five eight-company battalions for the defense of New York, and a number of militiamen from every county were mustered as "levies" for five months of active service and sent to the city under the command of Nathaniel Heard, now a brigadier general.[9]

In an operational style that would become characteristic, Howe took his time before assuming the offensive against the Americans. After landing at Staten Island in early July, a move that caused more than a bit of panic in New Jersey, where frantically digging militiamen could plainly see the enemy across a short span of water, the British commander consolidated his command as reinforcements from England and the failed British expeditionary force to Charleston arrived, until he had a total of 25,000 men fit for action, supported by thirty ships of the line and frigates mounting 1,200 cannons. As the British force grew before their eyes, and in fear of a Loyalist insurrection, New Jersey's nervous Patriot leaders called for their militia to return and establish a "Flying Camp" near Perth Amboy, intended to respond quickly to British incursions but be available for state service. When the Jersey militiamen returned, however, many were discharged from any duty at all.

By mid-July a majority of the state's citizen soldiers had been "temporarily excused from service to gather their harvest," and replaced by Pennsylvanians. Subsequent attempts to call the Jerseymen back to duty were fruitless; none of the 2,000 called up on July 18 had responded by August 1. Of the 3,300 militiamen initially called to duty in June, only 1,458 were still serving in mid-August, and desertion and insubordination ran rife among those remaining. Militia brigadier general William Livingston made do with what he had, and, although lacking in military experience, managed, though organizational skill and energy, to keep the state's military from disintegrating entirely. Livingston became the state's first governor in July, and turned over the militia to Philemon Dickinson, an equally capable commander. New Jersey Loyalists observing the chaotic events of the summer of 1776 were heartened by both the arrival of overwhelming royal forces and the apparent decline in enthusiasm in Patriot ranks and began, here and there, to plan their own counter-rebellion.[10]

## NEW JERSEY'S LOYALISTS

Loyalist rumblings did not go unnoticed. On June 26, 1776, the Provincial Congress, meeting in Trenton, ordered militiamen to suppress Tory demonstrators in Hunterdon County and directed the arrest of others in Monmouth County's Upper Freehold and Shrewsbury Townships, where Loyalist agents were active and somewhat successful in exploiting Quaker ambivalence about the war and translating it into active opposition to the Patriot cause. Within weeks of the British arrival off Sandy Hook, some sixty volunteers from Upper Freehold and forty-eight from Perth Amboy, home town of Governor Franklin's attorney general and prominent Tory Cortlandt Skinner, made their way through American lines to offer their services to

General Howe. In July, British forces on Staten Island were advised that "there are thousands in the Jerseys will Join us, as soon as we get footing in that province." Under advisement from Washington, Governor Livingston ordered a number of Perth Amboy Loyalists detained and moved inland to prevent them from communicating with the British on nearby Staten Island, and militia guards were assigned to patrol the Monmouth County coast. As it seemed likely the British might move up the Hudson, Powles Hook, in old Dutch Pavonia across the river from Manhattan, was fortified and garrisoned with New Jersey militiamen and Connecticut Continentals.[11]

In early August, the New Jersey legislature, concerned that militiamen released from duty to gather the harvest had not returned, reorganized the state's military. All men between the ages of 16 and 50 were divided into two classes, and assigned to serve full time duty in alternate months—or provide substitutes to serve in their places. The order bore fruit, and the Flying Camp, now under the command of Continental army brigadier general Hugh Mercer, was reinforced by a new infusion of militiamen, who were ordered to garrison critical points. By the middle of the month, Mercer counted nine regiments of Jerseymen among his troops, but many were detailed to construct fortifications along the Palisades. By then the Pennsylvanians, who had had enough of duty, began to leave for home, with or without authorization. One Pennsylvanian reported that the Jersey meadowlands around his duty station at Bergen presented "a frightful appearance . . . as far as the eye could see." On the other hand, many New Jerseyans wanted the Pennsylvanians to leave, as tensions rose when they foraged off the countryside due to an erratic supply chain.[12]

## THE BRITISH OFFENSIVE AROUND NEW YORK CITY

In late August General Howe, finally moved to action, began what would be a series of successful operations by crossing from Staten Island to Long Island and decisively defeating the Patriot force there. After putting up some stiff resistance, General Heard's Jersey levies were outflanked and rapidly retreated. Some drowned trying to cross a pond. Despite the American tactical disaster on Long Island, also known as the Battle of Brooklyn, the British offensive enabled George Washington to begin building a reputation as an extraordinary and resourceful commander, as he successfully extricated his beaten army through a cover of fog and darkness from Brooklyn to Manhattan under the noses of the enemy.[13]

Manhattan Island, as Lee had perceived, proved to be indefensible, especially with the unseasoned and inadequately trained force of Continentals and militiamen Washington had at his disposal. Discouraged by defeat on Long Island, and concerned about their families at home, many remaining American militiamen began to drift away. The British landing at Kip's Bay on the East River signaled the advent of another series of American tactical setbacks, which accelerated the deterioration of the army. Although continually bested in a series of battles lasting into November that drove his men north and out of Manhattan to White Plains, Washington, aided by Howe's hesitation, managed to preserve a battered but steady core force, and eventually crossed over into New Jersey.

In early September, Washington ordered General Mercer to erect a supporting fortification across the Hudson River from Fort Washington, the last American toehold on Manhattan Island. The result was Fort Lee, located atop the Palisades. The forts, in conjunction with several armed galleys, were intended to block the advance of British ships up the river. As work began, Powles Hook was fired on by a British ship, and the New Jersey militia regiment garrisoned there panicked and fell back to Bergen, leaving behind 300 Connecticut Continentals, who in turn abandoned the now exposed post on September 23. Shortly afterward the king's soldiers landed at the Hook, taking possession of New Jersey soil for the first time in the war. With the enemy now lodged in a secure beachhead, however, the British inexplicably halted their offensive juggernaut for almost two months.[14]

## THE LOSS OF FORTS WASHINGTON AND LEE

In the interim, Washington moved his headquarters to Hackensack. Major General Nathanael Greene, now in command of Forts Lee and Washington, reinforced the latter, believing that withdrawal from the increasingly isolated position would harm morale. On November 16, however, a British and Hessian force stormed Fort Washington and captured 2,600 Americans. Morale on the Jersey side of the Hudson indeed plummeted, and the Americans started to evacuate supplies inland as British raiders began to cross the river, isolating Fort Lee. With the Hudson to its front, and the Hackensack River and limited roads and bridges to its rear, the garrison feared being trapped, and that, no doubt, was what Howe had in mind when he ordered General

Gen. Charles Cornwallis's troops ascending the Palisades on November 20, 1776, before moving on Fort Lee, sketched by Thomas Davies, an artillery officer serving under Cornwallis.

Charles Cornwallis to lead a force of 4,000 men, guided by local Loyalists (including Isaac Perkins of English Neighbourhood, a Loyalist ferryman whose property adjoined Fort Lee), across the river and up the Palisades north of the fort. Foreseeing potential disaster, an apprehensive General Washington had already ordered the garrison of less than 3,000 "irregular and undisciplined" Americans to abandon the position before Cornwallis's November 19 crossing. Greene moved as much of the food and equipment stored at the fort to safety as possible, but a lack of wagons and boats led to a considerable loss of supplies, including valuable artillery, both in the fort and on the road. Much of the artillery had previously been captured from the British and was returning to royal custody.[15]

Although the dispirited American army regrouped at Hackensack, it was still in a vulnerable position. Then it began to rain. Washington retreated to Newark with about 4,400 men and ordered the remainder of his active force, about 7,000 additional soldiers, to concentrate near White Plains, New York, under General Lee, as defense against a possible British thrust north up the Hudson. He then assigned the Connecticut militia to defend the back door to New England. The American commander called on the New Jersey militia to augment his diminished immediate command, but to no avail. The men of the New Jersey and Maryland militia brigades stationed at the Flying Camp, their tour of duty ended, returned home. No one came forward to replace them.[16]

## THE CONTINENTAL RETREAT ACROSS NEW JERSEY

Howe dispatched a sea-borne force to seize Newport, Rhode Island, while

Cornwallis continued to chase the Americans across New Jersey. Washington fell back before his pursuer, who was joined by Howe, through New Brunswick and Princeton to Trenton, which he reached on December 2. On December 7, the Americans advanced on Princeton but fell back again on Trenton and then crossed the Delaware River to Pennsylvania. Howe and Cornwallis continued the pursuit, but found when they reached the river that Washington had brought all available boats to the Pennsylvania side. British artillery traded fire with American guns across the river while British light infantry and Hessian Jaegers vainly searched for a fordable crossing point. Washington had escaped, but many on the British side, including prominent Pennsylvania Tory Joseph Galloway, a prewar friend of Benjamin Franklin, felt that Howe had not pursued the American army with the persistence and aggressiveness he should have. Howe, on the other hand, believed the American army was truly a broken force, and a more vigorous pursuit unnecessary, as the Rebels would soon come to a reasonable peace and reconciliation agreement. No matter the rationale, it was a decision the British general would soon come to rue.[17]

On November 21, as the main American army withdrew across New Jersey, Governor Livingston ordered his militia to rally in support of Washington's strategic retreat and also control potential Loyalist uprisings. The initial response was less than stellar. Many Bergen County militiamen, in fact, had defected to the British in the days after the fall of Fort Lee. In early December Militia brigadier general Matthias Williamson established a headquarters at Morristown, a position securely tucked west of the Watchung mountain ranges from

British-controlled eastern New Jersey, and awaited the appearance of the state's citizen army. Early evidence suggested Williamson might have a long wait. As of December 8, less than fifty men from Essex County had reported to the general, and only a few more showed up from Sussex shortly afterward. Eventually enough part time soldiers appeared, however, to provide, as Morristown's Colonel Jacob Ford Jr. noted, an "appearance of defence," which fortunately would not be severely tested. Washington found few Jersey militiamen on hand to support him when his army arrived at Trenton. The Continental commander and his generals let it be widely known that they were disgusted with the New Jersey militia; Nathaniel Greene characterized the behavior of the state's citizen soldiers as being "scurvily." Desperate for manpower, in November the state enlisted four battalions of state troops, promising them Continental army pay, six dollars' bounty and a pair of shoes and stockings on enlistment.[18]

All in all, in early December 1776, New Jersey appeared, as Leonard Lundin has put it, "almost as completely cowed by the deliberate and nearly bloodless advance of the royal army as it would have been had Washington's force been crushed in fierce battle." Several New Jersey legislators and other Patriot leaders, including Trenton's Samuel Tucker, president of the Provincial Congress, along with Princeton's Richard Stockton, a signer of the Declaration of Independence, had been captured by the British, as had the New Jersey treasury. Formerly discreet Loyalists come out into the open and wavering citizens across the state declared publicly for the king; even some Jerseymen who had espoused the Patriot cause accepted what seemed to be the new reality and switched sides. Commissioners appointed by Howe instructed local citizens to report to towns like Freehold in Monmouth County to sign loyalty oaths, and recruiting for Loyalist military units was brisk in Bergen, a county Livingston declared "almost totally disaffected." Cortlandt Skinner, who accompanied the British into Bergen, told Loyalist Isaac Noble of Ramapo to "let the people know now is the time to evince their Loyalty by actions, not words." Noble immediately went to work as a guide and recruiter for Skinner, with the rank of major. Noble's military career for the king came to an abrupt end, however, as he was "attacked by a skulking party of Rebels near the camp at Acquackanonk" and bayoneted in the eye. To cap it off, Charles Lee, who the British thought the best American officer, was captured while dallying at Basking Ridge on December 13. The British were riding high, and General Howe decided to temper might with mercy, at least in principle, issuing "protections" from British army plundering and requisitions to those who signed a loyalty oath. In one instance British supply officers actually issued food to hungry civilians. The war seemed to be coming to a close.[19]

But things would change, dramatically and rapidly. Just as all appeared lost, the New Jersey militia, responding to indiscriminate British pillaging, began to revive and harass the enemy in small actions across the state. Thomas Paine's pamphlet *The Crisis*, inspired by the author's experience as a militiaman and correspondent during the retreat from Fort Lee, was widely circulated and fired up men in both Pennsylvania and New Jersey. Enough militiamen made it to Morristown by mid-December to blunt the advance of an 800-man British probing force at Hobart's or Springfield Gap beyond the village of Springfield, the

only feasible approach for an army to the Patriot stronghold beyond the almost impenetrable Watchungs. The British retreat from Springfield secured Morristown as headquarters for a potential American comeback. While General Howe lived in comfort in New York, Colonel Johann Rall, commanding a three regiment force of around 1,400 Hessians in Trenton, complained to British higher headquarters that his men were being shot at by local civilians as soon as they ventured beyond friendly lines. Colonel Carl von Donop's Hessians at Bordentown, Mansfield Square, and Black Horse Tavern were in a similar situation. Pennsylvania militiamen rolled cannons down to the Delaware and kept up a drumbeat of fire on the hapless Trenton garrison. British general James Grant, parroting the official line that the Rebels were done for, however, refused to honor Rall's request for reinforcements. Von Donop, meanwhile, skirmished with and pursued American militiamen near Mount Holly, limiting the amount of support he could provide Rall. One Hessian officer wrote "It is now very unsafe for us to travel in New Jersey. The rascal peasants meet our men alone or in small unarmed groups."[20]

As the year came to an end Washington saw an opportunity to strike at the British outpost line in New Jersey by taking advantage of the fluid tactical situation that had developed during December before it once again ebbed. Although finally reinforced by some troops from Charles Lee's command and another detachment from Fort Ticonderoga, as well as 1,000 Pennsylvania militiamen later in the month, the American commander had to deal with the expiring enlistments of most of his soldiers, so he had to act quickly.

## THE BATTLES OF TRENTON AND PRINCETON

In the days that followed, George Washington conducted the most brilliant and successful series of tactical moves of his career. On Christmas night he led 2,400 men across the Delaware in rain, sleet, and snow at McKonkey's Ferry, north of Trenton. At 4:00 a.m. the following morning the force marched south in two columns; one, under General Greene, which Washington accompanied, followed an inland route, and the other, led by General John Sullivan, moved on Trenton along the river road. In an effort to completely isolate the Hessian garrison, General James Ewing was ordered to cross the Delaware from Pennsylvania with 700 New Jersey and Pennsylvania militiamen and block any escapees crossing Assunpink Creek just south of Trenton, while General John Cadwallader's 1,900-man division crossed from Bristol to divert von Donop's force in the Bordentown area from marching north to reinforce Rall. Once Trenton was taken Washington planned to concentrate all three commands and move on Princeton.[21]

Following a hard march in horrible weather, Greene's troops overran a Hessian outpost on the Pennington road just before 8:00 a.m. and then poured into Trenton, battering Rall's attempt at a counterattack with musketry and artillery and mortally wounding the German commander—in an interesting tactical decision, the Americans had brought a much higher proportion of cannon to infantry than usual to the fight—and drove the routed enemy through the town. Some panicked Germans tried to rally in an orchard, where they were forced to surrender. Meanwhile, Sullivan's men entered Trenton

from the river road, pushed the Hessians from the area around the French and Indian War barracks and seized the bridge over Assunpink Creek, capturing much of the remainder of the fleeing garrison. Unfortunately, Ewing and Cadwallader failed in their assignments, and before Sullivan closed the trap, several hundred Hessians escaped across the creek and made their way south to von Donop. In all, the Hessians lost 100 men killed or wounded and almost 1,000 as prisoners at Trenton. American losses were a mere four men wounded, although two soldiers apparently froze to death on the march. Despite legend, perhaps initiated by British sources trying to cover up their own incompetence, there is no evidence that the Hessians at Trenton were drunk. They were undoubtedly, however, surprised, outgeneraled, and outfought.[22]

Although he had planned to march on Princeton and even New Brunswick following the taking of Trenton, Washington, his little army exhausted and with Ewing and Cadwallader's men still on the Pennsylvania shore, ended his grand raid by returning to McConkey's Ferry and recrossing the Delaware that afternoon. In response to the Trenton disaster, a shocked General Howe recalled Cornwallis from his intended return to England and dispatched him across New Jersey with reinforcements. In an attempt to counter the British move, Washington returned to Trenton on December 30. Although much of the Continental army was due to dissolve as enlistments expired the following day, he had cajoled a majority of the men to stick by the colors a bit longer by appealing to their patriotism and offering each a $10 bounty (which he did not have in hand when making the promise) for a six-week extension of service. Aware that there were more than 8,000 British and Hessian troops scattered around New Jersey and that Cornwallis was now moving across the state with most of them, Washington ordered all available men, militia and Continental, to march to Trenton, then dispatched a small force, composed largely of riflemen under Colonel Edward Hand, to fight a delaying action against Cornwallis's advance beyond Princeton. The British commander had 5,500 men under his immediate command, with 1,500 of them in an advance guard skirmishing with Hand's men. When the exhausted British reached Trenton near nightfall, they were stymied in an attempt to cross Assunpink Creek in a sharp but limited firefight. Both sides disengaged, presumably to reopen the contest again in the morning.[23]

Hand's delaying action gave Washington time to create a defense in depth along Assunpink Creek, but Cornwallis remained confident he could outflank and destroy the American army. At around 1:00 a.m. on January 3, however, the American commander, leaving a rear guard of 400 men to tend otherwise abandoned campfires and dispatching his heavy artillery and excess baggage south to Burlington, stole a march on the enemy and headed to Princeton, where Cornwallis's rear guard of 1,200 men under Lieutenant Colonel Charles Mawhood was stationed. It was a hard march down a logging trail through the woods, but the American army crossed Stony Brook near Princeton at morning light, then divided, with a brigade under General Mercer splitting off from the main force with orders to tear down a bridge

in order to block any enemy reinforcements moving up from Trenton. The rest of the force moved directly on Princeton.[24]

Lieutenant Colonel Mawhood had already started two of his three regiments, the 17th and 55th, on the road to Maidenhead, leaving the 40th behind to secure the town and army baggage. By the time Mercer wheeled left from the American line of march, Mawhood had already crossed the Stony Creek bridge. British cavalry scouts, however, discovered Mercer's column and reported it to Mawhood, who turned his troops around, recrossed the creek and began to move toward the high ground between him and Mercer. Mercer spotted the British and adjusted his own advance to meet them and, at the same time, protect the flank of the main American column, which was marching down the "Back Road" towards Princeton. The Americans first engaged Mawhood's cavalry detachment, which had dismounted behind a fence at the Clark family orchard, and drove the horsemen back on the advancing 17th Regiment. After exchanging fire with Mercer's men the 17th launched a bayonet attack which routed the Americans and killed and wounded a number of them, including Mercer himself, who was unhorsed, beaten with a musket butt, and bayoneted seven times. The British ran amuck, and also killed a number of injured men who fell into their hands, including a lieutenant who suffered thirteen bayonet wounds.[25]

As General Sullivan's column continued on towards Princeton, Cadwallader diverted his men towards the combat he could see developing at the Orchard,

Overleaf: William Faden's map of the British and Continental troop movements during the Trenton and Princeton campaigns, published in London in 1777.

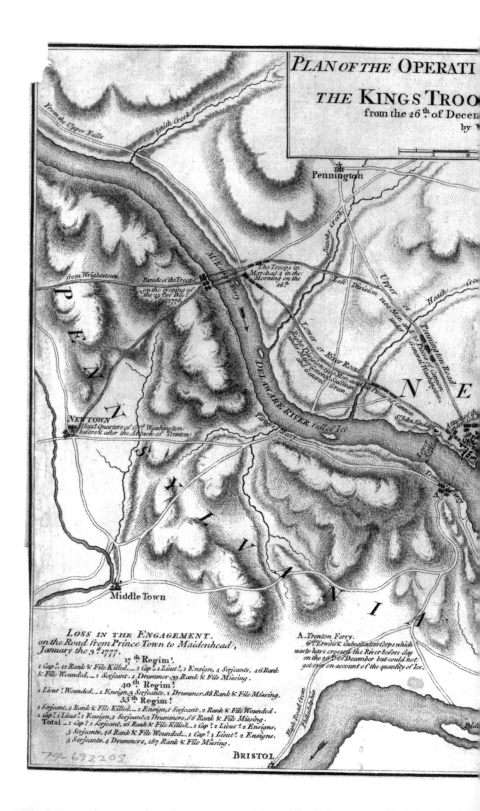

PLAN OF THE OPERATI

THE KINGS TROO

from the 26ᵗʰ of Decen

by

LOSS IN THE ENGAGEMENT.
on the Road from Prince Town to Maidenhead,
January the 3ᵈ 1777.

17ᵗʰ Regimᵗ.

55ᵗʰ Regimᵗ.

A. Trenton Ferry.

BRISTOL.

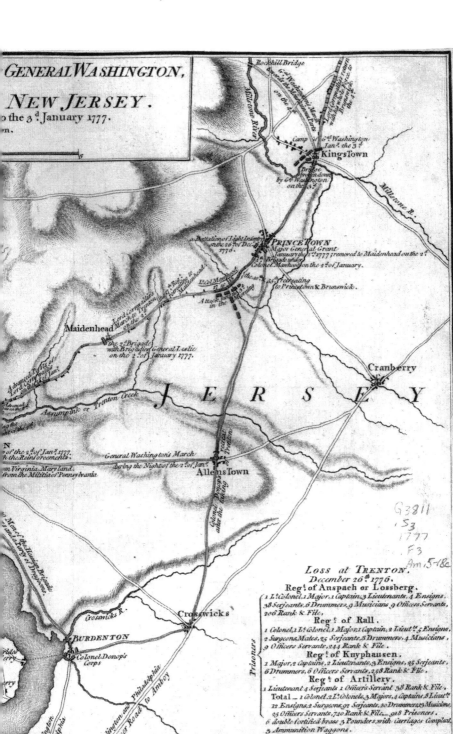

The Princeton battlefield today, with the Thomas Clarke House, which was built in 1772 by a Quaker family, in the distance. The house is furnished as it would have been in the Revolutionary era and has holdings of military artifacts and battle exhibits, as well as a research library. Hugh Mercer was brought to the house for treatment after being bayoneted during the battle.

pushing through Mercer's fleeing force to confront the British, who had temporarily halted. He deployed artillery and riflemen to drive in the 17th's light infantry skirmishers and advanced in line of battle in an attack that sputtered, then failed when his militiamen broke and fled under heavy enemy fire. A well-served American artillery battery held the British at bay, however, until Washington arrived with a force of Virginia and New England Continentals and a detachment of riflemen. The American commander rallied the militia and personally led the better disciplined Continentals forward. Washington emerged unharmed from a hail of bullets fired at close range and the British line broke and ran under the attack, although Mawhood managed to cut his way out with a small detachment. Sullivan, meanwhile, routed the 55th and 40th Regiments at Frog Hollow, driving them into Princeton, where some took refuge in Nassau Hall. A few well-placed cannon balls and an infantry assault on the main door led

to the surrender of 194 British soldiers holed up in the building. Princeton was won. Total casualties in killed, wounded, and missing that day are, as is often the case, in dispute. The British admitted to 276, although it is likely there were more, considering the haul of prisoners from Nassau Hall. Washington, who had totally wrecked a British brigade, claimed enemy casualties were between 500 and 600, while the Americans lost forty-four men killed, including General Mercer, who died of his bayonet wounds over a week after the battle.[26]

Washington's victories succeeded in tumbling the enemy outpost line back across New Jersey, and the American commander was in a position to threaten New Brunswick, where a hefty British payroll was reputedly stored. Instead, he decided that the best course was to march his victorious but battered little force north into winter quarters at Morristown, where many of his men would shortly be discharged. Protected by the hills, surrounded by a loyal Patriot pop-

President Warren Harding dedicating the Princeton Battle Monument in May 1922.

ulation, and supplemented by New Jersey militiamen who remained on duty through the middle of February, he began the slow process of rebuilding the army through the winter and into the spring of 1777. His troops encamped in the Loantaka Brook valley between Morristown and Madison, while Washington himself headquartered in the Arnold Tavern in town. All that survives of the camp is "Fort Nonsense" built in the spring and somewhat creatively reconstructed by the Civilian Conservation Corps in the 1930s. Recruits for new Continental regiments came in slowly after the catastrophes of the summer, but when they did they mustered in for three years or the duration of the war, as opposed to the one year enlistments of the first generation of Continentals. The new regiments would provide a solid basis for the army's future.[27]

## THE WAR AGAINST NEW JERSEY'S CIVILIANS

Rebel resistance across New Jersey continued to stiffen into the new year of 1777, as the militia, buoyed by its own and Washington's successes, began to restore Patriot political control across the state. Counterrevolutionaries like the fighting Quakers who took control of Upper Freehold Township in the name of the king towards the end of 1775 were routed, their leadership fleeing to the Pine Barrens or New York. The American revival was also ironically abetted by the enemy's conduct in the state. Dispirited Jerseyans had flocked to the seemingly triumphant British in the autumn of 1776, with, according to General Howe, at least 2,500 of them signing loyalty oaths. The British army, however, perhaps surprisingly considering its reputation as a well drilled and disciplined force, clearly violated what would today be considered the basics of good counterinsurgency policy. Allowing for a measure of Patriot propaganda exaggeration, there is no doubt that the British and their German auxiliary allies, despite official orders from Howe, who genuinely believed a rapprochement between king and colonists possible, ignored orders to treat the local population well and in fact abused them, even by the standards of European eighteenth-century civil-military relations. While foraging in Bergen County in November 1776, Hessian colonel von Donop observed that "infamous plundering" was engaged in by the English "in spite of orders to the contrary." Martin Hunter, a British junior officer then serving in New Jersey, recalled years later that "there was never a more expert set than the Light Infantry at either grab, lob or gutting a house."[28]

New Jersey's populace was pillaged, often regardless of loyalty or proffered paper "protections." Newark Presbyterian pastor Alexander McWhorter noted that "Whig and Tory were all treated in the same manner ... one Nuttman, who had always been a remarkable Tory, and who met the British troops with huzzas of joy, had his house plundered of almost everything; he himself had his shoes taken off his feet, and threatened to be hanged." Even higher ranking officers apparently engaged in looting, including Colonel Sir William Erskine, the British quartermaster general, "who lodged at Daniel Baldwin's [and] had his room furnished from a neighbouring house with mahogany chairs and tables, a considerable part of which was taken away with his baggage when he went to Elizabeth-Town." Other colonels were also accused of looting, including one who allegedly "took away a sick woman's bed." Howe personally promised protection to a woman who cooked a meal for his entourage, but had no sooner left the premises when "his soldiers Come in And plunder[ed] the Woman of Every thing in the house, Breaking And Destroying what they Could not take Away, they Even tore up the floor of the house." Some latter day accounts maintain that the British behaved well towards the civilian population compared to the European military standard of the day, one noting that "the forces of George III manifested unusual respect for the persons and property of noncombatants." Overwhelming evidence, however, suggests that this was clearly not the case. One perceptive recent historian notes that to the contrary, "damage claims reached the modern equivalent of millions of dollars."[29]

Jason Wickersty, who has done an exhaustive study of the New Jersey property damage claims filed in 1782, has concluded that the total value of destruction attributed to the British army in the state from 1776 on was £226,949. Continental soldiers were not entirely guiltless either, but the total attributed to them is a mere £17,317. Wickersty cautions that it is difficult to establish a close modern equivalent of these sums due to wartime inflation and other variables.[30]

Such accounts of civilian abuse, coupled with stories of sexual assaults perpetrated on New Jersey women by Howe's soldiers, spread like wildfire across the state, with inevitable results. By early 1777 British and Hessian troops venturing out of their diminishing chain of New Jersey posts in search of food for themselves and fodder for their animals found their paths barred by angry men wielding muskets and determined to make their forays as costly as possible. British stragglers found themselves, as one militiaman described it, "caught in their rambles." Some of these citizen soldiers had signed loyalty oaths to the British a few short months before—a British raiding party from Staten Island into Monmouth County in February 1777 captured militiamen who "had certificates about them of their having taken the Oaths of Allegiance." On January 4, a New Jersey mounted militia force captured a British supply wagon train in Somerset County. Sporadic fighting subsequently sputtered in an arc around Elizabethtown, which was held by Scottish Highlanders and German mercenaries. A combined British-Hessian foraging force was crushed at Springfield, with the entire German detachment, numbering between fifty and sixty men, killed or captured. On January 6, Howe ordered Elizabethtown abandoned. The town's garrison fell back to Perth Amboy, losing 100 prisoners and a large amount of supplies to pursuing Jersey militiamen along the way. The British commander soon withdrew all of his detachments from the state save those at New Brunswick and Perth Amboy and the Loyalist haven at the Sandy Hook lighthouse, which was protected by the guns of the Royal Navy. The New Jersey legislature felt comfortable enough to repeal the six dollar plus shoes and stockings bounty for state troops. Although New Jersey would continue to supply a substantial number of recruits to the Loyalist cause, the state as a whole would never be in serious political play for the remainder of the war.[31]

PETIT GUERRE IN NEW JERSEY

In the wake of Washington's winter miracle and the revival of the militia, some lukewarm British sympathizers, resentful at abandonment by their sworn protectors, professed a new loyalty to the Patriots. One account, perhaps apocryphal, had former Loyalists using their Howe-issued Oaths of Allegiance to roll paper musket cartridges for use against the British. Of thirty-five Tories sentenced to hang by a Morristown court in January 1777, thirty-three opted to join the regiments of the Continental army's New Jersey Brigade when that option to the scaffold was offered them. The upshot of the British withdrawal from most of New Jersey was the effective end of any significant Loyalist chance of seizing political and military control of the state. Instead, the Loyalists had come out into the open and exposed themselves to defeat and Patriot retribution, which resulted in flight and "refugee" status for many and eventually led to a vicious civil war within the Revolution in parts of New Jersey. By early 1777 New Jersey Loyalist property was being confiscated by official state orders and even those

who declared themselves neutral became subjects of suspicion and harassment. In July 1777, militia light horsemen carried off all of the "cattle, Sheep, Hogs and Horses" belonging to Thomas Crowell of Shrewsbury and told his wife they were coming back for her furniture and that the Crowell house and farm would be confiscated and put up for sale.[32]

Governor Livingston ordered Philemon Dickinson, who had initiated the early Patriot revival in Hunterdon County, to "compel all such Delinquents" avoiding militia service to come to the colors. Dickinson organized and maintained an active citizen-soldier presence in the field by rotating duty stints through the winter. Another key leader in the American counteroffensive was Continental brigadier general William "Scotch Willie" Maxwell. In December 1776 Washington had assigned Maxwell, a veteran of the ill-fated Canadian expedition of 1776, to report to Morristown and begin organizing new New Jersey Continental units, since the original battalions' enlistments were expiring. Maxwell was also assigned to operate alongside the militia in a continuous harassment campaign against remaining British garrisons in the state. Maxwell used his soldiers to stiffen Dickinson's men at critical junctures in what proved a seamless campaign.[33]

While the British garrisons in Middlesex County remained beleaguered, their living conditions were enhanced somewhat after General Cornwallis took command in New Brunswick and improved supplies of food and clothing for his men. The British still staged expeditions into the local countryside to acquire forage for their animals, however. Forage was a serious logistical need, equivalent to gasoline for a modern mechanized force, and so the armies continued to spar with each other on a regular basis into the spring. A New York Loyalist observed that "not a stick of wood, a spear of grass or a kernel of corn could the [British] troops in New Jersey procure without fighting for it, unless sent from New York." On February 23, Colonel Mawhood led a strong British force on a sortie from Perth Amboy to Rahway. Maxwell, his men's confidence on the rise, was happy to accommodate the colonel's apparent desire for a fight. Mawhood tried to outflank a line of militiamen with a company of grenadiers from the 42nd Highland Regiment, but Scotch Willie had deployed more Jerseymen, who remained unseen, in a position outflanking the Scottish advance, and at the appropriate moment, they rose and shot the regulars to ribbons. The whole British force fell back towards Perth Amboy, harassed by Maxwell's men all along the way, and two weeks later Maxwell repeated his stellar performance against another enemy column. Historian David Hackett Fischer calculates that over the winter following the battles of Trenton and Princeton, General Howe's army lost "more than nine hundred men . . . killed, wounded, captured or missing," in its "forage war" operations in New Jersey. That damage was inflicted by the aggressiveness and military skill of the New Jersey militia and Continentals led by Dickinson and Maxwell.[34]

The *petit guerre* not only battered and bled the British, but provided much needed military experience and confidence to the Americans, both militiamen and newly enlisted Continentals. Howe's officers realized this as fully as did Washington. In March 1777, a British major involved in the New Jersey fighting wrote that the "rebel soldiers from being accus-

tomed to peril in their skirmishes, begin to have more confidence." He added that "although they do not always succeed, following our people as they return . . . wounding and killing many of our rearguards gives them the notion of victory." A colonel worried that the forage war was creating a more difficult to defeat enemy, declaring that the constant skirmishing was "a plan which we ought to avoid most earnestly, since it will certainly make soldiers of the Americans." If newspaper reports were correct, by spring even New Jersey's ladies had joined the fight. According to one account, a Woodbridge woman, spying a "drunken Hessian" pillaging a house, "went home, dressed herself in man's apparel and armed with an old firelock" took him prisoner and delivered him to one of Maxwell's patrols.[35]

There were also British incursions into Bergen County in the spring of 1777. In May, Lieutenant Colonel Joseph Barton led a force of 300 Loyalists of the Fifth Battalion of New Jersey Volunteers from New York City into the county in an attempt to surprise a contingent of militiamen at Pompton. In a confused firefight in fog and haze, the militia successfully turned the tables on the invaders and forced them to withdraw.[36]

As the spring campaigning season approached, American and British commanders considered larger operations. Washington had assumed the tactical offensive at Trenton and Princeton and the swift reaction time and combativeness of the New Jersey militia and Continentals had proved decisive during the "forage war." Despite this, General Howe, with his large army centrally located in New York City and in command of American coastal waters, with another British army forming in Canada under General John Burgoyne and poised to move down

Lake Champlain to the Hudson, would retain the overall strategic initiative in the spring of 1777. Howe could strike wherever and however he wished. Washington, burdened with the defense of the American capital at Philadelphia and the Continental Congress meeting there, and committed to holding his Hudson River forts north of New York City, was in a necessarily reactive position.

## THE PHILADELPHIA CAMPAIGN

As winter waned, Howe began to strengthen his New Jersey outposts by transferring six battalions of infantry from Rhode Island to Perth Amboy. In February, the British chief made a personal visit to New Brunswick, where he put out the word, quickly picked up by American spies, that a Loyalist column was preparing to march into Sussex County and that British engineers were building a pontoon bridge to cross the Delaware. Howe's apparent preparations suggested to Washington that the British commander might be ready to either launch an attack on the main American army or renew his push across the state to capture Philadelphia. From his Morristown headquarters, the American commander made plans to counter any British moves, but he was far from confident that his army, still in the process of rebuilding, was in any condition to meet the enemy in the open field. Howe may have been planning an offensive but more likely he was making a feint to test the American reaction.[37]

George Washington was cautious, despite the fact that his army had grown over the winter. By May 21 the force under Washington's direct command at Morristown reported 7,363 officers and men "fit for duty and on duty." Arms and ammunition were arriving in large quan-

tities from France, with 19,000 muskets and 1,000 barrels of gunpowder imported during the month of March alone. These facts may have influenced the American commander's decision to push on the enemy's New Jersey lines in hopes of striking a lucky blow and driving the British from the state. In late May Washington advanced towards Howe's garrisons in eastern New Jersey, carefully establishing his main force, reinforced by more than 700 militiamen from Elizabethtown and Newark, at Middle Brook, on high ground less than ten miles from New Brunswick. The Middle Brook deployment gave the Americans an interior line *vis a vis* the enemy, which enabled Washington to move troops on an inside arc quickly to check a British advance from Perth Amboy or New Brunswick as well as any attempt by Howe to probe up the Hudson River.[38]

The American commander initially assumed that when the British resumed campaigning they would probably take up where they had left off and reinitiate their overland advance on Philadelphia. By mid-June, however, that did not appear to be the case. American spies reported a large amount of naval activity in the waters around New York, indicating that Howe was considering some sort of sea-borne movement, which could be directed at several possible targets, including Philadelphia and coastal cities to the north and south. In order to confuse the Americans as to his actual intentions, on June 11 Howe advanced 18,000 troops into New Jersey in two columns, concentrating them at Somerset and Middlebush in hopes of drawing Washington out of his Middle Brook position or perhaps cutting off part of the American army under General Sullivan stationed in the vicinity of Princeton. On June 21, after several maneuvers to bring the Americans to battle failed, Howe abandoned his advanced posts and New Brunswick and withdrew to Perth Amboy, where the British hunkered down, while American observation forces deployed at Quibbletown (New Market in today's Piscataway) and Metuchen.[39]

On June 26 Howe marched two columns out of Perth Amboy in an operation aimed at cutting off and defeating the Metuchen force commanded by New Jersey general William Alexander, usually referred to as "Lord Stirling" after the Scottish title he laid claim to on rather tenuous grounds. Although initially positioned on good defensive terrain, Alexander, who was outnumbered, aggressively moved his men forward and engaged the advancing enemy until he was almost cut off by a flanking movement initiated by Cornwallis. Alexander's hasty retreat cost him three artillery pieces and about seventy men as prisoners. Cornwallis followed the Americans to Westfield while Washington fell back with his main army on Bound Brook. Howe then withdrew his army once more to Perth Amboy, from where he began to cross to Staten Island, a move completed by June 30. A little known aspect of British operations in New Jersey in June 1777 was that they may have provided the occasion for the first use of breech loading firearms in combat in America. Captain Patrick Ferguson, inventor of a breech loading flintlock rifle, had arrived in New York on June 1 with a company armed with the experimental weapon and he and his command participated in Howe's offensive that month.[40]

Back in New York, Howe continued his dilatory preparations for the Philadelphia Campaign into July. When General Henry Clinton arrived from London on July 5 to take charge of the New York garrison, he was surprised to see that Howe had not yet left, and was dismayed when he discovered that Howe planned a seaborne movement against Philadelphia, rather than an overland one, as the latter option would, Clinton believed, help defend New York by screening that city from American attack. Howe, who disdained Clinton, refused to change his plans and, convinced that Burgoyne's army, by mid-July approaching Fort Ticonderoga, along with the New York garrison, were in no danger from any American forces, finally began a leisurely campaign to capture Philadelphia.

On July 23, Howe's 15,000-man force weighed anchor off Staten Island and sailed south in a 250-ship armada, confronting Washington with a number of possibilities, which changed as reports of the fleet's location came in. When the enemy was reported sailing north in Chesapeake Bay, then landing at Head of Elk, Maryland, in the upper Chesapeake, Washington correctly concluded that Howe's objective was Philadelphia. The American commander marched his 11,000 men south, parading directly through the capital city to boost Patriot morale. Congressman John Adams for one, was somewhat impressed, and wrote his wife that the Continentals appeared "an army well appointed" despite the fact that "they don't step exactly in time."[41]

On arrival at Wilmington, Delaware, Washington halted his army and pushed a small elite force forward to observe and report on enemy activities and movements and engage in limited combat when appropriate. Choosing a qualified officer to command the light infantry proved a simple task. Jerseyman William Maxwell had proved a master of the *petit guerre* during the New Jersey forage war and was assigned to the position on August 30. Washington cautioned Maxwell to "be watchful and guarded on all the roads," to "annoy" the enemy whenever possible," and to be careful when and where he fought, only engaging the British when he had a good chance of success.[42]

While the light infantry, reinforced by Pennsylvania and Delaware militia, moved south, with the main American army cautiously following, Howe dispatched several supply ships back to Delaware Bay with orders to establish a forward base at Newcastle. Howe then marched north in two columns, one commanded by General Cornwallis and the other by Hessian general Wilhelm von Knyphausen. The slow and deliberate British advance was preceded by a screen of light infantry units and rifle-armed German Jaegers, including a company under the command of the highly observant Captain Johann Ewald.[43]

After halting his main army at Red Clay Creek, Delaware, Washington ordered Maxwell to move forward and confront the British advance guard. On September 2, Maxwell established a base in the vicinity of Cooch's Bridge, which crossed Christiania Creek, deployed a defensive line along the front of Iron Hill, and then sent most of his men forward down the Aiken's Tavern Road, which he perceived would be the main axis of the British advance, ordering them to fire on the enemy and fall back towards the main position. The Americans made contact with a detachment of Jaegers and light infantrymen under the command of Lieutenant Colonel Ludwig von Wurmb early the following morning.

Maxwell's men conducted a two mile fighting withdrawal against von Wurmb to the Cooch's Bridge line, made a short

stand and then retreated again, through woods and across fields and up the slope of Iron Hill itself. At that point General Howe personally appeared on the field, reinforced Wurmb with the Loyalist Queen's Rangers as well as artillery, and ordered a rapid bayonet charge on the American position. The British bayonet charge, a tactic perfected on Long Island, was designed more to rattle the American defensive line so that it would break and run rather than to actually close and fight hand to hand with bayonets—although, as seen at Princeton, that happened once in a while. The British charge succeeded. Maxwell's outgunned and outnumbered light infantry, which had held the British advance up for seven hours, rapidly fled the field, some men tossing away their blankets and muskets. Unlike his actions in New Jersey, Maxwell's conduct of the operation drew mixed reviews. The young and inexperienced Marquis de Lafayette caustically and presumptuously condemned the Jersey general's conduct and characterized him as "the most inept brigadier general in the army." General Washington, however, who along with Lafayette witnessed the last stages of what had been a long fight, concluded that Maxwell had done a good job until he "had to retreat" due to overwhelming odds.[44]

## THE BATTLE OF BRANDYWINE

Skirmishing continued as Howe moved north and Washington eventually deployed his army along the north bank of Brandywine Creek, adjusting as Howe concentrated at nearby Kennet Square (spelled Kennett Square today) along the main route to Philadelphia (approximating today's U. S. Route 1). Unfortunately, the Brandywine, which divided into west and east branches beyond the American right flank, was fordable by troops at a number of locations, including seven official crossings, a fact that proved detrimental to the Americans. On September 11, the American commander placed his best units in a position to contest a British passage of the Brandywine in the vicinity of Chadds Ford, then strung out militia to protect his left flank and covered his right flank with a light cavalry screen, a few infantry detachments, and some more militiamen. On arrival at Kennet Square, where the road forked, Howe divided his force, with Knyphausen's 5,000 men moving north along the Nottingham Road while Cornwallis took 7,500 soldiers up the Great Valley Road to outflank the Rebels.[45]

Major John Simcoe's Loyalist Queen's Rangers and Ferguson's riflemen, the latter armed with the captain's breech loading rifles, led Knyphausen's advance and were promptly ambushed by Maxwell's men, who had rallied from their defeat. Captain Ferguson reported that "nearly half of the two corps was either killed or wounded," but subsequently claimed that since his men were armed with breechloaders, more easily loaded and fired lying on the ground, they were saved from even heavier losses. Maxwell had already handled Ferguson's company roughly on the road north, and one scholar estimates "only some 24 to 30 men" were left in action by Brandywine. Knyphausen stepped up the attack and gradually drove Maxwell's men back in a running fight to a rise near the banks of the Brandywine, where the Americans took shelter behind some quickly erected field fortifications. In a repeat of Cooch's Bridge, British artillery shelled the position and infantrymen filtered around the American flanks until Maxwell withdrew across the creek. Ferguson shouldered a rifle himself and joined his men in the

front line, later claiming he passed up a shot at Washington, who was observing the fighting.[46]

Knyphausen spent much of the rest of the day skirmishing with the Americans across the Brandywine, providing a distraction for the outflanking maneuver, and by late afternoon Cornwallis was fording the creek in the American rear. Although Washington had been notified by mid-morning that an enemy column was marching north, he believed Cornwallis to be farther upstream than he actually was, and considered attacking Knyphausen in an attempt to defeat the British in detail. Before he could implement this plan, however, the American commander discovered to his chagrin that the enemy had successfully crossed at Trimbles's and Jeffries's fords and posed a serious threat to his right. In response he ordered troops to leave the Chadds Ford line to confront Cornwallis.

The Americans rushed to engage the enemy flanking force and soon there was heavy fighting around Birmingham Meeting House. As the tide of battle on the right began to turn against his men, Washington left Chadds Ford with reinforcements to take personal command of the growing fight. With opposing forces to his front thus weakened, Knyphausen launched his own offensive, spearheaded by German Jaegers, the remains of Ferguson's riflemen, and the Queen's Rangers, who splashed across the Brandywine under heavy fire and then pushed up the hill on the other side, capturing an American battery, but losing Ferguson, who was put out of action when a musket ball broke his right arm. By 7:00 p.m. the Americans were driven from the entire field in heavy fighting, leaving the way to Philadelphia open to Howe. Although beaten, Washington's army once again escaped destruction, and fell back to Chester to reorganize. The Americans reportedly suffered around 1,200 casualties, including killed, wounded, and missing or captured; the British about half as many.[47]

Although the Rebel army survived, Washington's defeat at Brandywine guaranteed that Philadelphia would fall to the enemy. As Howe advanced on the city, Congressmen took to their heels, but not before ordering the arrest of a number of accused Loyalists, many of them Quakers. Those who would not agree to comply with a series of restrictions were packed off to imprisonment in Virginia. Military supplies, government paperwork, and money were rapidly evacuated from the capital before the British marched in on September 26, 1777. The British army had not gained any local sympathy after Brandywine, when pillaging the local farms, as had been the case in New Jersey the previous year, became the order of the day. According to a local doctor, "the officers sent their servants round among the farmers of the vicinity to collect poultry and other provender for their own tables. These marauders regarded as lawful plunder everything they could lay their hands upon and deemed worth carrying away." Personal property was plundered as well, including "clocks, spice boxes, and looking glasses." Birmingham, Kennet, Pennsbury, Thornbury, and Westtown Townships subsequently filed claims totaling £8,602; Birmingham Township alone filed claims worth £5,844 in stolen property.[48]

## THE BATTLE OF GERMANTOWN

Howe pushed 9,000 men forward to Germantown to occupy the attention of the main American field force, which continued to hover within striking distance of the city, and dispatched his remaining troops to accomplish other vital tasks, including securing his overland supply line back to Delaware. After rallying his beaten army and supplementing it with several thousand militiamen, Washington decided to strike at the British in Germantown in early October, dividing his force, with one column fixing the enemy's attention while other troops worked their way around the British flanks. This was a tricky move with well-trained troops, made much more so when attempted with militia and half-trained Continentals.[49]

To complicate matters, as the Americans approached the British positions on the early morning of October 4, a dense fog set in. Although it initially provided cover for the Americans' advance, and first contact resulted in a confused British retreat, things fell apart as the main column was held up by a small British force holed up in the Chew House. The Americans, including Maxwell's New Jersey Brigade, bounced thousands of musket balls off the building, but the British inside held on. The attack stalled, and one of the American flanking divisions fired on the main column in the haze, causing a panicky retreat.[50]

Although Washington and his officers eventually got their retreating men under control, and the British pursuit was not aggressive, the battle was lost and Washington ordered a withdrawal. American casualties, including around 400 men captured, mostly from one Virginia regiment, totaled around 1,000, with British losses around half as many. Although Washington was defeated once more, his ambitious Germantown offensive almost succeeded, which was recognized by the troops themselves, and the fact that the American army once again survived potential disaster intact and was able to withdraw to fight another day was a significant morale booster. In the wake of the battle, Washington remained outside Philadelphia and his outposts continued to spar with Howe's patrols into the countryside.[51]

## ATTACKS ON FORTS MERCER AND MIFFLIN

Washington's Germantown failure left one final act to be played out in the Philadelphia drama, as the British contested American control of the lower Delaware River. Prior to the campaign, the Americans deployed ships, strung underwater obstructions, and garrisoned Fort Mifflin on Mud Island and Fort Mercer at Red Bank on the New Jersey side of the Delaware south of Philadelphia to block a British advance up the river. Howe now controlled Philadelphia, but his supply line remained blocked. Although it appeared impossible for the Americans to hold the forts indefinitely with Philadelphia lost, Washington reinforced Mifflin and Mercer.[52]

When a British bombardment of Mifflin failed to force its surrender, Howe decided to capture Mercer, which would enable his men to fire into the rear of Mifflin. Colonel von Donop volunteered to attack the fort with 2,000 Hessians. In the ensuing October 21 battle, the American defenders exacted a heavy price, inflicting 400 casualties, including von Donop himself, who was mortally wounded and captured. A simultaneous naval attack on Mifflin was defeated as well. The British in Philadelphia continued to suffer from a severe lack of supplies and warm clothing until both forts were evacuated in November and the American river defense fleet was aban-

doned and burned. Washington, still on the lookout for opportunities to successfully bring on battle with the enemy, kept his increasingly ragged army in the field near Philadelphia at Whitemarsh until mid-December. Reinforcements from General Horatio Gates, who, with assistance from the leadership of Benedict Arnold, had bagged Burgoyne's invading northern army at Saratoga on October 17, were slow in coming, although Colonel Daniel Morgan's riflemen, followed by three infantry brigades, arrived in November.[53]

## VALLEY FORGE ENCAMPMENT

As the weather worsened, Washington fended off yet one more British probe of his lines and the British, no doubt recalling Bunker Hill, declined to attack his fortified position in force. Howe withdrew to Philadelphia on December 8, leaving the next move to Washington, who went into winter quarters at Valley Forge, eighteen miles from Philadelphia. At Valley Forge the American army was well positioned to cover Philadelphia and also provide a protective roadblock against any British expedition launched to capture the Continental Congress, then meeting at York. Unfortunately, many men were still living in canvas tents as late as February, and the poorly constructed and unsanitary huts many of Washington's 10,000 soldiers eventually erected were not much better.[54]

During the winter of 1777–1778, some 12,000 troops were quartered at Valley Forge at one time or another, and as many as 3,000 of them died there. The deaths were not the result, as legend might have it, of severe weather conditions, but of malnutrition and disease. The army's supply system, crippled by corruption, administrative incompe-

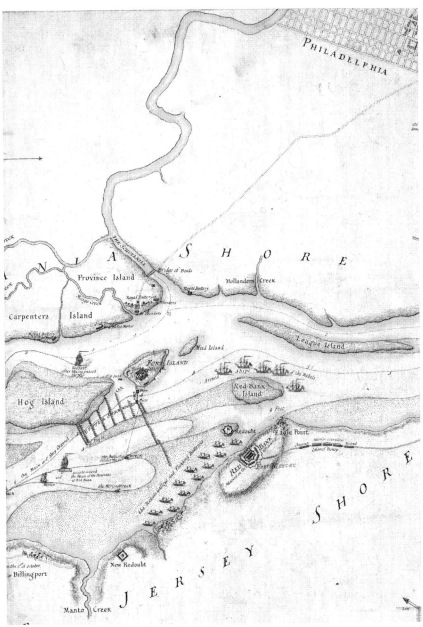

A detail from William Faden's 1777 map of the Delaware River showing the British attacks on Fort Mercer at Red Hook and Fort Mifflin on Fort Island.

tence, and poor roads, simply collapsed. As early as October 1777, General Maxwell petitioned Governor Livingston for a supply of clothing for his Jerseymen, as the Continental Congress had not provided any. Maxwell advised the governor that "we are in great need at present of shoes, stockings, breeches, shirts, good jackets and some caps, for the want of which many valuable men are rendered useless." To make matters worse, while American soldiers suffered, some nearby Pennsylvania and New Jersey farmers sold food to the British garrison of Philadelphia. Salem County New Jersey residents, some of them professed Patriots, supplied the British in exchange for "specie coin, as well as sugar, tea, syrup and strong liquors, which are much used here."[55]

Despite its tribulations, Washington's army emerged from Valley Forge a more capable force than it had been the previous year. The belated appointment in March of Nathanael Greene as quartermaster general improved the supply system, while the arrival of "Baron" Friedrich Wilhelm von Steuben and his institution of a uniform training regimen dramatically improved the army's discipline and drill. Steuben, born in Magdeburg, Prussia, in 1730, the son of a Prussian army officer, joined the Prussian army at the age of seventeen, eventually rising to the rank of captain and serving as a staff officer. Discharged as the army down-sized in 1763 at the end of the Seven Years War, he found subsequent employment at another German principality, and then moved to France. Along the way he began to style himself as "Baron Von Steuben." The ersatz baron was down and out in Paris and living on a shoestring budget when the Revolution broke out. After impressing Benjamin Franklin by exaggerating his former level of command responsibility, he was accepted as a volunteer by Congress. Steuben traveled to America in December 1777, and arrived at Washington's headquarters at Valley Forge in February 1778.[56]

Although Steuben could not speak English, and Washington neither German nor French, Colonel John Laurens of Washington's staff was on hand to serve as interpreter, and Steuben impressed the American commander in his initial interview. Although he respected Washington's abilities as a commander and thought the Americans fine "raw material," the German was not impressed with the Continental army itself. After a few days of observations, he perceived that the army's chief problem, aside from a lack of food and clothing, was its poor marching and maneuvering ability. Ability to move in a rapid and disciplined manner was essential to an eighteenth century army, and the lack of these skills had demonstrably hindered the American performance from Long Island to Germantown.

Steuben wrote an entirely new and simplified drill manual combining British, Prussian, and American ideas and then established a cadre system of training to instill its lessons throughout the army. The Prussian personally instructed selected officers and enlisted men from different units in the new simplified drill and sent them back to their units to train their comrades. Swearing and yelling in various languages, with an interpreter close at hand, Steuben shouldered a musket himself and drilled his Continental charges into the spring. His system proved so effective that it endured long after the Revolution as the standard drill text of the American army.[57]

## BRITISH AND AMERICAN FOR-AGE RAIDS

There were supply problems in Philadelphia as well, complicated by British behavior. While General Howe tried to assist impoverished civilians in the city, many of his troops looted the citizenry, in a manner that was now becoming familiar. Howe often used Loyalist units for foraging expeditions into the countryside, even though his attempts to recruit soldiers from among loyal Pennsylvanians failed to live up to expectations. Some of these organizations were little more than gangs of bandits, who "live[d] from pillage." While Steuben trained the Continentals, American militiamen skirmished with Howe's foragers in Delaware, Pennsylvania, and New Jersey throughout the winter as both armies scoured the surrounding countryside for food and fodder.[58]

In February 1778, American general Anthony Wayne led a foraging force through the Swedish settlements along the Jersey shore of the Delaware. Reverend Nicholas Collin, pastor of the Swedish Lutheran Church at Penn's Neck, recalled that some of Wayne's men marching past his parsonage were "without boots, others without socks." The Americans were hotly pursued by a British force that scattered the local Swedesboro militia. Although neutral with a tendency to sympathize with established authority, Collin reported that "many people here were plundered," as "the English soldiers are undisciplined and cannot always be controlled." Collin wrote that "often both friend and foe were robbed in the most despicable manner, and sometimes with the permission of the officers." Throughout the winter and into spring the southwestern part of New Jersey was subjected to

The Hancock House along Alloways Creek, New Jersey, is a New Jersey State Park site.

wholesale theft, raids, kidnappings, and random violence.[59]

Perhaps the most egregious New Jersey raid was conducted by a party of Howe's Loyalists, including Simcoe's Rangers and the New Jersey Volunteers. On March 17, 1778, a force under Colonel Mawhood landed on the Jersey shore in Salem County and pushed inland, luring an American militia detachment into an ambush at Quinton's Bridge. Mawhood, no doubt still smarting from Princeton and the forage war, assigned Major Simcoe to remove another perceived threat to his rear, a militia detachment guarding Hancock's Bridge on Alloways Creek. On the night of March 20–21, Simcoe's Loyalists conducted a surprise attack on the Hancock's Bridge garrison, killing everyone they could find in the vicinity, including men they encountered along the road, twenty to thirty militiamen sleeping in the Hancock house, and the house's owner Judge William Hancock and his brother, who happened to be noted local

Loyalists. Following the massacre, Mawhood threatened to use local Loyalists to "attack all such of the Militia who remain in Arms, burn and destroy their Houses and other Property, and reduce them, their unfortunate Wives and Children, to Beggary and Distress." In response to such incursions Washington dispatched Colonel Israel Shreve's Second New Jersey Regiment from Valley Forge to the state. Mawhood tried to bag Shreve's regiment at Haddonfield, but the colonel slipped away to Mount Holly. When Mawhood returned to Pennsylvania on March 31, the Second remained in New Jersey. After the war Simcoe bragged about the massacre of the militiamen as a stellar surprise operation, but expressed sorrow at the "unfortunate circumstances" of the bayoneting of the Judge and his brother, stating that "events like these are the real miseries of war."[60]

Although newspapers in British occupied Philadelphia argued that Mawhood's expedition actually won over a populace that "lamented much that the army was to depart and leave them again to the tyranny of the rebel faction," it seems more likely that it merely elevated the general climate of chaos in the area. The violence created a situation that Reverend Collin described as a climate of "distrust, fear, hatred and abominable selfishness" and spawned, not for the first or last time in Revolutionary War New Jersey, a civil war within the context of the general war. The struggle in the lower Delaware Valley led "parents and children, brothers and sisters, wife and husband" to become "enemies to one another," Collin recalled. The minister wrote that "militia and some regular troops on one side and refugees with the Englishmen on the other were constantly roving about in smaller or great numbers, plundering and destroying everything in a barbarous manner." Things were not quiet on the other side of the state, either, with constant skirmishing between Loyalist and British troops and American militia, from Bergen County to Monmouth. On November 27, 1777, General Dickinson led a force of 1,400 militiamen on a massive raid on Staten Island and captured 200 men of the Loyalist New Jersey Volunteers, most of them recruited in Bergen County.[61]

To add to the confusion, a number of Jerseymen switched sides, often for economic reasons. One Isac Josten, "a Swede" from Salem County who had been a "strong Republican and officer in the militia" went over to the British "after he had begun to trade [with them]." Fickle loyalties were also apparent in both field armies, with desertions fairly common. Unsurprisingly, considering the situation at Valley Forge, where soldiers were poorly clothed and fed and sporadically paid, some 2,000 Americans either took unauthorized leave or deserted over the winter, either heading for home or to the British lines around Philadelphia. Less understandably, considering their superior logistical position, Hessians and other Germans often deserted from Howe's redoubt ring. Eleven British and German deserters entered the American lines at Valley Forge on one day, December 30, 1777.[62]

# 4. New Jersey and the American Revolution, 1778–1783: Fighting for Victory

By the spring of 1778, the course of the war had taken a dramatically different turn. The American victory at Saratoga in October 1777 led to active French intervention in the conflict, changing the chessboard of combat across the Atlantic. The new military realities in the American war demanded a change in British strategy. Troops and ships had to be detailed to defend against potential French moves against Britain's West Indian possessions, which had more commercial value than the mainland colonies, as well as to initiate attacks against French islands in the West Indies. These new priorities led to a scaling down of operations in the Middle Atlantic region. The consolidation needed to provide troops for other missions required that the main British army in America in Philadelphia move back to New York—and initiate that change of base as soon as possible.[1]

On April 20, Washington, not privy to the British strategy, convened a council of his generals to consider the army's initial moves for the 1778 campaign season. Three options were available, attacking Philadelphia, moving north against New York, or remaining at Valley Forge and

continuing to train and strengthen the army. Although some generals wanted to pursue a more aggressive policy elsewhere, the final conclusion, reached on May 8, was that recovery of Philadelphia was the most important item on the American agenda, and that the army should closely monitor British activity in and around the city. American morale soared when word arrived at the end of April of the French entry into the war. On May 6, following a rollicking May Day celebration in which the men of Maxwell's Jersey Brigade, some dressed as Indians and well-fortified with whiskey, their hats adorned with cherry blossoms, marched with "mirth and Jollity" in honor of "King Tammany," the whole army gathered for a formal announcement of the French alliance, followed by salutes of cannon fire and a musketry *feu de joie*.[2]

On May 8 Washington launched a 2,200-man expeditionary force of Continentals and militiamen supported by five artillery pieces under the Marquis de Lafayette across the Schuylkill River to disrupt British foraging parties and gather intelligence on enemy intentions. Lafayette camped at Barren Hill and deployed in a defensive position, and Howe ordered General Clinton, his soon to be successor, to try to bag Lafayette and his entire force. Clinton moved out of Philadelphia with 12,000 men in three columns intended to converge in a complicated tactical scenario on the small American force, but Lafayette eluded him.[3]

Subsequently given the army command, Clinton would have preferred to withdraw by sea, down the Delaware River, around Cape May and north to New York. The threat of intervention by a French fleet made such a course dangerous, however. A lack of available transport ships would have made it necessary to move the British army and its entourage, including some 3,000 panicked Loyalists eager to leave town before the Continental army arrived, in relays. Clinton decided to load his heavy gear and baggage aboard ship, along with all of his sick and disabled soldiers and the Tories, then march across "the Jerseys" with his able-bodied troops and the remainder of his supplies and equipment; the latter hauled in some 1,500 wagons.[4]

By mid-May it was becoming apparent to Washington that the enemy was up to something. Maxwell's brigade, reinforced by nine-month service "levy" militia draftees and substitutes and militiamen under General Dickinson, took up a position at Mount Holly and awaited developments. The Jersey general had had a few rough spots over the winter; he was found innocent at a court martial accusing him of being drunk during the Brandywine fight and survived lobbying by some of his officers to have him removed from command. With the arrival of the campaign season, however, "Scotch Willie" was ready for action.[5]

By early June, Hessian captain Johann Ewald noted that terrified Tories were "packing up and fleeing [Philadelphia] before the wrath of Congress" as British troops in small numbers began to cross the Delaware into New Jersey at Cooper's Ferry. In the early morning hours of June 16, Clinton removed his artillery from the redoubts Howe had built to defend Philadelphia and began to march his army down to the river. Within two days the entire British force had crossed once more into New Jersey and the supply train was well on its way to Haddonfield. Once he became aware Clinton had evacuated the city, Washington began to move his own army from Valley Forge, sending troops to Philadelphia and heading northeast with his main force to Coryell's Ferry, (modern New Hope, Pennsylvania) to cross the Delaware to New Jersey. The Americans marched swiftly and efficiently, by divisions, revealing the professionalism that had permeated their ranks over the winter at Valley Forge.[6]

## THE BRITISH WITHDRAWAL ACROSS NEW JERSEY

As Clinton's army began its march across "the Jerseys," resistance, unlike in 1776, was quick and stiff. The New Jersey militia and Maxwell's Continentals harassed the column continually, wrecking bridges, filling in wells, and delivering sporadic bursts of musketry into the line of march. Captain Ewald recalled that on the route across the state, "skirmishing continued without letup. Many men fell and lost their lives miserably because of the intense heat, and due to the sandy ground which we crossed through a pathless brushwood where no water was to be found on the entire march." One militiaman who carried a rifle, which was rare for the usually musket-armed Jerseymen, dropped a British soldier, one of a group plundering a house, at 100 yards distance.[7]

Clinton divided his army into two divisions, under Generals Knyphausen and Cornwallis, to protect his twelve-mile-long baggage train. He issued strong orders against "marauding," and threatened soldiers caught pillaging with "execution on the spot." Even John Simcoe advised his men that "an abhorrence of plunder . . . distinguishes the truly brave from the cowardly ruffian," and ordered his officers to march in the rear of their companies to make sure that "no soldier quitted his rank on any pretence."[8]

At Evesboro the British engaged in a running fight with New Jersey Continentals and militiamen. Militia captain Jonathan Beesley died of his wounds in British custody and Clinton ordered him buried "with all the honors of war" because "he was a brave man." Despite Clinton's proclamation banning marauding under penalty of death, however, his men "plundered the [local] inhabitants of their household goods, their grain, horses and cattle . . . at every opportunity." Major Richard Howell of the Third New Jersey reported that the local people were "villainously plundered." Many farmers drove their stock into hiding places like Deer Park Swamp near Moorestown to conceal them from the British.[9]

At Mount Holly, British soldiers burned an iron works and the homes of Colonel Israel Shreve of the Second New Jersey and local Committee of Safety chairman Peter Tallman. Clinton offered a reward of twenty-five Guineas for information as to the perpetrators, further evidence of the inefficacy of the general's warnings about "marauding." No one collected. On June 21, Lieutenant Colonel Clarke of the British 7th Regiment

A soldier of the 3rd New Jersey Regiment in 1777.

issued an order condemning the "irregularity and excesses that have been committed these few days," adding that his officers should "prevent its happening again," and threatened punishment "with the utmost Severity." Although Captain John Andre wrote that "a good deal of attention was paid to enforcing the Orders respecting plunder," another officer recorded that even with "all the precautions taken, a good deal of plundering [was] going on." A Hessian major wrote that "there was much plundering, which disturbed General Clinton . . . It has made the country people all the more embittered rebels."[10]

The British marched on through appalling heat, and, at Allentown, Clinton decided to push on to Sandy Hook rather than take a route to the city through New Brunswick to Perth Amboy and Staten Island. The shorter route would save time and remove the risk of crossing the Raritan River at New Brunswick with his potentially vulnerable baggage train, and, at the same time, pull away from the American army, which was now in New Jersey.[11]

## THE BATTLE OF MONMOUTH COURT HOUSE

On the morning of June 25, after struggling over sandy roads in increasing heat, the British halted a few miles south of Monmouth Court House. The tempo of American harassment had steadily increased, and a combined Continental and militia force under New Jersey major Joseph Bloomfield hung within a quarter-mile of the British rear, closing with and firing on the enemy "several times during the night." Bloomfield's detachment "took 15 prisoners & had several skirmishes with the Jagers," with the major personally claiming three Jaeger prisoners.[12]

The following afternoon, the British reached Monmouth Court House and Clinton decided to halt and rest his exhausted army. After pushing out patrols beyond the town, he established headquarters in the house of Mrs. Elizabeth Covenhoven. Most of the town's inhabitants had fled, taking everything they could carry with them, before the British arrival, but that did not stop soldiers from looting what remained. A Hessian lieutenant recalled that "every place here [Monmouth Court House] was broken into and plundered by British soldiers." While the Hessians watched, "the English

An officer of the 2nd New Jersey in 1778.

soldiers had . . . been breaking and destroying everything in the city-hall-house, even tearing down the little bell in the steeple."[13]

On the morning of June 24, Washington called a council of war at Hopewell. General Charles Lee, who had returned to the army following a comfortable British captivity in New York, maintained that the American army was absolutely unable to stand up to Clinton's and that Washington should limit himself to harassing the British along their way, a concept known as providing a "bridge of gold" passage out of one's territory. Generals Alexander and Knox concurred with Lee, but Generals Wayne,

Greene, Duportail, Lafayette, and Steuben wanted to fight, as early as possible. Lafayette believed it would be "disgraceful and humiliating" for the American army to allow the British to withdraw without a battle, and Steuben, who was confident of the combat readiness of the troops he had trained, agreed. These officers lobbied for aggressive offensive action against the enemy which Lafayette, for one, thought could produce a decisive war-winning battle.[14]

In the end, Washington took a middle course. The Steuben drill had improved the ability of soldiers from different regiments to work together and Washington ordered a force of "picked men" from different regiments, more than 1,400 strong with four artillery pieces, under the command of Brigadier General Charles Scott, to harass the British left flank and rear guard. Fiery young Lieutenant Colonel Alexander Hamilton, as eager for a fight as Lafayette, was not satisfied, and is quoted as saying that Washington's decision "would have done honor to the most honorable body of midwives and to them only." Still, the order moved more American forces to the front and increased the likelihood of a battle. Despite Lee's misgivings, the American army was actually spoiling for a fight.[15]

On June 25, Washington added 1,000 more "picked men" and two artillery pieces under General Wayne to the advance, ordering Lafayette to bring that force forward, merge it with Scott's and assume overall command of what by this point was a sizeable detachment, and harass the enemy with "every degree of annoyance." Lafayette was instructed to attack the British "as occasion may require by detachment," but also, "if a proper opening sh[oul]d be given, by

operating against them with the whole force of your command." British march discipline was largely effective, however, and the enemy were "in so compact a body" that the Americans could not inflict any significant damage on them."[16]

General Lee, who had disdained command of the advanced forces, now complained that he should have Lafayette's job by right of seniority. Acceding to Lee's demand, Washington ordered him forward with a 600-man detachment and authority to take command from Lafayette. On June 26, Lee arrived at Englishtown, within five miles of the British at Monmouth Court House, and began concentrating all the advance troops.[17]

Clinton had deployed his men in a defensive posture, in a line about four miles long. Dickinson's New Jersey Militia hovered to his west, and Morgan's riflemen were deployed to the east, while the small American mounted force patrolled the roads around the enemy position. At 4:00 a.m. on June 28, General Clinton's army, led by Knyphausen's division, began to pull out of Monmouth Court House towards Middletown. An hour earlier, Lee had ordered Colonel William Grayson to probe the enemy, without starting a major fight. Grayson and his soldiers met Lee at 6:00 a.m., briefly halted for instructions, and then marched out in relative morning cool towards Monmouth Court House.

Grayson led his 600 men, supported by two artillery pieces, cautiously forward and was followed by other detachments under Colonel Richard Butler and Colonel Henry Jackson, Brigadier General Woodford's brigade, and the rest of Brigadier General James Varnum's brigade, commanded by Colonel John Durkee, as well as two additional artillery pieces. Anthony Wayne's 1,000-man detachment with four artillery pieces and then Scott's men with four more guns followed Varnum's brigade. "Scotch Willie" Maxwell brought up the rear with his Jerseymen, supplemented by two artillery pieces. Since almost forty percent of his men were minimally trained new militia levies, Maxwell conceded the seniority of a position farther forward. Lee's total strength was around 4,000 men, although the force under his immediate command when he actually engaged the enemy was significantly smaller—one estimate has it at 2,100.[18]

The terrain between Englishtown and the small town of Monmouth Court House was a mix of farmland and wood-lots, with creek beds bordered by marshy wetlands or "morasses" wending through it. General Dickinson's militiamen were in much closer contact with the enemy than Lee, and before dawn Dickinson had advised both Lee and Washington that the British advance had left Monmouth Court House and was on the road to Middletown. The militia, supplemented by some Continental Light Dragoons, launched limited attacks on the British baggage train and had some success in disrupting the column, as Captain Joshua Huddy's company bayoneted some horses and drivers.[19]

Grayson crossed the bridge over Spotswood Middle Brook, but had two more creek bed wetlands, the middle and east morasses, between him and the enemy. Shortly afterward, some American dragoons reported that the militia had made enemy contact. Cornwallis's division was just north of town and his strong rear guard of over 2,000 men was still deployed near the Court House. Washington, afraid the British would slip away unharmed, dispatched an aide to Lee with instructions to engage the enemy, presumably the rear guard, "as

soon as possible," and ordered the main army, then several miles away from Englishtown, to reinforce Lee's division.

Washington understandably wished to engage the enemy "as soon as possible," since Monmouth Court House was his last best chance to initiate a limited fight for limited ends on ground in any way favorable to the Americans. As Nathanael Greene told his chief, "people expect something from us."[20]

The Continental army was prepared, in both morale and tactical skill, to confront the enemy, allowing Washington to fight with reasonable expectations of success by his standards. The Continentals would stand up to the British and, with some luck, inflict damage on them with minimal risk of forcing a major action. Although it was unlikely that Clinton, with his entire force, or even a significant portion of it, could be "Burgoyned" (printed fliers referring to Burgoyne's surrender at Saratoga left along the British line of march deridingly suggested such a fate), and Washington certainly did not have such a prospect in mind, the longer Clinton was delayed, the worse his overall outcome would be in terms of casualties, desertions, and a potentially embarrassing, albeit limited, combat action. Whether Lee understood this is unclear, but seems doubtful.

As Grayson advanced, Hunterdon County, New Jersey, mounted militiamen escorting General Steuben and several staff officers were attacked by Simcoe's Queen's Rangers. It was a close run affair, but Steuben and his party successfully escaped and Simcoe broke off the action when militia reinforcements arrived and he saw Grayson's Continentals in the distance. The British lost five men wounded, one mortally, but the slightly injured Simcoe carried off Steuben's hat as a war trophy.[21]

A historical interpreter looks out over the Monmouth Battlefield from Combs' Hill, the highest point on the field.

Lee caught up with Grayson, and, with the rest of the division halted and strung out behind them, held an impromptu conference with the colonel and General Dickinson. Lee had no idea where the enemy was and soon got into a squabble with Dickinson, who reported that if Lee's men crossed the bridge over Spotswood Middle Brook, they would be vulnerable to a British attack with no easy way to withdraw. In the end Lee decided to continue the advance. He ordered Jackson's force to the front and placed Wayne in command of the advance.[22]

Around 11:00 a.m., Lee began to redeploy his men for a possible fight with the British. His progress was slow and careful, and the Americans stuck to the woods as closely as they could, both for concealment and as relief from the debilitating heat. One important American detachment, Colonel Morgan's riflemen, was absent from the field. Although ordered by Lee to attack the enemy as they moved out of Monmouth Court House, Morgan halted three miles south of the developing battle and remained there, apparently confused by Lee's instructions, awaiting further orders that never arrived.[23]

Once he was convinced that the British were moving out, Lee pushed his troops forward more aggressively, in hopes of encircling their rear guard. Lee ordered Wayne to attack the enemy, then north of town, and ordered Lafayette, now leading Wayne's former command, to march northeast in hopes of cutting off the enemy rear guard. Unfortunately, the terrain blocked Lee from seeing that the rest of Cornwallis's division was on the road only a short distance beyond and he apparently thought he was only confronting a total of about 600 British troops.[24]

Anticipating success, Lee now ordered Wayne to advance up the Middletown road, where he encountered British light infantry and artillery and halted. By this time Lee was beginning to lose control of the overall situation, even to the point of confusing his own men with the enemy. The situation rapidly deteriorated as Clinton, seeing a chance to bag the American force, ordered a full counterattack by the rear guard, buttressed by men from Cornwallis's division ordered to return to Monmouth Court House. Wayne could now see large numbers of the enemy moving in the distance, and sensed that his command was in danger. He repulsed a few British probes and launched limited attacks of his own in an attempt to gauge the strength of his opposition, but soon began to suffer casualties from enemy artillery fire and considered falling back.[25]

Lee, meanwhile, had joined Lafayette's detachment, which he had ordered north to the vicinity of Forman's Mill Pond (today's Lake Topanemus) while Cornwallis's division, unbeknownst to him, was now marching rapidly south. Apprehensive about the security of his whole force, Lee tried to accelerate Lafayette's attack and issued a flurry of orders, which one officer later recalled as erupting "with a rapidity and indecision calculated to ruin us." It was all too little too late, for Cornwallis's men were rapidly approaching the American right flank. And, across the field, the Continentals began to leave.[26]

There would be dispute over exactly when and where the overall American retreat began, but it may have been initiated by the artillery supporting Butler and Jackson, which, out of solid shot and with two men and two horses killed, hitched up and headed for the rear. With Cornwallis's grenadiers moving towards the open American right flank, the infantry shortly began to follow. As first

one unit, then another, realized that supporting units had withdrawn, fell back, as the retreat became general. Around 12:30, Lee formally ordered a general retreat, although the order was hardly necessary. With 6,000 British soldiers now bearing down on his fragmented command, Lee was no longer the hunter, but the hunted.[27]

Many of the Continentals, prepared to fight, were puzzled by the retreat. Private Martin recalled that his company commander had announced that "you have been wishing for some days past to come up with the British, you have been wanting to fight— now you shall have fighting enough before night." Martin added that "the men did not need much haranguing to raise their courage," noting that even invalids tried to join the advance that morning. The retreat was the inevitable result of Lee's haphazard battle preparation and lack of terrain knowledge, combined with Clinton's aggressive desire to bring on an action to protect what he perceived was a serious attempt to seize his valuable baggage.[28]

The American retreat never became a rout. This would not be a repeat of Long Island. There was confusion on the British side as well, at least among some junior officers. Lieutenant William J. Hale of the 2nd Grenadier Battalion thought Lee had actually baited a clever trap to suck the British in. Turning his spyglass on some troops who seemed to be heading for his rear, Hale "saw from their variegated cloths they did not belong to our army" and feared encirclement. The British officer's perceptions to the contrary, however, a slow but steady swarm of American soldiers was moving towards their own rear as rapidly as the increasingly hot day allowed.[29]

The British paused briefly to consolidate, and Clinton dispatched a force to

British troops advance during the 200th anniversary reenactment of the Battle of Monmouth, fought on the same ground as the original action.

move around the American left flank. The Americans had temporarily halted, but Lee, desperate to find a secure place to make a stand, ordered another pull-back, seeking the advice of local farmer and militia officer Captain Peter Wikoff, who said either Combs' Hill or a ridge east of the Tennent Meeting House were the best defensive positions in the area. Lee perceived that Combs' Hill, while it dominated the battlefield (and still does) could not be easily occupied since his men and guns would have to navigate a thick wet hay meadow and marshy terrain, and ordered Wikoff to begin guiding troops to a position near the Tennent Meeting House.[30]

As Lee fell back, units of the 8,000-man main American army, personally led by Washington, were marching east to reinforce him. Washington, riding ahead, was advised that Lee had made

contact with the British rear guard, but then received word that Lee was rapidly retreating and dispatched aides to discover the true situation. One of these staff officers encountered Colonel Matthias Ogden of the First New Jersey Regiment, who said he had no idea what caused the retreat.[31]

Although initially reluctant to pursue Lee, Clinton decided to escalate the action. He had his best men, guards, grenadiers, and light infantry, as well as half of his dragoons, on the field, which made it seem worthwhile to push the issue and perhaps score a significant victory. The elite British infantry deployed into two battle lines and came on hard and fast. Lieutenant Hale of the 2nd Grenadiers recalled that cross-country pursuit of Lee as "a march may I never again experience," along "sand [roads] which scorched through our shoes with intolerable heat; the sun beating on our heads with a force scarcely to be conceived in Europe." Men dropped with exhaustion, and "two [soldiers] became raving mad, and the whole road, strewed with miserable wretches wishing for death, exhibited the most shocking scene I ever saw." It was equally bad on the other side; Private Martin recalled that by 11:00 a.m. the air was like that in a "heated oven" and was "almost impossible to breathe."[32]

Washington encountered Captain Wikoff guiding the Second New Jersey toward Perrine Ridge and ordered him to lead the Jerseymen to a woodlot to rest as reserves and then rode on to meet Lee. Most accounts of this encounter have been considerably elaborated, including stories that Washington called Lee a "damned poltroon" among other things. Private James Jordan, a nine-month levy in the 2nd New Jersey Regiment who claimed to be a witness, gave a more nuanced account of Washington's words, recalling that he merely asked Lee "What is this you have been about today?" A New Jersey militiaman remembered years later that he had been told that Washington asked Lee "what all this disorder was." Lieutenant Colonel Tench Tilghman, Washington's military secretary, remembered that Lee appeared confused, and said he had poor intelligence. Lee allegedly claimed that he had been willing to obey Washington's orders but that the situation had prevented him from doing so and that a major attack on the enemy was not in the interest of the army or the country. Unsatisfied with

Lee's rationale, Washington assumed direct command of the fight, but did not, contrary to popular myth, formally relieve Lee on the spot. Instead, he ordered him to organize the rear guard.[33]

Washington came upon Lafayette and other commanders who were withdrawing, and who advised him of the events of the battle thus far. The American commander then ordered a delaying action east of the bridge over Spotswood Middle Brook until he could establish a defensive line to the rear. In the event, two forward lines were established, one on a hill slightly south of an American position in a woodlot, extending it southward, and another, the "hedgerow" line, composed of rails and cut brush, still farther to the rear and closer to Spotswood Middle Brook.[34]

The British first encountered stiff resistance about 200 yards east of today's Wemrock Road, where Anthony Wayne's men opened fire and dropped as many as forty British killed and wounded, including Lieutenant-colonel Henry Trelawney of the Foot Guards. The British rallied for a bayonet charge into the woods and pushed the Americans out onto open terrain, where British dragoons rode some down as they retreated towards Spotswood Middle Brook. Colonel Nathanial Ramsay of the 3rd Maryland Regiment was dismounted, wounded, and captured in hand-to-hand combat. Heat exhaustion slowed the British pursuit, as they "had several Men Dye on the spot with Thirst & Extreme Fatigue & still a greater Proportion not able to defend themselves."[35]

Opposite: A map of the Battle of Monmouth, c. 1778. Letter G in front of the hedgerow indicates the principal battle.

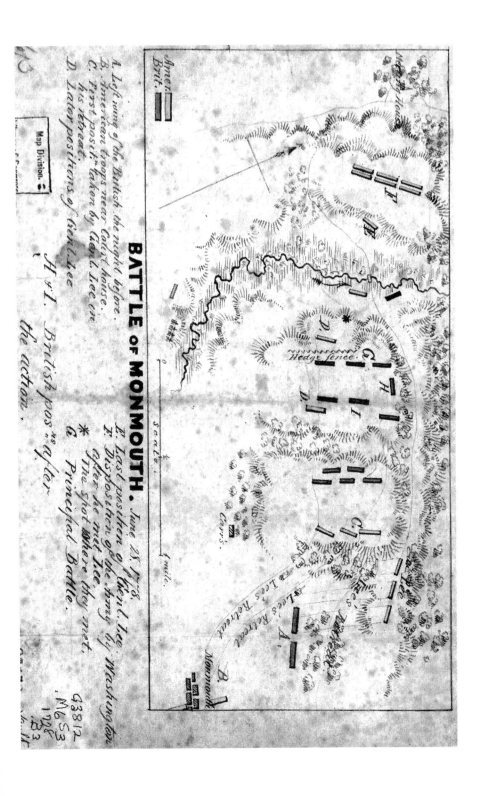

BATTLE OF MONMOUTH. June 28, 1778.

Amer.
Brit.

A. Left wing of the British, the night before.
B. American troops near Court house.
C. First posit." taken by Gen.l Lee in
D. his retreat.
D. Later positions of Gen.l Lee

E. Last position of Gen.l Lee.
F. Disposition of the Army by Washington
G. after he met Lee.
* The Spot where they met.
G. Principal Battle.

H. y I. British pos.ns before
    t the action.

Map Division.

G3812
.M6 S3
1778
.B3

Dragoons and grenadiers pursued the Americans towards the hedgerow, where Clinton rode into the thick of the fight, "galloping like a Newmarket jockey at the head of a wing of Grenadiers," and yelling "Charge Grenadiers, never heed forming!" His grenadiers rushed into a blizzard of American bullets and artillery canister shot, which one British officer described as "the heaviest fire I have yet felt," and swarmed over the hedgerow in a five-minute fight. The Americans successfully disengaged and conducted a disciplined withdrawal across the brook and bridge, followed quickly by British grenadiers. American artillery had deployed in force on Perrine Ridge, however, and blasted the pursuing enemy with grapeshot and canister, killing Lieutenant-colonel Henry Monckton of the Grenadiers, whose men were unable to retrieve his body as they hastily retreated back across the brook.[36]

The rear guard had actually done well while under aggressive attack by some of the best units in the British army in heat so debilitating that men were literally dropping dead from it on both sides. The Continentals maintained unit cohesion and managed to cross Spotswood Middle Brook and its narrow bridge without losing a single color or gun and suffering relatively light casualties. Steuben's instruction paid off once more, allowing the Americans to perform a retrograde movement in the face of the enemy that might have produced panic in the same army the year before. It was yet another remarkable demonstration of how far the Continentals had come.

The delaying actions proved critical to the outcome of the battle, allowing Washington to improve his tactical position so that it was impregnable. Perrine Ridge bristled with artillery, thwarting frontal attacks; a swamp prevented the enemy from turning the American left and the woods behind the ridge provided a safe and shady haven for reserves. General Alexander deployed his troops to the north along the ridge, while Nathanael Greene extended Alexander's line to the south, and later sidled to the right to make room for Wayne, who anchored the American center with five regiments. Greene, who had been ordered to prevent a British flanking attack from the south, also made a personal reconnaissance to and beyond Combs' Hill.[37]

The rear guard troops marched through the new line to the rear and those most actively engaged in the morning fighting moved, along with General Lee himself, towards Englishtown for reorganization and rest while Washington, aided by Steuben, built a defense in depth. The enthusiastic German, his fighting blood up, reorganized Lee's men and merged them with the army reserve, then turned command over to Maxwell and returned to the front. Lee wandered forward again, apparently in an effort to continue his conversation with Washington, but the still unhappy commander was too busy organizing the defense to listen to him. General Lee's command time at the Battle of Monmouth, and in the war, was over.[38]

Clinton was not quite done. He pushed a force under Quartermaster General Erskine to the north to outflank Perrine Ridge. After a long hot march, skirmishing with militia and with men dropping dead or exhausted from the heat along the way, however, the British were halted by difficult terrain and fatigue. Erskine concluded that he could not turn the American flank and withdrew a short distance to rest his men. Had he persisted and made it a bit farther on, however, he would have run into a solid reserve line of Continentals under Lafayette anchoring the American line.[39]

With the fight stalled by early afternoon, Clinton brought up artillery to engage the American batteries in a two-hour duel, one of the longest of the war. The results were inconclusive, however, as the range was extreme. No guns were dismounted and casualties were limited, but the cannonade supplied a future American heroine, "Molly Pitcher." "Molly," whose real name was apparently Mary Hays, was described by Private Martin as "a woman whose husband belonged to the artillery" and helped serve a gun alongside her spouse on the Perrine Ridge line behind and north of Martin's position.[40]

Clinton also came under fire from Combs' Hill, now occupied by Greene. The Americans moved infantry and artillery pieces to the crest and the guns, personally sighted and under the direct command of Chevalier de Maudit du Plessis, chimed in during the artillery duel. The Combs' Hill cannons were positioned to deliver a raking enfilade fire on any infantry attack on Perrine Ridge, and could also discomfit the British gun line somewhat, although the distance was great.[41]

Eventually Clinton, realizing that victory was not likely and that he was running short of artillery ammunition, but with his baggage safely on the road to Middletown, ordered a withdrawal to consolidate his forces closer to Monmouth Court House. As the British began to fall back, leaving a number of dead, dehydrated, and seriously wounded men behind, Washington launched several limited attacks, including an assault on the position of the 42nd Foot in the Sutphin Farm orchard by Colonel Cilley's battalion of New England "picked men."[42]

A romanticized nineteenth-century view of "Molly Pitcher" at the Battle of Monmouth.

Under pressure from Cilley, the Scots fell back through the orchard into a field beyond and up a slight rise, where they were safe from Continental artillery, fired a volley at their pursuers and marched off farther to the rear, where they took another position supported by two three-pounder guns. Cilley pursued, advancing through artillery fire and musketry to deliver a volley into the enemy's faces at short range. The Highlanders retreated again, across the headwaters of Spotswood Brook. Cilley did not follow. Casualties were light on both sides, although Private Martin, acting as a battalion skirmisher, recalled that he "singled out a man and took my aim directly between his shoulders" as the 42nd fell back out of the orchard. This often overlooked skirmish provides concrete evidence of the cohesiveness, discipline, and tactical ability of the Continental army in June 1778.[43]

Washington pushed back on the right as well, ordering Wayne to attack the 1st Grenadiers, who were preparing to retreat. The Grenadiers successfully disengaged and moved beyond the hedgerow as the 33rd Foot advanced to support them. Wayne pursued with three small regiments and the British turned and launched a counterattack near today's Wemrock Road that drove Wayne's men back to the hedgerow and into the fields of the Tennent Parsonage farm beyond. As the British surged forward, however, they were caught in enfilade by the guns on Combs' Hill and abandoned their pursuit. Both Cilley's and Wayne's attacks were minimally risky to Washington. Even if one or both forces were smashed, his army would remain intact.[44]

Following Clinton's withdrawal, Washington advanced all along the line and instructed the Virginia Continentals on Combs' Hill to attack the enemy's left flank. Heat exhaustion and, in the case of the Virginians, difficult terrain, slowed the American advance to a crawl and then halted it. By the time Lee's reorganized division arrived on the field from Englishtown under the command of Steuben it was after 6:00 p.m. and Washington officially ended the pursuit, ordering his men to sleep on the battlefield and be prepared to renew the fight in the morning. Washington himself dozed under the stars, Lafayette alongside him, near the Sutphin farmhouse.[45]

## AFTERMATH OF THE BATTLE OF MONMOUTH COURT HOUSE

The fight would not be renewed. While the Americans slept, Clinton moved out of Monmouth Court House. The British march up the Middletown road was conducted in a thoroughly professional manner, and with so little noise that Washington apparently did not realize the enemy was gone until morning, although some have suggested that the American commander, usually well informed by his militia scouts, simply decided that since he had fulfilled his

immediate ends that day, it was time to provide Lee's "bridge of gold." Clinton rested at Middletown, moving on to Sandy Hook on June 30, where he rendezvoused with Admiral Richard Howe's fleet. Today Sandy Hook is a peninsula, but in 1778 it was an island, separated from the mainland by a narrow sixty-yard tidal-cut channel. The British constructed a pontoon-style bridge of barges to march over to the island, and subsequently boarded ships in an efficient four-day evacuation operation.

The exact human toll of the fighting at Monmouth Court House is difficult to determine. Casualty reports were inconsistent and often framed to meet the propaganda goals of either side. Clinton's secretary Andrew Bell, who estimated the American force at a hyperbolic 25,000 men, reported in his diary that "Tis generally thought the rebels have lost 2,500, as General Clinton was master of the field [which he was not] and had an opportunity of observing. 'Tis said Lee is killed, and a French General."[46]

On July 1, Lieutenant Colonel Laurens reported 356 American casualties, including sixty-nine men killed in action, 161 wounded, and 132 missing. Some of the latter simply collapsed from the heat and later rejoined their units, but others, an estimated thirty-seven, died from the severe heat in various locations around the battlefield. Some may have simply deserted and some may have been prisoners, as Andrew Bell reported that the British captured sixty men.[47]

British losses are more problematic. On July 6, the *New York Gazette and Weekly Mercury*, a Loyalist newspaper, reported a total of 358 British casualties, including 124 dead, 170 wounded, and fifty-six missing, the vast majority of whom were probably dead, prisoners, or deserters. Lieutenant Hale of the heavily engaged 2nd Grenadier Battalion listed total casualties in that unit as "98 with 11 officers killed and wounded," including four fatalities in his own company. Another junior officer recalled that "our loss altogether was upwards of four hundred men killed, wounded and who died from the sun and want of water." A Hessian major noted that the British casualties totaled 286, including 112 killed, 62 died of sunstroke, and 174 wounded. An American after-action report summarizing the interments of various burial details, as well as accounting for British dead buried by local residents, came up with a total of 217, and added 29 Americans, but some doubt has been cast on the accuracy of that number. Washington wrote his brother that his army buried 245 enemy dead left on field and took 100 prisoners; several other accounts are close to those numbers. Deserters, not listed in official British returns of losses, began leaving the ranks as soon as the army began to leave Philadelphia. There were at least 200 deserters from Hessian ranks during the campaign, and one American account cites a total of 600 deserters, 440 of them Germans, returned to Philadelphia by July 6. Some modern historians question the casualty totals of both armies, since the ratio of killed to wounded seems higher than it should be. Estimates range as high as 1,134 British and 500 Americans killed, wounded and missing in the battle itself. None of these accounts include casualties incurred on the march before and after the battle.[48]

On July 1 the American army began to march away from Monmouth Court House. The Continentals moved on in stages to White Plains, New York, with Maxwell's Jerseymen detached to Elizabethtown to keep watch on British activity on Staten Island and provide a trained defensive force to reinforce the militia in case of any British or Loyalist incursions into eastern New Jersey. While the army marched, it court-martialed General Lee, who had imperiously demanded a trial for perceived insults he was subjected to by his commander on the field at Monmouth. He was convicted and his military career brought to an end.[49]

Monmouth Court House, the largest and most intense battle ever fought within the boundaries of the state of New Jersey, was the last major battle of the conflict fought in the north, although the June 1780 battle at Springfield, New Jersey, which occurred when Continentals and militia resisted a British incursion, was a fairly substantial action, and the state was plagued with guerilla raiding until the actual conclusion of hostilities.

The Monmouth Campaign established that the Continental army had achieved a new competence, and provided an opportunity to perfect the army's cooperative tactics with the local militia that had originated in the New Jersey Forage War. A tough professional standing force, working with an aggressive militia and effective local political organization, spelled doom to British hopes for returning New Jersey, a state that had seemed a significant source of sympathizers less than two years before, to the loyal fold.[50]

## THE GRAND FORAGE WAR

Following the Battle of Monmouth Court House, Washington marched his army north and crossed the New York border into Westchester County, and two years of intense military activity in New Jersey, in the words of one chronicler, "relapsed into quiet." This may have been true as far as major battles were concerned, but British forage raids from New York into the New Jersey countryside, coupled with sporadic violence by vengeance-seeking Loyalists, primarily in Bergen and Monmouth Counties, continued to be features of life in the state for the next five years.[51]

Like Monmouth to the south, Bergen County was a divided polity from the outset of hostilities, and a number of the county's citizens, even nominal members of the militia, had signed loyalty oaths proffered by the British in 1776. Monmouth County's Quakers had been reluctant to rebel and there was a religious element to the loyalty of many of Bergen County's predominantly Dutch citizens as well, with a pre-war schism in the Dutch Reformed Church into a more structured conservative and a more diverse liberal faction mirrored in politics. The conservative "Conferentie" pastors and their flocks tended to remain loyal to the Crown, while the churches inspired by the teaching of Domine John Henry Goetschius, who had preached a theology with broader appeal during the "Great Awakening," tended to the Rebel side.[52]

The British garrison in New York was in constant need of food and forage. On September 22, 1778, General Clinton ordered General Cornwallis and General "no flint" Grey to organize a large raid into Bergen County to gather supplies, perhaps tempt Washington into battle, and also divert attention from a New Jersey coastal expedition he was organizing. Cornwallis initially occupied the village of English Neighbourhood, as diversionary activity on Staten Island that kept the New Jersey Continentals under General Maxwell in place. Washington cast a wary eye on the expedition, as the American command was not sure if this was a major operation or a massive yet tempo-

The memorial at the site where six American dragoons were buried in the aftermath of the "Baylor Massacre."

rary foraging mission to secure supplies for the winter.[53]

Colonel George Baylor's Dragoons, a mounted unit mustering 116 officers and men, were detailed as an observation force at a Hackensack River crossing, and moved to Overkill (today's River Vale) where they were quartered in various local homes. The Continental dragoons, principally Virginians, did a bit of foraging themselves, and were not welcomed by some of the local farmers. When Grey learned of the Continentals' location, he ordered a night bayonet attack by 650 of his men. On September 28, in an action forever after known locally as the "Baylor Massacre," the British overran the dragoons, who had unaccountably neglected to post sentries. The Americans lost 15 men killed and 54 wounded and captured. Colonel Baylor, who was wounded and among the prisoners, died several years later as a result of his injuries. Six of the dead Americans were hastily buried in abandoned leather tanning vats near the bridge by local militia on the day after the massacre.

In November 1778, Washington detailed two North Carolina Continental infantry regiments to reinforce local

Bergen County militiamen in resisting further incursions. The Carolinians were initially stationed at Ramapough (Ramapo) and then moved to Paramus in December for winter quarters.[54]

In the wake of the British sweep through the county, many Loyalists who had remained in Bergen returned to Manhattan with Cornwallis's force, which picked the farms between the Hudson and Hackensack Rivers clean. Loyalist irregular guerilla activity in this area, Bergen's "Neutral Zone," was not as extensive as it was in Monmouth, probably because of the presence of a large number of British regulars, including the Loyalist New Jersey Volunteers, a unit which included many Bergen County men. Bergen County Loyalist civilians often acted as guides for regular British raiding and foraging parties, and there was much profitable "London trading," a euphemism for selling produce to the British in New York, by people of all political persuasions.[55]

Unsurprisingly, considering their policies elsewhere in New Jersey, the British failed to recognize that ravaging the Bergen County countryside and acting on biased intelligence from angry Loyalist refugees, including William Franklin and his associates, did not make for an effective counterinsurgency program. In the words of Adrian Leiby, whose comprehensive history of the war in Bergen was a pioneering work on the subject, the Loyalists "carried into New York a source of misinformation about American patriots which was as great a handicap to the British command as any false intelligence it received about Washington's army; men who could only deceive Britons, as they had deceived themselves, with the comforting assurance that American leaders were knaves and their followers fools."[56]

## PRIVATEERING IN NEW JERSEY WATERS

As the conflict continued, entrepreneurial war in the form of privateering flourished in the waters around New Jersey. Some with government issued letters of marque and reprisal and others without, enterprising New Jerseyans captured numerous British ships attempting to make port in New York, sold their goods, and split the profits with state government. With New Jersey safe from British occupation in the final years of the war, business was good for coastal privateers, as well as salt producers, from Raritan Bay to Cape May. Henry Clinton intended to put a stop to, or at least curb, this activity, and he chose breech loading rifle inventor Patrick Ferguson as his implement. Badly wounded in his right elbow joint during the Battle of Brandywine, Ferguson had gamely refused amputation and painfully convalesced in British occupied Philadelphia for the next eight months, undergoing several operations without anesthetic to remove bone fragments from his now permanently disabled arm and teaching himself to write left handed.[57]

Although disabled, Captain Ferguson, whose original orders stated that he should return to his regiment at the close of the Philadelphia Campaign, remained with the main British army, and probably participated in the 1778 march across New Jersey. After the army reached New York, he was promoted to major and assigned to command of a composite force of Loyalists and regulars. In October 1778, following Cornwallis's thrust into Bergen, Ferguson led this unit on a raid on the "nest of rebel pirates" at Little Egg Harbor, New Jersey, burning privateer ships, salt works, and the village of Chestnut Neck on the Mullica River.

General Casimir Pulaski's Legion and other troops were dispatched to Mullica to reinforce local militia and prevent Ferguson from capturing Batsto, a bog iron forge town that also served as an auction site for privateers. After Pulaski's men arrived at Little Egg Harbor, Ferguson, acting on information from an American deserter from Pulaski's unit, nineteen-year-old Lieutenant Carl Wilhelm Joseph Juliat (who had previously deserted from a Hessian regiment to the Americans) staged a successful surprise night bayonet attack in the style of General Grey, killing as many as fifty soldiers as they slept, and then returned to New York. Although the privateers were soon back in business, Ferguson's star was on the rise once more, and he was subsequently given command of an "American Volunteer" corps of 175 soldiers drawn from New York and New Jersey Loyalist battalions and deployed in the south after the capture of Charleston, South Carolina, in 1780. Ferguson, some New Jersey Loyalist Volunteers and the Loyalist force he recruited in the South came to a bad end at King's Mountain, North Carolina, on October 7, 1780, where he, along with many of his men, was killed, and the remainder captured or scattered.[58]

## NEW JERSEY SOLDIERS OF COLOR

As the low intensity conflict in New Jersey simmered, there were periodic calls to reinforce the New Jersey Continental Brigade. Recruiting was not brisk, but drafts from the militia usually resulted in soldiers, many of them substitutes for actual draftees, coming to the colors for brief periods of service. As with the "Jersey Blues" of the French and Indian War, the enlisted ranks of the brigade were drawn primarily from small farmers and farm laborers. Some recruits were actually British deserters. Surprising to some today, the line regiments were, unlike future American military units, racially integrated. It is estimated that two percent of the men who served in New Jersey's "Second Establishment" brigade of Continentals in the Revolutionary War were nonwhite. Although some of these soldiers were Native Americans, most, like John Evans, who enlisted from Reading Township, were black. The most well-known New Jersey African American Revolutionary War soldier was Oliver Cromwell, a Burlington County man who served in the 2nd New Jersey Regiment from 1777 through 1783. Cromwell, of mixed African, Caucasian, and Native American ancestry, fought in a number of engagements, including the Battle of Monmouth, and lived until 1853. Jacob Francis, a twenty-one-year-old newly freed New Jersey slave, found himself in Massachusetts at the outbreak of the war. Francis served over a year in a Massachusetts Continental Line unit, fighting at Long Island and Trenton. When discharged, he returned to his home in Amwell, New Jersey, and served numerous tours of active duty in the militia until the cessation of hostilities. The New Jersey legislature was often inconsistent in its enlistment policies. In 1779 it banned slaves from serving in militia units but on three occasions it specifically freed slaves, including Peter Williams and Cato, owned by Loyalists, so that they could join the state or Continental ranks.[59]

New Jersey law, like that of other states, allowed draftees to provide substitutes to serve in their place in the military when a militia conscription for Continental service occurred, and at least some men sent their slaves. Samuel Sutphen, a Somerset County slave sol-

As this reenactor at the 200th anniversary of the Battle of Monmouth illustrates, the New Jersey Continental army and militia units were racially integrated to a degree, with both African Americans and Native Americans serving in the ranks.

dier, substituted for his master, Caspar Berger, for several tours of duty in both the militia and the New Jersey Continental Line between 1776 and 1780. He was present at the battles of Princeton and Monmouth, fought in numerous engagements including the battle of Long Island and was wounded in a New York State skirmish with British troops following his return from the 1779 campaign against the Iroquois Indians. General Dickinson personally presented Sutphen with a musket for capturing a prisoner during an action at Van Nest's Mill during the Forage War, and he kept the gun for the rest of his life. Sadly, Sutphen's expectation of personal liberty at war's end in return for his sacrifice was denied, although he eventually pur-

chased his freedom and then that of his wife. In his old age Sutphen was denied a pension by the Federal government, apparently because he served as a slave and substitute, rather than a free man, despite the testimony of numerous witnesses to his loyal service. Eventually the New Jersey General Assembly did the right thing, awarding the old veteran a special stipend in 1836. Samuel Sutphen, a good man and a good soldier, died at the age of ninety-four, on May 8, 1841.[60]

While Quaker-dominated West New Jersey had been largely pro-abolition in the years leading up to the Revolution, slavery was a firmly established pillar of East New Jersey's economic life, with most farmers owning from one to six slaves by the time of the war. Revolutionary rhetoric about freedom, especially in the wake of the Declaration of Independence, often seemed hypocritical in a society that condoned human bondage, and this was recognized by a number of New Jersey revolutionaries, including Governor Livingston and New Jersey Brigade officer and future governor Joseph Bloomfield. British efforts to undermine Patriot control included promises of freedom to slaves who escaped to New York and aided the British war effort, exacerbating existing fears of slave insurrection that haunted the dreams of slaveholders. For their part, Patriot officials confiscated the slaves of Loyalists who fled the state as state government property, even if they had escaped from their Loyalist masters. One such slave, Prime, was allowed to serve as a teamster with the New Jersey Brigade in compensation for his master's defection. Prime was freed at the end of the war, but then returned to slavery when claimed by a new master who stated that he had purchased him from the Loyalist's wife, a claim that New Jersey courts then

declared invalid. The complex history of
slavery in New Jersey was made more so
by the Revolution.[61]

## LOYALIST ACTIONS

While the New Jersey Continentals
struggled to maintain their unit strength,
former governor William Franklin firmly
established himself in New York as a Loyalist leader. By 1779, he, along with other
leading exiles in the city, was advocating
a scorched earth raiding policy by British
and Loyalist forces against all nearby Pa-
triot-held territory that could be reached
in New York, Connecticut, and New Jersey. Buoyed by wish-fulfillment, Franklin
and his associates, hearing what they
wanted to hear from American deserters
and local Tories, convinced themselves,
once again, that New Jersey was a hotbed
of Loyalist sympathy and that all they
needed to do, paradoxically, was to
launch brutal raids into the state to convince fence sitters to turn against the Patriot cause. The winter of 1779–1780 was
the most severe of the eighteenth century, and the American army, wintering
once again near Morristown in Jockey
Hollow, had suffered severely, especially
when snow covered roads hampered an
already shaky supply system. Rumors
persisted that the army was about to disintegrate, and that perception, coupled
with the persistent idea that a loyal population was pining to come to the Royal
standard, led the New York Tory clique
to push for one more invasion of New
Jersey.

As Franklin and his associates plotted,
the British government was chasing yet
another chimera not unlike the one that
had inspired the first invasion of New
Jersey and the subsequent expedition to
Pennsylvania—the idea that local Loyalists were merely awaiting the arrival of a

William Franklin (1731–1813), son of
Benjamin Franklin and the last royal
governor of New Jersey.

large British army to rally around and return to the Crown. This time the golden
fleece was in the South, and, following
the December 1778 capture of Savannah,
Clinton himself led a force to attack
Charleston in October 1779. Charleston
and its 4,500-man garrison fell to the
British on May 12, 1780, and as a result,
the main British offensive effort in
America was subsequently dedicated to
an ultimately failed policy to regain the
South. The southern campaign had an
impact on the New Jersey theater of the
war because Washington had to respond
to the enemy effort by sending Continental units south from Morristown.

## BRITISH RENEW THE FIGHT FOR NEW JERSEY

While Clinton was away the command
in New York fell to General Knyphausen,
who had proved himself a competent
and cautious officer during the 1778

Monmouth Campaign. Encouraged by the Franklin clique, however, the German commander decided to make a move on Morristown by using the easiest approach, through Hobart's Gap in the Watchung Mountains at Springfield. Once through the gap it was a relatively easy eleven-mile march over level ground to the town, where, presumably, after brushing aside New Jersey militiamen, he would scatter an already demoralized American army and perhaps, even with the aid of some of Washington's demoralized and mutinous Continental troops, if Tory informants were to be believed, bag the general himself.[62]

On June 6, 1780, Knyphausen moved 6,000 British and Hessian troops from Manhattan to Staten Island, and then crossed over to Elizabethtown, New Jersey, at midnight. Although initial resistance from the Jerseymen was light and sporadic, a lucky shot, most likely from a detachment commanded by Ensign Moses Ogden of Spencer's Regiment, part of Maxwell's Jersey Brigade, severely wounded the commander of the British advance, confusing and delaying the progress of the operation. By the time the enemy had pushed a combined force of New Jersey Continentals and militia under Continental colonel Elias Dayton back to Connecticut Farms (today's Union, New Jersey), Scotch Willie Maxwell had arrived on the scene with more militiamen and the remainder of his brigade. By this stage of the war Maxwell was perhaps the best man in the army to command in such a situation. His experience with combining militia and Continentals initially gained in the Forage War, honed at Brandywine, and perfected in the Monmouth Campaign, stood him in good stead. His men were by now used to fighting this kind of war as well.[63]

Maxwell held off the British advance guard for three hours until the Redcoats were reinforced to over 3,000 men, then conducted a fighting withdrawal from house to house, fencerow to fencerow, and woodlot to woodlot, gradually falling back beyond Connecticut Farms and across the Rahway River towards Springfield. As the running fight continued, militia reinforcements continued to arrive on the scene, and Washington dispatched his crack bodyguard detachment to stiffen the defense. By nightfall on June 7, Knyphausen had not yet reached Springfield, and all hope he might have had of a surprise dash through Hobart's Gap to the level ground beyond was gone, even though the Americans were exhausted and low on supplies. The following day he withdrew his main force to Staten Island, but retained a beachhead at Elizabethtown.[64]

As they had since first entering the state in 1776, British troops looted homes in Connecticut Farms and burned a number of them. One nervous British soldier, perhaps mistaking movement inside a house for an American militiaman ready to fire at him, shot through a window and killed Hannah Caldwell, wife of prominent local Patriot leader Reverend James Caldwell. The killing itself was no doubt an accident, but the fact that British soldiers apparently knocked down the door of the house shortly afterward and searched Mrs. Caldwell's body for jewelry epitomized British behavior in New Jersey.[65]

## KNYPHAUSEN'S OFFENSIVE TO REGAIN NEW JERSEY

Following Clinton's return from Charleston on June 17, 1780, the British, still in the belief that Washington's army at Morristown was on the brink of dissolution, decided to try one more time to force a passage through Hobart's Gap. This time the plan was more complex. On June 23, a strong force under Knyphausen landed once more at Elizabethtown, but the German general, more cautious this time, deployed a significant number of men to guard his rear area and lines of communication against militia raids. He then divided the remainder of his force into two columns, which would advance via separate routes on Connecticut Farms and then Springfield. One column, under Knyphausen himself, moved on Galloping Hill Road and another advanced further north along the Vauxhall road. A third British force crossed the Hudson from New York City and marched towards the north end of the Watchungs and New York's Westchester County, to threaten West Point and act as a diversion but also to be in position to attack Washington should he try to come down on the right flank of Knyphausen's command. Clinton, who was, at the time, receiving intelligence from Benedict Arnold, was aware that a French fleet was approaching Rhode Island to land an army to assist the Americans and his move north was also intended to block a possible juncture of the American and French armies.[66]

Wilhelm von Knyphausen (1716–1800), general officer of Hesse-Kassel, commanded Hessian troops in British service during the American Revolution.

Following his initial move into New Jersey from Staten Island, Knyphausen built a pontoon bridge to Elizabethtown, so the initial stages of his new offensive were quicker and less problematic than before. Washington, who was apprehensive regarding Clinton's moves to the north, took a personal interest in that front but assigned General Nathanael Greene to take over operations beyond Elizabethtown. Greene had Philemon Dickinson's militiamen on call to back up his regular force of around 1,000 Continental soldiers, which included Maxwell's Jerseymen, John Stark's brigade of New Englanders, and Major Light Horse Harry Lee's Legion. In the early morning hours of June 23, the British advanced from their stronghold on Elizabethtown Point. Greene was expecting them and had deployed Colonel Israel Shreve's 2nd New Jersey and Colonel Israel Angel's 2nd Rhode Island to defend the first two bridges on the Galloping Hill Road and posted Colonel Matthias Ogden's 1st New Jersey and Colonel Henry "Light Horse Harry" Lee's Legion at the Vauxhall Road bridge, holding the remainder of Maxwell's and Stark's brigades in reserve. Many of the local militia, lulled into a false sense of security following the failure of Knyphausen's first offensive, had drifted home. Some of those who remained sniped at the advancing British, while about 500 responded to a call from Dickinson and were ordered by Greene to back up Shreve's regiment.[67]

At what remained of Connecticut Farms, the British advance party, men from the Loyalist New Jersey Volunteers, encountered fellow Jerseymen from the Jersey Continentals and militia and were unsuccessful in forcing a passage west. Simcoe's Rangers managed to eventually penetrate the American line and rout the militia, at which time the Jersey Continentals conducted a fighting retreat. On the Vauxhall front, German Jaegers were stalled by the Rhode Islanders and an artillery piece, but British reinforcements arrived and British artillery counter-battery fire disabled the American gun. Two British regiments forded the stream, which was only a few feet deep, and the outflanked Americans slowly retreated towards Springfield. The battle seesawed back and forth, but the British, with the advantage of superior numbers, steadily pushed the Americans west.

Outflanked themselves on the Vauxhall road by militia gathering on a nearby hillside, the British column then abandoned that path and traversed a side road to join Knyphausen, who had by this time fought his way into Springfield. Greene pulled his men back, reorganizing his defense so that he was directly blocking Hobart's Gap, with Maxwell holding the mountainside behind in a reserve position. Checked once more, Knyphausen made a command decision that clearing the gap and moving on to Morristown, with a force of determined Continentals in front of him and increasing numbers of militiamen joining the fight, was not possible. He ordered his men to burn the town of Springfield and prepare to retreat.[68]

The tale of Reverend Caldwell coming out of his church with an armload of Watt's hymnals and handing them out to militiamen or Continentals for "wadding" for their muskets while crying "Let them Eat Watts boys," has long been part of the folklore of the battle of Springfield. A colorful footnote to New Jersey history, the story is best taken with more than the proverbial grain of salt. While Caldwell may well have been present and, as a firebrand Patriot whose wife was killed by a British soldier a few weeks previously, vigorously supporting the Continentals and militiamen, it is unlikely they used his hymnal pages for "wadding." Continental soldiers, and militiamen as well, came to a fight with prepared musket cartridges of powder and ball wrapped in paper, and would have had no need for "wadding," as the cartridge paper, rammed down the barrel along with the musket ball, provided it. In March 1780, the New Jersey Assembly authorized the purchase of, among other war materials, a large amount of gun powder and cartridge paper for the militia, and hired people to make up cartridges and pack them into storage boxes; so there was certainly no lack of available prepared ammunition at Springfield. It is possible that the minister ran out of the church with armfuls of books to save them from impending fire, and that somehow was responsible for the legend. It has also been suggested that the "wadding" was offered for use by artillery, which is equally unlikely. The story seems to have its origins in a nineteenth century poem by Bret Harte.[69]

The British retreat from Springfield, as with the advance, followed both Vauxhall and Galloping Hill Roads, with Simcoe's Legion and German Jaegers providing a rear guard in the face of increasing swarms of angry militiamen harassing the withdrawal.

And so the last serious British attempt to regain New Jersey for the Crown ended ignominiously, failing in the face of effective militia response and cooperation between Continentals and the militia. With the conclusion of the battle of Springfield, major British operations in New Jersey came to an end.

Loyalist guerilla raids fostered by former governor Franklin did not abate following Knyphausen's failure, however, and, if anything, took on a more desperate tone as the inexorable downslide to British defeat in America took hold. The violence became especially vicious in Monmouth County. Monmouth, like Bergen County, had a large Loyalist population at the outbreak of the Revolution, many of whom fled during the Patriot ascendency, leaving valuable property behind, and were eager to extract revenge. The county's extensive coastline was impossible to effectively control although mounted Militia "Light Horse" units patrolled the beaches in rotational duty stints.

## "REFUGEETOWN" AND "CIVIL WAR"

In 1778, following the Battle of Monmouth, a runaway Shrewsbury slave named Titus began a brief but notorious career as "Colonel Tye" after being hired on as a raider by Franklin's Associated Loyalists. Throughout 1779, Tye and his multiracial band descended on the households of known Patriots, killed or captured any military age men who happened to be present, and gathered up valuables, livestock, and other property. Following a raid, the Loyalists would retreat to "Refugeetown," a fortified community on Sandy Hook, which had been

held by the British since Howe's arrival in 1776. By 1779, Refugeetown was a busy base of operations for those who saw an opportunity to deal a blow to the Patriots and also pocket a profit in a convenient blend of ideology and entrepreneurism.[70]

As in Bergen, Continental army troops were sent to Monmouth to stiffen the militia. On April 25, 1779, however, the Continentals fell back in the face of a 700-man expeditionary force of Loyalists and Regulars advancing on Tinton Falls, a town with an iron forge that also served as a militia supply point. The enemy force looted the town after scattering ineffectual militia opposition. Following the attack, Washington withdrew the Continentals, whose presence he felt had actually motivated the raiders, rather than deterred them. A subsequent raid on Tinton Falls by around one hundred Refugee irregulars in June succeeded in capturing the Patriot leadership of the town. The Refugees then carried off all the livestock they could find, burned houses and public buildings, and "behaved like wild or mad men" according to one witness. Militiamen caught up with them as they embarked for Sandy Hook at Jumping Point and fourteen militiamen and two raiders were killed in a vicious hand-to-hand battle, the bloodiest encounter to date between Loyalists, many of them former local men, and local Patriot forces.[71]

There was marauding in the other direction as well, most notably General Dickinson's assault on British occupied Staten Island, and many Loyalists viewed their forays into Monmouth as justified payback for Patriot excesses. On March 30, 1780, raiders looted the home of John Russell, a man reviled for his own attacks on Staten Island, killing him and wounding his son. In June 1780, Loyalists killed

Monmouth County militiaman Joseph Murray in retaliation for his alleged summary executions of several captured Tories. A few days later, Refugees captured Captain Barnes Smock and twelve other Patriot militia leaders and hauled them off to New York.[72]

As Loyalists from Refugeetown and Staten Island continued to wreak havoc in Monmouth County, panicked residents frantically petitioned Governor Livingston for assistance. In response the governor established martial law in the county, but he had few men available to enforce it; militia recruiting was often problematic in Monmouth, and many farmers with Patriot leanings were more interested in tending to the planting season than policing far and wide. Others simply wanted to stay out of the growing civil war and make some money from "London Trading." The governor did authorize bounties to enlist some state troops to garrison various points in the county.[73]

COLONEL TYE'S RAID

In August 1780, Colonel Tye, whose reputation had soared with the capture of two members of the New Jersey legislature in addition to several militia officers, embarked on a raid that would become his most famous endeavor and also prove his undoing. The African-American guerilla and his band, accompanied by a detachment of regular Loyalist troops, attempted to capture prominent Patriot captain Joshua Huddy in his Colts Neck home. Huddy held the raiders off for hours by running from one window to another firing off shots as his mistress, Lucretia Emmons, reloaded muskets for him. He eventually surrendered but later escaped. Tye was wounded in the wrist during the fight,

and the injury became infected and led to his death, apparently from tetanus, within days.

Although Stephen Blucke replaced Tye as leader of the raiders, the African-American Loyalist guerilla's fame resonated across Monmouth County for years afterward. The *New Jersey Gazette* referred to "the famous negro Tye" in an April 1782 article, judging him "justly much more to be feared and respected, as an enemy, than any of his brethren of the fairer complexion."[74]

THE CIVIL WAR CONTINUES

The actions of Tye and other Loyalist guerillas and their Patriot militia opponents reveal the evolving nature of the Revolution in New Jersey in the closing years of the war. The conflict had transitioned from large scale foraging expeditions by regular troops and the formal battles of Trenton, Princeton, and Monmouth into bushwhacking and banditry. Although the tendency of eighteenth century armies, particularly the British in New Jersey, to engage in pillage and other bad behavior toward noncombatants had always meant that distance from the front lines, garrison towns, or an army on the march did not guarantee safety from the ravages of war—such losses were often unlucky matters of happenstance. British army excesses were geographically limited, although the Patriot propaganda they fed magnified their effect. With the advent of partisan raiding parties, however, homesteads across widespread areas were transformed into potential military targets. The paramilitary units spawned by William Franklin and his Associated Loyalists often had specific revenge in mind, rather than wanton pillaging, kidnapping, and killing.

In September 1779, a proposal to compensate victims of Tory raids in Monmouth directly from the sale of the confiscated estates of Loyalist refugees who had fled the county was defeated in the New Jersey Assembly by a margin of thirty to six; despite its general unpopularity, all three Monmouth representatives, on the front lines of the raider war, supported the bill. Patriotic Monmouth men were feeling considerable pressure from the frequent raids from Refugeetown that struck along the shore, bands of horse thieves active in the northern part of the county, and "Pine Robbers" hiding in the Pine Barrens region to the south.[75]

## THE RETALIATORS

In early 1780, a group of Monmouth Patriot leaders convened to form the Association for Retaliation. This extra-legal organization was created for the sole purpose of harassing known local Loyalists and their suspected sympathizers still residing in the county by using some of the same tactics employed by Tory refugee groups: violence, theft, and murder. The participants in the meeting drafted a constitution entitled "The Articles of Association for Purposes of Retaliation," a document that clearly exemplifies the principle of an "eye for an eye."[76]

By the time the "Retaliators" were organized, the war in Monmouth had degenerated into a bitter civil conflict with political agendas, personal revenge, and economic opportunities all in the mix. The Retaliators were at the center of this maelstrom, and despite the questionable nature of their actions they continued to seek official recognition from the state, petitioning the legislature in June 1780 to recognize them as a legal entity. Liv-

ingston and his legislature declined to endorse them, however.[77]

The Retaliators did not wait for a response from the state government before holding their first public gathering on July 1, 1780. During this meeting they elected former Continental colonel and militia brigadier general David Forman, an active Patriot from a prominent Freehold Township family, to serve as chairman of their nine-man board. Forman's increasingly controversial status would dash any chances the Retaliators may have had of achieving official status for the Association.[78]

Although opposed by moderates within the Patriot community, including militia and state troop colonel Asher Homes, the Retaliators and the intense enmity that motivated both them and their Refugee foes would carry the violence in Monmouth far past the general cessation of hostilities that followed the Yorktown surrender in 1781, including the murder of Loyalist prisoner Philip White by Retaliators and the subsequent revenge lynching of Patriot prisoner Joshua Huddy, who had been captured in a blockhouse fight in Toms River, in 1782. The proposed hanging of a British regular officer in response to the Huddy lynching led William Franklin, who exercised direct control of the Loyalists responsible, to leave New York for London. In May and June 1782, David Forman, acting as a judge of the Court of Common Pleas, issued orders empowering militia officers to impress the horses of several suspected but uncharged Loyalist sympathizers; in July 1783 at Sandy Hook, even though the war was effectively over, a band of Retaliators fell upon, captured and severely beat three sailors from the British ship HMS *Vixen* as they completed a routine mission to collect fresh water from a well. It was not until the British evacuation of New York in the fall of 1783 that the Retaliators finally faded away. They were replaced by the Association to Oppose the Return of Tories, which exploited local animosities towards Loyalists but vowed to conduct itself moderately, utilizing legal channels, while apparently providing a political home for many former Retaliators in the post-war era.[79]

## THE END OF THE REVOLUTIONARY WAR

Following the battle of Springfield, Scotch Willie Maxwell, worn out from fighting the British and victimized by the political backbiting of the Ogden family cabal of officers in his brigade, who several times plotted to have him court-martialed or relieved from duty, resigned his commission and retired to his family farm in Warren County's Greenwich Township. Maxwell served in the New Jersey Assembly in 1783. Although maligned over the years by some, accused of being a drunkard by others, and forgotten by most everyone, Scotch Willie was one of the most talented generals New Jersey ever produced. He died on his farm in 1796 and was buried in the First Presbyterian Church burial ground in Greenwich.

Despite their good conduct in the success at Springfield, the New Jersey Continental regiments continued what had been a long manpower decline into 1780. Recruits were not forthcoming and what had once been a four regiment brigade gradually diminished. The 4th Regiment was disbanded, its men consolidated into the other three regiments, and the brigade reinforced by Spencer's additional Continental Regiment, which had been raised in New Jersey. In September 1780, the brigade mustered around 900 men. A temporary reinforcement levy of six-months militia conscripts were mustered out in June 1781, and the 3rd Regiment and Spencer's Regiment were disbanded by January 1781.[80]

Over the winter of 1780–81, the sadly diminished New Jersey Brigade wintered at Pompton, northeast of Morristown. The victors of Springfield were increasingly unhappy. Their pay came late, and when it arrived it was worth less than it had been the last time they were paid, due to the depreciation of Continental currency. Food and clothing were in short supply as well, and men complained that they had enlisted for three years of service and that their enlistments were being arbitrarily extended to the end of the war. Although the New Jersey legislature promised to redress the pay issue in January 1781, the Jerseymen, following the example of the Pennsylvania regiments that had mutinied over similar grievances, then largely had those grievances redressed, mutinied as well. About 200 mutineers marched from Pompton to Chatham, where Colonel Eilas Dayton was quartered, presented their demands and argued with their officers for several days before laying down their arms. Although Dayton promised pardons for all, a detachment of New England troops arrived from West Point and surrounded the mutineers, who surrendered. Subsequent court martial of the leaders resulted in two men being executed by firing squad.[81]

Although their new brigade commander, Lieutenant Colonel Francis Barber, characterized his Jerseymen as "a set of drunken, unworthy fellows," he ended up leading a picked light infantry detachment from the brigade to the siege of Yorktown, where they became part of the unit that successfully assaulted Redoubt Number 10 and were present for

Reproduction soldier winter quarter huts in Jockey Hollow in the Morristown National Historical Park.

the British surrender. The New Jersey Brigade spent the following winter in Morristown, and then, in August 1782, moved on to New Windsor, New York, the last encampment of the Continental Army. While at New Windsor, Lieutenant Colonel Barber was killed when a tree a soldier was cutting down fell on him, presumably accidentally.

Although there was no way to foresee it, the end of the Revolutionary War ended combat within the boundaries of the state of New Jersey to the present day. New Jerseyans would, however, travel far and wide as soldiers of the United States, engaging in battle over succeeding centuries in Ohio, Pennsylvania, Canada, Mexico, from Virginia to the banks of the Mississippi, and then on to the far corners of the world.

# 5. New Jersey Through the War of 1812

In the wake of the Revolution, it seemed to many, if not most, Americans that amateurs had indeed defeated the best professional army in the world. No one remembered the caveats of the situation; support for the war against Britain had been, especially in New Jersey, less than unanimous, the British army that fought the war had largely been raised in haste from the general population itself, long supply lines had hampered the British war effort, the regulars of the Continental Line, trained by Von Steuben in European-style tactics, had provided an anchor for the part time soldiers of the militia to rally round, and the intervention of France had proved decisive. The militia had indeed made a significant and vital contribution to ultimate victory, but as part of a more complex scenario. In fact, in contrast with popular folklore, many militiamen, despite the supposed obligation, did not own firearms, showed up for duty unarmed or with borrowed muskets, and were remiss in maintaining their weapons. The mythology that arose surrounding the Revolution did not permit thoughtful analysis of military affairs, however. Defeat usually results in more introspection

and innovation than victory. Like soldiers of many future wars, the dwindled Continentals of the New Jersey line, given short shrift by their political masters, were sent packing at the end of the conflict with, to paraphrase a modern cliché, a perfunctory "thank you for your service."[1]

## THE ARTICLES OF CONFEDERATION AND THE MILITARY

The idea that a standing army was a danger to the republic, rather than an instrument of security, quickly became the dominant philosophy among most of the new nation's leaders. Although the militia still existed on paper, it quickly became moribund in the coastal states, and even the citizen-soldier force that existed on the frontier during the period of the Articles of Confederation, approved as a national governing document in 1781, seems to have been little more than an armed mob for the most part. The regular army was almost nonexistent. As one scholar points out, "the term 'army' appeared only once in the Articles." The document required each state to maintain "a well regulated and disciplined militia," locally based and

equipped with small arms and accoutrements, with artillery and logistical
support available at the state level. All officers up to and including the rank of
lieutenant-colonel were appointed by the
states, with colonels and generals to be
named only by the Congress. In order to
fight a war, the federal government had
to ask for men and money from the
states, which could actually refuse the request. There was no specific legislation
enforcing any of those regulations, however.[2]

In 1784 the entire United States regular army consisted of a regiment of 720
volunteers recruited from Connecticut,
New York, New Jersey, and Pennsylvania
for one year's service. In 1785 the unit
was reorganized and reenlisted for three
years' service. The First United States
Regiment was responsible for guarding
military stores that were United States
property, as well as defending the frontiers; it was woefully insufficient for the
latter task. Under the terms of the treaty
of 1783 ending the Revolution, the
"Northwest Territories" came under the
nominal authority of the United States.
British traders based in Detroit still op-
erated in the area, however, and local Na-
tive-American tribes, including some
displaced New Jersey Lenape, now
known as the Delaware, were resistant to
American expansion. Sporadic frontier
warfare between whites and Indians,
with its origins in settler encroachment
even before the Revolution, became a
regular feature of the 1780s frontier, and
local militia forces proved inadequate to
the task of defending settlers who, in at
least some cases, began to rethink their
relationship with the United States and
flirted with the Spanish authorities to the
south. Revolutionary War hero George
Rogers Clark was given command of a
state force to secure the Virginia frontier,
but had almost as much trouble with his
own men as with the enemy. Drafted
militiamen reluctant to serve rioted in
protest, getting Clark's campaign off to a
shaky start, and once the unit arrived at
the frontier, continued insubordination
destroyed its effectiveness, leading him
to abandon the operation entirely.[3]

SHAYS'S REBELLION

Meanwhile, in western Massachusetts,
rebellion was in the air. In 1786, former
Continental army officer Daniel Shays
led 1,100 men, many of them veterans
and all of them at least theoretically
members of the Massachusetts militia, in
an armed protest against bankers who
held mortgages on their farms and refused to grant them debt relief. Governor
John Hancock called out the local militia
to suppress the rebellious little army, but
the militiamen simply stood by and
watched as Shays and his men marched
on the state Supreme Court. Fearful that
their money and status, and even personal safety, were on the line, well-to-do
Boston merchants hired an essentially
mercenary force of volunteers from the
eastern Massachusetts militia to finally
put down the rebellion. Shays fled the
state. That incident, coupled with frontier troubles and interstate rivalries and
monetary problems, scared the American political and economic elite into
subsequently gathering in Philadelphia
at a constitutional convention intended
to establish a stronger government able
to control both its borders and internal
security.

THE CONSTITUTION AND THE
MILITARY

The Constitution adopted in 1789 to
supplant the Articles of Confederation
was, like the Articles, created by men

who mostly regarded a standing army as an inherent danger to civilian government. Provisions made for the militia in the new governing document were vague, and legislation framing the organization yet to be determined, but it seemed clear that control of the militia was mostly deferred to the states. The tiny one-regiment regular army of the Confederation continued to exist as a federal force, primarily to police the frontier. And the frontier continued to sputter with violence, as white settlers pushed farther into territory Native Americans considered their own.

### THE HARMAR EXPEDITION

In the summer of 1790 Judge Harry Innes claimed that some 1,500 settlers had been killed or captured and 20,000 horses stolen in Indian raids along the Kentucky frontier since 1783. Although the United States initially sought a peaceful negotiated solution to these hostilities, in 1790, following the recommendation of Secretary of War Henry Knox, President George Washington ordered General Josiah Harmar to pacify the Indians of the Ohio country through the use of military force.

After a struggle to accumulate supplies and ammunition, Harmar assembled his task force, which was composed of a small regular army detachment supplemented by 1,500 Kentucky and Pennsylvania militiamen, at Cincinnati's Fort Washington. Although it might be assumed that a frontier militia force called to active service against Indians would be composed of hardy woods-wise part-time soldiers, such was not the case. The men who filled the Kentucky militia ranks were mostly draftees and substitutes for draftees who had little to no knowledge of military discipline or conduct or even familiarity with firearms. One officer characterized the 1,000 Kentuckians as "unused to the gun or woods." Many of their weapons were broken and useless. The Pennsylvanians, also a mix of draftees and substitutes were, if anything, even worse. Only 300 of the promised 500 showed up, and they were mostly "old, infirm men and young boys." Despite the militia requirement to bring one's own firearm to active service, many had no weapons, and their commander confessed that many of them "probably had never fired a gun." Most did not know how to disassemble what weapons they had, or even how to fix a flint in the jaws of a musket's hammer.[4]

This haphazardly organized force marched north out of Cincinnati at the end of September 1790, to fight what turned out to be 1,100 seasoned warriors defending their homes under the leadership of capable Native American commanders. Just before Harmar left he received a letter from Knox alleging that he was known to be a drunk and that if the expedition failed Knox would know why. The portly secretary of war knew as well as any modern politician how to hedge his bets when a policy he advocated appeared to be on the edge of failure. And fail it did.

Harmar's goal was to destroy the Miami village of Kekionga, which was the major settlement as well as trading post of the Ohio tribes, including the Shawnee and the Delaware. As Harmar closed in the Indians abandoned Kekionga, which was looted by a force of mounted Kentucky militiamen on October 15. Discipline among the Kentuckians, never very strong, broke down completely in a festival of plundering as they spread out to other nearby abandoned Indian villages. On October 19 Miami chief Little Turtle launched a counteroffensive, ambushing a force of Kentuckians and some regular army soldiers. The Kentuckians fled the scene, some not stopping until they reached home, leaving the outnumbered regulars to cover their hasty retreat. Harmar dispatched another force a few days later and it too was ambushed. Following these multiple defeats, Harmar declared victory and withdrew to Fort Washington, his casualties totaling 183 men killed or missing. True to his word, Knox initiated court-martial proceedings against Harmar, who was eventually acquitted, but left the army.

## ARTHUR ST. CLAIR'S DEFEAT

The poorly executed Harmar expedition exacerbated the frontier problem, and led to an attempt to remedy its faults and launch another effort. President George Washington appointed Arthur St. Clair, governor of the Northwest Territories, who had served with him as a general in the Revolution, to the rank of major general with orders to resolve the issue once and for all. Before St. Clair's assumption of command, Washington called the general to Philadelphia and advised him, based on the president's own French and Indian War experiences, to be wary of ambushes and secure his camp with at least rudimentary fortifications every night. St. Clair would have, on paper at least, a better army than his predecessor. Congress authorized the raising of a second regiment of regulars and, in addition, in an experiment attempting to bridge the gap between regulars and worthless militiamen, authorized the enlistment of 2,000 "levies" from New Jersey, Pennsylvania, Maryland, and Virginia for six months of service. These troops would serve as a semi-regular force under officers appointed by the federal government rather than militia commanders and be uniformed and equipped and paid a bounty and the same salary as regulars. In addition, St. Clair had the authority to call up militiamen if necessary.[5]

Had all the troops authorized been enlisted, St. Clair would have led a formidable 4,000-man army to Kekionga. In the event, however, things were far more muddled. Many men of the 1st United States Regiment refused to reenlist because their pay, which they had not seen in some time, was actually reduced by Congress. Of 420 men whose enlistments expired in 1790, only sixty reenlisted. The new 2nd United States Regiment had difficulty securing recruits for the same reason. The entire strength of the 1st Regiment in the summer of 1791 was 299 men, mostly new recruits, with veterans scrounged from garrisons around the territory. The 2nd Regiment mustered less than 500 recruits, many of them "urban riffraff . . . former prisoners [and] inveterate drunkards . . . all totally unfamiliar with army methods and frontier life." The levy battalions did a bit better with a total of 1,674 officers and men enrolled out of an expected 2,000, although the quality of recruits was considered similar to that of the 2nd Regiment.[6]

The levies were assembled into state-identified battalions and assigned to the 1st and 2nd Levy Regiments, which differed from the longer service 1st and 2nd United States Regiments. The New Jersey levy battalion, recruited in four companies initially totaling 328 officers and men, traveled to Carlisle, then Pittsburgh, and then down the Ohio River to Cincinnati's Fort Washington to join St. Clair's makeshift army, which was hamstrung by erratic and poor logistical support. William Duer, a maker and shaker with shady connections all over the government who had conned President Washington into giving the bride away at his Basking Ridge, New Jersey, wedding to Kitty Alexander, daughter of William Alexander, the New Jersey general who styled himself as "Lord Stirling," was appointed as provision contractor to the army. Duer, a British-born former member of the Continental Congress, who historian Wiley Sword accurately characterized as an "unscrupulous New York financier," was a good friend of Treasury Secretary Alexander Hamilton and Secretary of War Henry Knox and Knox's business partner as well. He spent part of the money he was allotted to acquire supplies on land he hoped to sell to refugees from Revolutionary France for inflated profits, and loaned $10,000 of it to Knox.[7]

The army that eventually marched north out of Fort Washington on October 4, 1791, led by the increasingly gout-disabled General St. Clair, never mustered anywhere near the 4,000 men it was supposed to. Things deteriorated as the army marched. Many of the Virginia levies, maintaining that their six month enlistments were up, went home. The army was further diminished by shedding soldiers—mostly from the 1st United States Regiment, the most experienced unit despite its large number of recruits—needed to garrison posts established to guard the main supply route hacked out of the wilderness. More men were lost to illness and desertion. To compound St. Clair's problems, frosts destroyed forage for his horses and mules, and he was confronted with the impending expiration of the six month enlistments of the Jerseymen and other remaining levies. After establishing Fort Jefferson and leaving a garrison there, St. Clair pushed on towards Kekionga, in-

tent on forcing a battle before his army, now mustering around 1,700 men, disintegrated.[8]

St. Clair ignored Washington's advice and took his Indian fighting clues from Knox, who subscribed to the idea that a display of "disciplined valor" was all that was needed to send the enemy flying. His little army struggled along into the increasing cold weather, and camped near the Wabash River in sporadic snowfall on the night of November 3, 1791. Although St. Clair laid out his camp in a tactical manner, with artillery guarding the main approaches, front and rear, he made no attempt to fortify the position and so his force, now down to around 1,400 soldiers and composed of the 2nd United States Regiment and levies, including the New Jersey battalion, now reduced to 180 men, in addition to some Kentucky mounted militia rangers, was not well prepared to repel a determined attack. In an attempt to provide an early warning of any enemy activity, St. Clair posted the Kentucky horsemen a short distance to his front.[9]

The American commander had believed from the start that the campaign would end with one big battle. His thoughts were confirmed, but the event did not turn out as he had anticipated. As St. Clair worked his way north, Little Turtle had massed over 1,000 well-armed warriors from a number of different tribes, including some from far to the west, at Kekionga, and on the morning of November 4, at around 6:00 a.m., he launched them at the Kentucky militia. The Kentuckians responded by running for their lives, and as the militiamen raced through St. Clair's camp in terror, the levies and the 2nd Regiment formed up to fight.[10]

Although a disciplined volley of musketry initially halted the Indian advance,

Little Turtle's men hit the ground and began a steady drumbeat of fire into St. Clair's camp, while maneuvering left and right to envelop his little army. Successive bayonet charges by the Americans pushed the enemy back from the perimeter, but the soldiers then found themselves isolated from flank support and forced to retreat, and the Indians would pursue them back to their original line and recommence firing. Little Turtle's marksmen shot down so many artillerymen that the remaining gunners had to spike their cannons. St. Clair's second in command was mortally wounded and the general had several horses shot out from under him attempting to supervise the defense. By 8:00 a.m. the situation had so deteriorated that the American commander ordered a retreat. Fortunately, the uninjured and walking wounded were able to break out of what had become an encirclement and struggle back down the road to Fort Washington. Most of Little Turtle's men abandoned the pursuit to plunder the camp and kill the wounded left behind, which enabled the majority of the survivors to escape, as St. Clair's retreat turned into a panicked rout. Among the casualties left behind, some killed and others taken as prisoners, were a number of the women and children who had accompanied the army as camp followers.[11]

Several days later, as the decimated force fell further back towards Cincinnati, officers totaled up the butcher's bill. The number of dead and missing, the latter presumed dead, came to 630; 230 wounded men managed to escape, a number to die afterwards. Scarcely 500 men of the original force engaged in the November 4 fight escaped uninjured. Indian casualties were negligible, most estimates being less than one hundred killed and wounded. The four New Jer-

sey companies under the command of Major Thomas Paterson, a former captain in the Revolutionary War 3rd New Jersey Regiment, were badly shot up in the disaster. Over the course of its service, from May through November 1791, 328 officers and men served in the New Jersey battalion. Of these, thirty-four deserted, five died of undisclosed causes, fifty-one were killed or went missing on November 4 "near Fort Recovery," and eight were wounded but escaped. Two of the four company commanders, Captains Jonathan Snowden and William Piatt, had served with the 1st New Jersey Regiment in the Continental army. Piatt was killed in action on November 4. Another company commander, Captain Zebulon Pike, descendent of an early English settler and founder of Woodbridge, New Jersey, who also had Continental army service, survived the expedition. His son, Zebulon Pike Jr., would be heard from in the future, as both a Jerseyman and a national figure. With their term of service up, the Jersey levies were discharged; a few enlisted in the regular army, but the vast majority of them seem to have had enough of soldiering.[12]

## UNIFORM MILITIA ACT OF 1792

Although the regular army was upgraded significantly after the disaster under the leadership of General Anthony Wayne, who created the combined arms "Legion of the United States" and avenged St. Clair's defeat at the Battle of Fallen Timbers in 1794, the national defense continued to be basically entrusted to a militia establishment, formalized to a degree by the Uniform Militia Act of 1792, which became law in May of that year. The law specified that militia duty was an obligation of free, able-bodied white men between the ages of eighteen and forty-five, who were to provide themselves with weapons and accoutrements at their own expense. Certain exemptions, primarily created by the individual states, applied to citizens otherwise obligated.[13]

There was little direct instruction in the Militia Act as to how the militia should be organized and commanded, although, in an attempt to provide some sort of basic uniformity should militias from different states be called up for federal duty together, states were encouraged, albeit not mandated, to organize their forces into regiments, brigades, and divisions. Each line battalion was supposed to contain elite companies of grenadiers, riflemen, or light infantry, and a limited number of cavalry and artillery.[14]

Every state was required to appoint an adjutant general to supervise its militia, and he was supposed to report to both the state's governor and the president on an annual basis. If actually implemented, the law would create a standby force of a half million men, but in the event, the lack of penalties for states that simply ignored the requirements made the legislation more of an advisory than an actual law. When President George Washington presented a plan devised by Secretary of War Knox that would further organize the militia as a national reserve for the tiny regular army, Congress rejected it, leaving militia command and control to the states. Another law which gave the president the authority to call up the militia to suppress an insurgency was balanced by the need for the chief executive to essentially allow a federal judge to make the final decision in the matter, although once that approval was gained, states were, unlike under the Militia Act, compelled to obey or suffer penalties.[15]

In the end, the militia obligations followed a simple-to-understand structure. The people of the then fifteen states subject to militia duty were required to keep and bear arms on a personal basis, and the militia was declared the official state military force, with each state's governor as its commander. Conscientious objectors like Quakers were exempt from militia service. Militiamen could be conscripted for service, but were allowed to procure substitutes to serve in their places, as they had during the Revolution when the Continental Line regiments were reinforced by "levies" of drafted militiamen. State laws varied in numerous ways as to specific local militia organization, as the Act of 1792 allowed. In addition, a second act passed in 1792 gave the president the power to call the militia into active service to "execute the laws of the Union, suppress insurrections and repel invasions."[16]

New Jersey passed its own Militia Act in 1792 to comply with the federal legislation. Although the entire able-bodied white male population was considered to be the "militia," and subject to service, the legislation authorized the counties to create companies of light infantry, grenadiers, cavalry, and artillery that would "dress themselves in uniform regimentals," as a more active force.[17]

## THE WHISKEY REBELLION

The New Jersey militia got its first call to duty for federal service in the "Whiskey Rebellion" of 1794. Farmers in western Pennsylvania made whiskey out of a considerable portion of their grain crop, a not unusual practice in an era of poor transportation and lack of refrigeration. In 1791, when Treasury Secretary Alexander Hamilton decided to raise money to consolidate state and national debts from the Revolutionary War and Articles of Confederation eras and establish the United States as a worthwhile credit risk, he backed a law imposing an excise tax on whiskey, which was passed in March 1791. Frontier farmers resisted the tax, initially through their legislators and by petition, but eventually an armed mob besieged the house of a federal tax collector in western Pennsylvania. President Washington dispatched mediators to solve the problem, and the tax was reduced, but the frontier continued to simmer. Mob violence escalated and in 1794 local militiamen rallied in support of those who refused to pay the tax. Shots were fired and a militia leader and Revolutionary War veteran officer was killed by United States soldiers from Pittsburgh.

It seemed as if full scale rebellion was about to break out, and Washington called up militiamen from Virginia, Maryland, eastern Pennsylvania, and New Jersey to enforce the law. A force of almost 13,000 men was mustered, including 4,318 from New Jersey, led by veteran officers of the Revolution. The Jerseyans were commanded in the field by Governor Richard Howell, a former major in the state's Continental Line who was later elevated to command of the impromptu army's right wing by Washington, who met the force in the field. The state's adjutant general, Anton White, a Revolutionary War cavalryman, was assigned to lead New Jersey's horsemen, and was subsequently assigned to command the entire force's cavalry. Brigade command was vested in Brigadier General Joseph Bloomfield, another New Jersey Continental Line veteran, while Major General Frederick Frelinghuysen, a militia commander in the Revolution, took charge of a mixed force of troops from other states.[18]

New Jersey militiamen who marched out to western Pennsylvania to defeat the Whiskey Rebellion were nattily attired, as this photo of a reproduction uniform on display at the National Guard Militia Museum of New Jersey in Sea Girt reveals.

The New Jersey militia assembled at Carlisle, Pennsylvania, marched to Shippensburg, then Strasburg and then crossed the Blue Mountains, passing through Bedford, Parkinson's Ferry, and Brown's Ferry and halting at Pittsburgh, where they joined militiamen from other states in an army led by General Henry Lee. The New Jersey records note that the militia did not actually engage in combat, but made a number of arrests, until finally, overawed by the approach of such a large force, the "'whiskey boys' succumbed, asked the clemency of the government authorities and pledged their future submission to the law." The Jerseymen began their return to the state on November 21, 1794, and arrived back in Trenton on December 20, where they were discharged over the next several days.[19]

## THE MILITARY RETRACTS

The years following the end of the Whiskey Rebellion witnessed the steady decline of the New Jersey militia. "Training Days" became public entertainment events, with those who chose not to attend paying a minimal fine used to finance militia expenses. Sylvia Du Bois, a freed slave, characterized a Training Day she attended in Flemington in 1805, as "filled with dancing, laughter, music, and, most of all, rum." The experience convinced her to open her own tavern during future Training Days.[20]

Although there was plenty of political infighting between Jeffersonian Republicans and Federalists, as well as the leadership of the old East and West Jersey sections of the state, New Jersey's military force, as with much of the militia nationwide, became moribund. Following the passage of the Alien and Sedition Acts in 1798, Republican militia officers refused to join Federalist officers in signing a petition of support for President John Adams. Governor Howell, a Federalist, condemned the officers and they, in turn, maintained that Adams had violated the Constitution. The feud went on in the partisan newspapers of the day, with Howell attacking the Republican officers as a "French faction" bent on political assassination and the officers responding that the governor was the "Prince of Blackguards." When civil strife broke out again in Pennsylvania in 1799, Howell volunteered New Jersey militiamen to restore order, but regular army troops were assigned the task instead. Howell was embroiled in a constant series of political fights before leaving office in 1801 and dying the following year, amidst charges that he had embezzled state money.[21]

Although Governor Howell proposed to raise a regiment when tensions with France spilled over into naval conflict in 1798, that event did not come to pass. New Jerseyans did, however, serve in the regular army, navy, and Marine Corps of the United States during the "quasi-war" naval conflict with France from 1798 to 1801 and the conflict against the Barbary pirates from 1801 to 1805. Joseph and William Bainbridge of Princeton, and Burlington-born James Lawrence, officers in both wars and heroes of the latter one, were Jerseymen and, ironically, the sons of Revolutionary War Loyalist fathers.[22]

Within a few years the moribund militia would awaken, as war with Great Britain loomed on the horizon once more. New Jersey, as a coastal state, was particularly vulnerable to the massive British fleet, and the state took that possibility seriously. New Jerseyans would join the regular army and navy as well, and the state's soldiers and sailors would do their duty in what many of their fellow citizens would consider an unnecessary conflict.

## THE WAR OF 1812

The War of 1812, the second and final conflict between the United States and Great Britain, grew out of a number of issues, many of them related to the former mother country's ongoing long war with France. The British navy interfered in the neutral United States' trade with France, and, in dire need of seamen, stopped American merchant ships at sea and impressed sailors into service, conscripting not only people they identified as deserters from the Royal Navy, but naturalized American citizens who had been born in Britain, and at least some native born Americans as well. An incident on June 22, 1807, in which the British ship HMS *Leopard* attacked the USS *Chesapeake*, killing and wounding a number of American sailors and impressing several alleged British citizens, brought the two countries to the brink of war, but President Thomas Jefferson stepped back, attempting, unsuccessfully in the end, to divorce neutral America's interests from foreign conflicts through a trade embargo that was widely disregarded. In addition to affairs at sea, the British in Canada also continued to supply arms and encouragement to the Native American tribes of the Northwest, which they had been doing since the end of the Revolution in an attempt to limit American westward expansion. In response, many Americans were eager to expel Britain entirely from the North American continent and annex part or all of Canada to their new nation.

These ongoing tensions led to political feuding between the Jeffersonian-Republican and Federalist parties, the latter more sympathetic to the British, in the first decade of the nineteenth century. The squabbling came to a head in 1812. On April 10, Congress authorized "a Detachment from the Militia of the United States" of 100,000 men nationwide to ready themselves for six months of possible active federal service. If federalized, militiamen were authorized to receive regular army pay and supplies, but were exempted from the flogging administered in the regular army as a punishment for disciplinary infractions. Members of the militia on active service who committed military offenses could only be punished by "stoppage of pay, confinement and deprivation of part of the rations."[23]

Thomas Jefferson believed that militiamen were sufficient to defend the country, and he had cut the budget for the already small regular army and navy during his two terms in office. Despite the president's support of the militia, between 1800 and 1812 the force's military capability, never strong after the Revolution, steadily deteriorated. Militia musters in the iron forge towns of the southern New Jersey Pinelands, for example, often turned into drunken brawls, or, as one historian euphemistically characterized them, "fights and frolics." On one occasion, an officer drilling his company at Bodine's Tavern near Martha Furnace was court-martialed because he was "so intoxicated that he did not know the duty of a captain." Militia laws that allowed people of means to escape duty by paying a fine led to a military organization in which "men who served owned less than 1 percent of the property they helped to protect."[24]

Many of these citizen soldiers could not afford the rifle or musket they were supposed to provide at their own expense—one study concludes that only 10 percent of militiamen owned their own guns. As part of the militia law of 1808, Congress appropriated $200,000 to provide weapons to the states to arm militiamen, but the amount was far less than was needed. When New Jersey militiamen were called to service in 1812, a Cumberland County company commander whose men were "farmers, mechanics and shallop men" reported that they owned muskets "unfit for actual service, the most of them . . . old and of various sizes," with few bayonets. Another Cumberland captain complained that "the expense of arms and accoutrements, exceeding fifteen dollars" was the reason his company was under strength.[25]

The state helped out by purchasing and issuing firearms whenever possible. An 1804 inventory revealed that New

Jersey claimed ownership of "12,915 muskets, 3,302 bayonets and three rifles" all of them reportedly in the hands of militiamen in various locations. In 1808 the state treasurer provided the adjutant general with $9,205.14 to purchase militia firearms, the money apparently provided by fines levied on men who failed to show up for militia training days. At least some of the muskets acquired by New Jersey were manufactured in the state by John Miles of Bordentown. Three surviving brass mounted muskets by Miles are marked as the property of the Burlington Brigade.[26]

The federal militia legislation of 1812 further authorized President James Madison to call all or part of the newly created ready force into action as he deemed necessary. On June 1, 1812, Madison sent a list of complaints against Britain to Congress, which responded with a declaration of war on June 18. Some New England states, governed by Federalists, refused to cooperate with the president, and the war, like the Revolution, found New Jersey, with its many Quakers and Federalists, divided and unenthusiastic. New Jersey's congressional delegation was divided when considering President James Madison's request for a declaration of war against Great Britain, with some voting for the declaration and others against it, including Senator John Lambert, of Madison's own Republican party.[27]

The declaration was, however, supported by the majority of the state's Jeffersonian Republicans, and their sympathetic news outlets, including Elizabeth's New Jersey Journal, hailed the new conflict with "our ancient and inveterate foe." In contrast, a number of New Jersey Federalist legislators decried the war as "inexpedient, ill-timed, and most dangerously impolitick," as well as "un-

just" and called for a negotiated settlement as soon as possible. John Nielson, chairman of the group, demanded "a speedy and honourable peace and no alliance with France." The Federalists, hoping to gain Quaker votes, rechristened themselves the "Friends of Peace," much to the disgust of the Journal. A disgruntled Republican threatened a Federalist newspaper, Elizabeth's Essex Patriot, in a message warning "Your damd tory paper will be serve a Baltimore trick if don't quit printing federal lies. If your shop burn down . . . tis not any more than what you deserve." The paper's office was indeed torched on October 20, 1813.[28]

Governor Joseph Bloomfield, a fifty-nine-year-old Revolutionary War veteran and Jeffersonian-Republican who had been governor of New Jersey every year but one since 1801 (under the state constitution of 1776 governors were elected annually by the legislature—in 1802 they decided they didn't need one), authorized the organization of the state's assessed 5,000-man contribution to Madison's contingency force. Although ambivalent about the wisdom of the war himself, the governor ordered local militia commanders to select men for the state's allotment of "detailed militia" and called on New Jersey citizen soldiers to defend their country's honor and independence. Theoretically "detailed militia" would defend the state while "detached" militia could campaign outside its borders, but the distinction was hazy. The men in these units would, preferably, be recruited from the organized volunteer "uniform companies," rather than the whole militia, or all men of military age, although men could be (and were) drafted to fill vacancies, and the hiring of substitutes for drafted men was widely practiced and not considered as evading duty. One officer encouraging the practice proclaimed that substitutes were "widely available from New Jersey and Connecticut" and could be "paid weekly by the principal."[29]

New Jersey adjutant general James J. Wilson, a man who was more a master politician than a military officer, set about implementing the governor's orders. In August, New Jersey quartermaster general Jonathan Rhea had 1,000 "stands of arms" transferred from a federal government agent in New York City to Jersey City in order to equip militiamen who could not supply their own weapons. Bloomfield resigned as governor when he was appointed to the rank of brigadier general in the regular army and assigned to command of the Third Military District, with headquarters at New York City's Battery. The governor's Republican friends gave him a grand send-off from Trenton, toasting Bloomfield as a "genuine . . . Jersey Blue." With Bloomfield gone, Charles Clark, vice president of the New Jersey Council (forerunner of today's state senate), acted as chief executive until the election of a new governor by the legislature. Although the militiamen of states to the north and west of New Jersey engaged in active campaigning under federal commanders with less than stellar results, New Jersey's citizen soldiers were assigned a static coastal defense role. In all, a total of 808 New Jersey militiamen served the federal government as "detached" troops in 1812, apparently all on Staten Island, in comparison with 4,494 Pennsylvanians and 14,866 New Yorkers.[30]

Shortly after the declaration of war, a New Jersey militia detachment under Major Isaac Andruss of Caldwell established a camp by Paulus Hook, a location in today's Jersey City and scene of a Revolutionary War battle. The land, which

This Dickinson High School plaque commemorates the encampment and militia headquarters at Paulus Hook in 1812–1815.

had been purchased by the United States government in 1804, was occupied by the New Jersey militia on a rotating basis for the rest of the war. The Paulus Hook encampment, used to train militiamen in "military instruction and discipline" prior to their deployment on other assignments, was located on high ground overlooking the Hudson River at the current site of Dickinson High School. It was also a logistical nexus, used to supply troops on active service elsewhere in the Third Military District, as well as troops passing through, since Jersey City was on the main route to New York City. On July 24, 1812, the area was the scene of what was perhaps a historic first, the transport of troops across water by steam-powered craft, as "Fulton's steam ferry boat," described as "a most excellent machine"

The "Old Arsenal" at Jersey City, erected during the War of 1812 to store supplies for the New Jersey militia.

ferried a battery of "flying artillery," headed for upstate New York across the Hudson to Manhattan. It took four trips to get four guns, limbers, horses, and men across the river. Within a year two ferries were running from Paulus Hook to Cortlandt Street in Manhattan and back every half hour. In 1813, the federal government erected an arsenal building on the west side of the camp property for the purpose of storing arms and equipment intended for use in the defense of the port of New York. A mill on the site was used to "furnish flour and meal" to troops stationed at Sandy Hook and elsewhere in the New York area. Andruss's detachment, composed of companies from Hunterdon, Middlesex, Sussex, Monmouth, and Essex Counties, moved on to Fort Richmond on Staten Island on August 17, where they served through September 25.[31]

While the militia was trying to organize after the advent of war, the ocean off the New Jersey coast witnessed a most peculiar slow motion chase. On July 5, 1812, Captain Isaac Hull sailed the USS

*Constitution* north from Annapolis and, unfortunately for him, ran into a five-ship British squadron off New Jersey. The British gave chase and then the wind failed. Over three days Hull advanced his ship by any means he could, including using oar-powered long boats to pull it and "kedging," or dropping small anchors and pulling the ship towards them by turning the capstan. Hindered by the lack of wind themselves, the British failed to get close enough to engage the *Constitution*. When the wind came back Hull was prepared with wet sails to better capture it and pulled away, eventually making it to Boston.[32]

In November 1812 the New Jersey legislature, which had come under the control of Federalists in the election of that year, unsurprisingly selected a Federalist, Aaron Ogden, as governor. Ogden's cooperation with the national government in its war aims led to conflicts with his essentially antiwar legislature, to which he stressed that the war obliged cooperation with the Madison administration, although the lawmakers did award him a personal monopoly on steam ferry traffic between Jersey City and New York. The governor, like Bloomfield a Revolutionary War veteran, assumed office on November 29 and ordered the state's entire active "uniformed" militia, a force of under 2,500 men, only half the strength originally envisioned, on twenty-four-hour alert, each man to be equipped with "one good blanket, and four days provisions ready cooked." His adjutant general, John Beatty, advised Ogden that the New Jersey militia suffered from serious deficiencies in arms and ammunition, and that the Somerset Brigade was in "an extreme defenceless and unwarlike attitude." Nonetheless, the governor encouraged the state's men to "display their zeal in joining themselves to some one or other of these Uniform Companies, as circumstances of inclination may lead, thus proving themselves a race of Jersey Men, not unworthy of their Fathers."[33]

Governor Ogden held a dinner in Trenton for officers of the New Jersey militia and other influential people to encourage support for the war. A large number of toasts were offered and the governor gave toast number fourteen: "Let the horse and flying artillery of New Jersey be dashing and let them be covered by riflemen—and supported by brave musket men in uniform." A newspaper report indicated that things understandably got a bit hazy, and "a number of other toasts were given, which was not recollected."[34]

Perhaps strangely, considering the militia of the Revolution, proper uniforms did not present a problem to the New Jersey militia of 1812. Although one source states that the New Jersey militia was outfitted with "dark blue clothes with light blue facings, collars and cuffs," the state's Militia Law of 1804 was spe-

cific as to how soldiers of different units, grenadiers, light infantry artillery, or cavalrymen, should be dressed. That law and other legislation detailed proper uniform colors, cut, trim, buttons, etc. Infantrymen, for example, were to be issued "a short blue jacket with red collar and cuffs." Due to transportation problems resulting from lack of infrastructure, uniform issue was often a problem for American troops on the frontiers, but New Jersey, in close proximity to the uniform manufacturers in Philadelphia, never wanted for clothing for its citizen soldiers. The state bought over 500 bicorn hats in 1812 and had no delivery problems.[35]

The New Jersey militia's primary initial mission was the defense of New York harbor, where the militiamen were under the overall command of Brigadier General William Armstrong, a federal officer who succeeded Bloomfield in charge of the Third District. In early 1813, Federalist lawmakers in Trenton called for peace with Britain and tried to prohibit New Jersey's citizen soldiers from leaving the state, leading to a number of insubordination problems in the ranks. While the New Jersey militia struggled with its wartime role, former governor General Bloomfield led a regular army and New York militia force intended to spearhead an invasion of Canada north to Plattsburgh, New York. Bloomfield did not take the field, however (fortunately for him as the expedition proved a disaster), and was assigned to command the Plattsburgh garrison. Later in the year he returned south to take over the Fourth Military District, headquartered in Philadelphia and responsible for eastern Pennsylvania, southwestern New Jersey, and Delaware.[36]

For the rest of the war, in addition to Paulus Hook or on or near Sandy Hook,

Jersey militiamen on active duty were stationed at other posts, including Fort Richmond on Staten Island, Cape May, and Billingsport, on the Delaware River, usually in three month periods of rotating service. These militia units were composed of a mix of volunteers, draftees, and substitutes. In southern Monmouth County, potential draftees reportedly joined together in seven man "clubs" to pool funds to pay $50 to a substitute if one of them was conscripted. According to one family history, Daniel Drew, an underage farm boy from New York, made his way to Paulus Hook in 1814, where he became a New Jersey soldier and pocketed a $100 substitute fee for his trouble. Whether volunteers, draftees or substitutes, the desertion rate was high in some organizations. A south Jersey unit commanded by Major William Potter lost thirty-seven men to desertion in a single week. When service time was occasionally extended beyond the original three months proposed, morale became a serious problem with draftees and substitutes alike, and in September 1813 it was reported that Jersey militiamen who believed their term of service had ended became "restless, and some of them are said to be in irons for the crime of desertion."[37]

Sandy Hook peninsula was the farthest outpost of the New York harbor defenses. The "Highlands of Navesink" to its immediate rear provided an excellent position to observe the ocean for enemy vessels, and the shoals around the Hook itself provided security against an easy enemy landing. In 1812 two blockhouses, one on the Highlands and another near the Sandy Hook lighthouse, were erected to house and protect small garrisons. In early 1813, 280 workmen were sent to Sandy Hook from New York to build barracks and a fort, which was

equipped with heavy "32 pounder" artillery pieces, near the lighthouse, and to erect another blockhouse with three cannons at Spermaceti Cove on the bay side of the Hook. An elaborate "telegraph" signaling system involving cannon fire and the lowering or hoisting of large black and white balls on masts sited atop the Highlands was established to convey coded "information of the movements of the enemy . . . to Signal Hill on Staten Island and thence to Governor's Island or Brooklyn Navy Yard in fifteen minutes."[38]

Several companies, akin to the state troops of the Revolutionary War, were recruited in 1814 for longer periods of service along the coast. These units included Gloucester County artillery and infantry companies under Captain Robert Smith and Captain John R. Scull, which were stationed at Somers Point, Great Egg Harbor, and Leeds Point. An infantry company from Monmouth County was organized by Captain Jacob Butcher at the bog iron forge known as "Butcher's Works" (later Burrsville in Ocean County) and was responsible for coastal defense at "Long Branch, Deal and Barnegat Inlet." Butcher's men fielded a six pounder cannon in addition to their muskets. Another Monmouth infantry company covered Eatontown, Long Branch, and Highlands, and a Cape May artillery company served along a stretch of the south coast. Many of the records of these units were lost in a late nineteenth century fire, so that their exact periods of service are estimated, but most served from the summer of 1814 through to the end of the conflict.[39]

Throughout 1813 the number of New Jersey uniformed militia units available for detached or detailed service continued to increase gradually, until it consisted of sixteen troops of cavalry, eleven companies of artillery, thirty companies of light infantry, and seven companies of riflemen. Although uniforms and rations were apparently supplied by the state, with federal fiscal assistance, individuals were still theoretically expected to provide themselves with weapons, powder and ball, blankets, and knapsacks; although in reality most arms were now supplied by the federal government through the state. Cavalrymen were supposed to bring their own "Serviceable horse, at least fourteen hands and a half high, a good Saddle, Mall pillion, and Valise holsters, a breastplate and Crupper, a pair of Boots and Spurs, a pair of Pistols, a Sabre and Cartouche Box to contain cartridges for pistols." Additional supplies, including canteens, camp kettles, blankets, "bed sacks," and tents, were issued out of supplies in storage at Paulus Hook.[40]

Governor William S. Pennington, a Jeffersonian Republican who succeeded Ogden as governor at the end of 1813, when the Republicans regained control of the legislature, was not a member of the pre-Revolutionary War New Jersey aristocracy like his predecessors, but a self-made man commissioned from the ranks during the Revolution. In his annual message in January 1814, Pennington called for more attention to the coast below Sandy Hook, down to Cape May and along Delaware Bay. The governor, an old artilleryman, actually toured the coast, suggesting sites for gun emplacements and promising as much artillery and small arms support as he could scrounge, and his efforts led to the establishment of the longer service companies along the shore.[41]

In July 1814, with the British threatening invasion from Canada and coastal incursions as well, Pennington called for 5,000 militiamen from around the state to "hold themselves in readiness to march at a moment's notice." (The state's total potential military strength was estimated at 36,000 men.) The call fell short once more, as only 3,600 officers and men were mobilized in August. One brigade, about half the available force, under General Ebenezer Elmer, who had served as a lieutenant in General Bloomfield's old Revolutionary War company, was assigned to the defenses of Philadelphia at Bloomfield's request, and the remaining troops were deployed at Sandy Hook and Paulus Hook. Most of Elmer's men established a camp and defensive positions at Billingsport, while some went to Cape May. The brigades served through January 1815. Many militiamen in the 1814 call up were draftees and substitutes; only seventy-two men volunteered in all of Salem County. A number of these citizen-soldiers deserted during the final months of the year. In October 1814, a court-martial board was established at the Sandy Hook lighthouse to try deserters.[42]

Political problems at higher levels did not help the situation. When Governor Daniel D. Tompkins of New York was placed in military command of the Third Military District, Pennington protested to Secretary of War William Eustis that Tompkins, a New York official, should not have authority over New Jersey militiamen while they were stationed in their own state, but the secretary advised the governor that Tompkins did indeed have such authority, since he had been appointed commander of the district by the authority of the United States government. Joseph Bloomfield's active duty career ended in November 1814, when he was superseded as commander of the Fourth District by Major General Edmund P. Gaines.[43]

Fears of possible invasion in late 1814, in the wake of the burning of Washing-

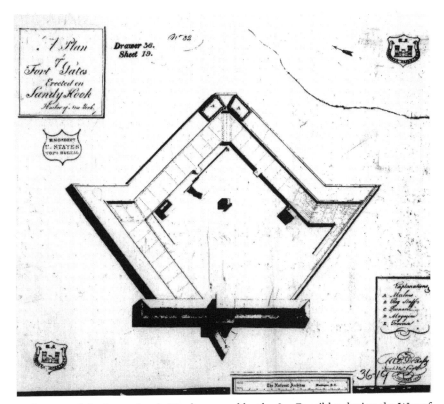

A diagram of the fort at Sandy Hook manned by the Sea Fencibles during the War of 1812.

ton, led to militia warning posts at "Elizabethtown, Newark, Springfield, Bloomfield, Caldwell and Patterson" with artillery positioned to fire signal shots as "an alarm in case of a threatened attack." Repelling such an attack was problematic, as militia infantrymen were still showing up without small arms. Essex Brigade major Peter Kean reminded his troops of their legal obligation in a brigade order of September 2, 1814, that stated: "Every militia man is required by the act of congress May 8, 1792, to provide himself with a good musket, or firelock, with a bayonet and belt, two spare flints, a cartridge box, with twenty-four cartridges fitted to the bore of his musket, each cartridge to contain a proper quantity of powder and ball—or with a good rifle, knapsack, shot pouch and powder horn, twenty balls suited to the bore of his rifle and a quarter of a pound of powder. Strict compliance with this act is now required." Despite this injunction, an order of September 26 noted that "arms and accoutrements for Infantry that are unable to provide for themselves" would be forthcoming.[44]

One soldier who reported to Paulus Hook in 1814 was Horace Holden, a Jerseyman studying law in New York City. Earlier in the year Holden had served, along with "all the bar and law students of the city" digging trenches in Brooklyn. Expecting to be drafted into a New York militia outfit, he volunteered as a private in a city company led by Captain John V. B. Varick. When Holden visited his home in New Jersey, his father, a Revolutionary War veteran who had served in George Washington's Life Guard, advised the young man that he could contact his old war buddy General William Colfax of Pompton and gain young Horace an officer's commission in Colfax's brigade of New Jersey Detailed Militia. On September 1, 1814, Holden was commissioned a third lieutenant in Captain Daniel Kilburn's artillery company in the Second Regiment of Detailed Militia. Before the day was done he was promoted to major and a position as aide de camp on General Colfax's staff, where he served through December 8.[45]

Many years later Holden recalled that his unit initially traveled to the Jersey City encampment and from there to the Navesink Highlands, "one of the most delightful spots ever presented to the human eye," where "Commodore Jacob Lewis commanded a flotilla of gunboats in lower bay within Sandy Hook." While some militiamen remained on the Highlands, others camped south of the Sandy Hook lighthouse at "Camp Liberty" or took up positions near a blockhouse. Although one writer characterized the duty rotations spent "throwing up fortifications" on Sandy Hook as "picnics," Holden described the peninsula as "the most inhospitable sand heap ever trod upon by the foot of man." The only dwelling on the "sand heap" was the home of the lighthouse keeper, a man named Schenck, which General Colfax took over as his headquarters. The fort near the blockhouse at the extreme end of Sandy Hook was manned by "a motley crew called 'Sea Fencibles.'" The Fencibles were part of a semi-regular federal force created in the fall of 1812 to man harbor defenses and gunboats and recruited from among sailors and watermen who were unemployed due to the British blockade. The Sandy Hook Fencible garrison came under Colfax's command for the duration of his unit's tour of duty. One account, based on interviews with veterans, maintains that the Sandy Hook militia garrisons spent most of their service time "uttering maledictions on commissaries for furnishing them with horse beef and other objectionable grub."[46]

Fortunately for Holden and his comrades, actual combat was not in the cards, although there were a few scares. The enemy, in the form of the British blockading squadron, including the *Bellephorus* and two other ships, floated offshore. The British were ready to pounce on any American vessels approaching or leaving the port of New York and fired on small coastal craft slipping around the Hook in shallow water when the opportunity arose. The Sea Fencibles sometimes returned fire with "hot shot," cannon balls heated red hot before loading and firing at ships in hopes of setting them afire. In October 1814, Captain John Logan of Peapack witnessed the escape of an American privateer's prize ship, "hugging close to the shore as possible," from the British as Lewis's gunboats rounded the Hook and the Sea Fencibles fired their "long gun" for cover, while militia riflemen rushed to the beach. A few nights later Logan's company was called out when "twenty or thirty muskets" were fired at militiamen camped near the lighthouse, in a probable "friendly fire" incident. Neither side caused any damage or inflicted any casualties during Holden's and Logan's tour of duty, although Logan found a drowned militiaman in the surf and Holden remembered some enemy rounds coming "near enough," before his service ended in December 1814.[47]

Although New Jersey was never actually invaded by British forces, there are a number of stories of small local ships chased and captured and landings by enemy raiding parties from the British blockading fleet. Much of this information is sketchy. An official roster of Captain Butcher's company notes that: "It appears they were engaged in one fight, called the battle at 'Brant Hill,' in which a British man-of-war, understood to be the "Effervire," carrying thirty-two guns, attempted to land at the mouth of the Squan River." According to the account, the British launched several small boats which attempted to capture and burn some ships in the river, but were repelled by "volleys of musketry" from Butcher's soldiers.[48]

Local lore, recounted in a late nineteenth century county history, has British sailors and marines from the blockading fleet landing near Barnegat Inlet to capture or destroy civilian vessels on several occasions, while civilians watched the action from rooftops in Forked River. In one incident the enemy reportedly set two coastal trading ships afire and took fifteen head of cattle. The raiders allegedly told local farmers that Commodore Thomas M. Hardy, commanding the British blockading squadron, would pay for the cattle, but the farmers refused payment, lest they be accused of trading with the enemy. Several other farmers subsequently claimed that their cattle had been forcibly confiscated by the British, but then admitted they had received payment, so the alleged refusal of compensation by some may be a storyline retroactively con-

cocted to avoid being accused of a repeat of the Revolutionary War custom of "London trading"—which indeed may have been the case.[49]

Cape May, located at the tip of a peninsula, was in an unusually exposed position, subject to seaborne depredation from ocean and bay. Although the county's state legislators, both Federalists, opposed war in 1812, Cape May officials had little choice but to prepare for the inevitable. In July 1812, the county Board of Freeholders brought two Revolutionary War cannons out of retirement, although Robert Holmes, the antiwar Federalist county treasurer, initially refused to pay for new gun carriages. In March 1813, the Freeholders appropriated $300 for the purchase of "amputating instruments, gunpowder," and '100 weight of large buckshot'" for issue to the militia. Shortly afterward, money intended to fund the Dennis Creek Causeway was diverted to buy 600 pounds of cannon balls, two kegs of powder, and material to make artillery cartridges. As the British blockade began to materialize that year, Cape May men built fortifications armed with log-barreled faux "cannons" at Goshen Creek.[50]

A British blockading squadron reached Delaware Bay in March 1813, and immediately conducted a loud if largely ineffectual bombardment of Lewes, Delaware, which spread panic on the Jersey shore side of the bay. People in inland New Jersey towns like Bridgeton feared incursions up the Cohansey or Maurice rivers, which, fortunately for them, did not occur, although the British threatened Cape May residents with shelling their houses if they warned coastal trade ships of the enemy's location. In May 1813, the British navy captured three sloops off the mouth of the Maurice River, and on May 30 a landing party reportedly skirmished with militiamen near Leesburg in Cumberland County. Raids and landings, as well as numerous false alarms, continued into late 1814, and nervous citizens drove their stock inland, buried their valuables in backyards or dropped them down wells when alarms were sounded. None of the raids, however, came remotely close to the size of British and Loyalist incursions of the Revolutionary War era.[51]

Incidents at sea, mostly involving the blockading fleet and local merchant ships, and occasional American privateers and British supply ships, also occurred off the New Jersey coast. According to one source, in late 1813 the *New Jersey*, a small coastal trading ship from May's Landing manned by a three-man crew, was captured by a British armed schooner off Cape May. The British put a small "prize crew" aboard but the Americans managed to recapture their ship and bring it in to Somers Point, where two Englishmen in the prize crew "hired out in the vicinity" and a third, an Irishman, joined the American navy as a gunboat sailor. On July 4, 1813, an American subterfuge of hiding an armed party of sailors below decks on a local fishing boat, the *Yankee*, succeeded in capturing the British schooner *Eagle* off Sandy Hook.[52]

A less successful foray by members of Elmer's brigade, garrisoned at Billingsport in 1814, occurred when an officer with some experience as a seaman manned a local schooner with militiamen and pursued a small British ship that had ventured up the Delaware. The enemy craft escaped when most of the Jerseymen became seasick in turbulent water and abandoned the chase. In another less than auspicious contest a gunboat squadron from Philadelphia conducted a daring assault upon a grounded sloop of the blockading squadron in Delaware Bay, but the fight ended when "gunboat 121" was captured by the British and towed out to sea. The gunboat was later abandoned and washed ashore with the tide at Absecon, where the locals scrapped it for the iron and brass.[53]

## NEW JERSEY AND THE REGULAR UNITED STATES ARMY

With the declaration of war between America and Great Britain the regular army of the United States, composed of two regiments of dragoons and seven of infantry as of January 1812, was considerably expanded. Enlistment terms in the regulars varied, and a recruit could sign up for a choice of enlistments for periods of "one year, eighteen months, for the war, and for five years." As many as 1,000 New Jerseyans served in the regular army, in a number of different regiments. The unit with the most Jerseymen in the ranks was the 15th U. S. Infantry, a regiment raised in Trenton, and known throughout the army as "the New Jersey regiment." Originally attached to General Bloomfield's command at Plattsburgh, the 15th participated in the invasion of Canada and fought at La Cole Mill in October 1812, the capture of York in April 1813, at Fort George in May 1813, and at French's Creek and Plattsburgh, New York, in September 1814. The regiment was back in Canada in September and fought at Fort Erie that month and Cook's Mills in October.[54]

The 15th was originally commanded by noted western explorer Colonel Zebulon Pike of Pike's Peak fame, a native of Lamberton, New Jersey, whose father had served as an officer in the Revolution and with the ill-fated "Jersey Levies" in the Indian War of 1791. Pike's combat career did not have an auspicious beginning, as the fight at La Cole pitted American regulars against American militiamen in a deadly case of mistaken identity, but his regiment was soon considered one of the best in the army, and he is considered to have been a "consummate professional." Pike developed a unique combat technique for the men of the 15th. Instead of two ranks with bayonets fixed on muskets in the advance, the colonel deployed his unit in three ranks, with the third rank armed with pikes, long considered obsolete weapons, and short muskets they slung over their shoulders, in order to provide a veritable hedgehog of sharpened steel in the attack. He also contracted with local Native Americans to provide snowshoes for his men to use in winter operations. Promoted to brigadier general in March 1813, Pike lost his life on April 14, 1813, following the capture of York (Toronto), when the withdrawing British detonated a powder magazine, killing Pike and a number of other Americans. His unique tactical formation was subsequently abandoned when it did not prove to offer any advantage over the standard drill. Among the other Jerseymen killed at York was Captain John Lambert Hoppock of Amwell, grandson of Senator John Lambert, who had voted against the war in 1812.[55]

Zebulon Pike (1779–1813) led two expeditions to the American West before losing his life in the War of 1812.

## NEW JERSEY AND THE U. S. NAVY

Jerseymen also served in the U. S. Navy in all ranks, but perhaps the best known natives of the state in naval service were two veterans of the Barbary Pirate war, Burlington-born James Lawrence and Princeton native William Bainbridge. Captain Lawrence, in command of the sloop-of-war USS *Hornet*, sank the brig HMS *Peacock* off the coast of South America in February 1813. His victory gained him the command of the frigate USS *Chesapeake*, which was outfitting in Boston harbor in May, and he impetuously sailed it out of the harbor with an untrained crew to engage the British frigate HMS *Shannon*. Lawrence lost the fight, his ship, and his life but contributed the phrase "don't give up the ship" to the American naval lexicon. Lawrence's friend Oliver Hazard Perry immortalized him by flying a flag emblazoned with the motto during his Lake Erie victory in 1814.[56]

Bainbridge learned of the outbreak of war while in St. Petersburg, Russia. Following an arduous journey, he finally arrived in America and was given command of the USS *Constellation* at Charlestown, Massachusetts. On December 29, 1812, while in command of the iconic USS *Constitution*, Bainbridge, leading, in contrast to Lawrence, a superbly trained crew, decisively defeated HMS *Java* off Brazil. Although Bainbridge was wounded twice himself, the fight demonstrated his men's superior marksmanship with both artillery and small arms.[57]

SOLDIERS OF COLOR DURING THE WAR OF 1812

Unlike in the ranks of the New Jersey Continental Brigade and militia fielded in the Revolution, the state's African Americans did not serve in integrated regular units in the War of 1812. There was considerable Quaker emancipation agitation prior to the Revolution, which resulted in freedom for a number of slaves, and both free men and slaves were allowed to serve as substitutes for drafted militiamen in the earlier conflict. New Jersey's gradual abolition law, sponsored by Governor Bloomfield, only freed children born to enslaved parents after July 4, 1804, once they reached the age of twenty-one for women and twenty-five for men, and the majority of black New Jerseyans were still enslaved in 1812 and theoretically ineligible to serve in a military capacity. Denied the vote as well, New Jersey African-American men, even those legally free, were not fully citizens.

British commanders employed black West Indian soldiers and encouraged slaves to flee their masters in the southern United States, but there is no mention of such a policy being initiated in New Jersey. In 1812 American general James Wilkinson proposed enlisting "colored volunteers" in Louisiana, but was barred from doing so by the newly elected state legislature. In November 1814, however, Andrew Jackson welcomed black and mixed race volunteers into his ranks as he prepared to defend New Orleans.

Although militia membership was officially limited to white males, African Americans did serve in New Jersey detailed militia units, albeit not as formal soldiers. A penciled note pasted into an adjutant general's "office copy" of the official roster of New Jersey War of 1812 soldiers compiled in 1900 noted that "all cooks, waiters and servants are not published." The reference is to black men who served in those capacities in militia units on active duty. Curiously, and without explanation, that same published roster lists, as an "addenda," a single black soldier, Thomas Lee. Lee, described as "colored," is recorded as a Jerseyman enlisting as a private in the 26th U. S. Infantry at Philadelphia in January of 1815 and being discharged in March 1815.[58]

THE END OF THE WAR OF 1812

The Treaty of Ghent, ending the War of 1812, was signed on December 24, 1814, and was ratified by the US Senate on February 17, 1815. Although the war had caused economic stress in New Jersey with the interruption of the coastal trade, privately owned turnpike companies chartered by the legislature had proved extremely profitable to their owners. The turnpikes, New Jersey's first toll roads, provided the land transportation infrastructure of the state and were used to transport massive amounts of supplies north to the armies operating in northern New York and Canada. Philadelphia, as previously noted, was a major uniform manufacturing center, and, due to the British blockade, Philadelphia goods had to cross New Jersey by road to get to New York. One historian estimates that the New Jersey legislature chartered fifty-one turnpike companies between 1801 and 1829 for periods of from fifty to ninety-nine years. Unfortunately, the heavy traffic, estimated at "4,000 wagons and 20,000 horses . . . rumbling back and forth across the state . . . demolished the roads," inspiring postwar solutions that further advanced New Jersey's economy while at the same time empowering a new industrial oligarchy and complicating its politics.[59]

Following the end of the conflict, the New Jersey militia resumed its downward spiral. While the federal government did its best to maintain an effective navy in the postwar era, the regular army's strength was cut in half by 1821, and the preparedness of the militia was left to the individual states. There was a great deal of bloviating political rhetoric celebrating the importance of the militia as the primary defense of American "homesteads and honor," but the institution itself was a veritable shambles. One motivation for making the militia, rather than a professional force, the bulwark of the republic, despite its ineptitude, was readily apparent: it was cheaper.[60]

New Jersey's War of 1812 soldiers and sailors were largely forgotten in the ensuing years, but in 1850 all surviving War of 1812 veterans in the United States were granted a bonus of 120 acres of federal government land, on application, with proof of service, at a U.S. Land Office. Henry Raymond, the last known New Jersey veteran of the conflict, reportedly passed away in Jersey City on September 20, 1878, although the state was still paying four War of 1812 pensions to surviving family members as late as 1893. In May 1916, the New Jersey State Society of Daughters of the War of 1812, along with a distinguished assembly of politicians including Governor James F. Fielder, and serenaded by the school band, installed a bronze plaque commemorating the old Paulus Hook camp and the men who served there and beyond at Dickinson High School. It endures.[61]

# 6. New Jersey on the Eve of the Civil War, 1826–1860

In 1826, a board of officers empaneled by James Barbour, President John Quincy Adams's Secretary of War, studied the nationally moribund militia and came up with a series of proposals to correct its most egregious problems, including reducing the overall size of the force, appointing an official in the War Department to oversee its development, issuing a standardized drill manual, and requiring an annual ten-day training period. The Barbour board's suggestions were, however, all ignored, as were subsequent efforts at reform. In the ensuing years, while the small regular army became a more professional force, with West Point-trained officers joining the ranks, the militia became even more of a nationwide laughingstock. Fines for non-attendance at drill went uncollected, inept commanders were deliberately elected as jokes, and the shortage of firearms became scandalous—one Iowa regiment mustered 950 men, but could only count sixty-three muskets. In 1845 Missouri refused to buy arms for its militia and then refused to build a state armory to store federal muskets issued to the state. While still held as the ideal, the concept of the militia as a genuine mili-

tary force consisting of the entire male population able to bear arms and subject to annual muster and training was largely abandoned by the 1840s, replaced by companies of volunteers who enjoyed the fraternal and social aspect of donning an often gaudy uniform and dabbling in quasi-military life a few days a year.[1]

Although most American militiamen, including those of New Jersey, had no potential national enemies in the post-War of 1812 era, some militia units on the frontier were actively engaged in military operations against Native Americans. Among these was an "untrained horde" of 10,000 men mobilized from the militia pool for the Black Hawk War of 1832. The poor performance of this force against the Indians resulted in a rout described by regular army colonel Zachary Taylor as "unutterably shameful." The subsequent conduct of some of these militiamen, who murdered captured Indian women, was even more reprehensible. The conduct of militia soldiers at the outset of the Florida Seminole wars was less than stellar as well, and Congress's response was to call for three and six-month service volunteers, paid at the same rate as regulars, in organizations similar to the "levies" of 1791 and the "detached militia" of 1812. Unfortunately, volunteers from other states often expended most of their enlistment time traveling to Florida and were minimally engaged in combat operations. One regular officer disparagingly characterized local Florida volunteer units as "dirty, ragged and dusty." Volunteers might not be the answer to a commanding officer's prayer, but on the whole they were considered more effective than mobilized random militiamen in wartime, and the volunteer concept was to grow and become an integral aspect of national military planning through the end of the nineteenth century.[2]

Daniel Haines, a Sussex County attorney and son of a wealthy Elizabeth-based New York City merchant who had married into the influential Ogden family, was initially a Federalist, but switched allegiance to the old Jeffersonian Democratic-Republican Party, now known as the Democratic Party. Haines was elected to the New Jersey Council in 1839 and quickly gained a reputation as a polished political operative. He was the last New Jersey governor elected by the legislature, serving two one-year terms in 1843 and 1844, the year a new constitution mandating popular election of the chief executive was adopted by the state. Haines took a personal interest in trying to resurrect the state militia, which he noted "seems to have fallen in great disrepute," but without much success. The New Jersey militia had been atrophying for decades, and a short-lived military academy founded in Orange in 1828 seems to have failed to interest a significant number of local youth in a part time career as militia officers.[3]

Although there were small volunteer companies around the state that mustered on a more or less regular basis, state militia reports from the county based brigades were seldom sent to Trenton, making compliance with federal requests for militia statistics impossible to accurately render. Strength reports were essential for the federal government to issue needed arms and equipment to the state. In January 1847, Adjutant General Thomas Cadwallader advised Governor Charles C. Stratton, a Whig farmer from Swedesboro and the first state chief executive chosen by popular vote for a three-year term under the 1844 Constitution, that "no regular returns have been made to this office for sometime past." As a result, Cadwallader had no idea how many men there were in the state militia, how many weapons they had or what their state of training was.[4]

Governor Haines, who returned to office succeeding Stratton as the second three-year-term state chief executive, remained as frustrated as he had been before. Haines complained that "the ordinary militia musters . . . are generally admitted to retard rather than to promote improvement; and to be a tax on the time and service of the citizen without any corresponding benefit." In the middle of this New Jersey militia muddle, there was a war.[5]

## THE U.S.–MEXICAN WAR

In 1845 the United States annexed Texas, a self-proclaimed independent country run by Americans following its successful rebellion against the Mexican government in 1836, as a state, despite protests and threats of war by Mexico. Democratic president James K. Polk's "Manifest Destiny" policy of westward expansion, which led to the annexation of Texas, was strongly supported in the South as an opportunity to expand the territory available to a slave labor based

An 1829 satircal cartoon of Philadelphia militia mustering. In the early nineenth century, militia were widely characterized as bands of drunken buffoons.

economy. In January 1846, Polk ordered
General Zachary Taylor to move American forces to the Mexican border in what
many saw as a deliberate provocation.
Failed negotiations and a subsequent
border incident, in which Mexicans attacked a small American force moving
into a disputed area in April, led to a declaration of war on Mexico by the United
States Congress on May 13. The subsequent conflict, an unqualified success by
American standards, both tactically and
strategically, resulted in a huge geo-
graphic expansion of the country.

The war was opposed by many, particularly opposition Whig Party members
from non-slaveholding states, including
both New Jersey senators and most of
the state's congressmen. One prominent
antiwar critic was Illinois congressman
Abraham Lincoln. New Jersey senator
Jacob W. Miller characterized the war as
a land grabbing "outrage," and the state's
other senator, William L. Dayton, expressed serious concern that it would

lead to a struggle over the expansion of
slavery. On the other hand, President
Polk was well received in New Jersey
when he visited the state in 1847, and the
Whig dominated legislature voiced support for the troops and General Taylor.
A prescient editorialist for the Trenton
*State Gazette*, however, agreed with Dayton, opining in September 1847, that
"the territories to be annexed ... will destroy the balance of the Union."[6]

In 1846, the New Jersey militia was as
moribund as it would ever be. With the
outbreak of hostilities, the president, totally ignoring the militia for the first time
in an American war, requested volunteer
regiments from the states, including one
from New Jersey, to supplement the
small regular army. On May 22, 1846,
Governor Stratton responded with a
proclamation calling on "organized uniform companies and other citizens of the
state to enroll themselves" in the regiment. Prominent early twentieth century
New Jersey historian Francis Bazley Lee,

in what can only be described as an ex post facto patriotic cover-up, claimed that the war "aroused the military ardor of New Jersey," conjuring up a scene of recruiting offices overrun with passionate patriots. In reality, the enthusiasm of Jerseymen for actually fighting in the Mexican War was, as in much of the Northeast, minimal. Although a number of existing volunteer uniformed companies allegedly offered to serve in the proposed regiment, all were well under minimum strength and none could enlist the additional men required by the federal government to meet that strength level, a situation Lee glossed over by claiming "none were accepted at the time."[7]

An embarrassed Governor Stratton blamed New Jersey's failure to produce a volunteer regiment on the "defective and prostrate condition of the militia system of the state," and encouraged the legislature to provide "encouragement in some way to the volunteer companies." Echoing Governor Haines's frustration with the general condition of the New Jersey militia, Stratton called for "some simple mode of ascertaining the number of the militia in the state," so that New Jersey could claim its fair share of federal militia aid in weapons and equipment.[8]

In April 1847, the War Department once again approached New Jersey for volunteer troops, this time deciding not to wait until a full ten-company regiment was raised, but to muster in each company as it attained minimum strength in hopes of raising a battalion that would be half the size of a regiment. A rendezvous point for recruits was established at Trenton. Curiously, as volunteers, they were, unlike regular army soldiers, expected to provide their own clothing, for which they were advanced $21 by the government. Only four of the proposed five companies (A, B, C, and D) were raised over the summer. They were placed under the command of Lieutenant Colonel Dickinson Woodruff and mustered into United States service in August and September. On September 29, 1847, two weeks after Mexico City fell to the American army, the battalion sailed from New York to Vera Cruz, Mexico, aboard the ship *Senator*. A review of the unit's published roster reveals no combat casualties. A fair number, however, died of disease, deserted, or were discharged by court martial or for other reasons at locations including Camden, Trenton, Vera Cruz, Jalapa, New York, and points in between. The battalion arrived back in New York aboard the ship *Indiana* on July 22, 1848, and the Jerseymen were discharged at Fort Hamilton in early August.[9]

In addition to the Volunteer battalion, the War Department authorized the enlistment of regular army soldiers in New Jersey. That recruiting effort, also headquartered at Trenton, resulted in three companies of the 10th United States Infantry, a regiment raised specifically for the war. Once recruited, the New Jersey companies, E, G, and H, reported to Fort Hamilton, where they were mustered into service in April and May 1847. Companies G and H shipped out on the brig *G. B. Lamar* on April 11 and arrived at Matamoros, Mexico, on May 6, 1847. Company E left New York on May 4 and arrived at Matamoros on June 14. As with the volunteer battalion, the New Jersey regulars were never engaged in a battle, although they suffered a rate of loss from disease, discharge, court martial, and desertion similar to that of their volunteer counterparts. The only known deaths from violent action were those of Private John McLaughlin of Company E, murdered in Matamoros, and Captain

The explosion of the "Peacemaker" aboard the USS *Princeton* on February 28, 1844, that killed six persons including the secretary of the navy.

Joshua W. Collet of Company H, killed in a duel with Captain Alexander Wilkin, another American officer, on January 21, 1848, at Camargo, Mexico. William S. Truex and Gershom Mott, two men who would make their military mark as leaders of New Jersey troops in the Civil War, gained their introduction to military life as junior officers in the 10th Infantry in Mexico.[10]

As with previous conflicts, other Jerseymen served in a number of units of the regular army, navy, and Marine Corps in the war with Mexico, although no comprehensive list is available. Two of the most notable New Jersey veterans of the conflict were Robert Field Stockton and Stephen Watts Kearny, who cooperated, then clashed, in California. Stockton was, at one time or another, a wealthy aristocrat, heroic naval officer, monopoly capitalist, self-interested political operative, social progressive, and apologist for slavery. In the course of all these twists and turns, he became one of the most influential and controversial

men in New Jersey and, indeed, America, in the first half of the nineteenth century. A grandson of Richard Stockton, New Jersey signer of the Declaration of Independence, and son of United States attorney, congressman, and senator Richard Stockton, Robert was born in 1795 in Princeton. He attended The College of New Jersey (Princeton University) but discovered early on that *academe* paled before potential adventure and dropped out to join the navy as a midshipman at the age of sixteen. During the War of 1812 Stockton was cited for bravery and rose to the rank of lieutenant. In the postwar years he challenged British naval officers to duels when they showed insufficient respect for the American navy, fought Algerian and Caribbean pirates, captured slave ships and, as the representative of the American Colonization Society, penetrated deep West African rain forests and negotiated at pistol point with local chiefs to acquire what would become Liberia, planned as a homeland for freed African-American slaves.[11]

After a stint at the helm of the "Joint Companies," a New Jersey canal and railroad transportation monopoly, Stockton returned to active naval service as a captain in 1838, and subsequently met Swedish ship designer John Ericsson, whom he convinced to come to America to design a steam-powered ship using a screw propeller rather than a paddle wheel for propulsion. Stockton directly supervised much of the construction of the new vessel, dubbed, in honor of his home town, the *Princeton*, which was launched in Philadelphia in 1843, and personally designed one of her large guns, the *Peacemaker*. On February 28, 1844, Captain Stockton took the *Princeton* for a pleasure cruise on the Potomac River, with President John Tyler, his cabinet, and 200 guests aboard. *Peacemaker* was successfully fired several times to entertain the guests, but then exploded and killed six people, including Secretary of State Abel Upshur, Secretary of the Navy Thomas Gilmer, and the president's soon to be father-in-law, as well as his personal valet. Tyler himself narrowly escaped death or injury. Twenty others were wounded, including Stockton, who sustained facial burns. In the aftermath, a quickly held court of inquiry absolved the captain from all blame, although he was the designer of the defective gun. Stockton's role as a political supporter and personal friend of President Tyler appears to have had something to do with the hearing's outcome. Despite the disaster, in the end Stockton's wooing of Ericsson paid off for the country, as the inventive Swede designed the Civil War ironclad *Monitor*.[12]

The explosion that nearly wiped out the United States government may have temporarily slowed Captain Stockton down a step or two, but he quickly recovered. By 1846, the outbreak of the Mexi-

can War found him, an acting commodore, sailing north along the California coast aboard the USS *Congress* on a mission to reinforce the American Pacific Squadron under Commodore John D. Sloat. On Stockton's arrival, the nervous and ailing Sloat, who had been nudging the Mexican authorities in California to accept an American takeover by diplomacy rather than military action, happily turned over command to the New Jersey officer. In a series of actions that earned him a reputation with one historian as "a competent seaman and an energetic officer," but also "vain, tactless, xenophobic, and glory-thirsty," Stockton's aggressiveness undid Sloat's careful work, inciting a *Californio* rebellion. Aided by Brevet Captain John C. Frémont, Stockton put together a rag-tag little force to fight the insurrection in a swift campaign that displayed his usual personal courage and revealed a surprising display of land-based tactical skills for a naval officer. By 1848, segueing seamlessly into his political persona, he gave a speech in Philadelphia advocating complete annexation of Mexico. Stockton's subsequent brief term in the United States Senate, attempted presidential run, and surmised Confederate sympathies in 1860 (his son was the New Jersey adjutant general at the time) make him one of New Jersey's most colorful characters.[13]

Stephen Watts Kearny never achieved the notoriety of his naval counterpart, and is far less well known than his storied nephew, Philip, who would become a hero in the fight for Mexico, where he lost an arm, and again in the Civil War. Born in Newark in 1794, Stephen W. Kearny lived in the city and nearby New York for much of his life when not on active duty with the army in the West. In 1812, he left Columbia College for a commission as a first lieutenant in the 13th United States Infantry. Promoted to captain in 1813, Kearny remained in the army at the close of the war. He was involved in the initial efforts to establish a military presence in the Louisiana Territory and accompanied several exploratory expeditions into what was then a little-known wilderness. Kearny commanded several of the first army posts beyond the Mississippi, including one at the site of Kearny, Nebraska, which was named for him. He was promoted to lieutenant colonel of the 1st United States Dragoons on the unit's formation in 1833 and elevated to the rank of colonel and command of the regiment three years later.[14]

With the outbreak of the Mexican War, Kearny was assigned to command of the "Army of the West," a less than impressive collection of Missouri mounted volunteer units, the Mormon Battalion, and some artillery, stiffened by his own dragoon regiment, with orders to capture Santa Fe and move on to California. Following an arduous overland march, Santa Fe fell to Kearny on August 18, 1846, without a shot being fired. After establishing a provisional government in New Mexico and leaving a garrison to secure the area, Kearny led 300 dragoons on to fulfill his orders to conquer California. He encountered Kit Carson heading east on the trail and learned that California had already fallen to Stockton and Frémont; he sent 200 of his men back to Santa Fe and continued west with the remainder.[15]

By the time Kearny arrived, however, the *Californios* were in the midst of their Stockton-inspired revolt. His exhausted and bedraggled American force of one hundred dragoons, mounted on played-out mules, encountered a superior enemy force at San Pasqual and lost

Col. Stephen Watts Kearny (1794–1848), claimed New Mexico for the United States in 1846.

eighteen men killed in a brief but nasty fight. Fortunately for Kearny, Stockton's ad hoc army of American adventurers, sailors, and marines came to the rescue and joined forces with the dragoons to crush the mini-rebellion. With the fighting over, Kearny considered his orders to claim California for the United States to supersede the opportunistic actions of Frémont and Stockton, and advised them of this. After Stockton left for the East in a huff, more army troops arrived by ship and Kearny dismissed Frémont and assumed the title of governor himself. He then escorted Frémont back across the prairie to Fort Leavenworth, where he had him charged, court-martialed, and convicted of mutiny and disobedience of orders. The court-martial sentenced Frémont to dismissal from the army. The captain's connections on high, including his father-in-law, Senator Thomas Hart Benton of Missouri, had the dismissal quashed but Frémont resigned in anger. Following his California adventure, Kearny was appointed military governor of Vera Cruz until the peace treaty of Guadalupe Hidalgo was signed, was awarded the brevet rank of major general, and then returned to his previous headquarters in Saint Louis, where he died on October 31, 1848, from yellow fever he had contracted in Mexico. He was buried in Belefontaine cemetery in Saint Louis.[16]

One long-forgotten Jerseyman who fought and died in Mexico and who was widely mourned at the time was Jacob W. Zabriskie. Zabriskie was born in Hackensack on April 11, 1817, and moved to Illinois in 1839, where he worked as a merchant. At the outbreak of the war he became a captain in the 1st Illinois Volunteer Infantry. Captain Zabriskie was mortally wounded at the battle of Buena Vista on February 23, 1847, and was temporarily buried on the field. His remains were subsequently disinterred and returned to Illinois and then disinterred once more for transportation back to New Jersey. The arrival of Zabriskie's coffin at Philadelphia on July 20, 1847, and the ensuing steamboat cortege, New York and New Jersey militia parades, artillery salutes, chiming church bells, and patriotic speeches, as his body wended its way through New Brunswick to Manhattan, then Fort Lee, and on to Hackensack for a lengthy eulogy by Reverend Cornelius T. Demarest and final interment, was a major news story. Zabriskie's obelisk-shaped monument still stands at the edge of the old cemetery across from the Bergen County courthouse in Hackensack.[17]

General Winfield Scott, a hero of the War of 1812, principal commander in the Mexican War, 1852 Whig Party presidential candidate, and commander of the United States Army at the outbreak of the Civil War, is counted as a Jerseyman by many, due to the residence he maintained in Elizabeth. Scott was actually born, raised, and educated in Virginia, and his familiarity with Elizabeth may well have come from the fact, surprising to many today, that the city was a popular summer resort area for Virginians and other southerners in the pre-Civil War era. Scott appears to have purchased "Hampton Place" on East Jersey and Madison Avenues in Elizabeth in 1848 on his return from Mexico and lived there "during intervals, sometimes short and sometimes lengthy" from then until his death in 1866. As commanding general of the United States Army in the 1850s, Scott maintained a headquarters in New York City, but apparently spent a lot of time in Elizabeth. The house was razed in 1928, but a replica was built on Westminster Avenue in 1931 and later occupied by the New Jersey branch of the American Cancer Society.[18]

Perhaps even more than the veterans of 1812, New Jersey's Mexican War soldiers, far fewer in numbers, are largely forgotten. There was but one small spark of recognition for some of these men a decade after the close of the conflict. In March 1858, the state legislature extended a belated recognition of the volunteer battalion's service by extending official thanks to the unit's officers and enlisted men, and then Governor William A. Newell presented one grade brevet or honorary promotions to the battalion's officers.[19]

## NEW JERSEY MILITIA

In the immediate postwar years, the annual message from Adjutant General Cadwallader to Governor Haines remained the same as it had been before the war. On January 3, 1850, Cadwallader, who had been adjutant general since 1842, advised that "no improvement has been made in the condition of the militia," and requested "different measures . . . to give life and energy to the system." The decade of the 1850s would witness a number of different approaches to the militia problem, with mixed success. In 1851, Cadwallader advised Haines that "a small tax could be laid upon all persons subject to the performance of military duty . . . as a special fund for the encouragement of volunteers," in place of fines for nonattendance, which went largely uncollected and ignored. The following year the adjutant general reported to Democratic governor George F. Fort that twenty-two new volunteer companies had been formed around the state and that Fort should consider his funding suggestion, which Haines had failed to act on. Fort was a physician whose involvement in politics reflected what today would be a gross conflict of interest due to his relationship with the monopolistic Joint Companies. Perhaps best known for solidifying the corporate role in politics, his view that New Jersey should support the Fugitive Slave Law of 1850, and his characterization of escaped slaves as "fugitives from labor," Fort appears to have had little interest in military affairs. To his credit on other matters, during Governor Fort's term the state did increase funding for public education, institute a ten-hour workday, and limit child labor.[20]

In his report for 1852, Cadwallader reported that the overall strength of the militia, males between the ages of eighteen and forty-five residing in New Jersey, totaled 81,985 potential soldiers statewide. The report broke down the number of men nominally assigned to each county brigade. How the counties produced those figures for the report went unsaid, but the census of 1850 is a likely source. The following year's reports were fragmentary and useless. Cadwallader complained that the state's militia laws ended up producing "no beneficial result" and that "the delinquency of the civil officers under the law must be corrected; otherwise, the state may be deprived of her quota of [federal] arms, and military supplies." The adjutant general concluded with yet another plea for the state to subsidize the volunteer companies with "some pecuniary allowance."[21]

Cadwallader must have felt himself redeemed when Sussex county native Rodman M. Price was inaugurated as governor in January 1854. Price, a former naval officer, had served under Robert Stockton in the conquest of California, and been appointed *alcalde* of Monterey. From 1848 to 1850 Price served as a financial agent for the navy in California, apparently engaging in a number of grandiose and rather dubious side business deals including land and commodity speculations, apparently often using government money, as well as participating in local politics. On leaving the navy and returning east, Price bought a mansion in Hoboken, became a Wall Street banker, and continued making long distance California deals. Encouraged by Stockton, he ran for Congress and won, and seems to have spent most of his time introducing private bills for constituents, although he once declared on the floor of the House that flogging in the navy led to "a well ordered, well-disciplined ship." Losing reelection, Price returned to New Jersey, where he succeeded in gaining the Democratic nomination for governor in 1853. As a candidate he spouted a great deal of anti-monopoly rhetoric, but as governor quickly caved to his friend Stockton's argument to extend the state's greatest monopoly, Stockton's Joint Companies.[22]

Despite his considerable baggage, which caught up with him in the 1890s, when he spent most of his final days in jail in Hackensack, Rodman Price, unlike his immediate predecessors, was a man with a thorough knowledge of military affairs, which appears to have reinvigorated long suffering Adjutant General Cadwallader, whose report for 1854 reflects that new-found enthusiasm. Cadwallader advised his "commander in chief" that New Jersey now fielded "regularly commissioned, armed and equipped, one hundred and fifty-two uniformed companies which, by averaging their strength, will be found nearly equal in numbers to the actual force of the regular army of the United States, reported as fit for duty," although he provided no actual figures. The militiamen in these new uniform companies, multiplying in other states as well, and characterized as 'belligerent amateurs" by one historian, were a diverse lot, from elite and exclusive units to urban companies "chiefly composed of clerks, artisans and—in the big cities—sometimes hoodlums."[23]

A number of the new companies were composed of German and Irish immigrants, concentrated in the state's growing industrial northeast. The tide of immigration in the two decades before the Civil War gave rise to the anti-immigrant nativist "Know Nothing" movement of the 1850s which, in turn, spawned the "American Party." Immigrant companies were often formed to counter nativist companies, which probably accounts for much of the increase in militia units in the 1850s. A riot in Newark in September 1854 involving armed nativists and Irish immigrants resulted in at least one death and the desecration of a German Catholic church, highlighting the growing tensions. Immigrants felt they needed to up the self-defense ante. Despite the fact that immigrant units were eyed warily by anxious American militiamen, Price, a Democrat who owed the newcomers something for their votes, readily signed commissions for their officers.[24]

Cadwallader attributed at least part of the apparent militia renaissance to "special legislation" passed in 1853 that provided "funds and facilities to the uniform companies in one brigade," a practice he wanted to see extended to the whole state. The adjutant general wanted to activate and fund "Brigade Boards" in every county to assume responsibility for reporting on militia strength and affairs, and to pay militiamen for their muster and service time. In his longest report ever, Cadwallader proved himself aware of evolving military technology as well, and advocated adopting "the Minnie [Minie] rifle" for the militia. The federal government was then in the process of converting older arms and developing a new "rifle-musket" to fire the conical, hollow based projectile developed by French captain Claude Minié, to replace the older smoothbore musket. The more accurate rifle-musket would extend the potential effective accurate range of infantry weapons considerably. Unlike older rifled arms that required a tight fitting patched ball to load, slowing the rate of fire, the new gun could be loaded and fired as rapidly as the smoothbore, an optimum three times a minute. Cadwallader's excitement dimmed a bit the following year, when a general order for the companies he had been so proud of the year before "to parade at certain convenient times and places" revealed that "in at least one half of the divisions it betrayed neglect and an entire want of efficient system." Although disappointed, the adjutant general continued to encourage Governor Price to set aside a sum to pay militiamen for drilling as well as upgrade their weapons. The governor, in turn, asked the legislature to approve a fifteen cent tax on military age males to fund the uniform companies, but the lawmakers declined his request.[25]

Governor Price, who viewed himself rather grandiosely, apparently decided to capitalize on his adjutant general's interest in evolving weapons technology. In 1856 he dispatched Cadwallader on a tour of Europe, with instructions to study, take notes, and comment on the status of European armies and their weaponry in order to "obtain correct information as to the most improved arms, tactics and drill, applicable to the efficiency and improvement of our militia system." At the same time, the federal government assigned a credentialed arms expert and ordnance officer of vast experience, Major Alfred Mordecai, who had previously traveled abroad on inspection tours, to conduct the same mission. Price and Cadwallader were evidently unaware they were duplicating the federal effort or didn't care. To his credit, for the first leg of his trip, the adjutant general picked Samuel Colt, the famed firearms inventor who began his small arms manufacturing career in Paterson, New Jersey, but was then located in Hartford, Connecticut, as a traveling companion.[26]

Cadwallader and Colt toured the Royal Small Arms Factory at Enfield Lock together, and the adjutant general correctly reported that the British government had adopted the "American System" of firearms manufacturing, with precise machinery creating interchange-able parts. When firearms needed maintenance in the field in the past, replacement parts had to be hand fitted, so the "American System" was a decided improvement. Cadwallader described the manufacturing process in some detail, including the use of American Blanchard lathes to produce gun stocks of identical dimensions. At the time of the adjutant general's visit, Enfield was producing the Model P53 rifle-musket, the AK-47 of its day, which would become one of the nineteenth century's iconic military small arms and, supplied by private contractors, the second most common arm used by both sides during the American Civil War.[27]

Cadwallader subsequently visited the British supply depot and production site for artillery pieces and artillery and small arms ammunition at Woolwich before crossing the channel to France, where he was impressed with the quality of the soldiers in the French army (over the British) but lamented the dictatorship of Napoleon III. On a more practical level he submitted a series of questions to French ordnance officers regarding firearms cost, cartridge making, bullet diameter and lubrication, gun finishes, arms making machinery, and trends in artillery.[28]

On leaving France, the adjutant general traveled through Belgium, where he visited the Waterloo battlefield and moved on to the German principalities along the Rhine and then Prussia, which impressed him considerably with the size and apparent quality of its army. Cadwallader was particularly interested in the fact that the Prussian army was using the breech-loading Dreyse "needle gun," which increased the infantry rate of fire dramatically. In Austria, he asked the American ambassador to forward a description of Austrian weapons manufac-

The Trenton Arsenal was a repository for New Jersey militia weapons and other supplies.

ture to him in Trenton, but it was apparently lost in transit. In a brief side trip to Piedmont, he concluded that the "Sardinian troops . . . will distinguish themselves . . . whenever called upon."[29]

The interaction between Cadwallader and Price suggests that they viewed themselves as valuable contributors to national policy. The adjutant general's conclusion at the end of his trip was that the political situation in Europe was dicey, most governments tended toward the despotic, and that America should not get involved in any "entangling alliances." Following this bit of foreign policy advice to the governor, the adjutant general returned to his usual annual report recommendations, including, once again, increasing the number of uniform companies and requesting they be paid for drilling, with the money to come from a tax on military age men who chose not to drill.[30]

In an attempt to get a grip on the state's supply situation, New Jersey quartermaster general Lewis Perrine inventoried the arms and equipment in storage

at the state arsenal in Trenton in 1856. He reported 8,970 weapons in various states of repair—4,740 were obsolete flintlock muskets still in their original packing crates. The quartermaster's attempt to get an accurate count on muskets and rifles and other state-owned gear, from cannons to cartridge boxes and tents, in the hands of the uniform companies, which averaged between twenty-five and fifty men each, proved less successful. Perrine complained that many weapons had simply disappeared. A number of companies had disbanded, and their commanders, who had originally posted bond for the arms and equipment they received, had either died or left the state. The quartermaster general recommended passing legislation to empower the state attorney general to "institute legal proceedings" against "delinquent officers" responsible for weapons issued their companies whenever they could be found. He also proposed hiring investigators to find and return guns that had disappeared into the civilian population. Perrine had a long way to go to straighten out New Jersey's property books, but he had at least made a beginning.[31]

The year 1857 brought a new governor. William A. Newell, a physician-politician from Allentown, had served as a Whig congressman from 1846 to 1850, when he declined renomination. Newell's crowning congressional achievement was introducing legislation that founded the United States Life Saving Service. As the Whig Party disintegrated in the 1850s, Newell joined the anti-immigrant American Party. In 1856, the New Jersey branches of the American Party and the new Republican Party allied themselves as the "Opposition Party" to nominate a single candidate for governor. Newell, who appealed to Republicans as a former Whig, was a member of the Americans, and was even respected by a number of Democrats, seemed a natural choice, and he eked out a victory over Democrat William C. Alexander. In order to maintain the Opposition coalition, Newell carefully apportioned patronage positions equally among Republican and American Party members, as patronage access was the glue that held the Republicans and Americans together.[32]

Unsurprisingly, Governor Newell's annual addresses stressed the need to limit the political influence of immigrants, a difficult task in the rapidly urbanizing state. His opposition as head of the Board of Pardons to pardoning James P. Donnelly, an Irish Catholic accused of murdering a Protestant over a gambling debt, and Donnelly's subsequent singling him out from the gallows, gained Newell the lasting enmity of the state's growing Irish population. It can be presumed that Governor Newell was not friendly to the ethnic militia units that had prospered under Governor Price, including Irish units like the "Emmet Light Guard" and

"Montgomery Riflemen" of Paterson, the "Montgomery Guard" of Jersey City, Trenton's "Sarsfield Guards," and the "Newark Volunteers," who, replete with green uniforms and "white facings and cross belts," marched in the New York City Saint Patrick's Day parade in 1858.[33]

It should be noted that uniform or volunteer militia companies in the 1850s, most of them organized in cities, were as much, if not more so, political bases, social clubs, and insurance societies than they were military organizations. A review of the notes of one unit, the "Continental Guards" of Jersey City, apparently outfitted with an approximation of a Revolutionary War uniform, revealed that the company elected slates of both military and civilian officers, the latter including a president, secretary, and treasurer. On one occasion the company raised a "subscription" to assist the widow of a deceased former captain. Following their annual inspection and drill in 1854, the Guards went on "an excursion to Ft. Lee" aboard a steamship, a fundraising trip that netted the company $150.25; a subsequent cruise conveyed the company to Keyport. The company, apparently affiliated with the American Party, was a selective organization, and aspirant members had to be voted into the unit. "Delinquents" who didn't show up for drill were "expelled" and "honorary members" were installed by vote of the membership. As the decade waned, the company changed its name to the "Independence Guard" and voted to adopt the standard militia uniform the state was advocating. Members who disagreed with the uniform decision seceded and formed their own organization. The onset of the Civil War proved to be the end of the Guards, as its men joined different active units and it was never reconstituted.[34]

Adjutant General Cadwallader's first report to the new governor, covering the year 1857, repeated the strength figure of 1852 for the militia. Cadwallader complained that "the sum total of efficient arms and other munitions of war in the State will be found to fall very short of a half supply for that number of men." Echoing Quartermaster General Perrine's complaints of the previous year, he conceded that he didn't even know where many of the state-owned weapons were, reporting that "we have a considerable number of arms in irresponsible hands, scattered all over the state." Cadwallader went on to enumerate some of his favorite concerns, including that New Jersey was the strategic key to America, that the militia needed rifled small arms, that the day of the six-pounder field artillery piece was done, and that any in service should be replaced by newer twelve-pounder guns. In conclusion, he tended the governor his resignation, ending a fifteen-year stint as adjutant general.[35]

Cadwallader's replacement, named on January 30, 1858, was twenty-six-year-old Robert Field Stockton, the son of the conqueror of California. A Princeton graduate and attorney, young Stockton unsurprisingly held a number of influential positions on the boards of New Jersey corporations, and had succeeded his father as president of the "Joint Companies."[36]

At the end of his first year in the job, Adjutant General Stockton reported some progress, with twelve new volunteer uniform companies formed, as well as some reorganization on the brigade level. He recommended more frequent drills and reiterated the need for adopting a standard uniform, at least for parade and training in larger formations, as each company having its own distinctive

dress, like the ersatz eighteenth century garb of the Continental Guards, created a patchwork look in regimental and brigade training exercises. Stockton also advocated the adoption of a standard drill manual, enforcement of militia laws, and a number of minor structural changes, all to be reviewed by a selected board of officers. The new adjutant general submitted an abstract of brigade reports to Governor Newell, which reflected that an inspection of the Newark Brigade revealed a total of 598 officers and men, while the Hunterdon Brigade mustered fewer than 200 part time soldiers. Inspection of the Bergen Brigade was, according to Stockton, haphazard at best, with only three companies, totaling less than one hundred officers and men, accounted for. There was obviously a lot of work still to be done if the militia was to become a viable force.[37]

## THE MILITIA AND LABOR UNREST

In September 1859, New Jersey militiamen were called up for active service for the first time since 1815, when Mayor (and Democratic gubernatorial candidate) Edwin R. V. Wright of Hudson City (today a part of Jersey City) proved unable to control a wage dispute between a largely Irish group of laborers and the New York and Erie Railroad. The workers blocked the railroad's tracks, and the Hudson Brigade, which Wright had once commanded as a militia general, was called on to assist the outmanned city police. The brigade assembled at the courthouse and confronted the disgruntled workers with fixed bayonets and artillery mounted on a railroad flatcar. Several thousand spectators assembled to witness what they thought would turn into a full scale battle, but in the end the workers, although they brandished weapons, tossed debris, and verbally abused the militiamen, avoided actual combat. Under the protection of the militia, the mayor and his police force made a number of arrests, and the crowd dispersed without any casualties to either side. The incident was a foreshadowing of the post-Civil War involvement of state troops across the country in union busting and defending corporate property, but ended without the violence often occasioned by such confrontations. The incident didn't seem to hurt Wright's high standing in the Irish community, which supported his unsuccessful run for governor in 1859, helped elect him to Congress, and mourned his death in 1871.[38]

### 1860: UNPREPARED FOR WAR

On December 31, 1860, eleven days after South Carolina declared its secession from the Union, Stockton reported a total of 4,400 men allegedly on the rolls of active companies statewide (the actual total was closer to half that), and equipped with "serviceable" arms. He was particularly impressed with the Camden Brigade, and the Newark brigade, which had adopted standard uniforms and "abandoned fancy names" for its companies. The guns of the Hudson Brigade, apparently older smoothbore flintlock muskets converted to percussion ignition and rifled to fire the Minie projectile, were found to be "in a

bad condition . . . easily put out of order, uncertain in aim, and liable to burst." Quartermaster General Perrine listed a total of 8,100 muskets in the state arsenal as of January 1, 1861, together with other equipment.[39]

War was in the air, and despite the efforts of Stockton and Perrine, New Jersey was not prepared for it. Following the end of the Civil War, the first historian of the state's role in the conflict characterized the condition of the militia in 1861 as "a system of shreds and patches, without organic unity, and almost entirely worthless." The heir to this system, inaugurated on January 17, 1861, was Charles Smith Olden of Princeton, the second and final governor from the makeshift Opposition Party. A former Whig state senator, Olden viewed himself as a moderate, opposing the extension of slavery but supporting the Fugitive Slave Act. A Lincoln supporter in the election of 1860, Olden participated, along with former governor Rodman Price and the ubiquitous Robert Stockton, in a peace conference held in Washington that February. He was the only serving governor to attend the conference, which attempted to find a solution to the growing secession crisis. Despite Olden's desire for compromise, reflecting the views of a fairly large number of New Jerseyans, once the Confederates fired on Fort Sumter on April 12, 1861, the state rallied to the Union cause.[40]

# 7. New Jersey and the Civil War, 1861–1865

In the 1860 presidential election, New Jersey voters, in a reflection of their ambivalence in a growing national crisis, split their electoral tally between Republican Abraham Lincoln and Democrat Stephen A. Douglas. In the tense months that followed the secession of South Carolina, as more states left the Union, New Jersey politicians, factory owners, and workers, already dealing with the aftermath of the economically disastrous Panic of 1857, were desperate to avoid war. They feared sectional conflict would result in the loss of Southern markets for cheap slave shoes and clothing made in Newark, Paterson, and other New Jersey cities, leading to further economic decline. Former governor Rodman Price, as afflicted by grandiosity as ever, even suggested that New Jersey secede from the Union itself and join the Confederacy. Price warned anxious New Jerseyans that if they remained in the Union their "commerce will cease . . . our state becoming depopulated and impoverished." Secession to join the Confederacy on the other hand, the former governor contended, would assure "our prosperity, progress and happiness uninterrupted . . . without any sacrifice of

principle or honor, and without difficulty or danger." On the slavery issue Price opined that race-based human bondage, which he regarded as mere "subordination to the superior race" was "natural and normal."[1]

In the century and a half following the Civil War, folklore tales, buttressed by Governor Charles Olden's Peace Conference appearance (he was the only Northern governor to attend), Price's disregarded suggestion, and the activities of other "Copperhead" antiwar activists in New Jersey, added to Lincoln's failure to carry the state's electoral votes in 1860 and 1864, gave rise to the idea that New Jersey was not only disloyal to the Union, but actually seriously considered joining the Confederacy. Historian Charles M. Knapp's flawed 1924 book, *New Jersey Politics during the Period of the Civil War and Reconstruction*, added academic fuel to the fire. Knapp's work was more recently characterized as "unsound in interpretation" by Rutgers University professor Dr. William Gillette, the leading modern scholar on the subject.

The myth, which has regrettably gained traction in certain quarters in modern times, with completely fabri-

cated enhancements, was no doubt amplified by the fact that eighteen aged people living in the state were considered
slaves by the 1860 federal census, although classified as "apprentices for life"
according to the 1844 law officially ending slavery by name in New Jersey, as well
as by the cases of a few New Jersey-born
men who had married Southern women
and moved south before the conflict and
later became Confederate officers.[2]

Aside from Rodman Price's ill-timed
and ignored call, which effectively ended
his own political career, the state was indeed home to a genuine antiwar element
in 1861, and that opposition would surface again as the conflict dragged on in a
seemingly endless and unsatisfactory
manner. Following the Rebel attack on
Fort Sumter in April 1861, however, such
sentiment was, for the time being, mostly
submerged in a flood of patriotism.

There were a few exceptions to the patriotic surge of 1861, however. While the
vast majority of New Jerseyans supported the Union, a vocal minority still
maintained an antiwar stance. Bergen
County, an antiwar "Copperhead"
hotbed throughout the conflict, was the
scene of a law enforcement raid on the
"American Guard," a forty-man militia
company in Schraalenberg, a village near
Hackensack, where a Confederate flag
had reportedly been flown. The men of
the Guard, commanded by a Lieutenant
Christie, were described as "secession-
ists" by the press. Threatened with imprisonment by federal marshals, the part
time soldiers quickly surrendered their
muskets and agreed to take an oath of allegiance to the federal government. In an
ironic twist, the unit's commander may
well have been either Garrett J. or James
Christie, both of whom subsequently
served as officers in the 22nd New Jersey
Infantry, a surly unit of reluctant war-

Charles Olden (1799–1876), the nineteenth governor of New Jersey.

riors enlisted in Bergen County for nine-
months service in 1862. The 22nd gained
the uncomplimentary sobriquet of the
"Copperhead Regiment."[3]

Perhaps the most dramatic antiwar incident of 1861 was the case of James Walter Wall, a Burlington County politician
and vocal Copperhead. On September
11, 1861, a posse of United States marshals appeared at his house to arrest him.
Wall resisted violently, knocking out one
of the officers before he was subdued
and conveyed to jail. He was never formally charged, but did sign a loyalty oath
before he was released two weeks later.
After his return home, Wall condemned
his treatment as a case of "wrong and
outrage" and notified authorities that he
was now armed and there would be a
"dead marshal" on his doorstep if the authorities attempted to arrest him again.[4]

In contrast, most New Jerseyans responded enthusiastically to President
Lincoln's first call for troops, although

raising and equipping an effective force from an admittedly moribund prewar militia proved a challenging task in 1861. At the end of 1860, Adjutant General Stockton reported a total of 1,863 men in the state's active uniformed militia volunteer companies, most of them significantly under strength and unable to produce the full brigade of four regiments for three-months service Lincoln had requested after the Fort Sumter attack without a large infusion of new recruits, which were, fortunately, forthcoming in the wake of Sumter. The state scrambled to outfit these new soldiers with clothing, and some uniforms were purchased by private groups of businessmen. Most of the militiamen were armed with obsolete .69 caliber smoothbore flintlock muskets converted to percussion ignition, although some companies were supplied with obsolescent .54 caliber Model 1841 rifles. The guns were provided from stocks in storage at the state arsenal in Trenton, and no New Jersey militiaman had access to the most modern .58 caliber rifle-muskets used by regular army troops.[5]

Within two weeks the militia mustered 3,075 men in a brigade of four regiments. Although on the eve of the war most of the uniformed militia companies were in the process of adopting the recently prescribed "brigade uniform," and rapidly acquired clothing for new recruits fit that pattern, some units retained their own unique garb, most notably the "Communipaw Zouaves" of Jersey City, a company of the 2nd New Jersey Militia with uniforms loosely patterned on the famous French Zouaves. The French soldiers' North African-inspired garb, fancy quickstep drill, and heroic exploits in the Crimean War and the Italian War of 1859 had inspired copycat organizations around the United States, especially in the wake of the 1860 national tour and drill team exhibitions of the "Chicago Zouave Cadets" commanded by Abraham Lincoln's law clerk Elmer Ellsworth. A newspaper described the Jersey City Zouaves as resplendent in "red caps, blue jackets with cuffs trimmed with red . . . [on] the front of their jackets there is a band of gold colored trimming as well as around the waist. They had brown leather gaiters that reached pretty near the knee with pants stuffed on the inside. The pants also have an orange colored band down the outside."[6]

The New Jersey militia brigade was organized at Trenton, and, under the command of Brigadier General Theodore Runyon, a Democratic politician from Newark, left the New Jersey capital by boat on May 3, 1861. The Jerseymen arrived in Washington on May 6, the first full brigade to reach the capital. Lincoln's subsequent call for three-year service volunteers also met with a warm reception in New Jersey, and a large number of men who had been denied the chance to join the militia brigade helped to fill out these regiments, the 1st, 2nd, and 3rd New Jersey Volunteer Infantry. Some men were reluctant to enlist for three years, but many naively believed the war would not last more than a few months anyway.[7]

The three-year volunteers left for Washington by train on June 28, arriving the following day. They remained briefly in the capital before crossing the Potomac into Virginia to join the state's militia brigade. Shortly afterward, the 3rd New Jersey Infantry suffered its first fatality as Private John Ellis of Company H was killed by a bullet fired by Private Samuel Middleton of the same company in a friendly fire incident while both were on guard duty.[8]

President Abraham Lincoln reviewing the New Jersey Militia Brigade in 1861. The Jersey Brigade was the first full brigade to reach Washington. The troops to the right are probably the Communipaw Zouaves from Jersey City.

The Jerseymen of both brigades were united into a division commanded by General Runyan and participated in the subsequent Manassas or Bull Run Campaign in late July. Runyan's men were deployed to protect the army's supply lines and were not engaged in combat, and, although the general Union rout swept around them, withdrew in good order towards Washington. In the army reorganization that followed Bull Run, the militia went home to be mustered out of service at Trenton, and the three-year regiments were formed into the 1st New Jersey Brigade. On August 7, one-armed New Jersey Mexican War hero brigadier general Philip Kearny, nephew of Stephen Watts Kearny, assumed brigade command.[9]

Back in New Jersey, the state was recruiting more three-year regiments. The 4th New Jersey Infantry joined the 1st Brigade in Virginia after Bull Run, and the 5th, 6th, 7th, and 8th New Jersey Infantry regiments were organized at Trenton's Camp Olden in late summer and early autumn. The sobering news of the Bull Run defeat may have dampened the military enthusiasm of some potential soldiers, but the new regiments left the state for Washington between late August and early October. When it appeared that the 5th regiment might be assigned to a brigade with regiments from other states, Governor Olden protested to the president, claiming that such a course "would be detrimental to the public service," since his Jerseymen should be afforded the opportunity "not only to serve the country, but to do honor to themselves and the state." Likely due to Olden's protest, the 5th was joined by the 6th, 7th, and 8th regiments to form the 2nd New Jersey Brigade.[10]

The last infantry regiment credited to the state in 1861 was the 9th New Jersey Infantry. The 9th was also the largest regiment New Jersey sent to war that year, with twelve rather than the usual ten companies, organized into four three-company battalions totaling 1,159 officers and men. The men of the 9th were recruited from all over the state in the autumn of 1861 for their shooting ability, as the unit was intended to be a "rifle regiment," of marksmen. When they were issued obsolete short range smoothbore muskets on arrival at Trenton's Camp Olden, the 9th's soldiers protested vigorously. Sensitive to the regiment's complaints, the governor lobbied the War Department for more appropriate weapons and the 9th was entirely re-equipped with scarce new Model 1861 Springfield rifle-muskets, shipped to Trenton directly from the arsenal in Massachusetts, before it left the state on December 4.[11]

1st Lt. William O'Connor, 2nd New Jersey Volunteer Infantry, 1863.

In addition to the infantry outfits, New Jersey also fielded a cavalry regiment, a "legion," and two artillery batteries in 1861. Cavalry was an expensive arm of service to maintain, and the organization of volunteer mounted regiments was initially discouraged by the authorities in Washington. In the wake of Bull Run, however, there was a change of attitude on the part of the federal government. On August 4, the War Department acceded to the request of seventy-year-old William Halsted, a prominent New Jersey Republican politician, to privately raise a cavalry regiment in the state. By the end of August, the unit, "Halstead's Horse," or at least its raw material, ten companies strong, was in camp on Washington's Meridian Hill. The regiment was a troubled organization from the start, rife with nepotism, incompetence, and internal feuding among the officers. At the end of the year, with Halsted on sick leave, Governor Olden appointed Joseph Karge, a dynamic Polish veteran of the Prussian

army, as a lieutenant colonel to reorganize the unit. Halsted, in and out of actual field command due to administrative troubles and various charges, ordered Karge arrested. Fed up with the bickering, the War Department formally handed over control of the regiment to New Jersey, redesignating it as the 1st New Jersey Cavalry. On February 19, 1862, Governor Olden finally relieved Halsted of command and appointed English soldier of fortune and adventurer Percy Wyndham as the regiment's new colonel.[12]

A similar "private regiment," known as the "Olden Legion" in honor of the governor, was raised in Beverly by William Bryan in the late summer and fall of 1861. The Legion was intended to be a combined arms unit, with nine companies of infantry and one of cavalry, but horses never arrived. Plagued with poor leadership, which was often intoxicated, "defective organization and the absence of all proper discipline," the Legion was turned over to the state in January 1862,

and—its horseless horsemen discharged—renamed the 10th New Jersey
Infantry. Under Colonel William Murphy, dispatched from Trenton to replace
Bryan, the unit was reorganized, and a
new infantry company replaced the departed putative cavalrymen. Still not
ready for field service, the 10th remained
part of the Washington garrison for the
remainder of the year.[13]

Prior to the war New Jersey militia
major William Hexamer commanded
the Hudson County Artillery, a battery
primarily composed of German immigrants and based in Hoboken. Hexamer
offered his unit's services in response to
the initial call for troops, but was turned
down, as artillery was, like cavalry, considered difficult to train up to regular
army standards and expensive to maintain. After Bull Run, however, the War
Department belatedly accepted the New
Jersey artillerymen, although Hexamer
had to take a downgrade from his militia
rank of major to that of a captain of volunteers.[14]

Hexamer's unit, designated as New
Jersey Battery A, was mustered in for
three years of federal service on August
12, 1861, and left for Washington eight
days later. Following their arrival at the
capital, the Jerseymen's six state-issued
six-pounder field pieces were replaced by
ten-pounder rifled Parrott guns, and the
battery was assigned to support the 1st
New Jersey Brigade. New Jersey's Battery
B, under Captain John Beam, was composed mostly of Newark men, many of
them veterans of the 1st New Jersey Militia who had been discharged after their
three months of service. The battery was
mustered into federal service at Camp
Olden, outside Trenton, on September 3,
1861, but did not leave for Washington
until October 22. On reaching the capital, Beam's battery, which arrived with no

guns, was issued four ten-pounder rifled
Parrott guns and two smoothbore
twelve-pounder howitzers.[15]

The 9th New Jersey Infantry was not
only a regiment composed of good
shots, but had a number of coastal "bay-
men" in the ranks who had valuable
small boat experience that could be used
in amphibious operations. This skill set
contributed to the 9th being the first of
the state's regiments to engage in actual
battle, as opposed to skirmishing on the
picket lines in northern Virginia. The
regiment, assigned to Major General
Ambrose Burnside's coastal North Carolina expedition, landed on Roanoke Island following a boating mishap that
resulted in the drowning of Colonel
Joseph W. Allen and Surgeon Frederick
S. Weller, on February 7, 1862. Lieutenant Colonel Charles A. Heckman assumed command of the regiment, and in
the subsequent battle of Roanoke Island,
Heckman's Jerseymen successfully attacked Confederate defenses through a
swamp, gaining the nickname "Jersey
muskrats." Captain Joseph Henry was
killed in the fight, gaining the dubious
distinction of being the first New Jersey
officer to be killed in action during the
Civil War.

Victorious at Roanoke, the 9th moved
on with the rest of Burnside's army to the
North Carolina mainland, fighting again
at New Bern on March 14, where Burnside was once more victorious and the
regiment played a critical role in breaking the enemy's line. In the aftermath of
that battle the 9th was one of the fortunate few units to remain on duty on the
North Carolina coast as part of an 8,000-
man occupation force. The regiment
would spend most of the rest of the war
in that state.

## THE PENINSULA CAMPAIGN

The 1st through the 8th New Jersey Infantry and both of the state's artillery batteries were assigned to Major General George B. McClellan's Army of the Potomac, and in the spring of 1862 all were involved in the Peninsula Campaign. Rather than fight his way directly south over the ladder of rivers between Washington and Richmond, McClellan, who had created an army out of the disorganized amateur soldiers encamped around Washington, decided to move by sea to the Virginia Peninsula and drive up the shorter distance to capture the Confederate capital. On March 17, 1862, the Jersey artillerymen of Batteries A and B boarded ships for Fortress Monroe as the campaign began to take shape. They were followed by the infantry regiments of both New Jersey brigades, while the 1st Cavalry remained in northern Virginia as part of the force left behind to protect Washington.

The first Jerseyans to arrive at the Virginia Peninsula were the Second Brigade men, who boarded ships "packed like herrings in a box" in April. After landing, they participated in the leisurely siege of Yorktown, spending weeks on mundane military tasks, including building roads, digging trenches, and standing picket duty. On the morning of May 4, 1862, after Union patrols discovered that the Confederates had abandoned Yorktown, the brigade, then part of the III Army Corps, joined the pursuit.[17]

Along with other Union forces, the Jerseymen caught up with the enemy on May 5 at Williamsburg. In the ensuing battle, a brutal close range encounter fought in a rainstorm, the Second Brigade had its baptism of fire. Total brigade casualties in the fight were 526 men killed, wounded, and missing in ac-

tion, 109 of them killed. After the battle, with the Confederates falling back towards Richmond, the New Jerseyans complained, with cause, that their sacrifice had been largely ignored by the national press, while New York regiments received most of the publicity and praise.[18]

When his dream of uniting the First and Second New Jersey Brigades into a New Jersey Division did not work out, and it appeared that his First Brigade might be left behind in the move to the Peninsula, General Kearny had accepted command of a Division in the III Army Corps. Colonel George Taylor of Hunterdon County, commander of the 3rd New Jersey, was promoted to Brigadier General and assumed command of the brigade, which then sailed to the Peninsula, landing initially at Cheeseman's Creek and then, after the Confederate withdrawal from Yorktown, moving to West Point, where the brigade skirmished with the Rebel rear guard. Shortly afterward Taylor's brigade became the First Brigade of the 1st Division of the VI Army Corps, a designation it held until the end of the war.

While New Jersey's infantry and artillerymen pushed up the Peninsula, Colonel Wyndham led the 1st New Jersey Cavalry on a march to Fredericksburg. Brigaded with Colonel George D, Bayard's 1st Pennsylvania Cavalry, the Jersey horsemen raided across northern Virginia in May, destroying Confederate government property wherever they found it until they were transferred to the Shenandoah Valley, where several Union forces were trying to corner General Thomas J. "Stonewall" Jackson. During the pursuit of Jackson, the 1st charged and overran a Confederate battery, and, on June 6, 1862, was sucked into an ambush and suffered forty casualties, including Colonel Wyndham, who was captured, and Captain Thomas Ryerson Haines, son of former New Jersey governor Daniel Haines, who was killed in action. Although driven back, the Jerseymen did not give up easily, and highly regarded Confederate general Turner Ashby lost his life in the fight as well. Following the defeat, the 1st, under the command of Lieutenant Colonel Karge, subsequently guarded wagon trains and then fought in a delaying action at Cedar Mountain during the Second Bull Run Campaign.[19]

Along with the rest of the Army of the Potomac, both New Jersey brigades followed the retreating enemy up the Peninsula towards Richmond, and the Second Brigade fought once again at Seven Pines, driving a Confederate brigade from the field. Confederate commander general Joseph Johnston was wounded at that battle, and replaced by General Robert E. Lee, a command change that would have a profound effect on the subsequent conduct of the war in the East. Following Seven Pines, McClellan continued his careful advance on Richmond, with a force divided by the Chickahominy River. Lee, now reinforced by "Stonewall" Jackson's command from the Shenandoah Valley, decided to attack the Union army.

The Rebel counteroffensive reached its climax in the battle of Gaines' Mills, on June 27, when the First New Jersey Brigade crossed the Chickahominy to reinforce a battered Union force. The brigade helped halt one Rebel assault, but was overwhelmed by another. A battery of "Coffee Mill guns," a type of primitive machine gun manned by the Jerseymen, was captured by the enemy as the 1st, 2nd, and 3rd Regiments fell back. The men of the 4th Regiment, detached to another area of the field, were com-

pletely overrun and most of them, including Colonel James H. Simpson, were captured. As the Union line began to disintegrate, Private Charles F. Hopkins of Boonton and the 1st New Jersey, although wounded twice himself, carried wounded Sergeant Richard Donnelly through a gauntlet of enemy fire to a place of safety, and was wounded once more in the effort. Hopkins would be awarded the Medal of Honor for his heroic actions.[20]

In the wake of Gaines' Mill, McClellan retreated back down the Peninsula. The two New Jersey brigades were, fortunately, not heavily involved in the resulting "Seven Days Battles," although Battery B's Captain Beam was killed when hit by a Confederate shell at Malvern Hill. The New Jersey regiments were soon shipped back to northern Virginia, however, where Major General John Pope had initiated an offensive over the old Bull Run battlefield, where the Second Brigade was heavily engaged on August 29, 1862. The following day the brigade was shifted around the field, and then withdrew. The Jerseyans helped cover Pope's retreat to Washington and supported General Kearny's division in an encounter at Chantilly, in which Kearny, the most famous Jerseyman of the war, was killed while making a reconnaissance of enemy positions.[21]

The First Brigade landed at Alexandria, Virginia, on August 24, and, as communications with Pope's army had been erratic, was ordered towards Bull Run in a reconnaissance in force to find out what was going on. The brigade traveled by train to Bull Run Bridge, then moved into enemy territory beyond on foot, where General Taylor led his men into a massive ambush. Still not recovered from Gaines' Mill, the brigade suffered 339 casualties, including 204 men captured.

Taylor was mortally wounded in the engagement and Colonel Alfred T. A. Torbert of the 1st New Jersey assumed brigade command. Torbert was promoted to Brigadier General on November 29, 1862.[22]

In the wake of his Bull Run victory, General Lee, in command of what he now called the Army of Northern Virginia, launched his first invasion of the North, capturing Harper's Ferry and pushing into Maryland. In the wake of the defeat, General McClellan resumed command of the reunited Army of the Potomac and cautiously pursued the Confederates. Units of the VI Corps, including the First Brigade, attacked Lee's outposts in the passes over South Mountain and the First Brigade, especially the 4th Regiment, with its recently exchanged POWs in the ranks, revenged its defeats at Gaines' Mill and Second Bull Run by overrunning the Confederate defenses. One soldier recalled that "we meant to pay them for what they had done to us, and we did it." Eugene Forbes of the 4th's Company A succinctly summed it up with: "Well, we licked 'em."[23] New Jersey's two veteran brigades were not engaged in the subsequent September 17 battle of Antietam, known as "America's bloodiest day." The First Brigade was on the field, but not ordered forward, and the Second Brigade spent the campaign in the defenses of Washington.

In the summer of 1862, the Lincoln Administration made two calls for troops, assigning quotas to the loyal states. In the first, for 300,000 new three year soldiers on July 7, 1862, New Jersey was assigned a quota of five ten-company infantry regiments. One regiment, which had been recruiting in a desultory manner since spring, while growing casualty lists lessened military enthusiasm,

was designated as the 11th New Jersey, and the other four as the 12th through the 15th. Instead of recruiting companies from around the state and organizing them into regiments at Trenton, as was the practice the previous year, Adjutant General Robert Stockton, son of the commodore, established regional regimental recruiting districts, and assembly camps in Newark, Flemington, Freehold, and Beverly for the four new units "to give an impetus to recruiting," as well as afford the recruit little time to change his mind. The 12th was recruited in the southern portion of the state, the 13th in the urban northeast, the 14th in central New Jersey, and the 15th in the rural northwest. Many of the junior officer slots in these regiments were reserved for experienced enlisted men from New Jersey units already in the field.[24]

Although all of the new regiments would see plenty of action and distinguish themselves before the close of the conflict, only one would engage in major combat in 1862. The 13th New Jersey, commanded by Colonel Ezra Carman, left Camp Frelinghuysen in Newark by train on August 31, 1862, and arrived in Washington on September 2. Assigned to the XII Army Corps, on September 6 the 13th began to march west, crossing the Catoctin Mountains on September 14 and arriving at Antietam Creek two days later. On September 17 the inexperienced regiment was ordered to advance towards the Hagerstown Pike, and soon encountered heavy fire. Captain Hugh Irish of Paterson climbed the roadside fence in an attempt to rally his wavering men but was quickly riddled with bullets. As the battle swayed back and forth, the disoriented Jerseymen retreated and advanced, only to retreat again, always under heavy fire, until they were allowed to rest in reserve. The day cost the rookie regiment 101 casualties, with seven men, including Captain Irish, whose statue adorns the New Jersey monument at Antietam, killed in action.[25]

Three of the other new regiments, the 11th, 12th, and 15th Infantry, were assigned to the Army of the Potomac but did not join the army until after Antietam. The 11th was assigned to the III Army Corps and the 12th to the II Army Corps, both to brigades with regiments from other states. The 15th joined the First New Jersey Brigade in the VI Corps and the 14th was stationed at Monocacy, Maryland, to guard the railroad bridge crossing the river at the town of Frederick.

Although the First Brigade was held in reserve at Antietam, its attached Battery A was engaged. The battery deployed around 700 yards east of the famed Dunker Church, and the Jersey gunners wrecked two enemy batteries in succession before running out of ammunition. Their work gained them praise from higher commanders and cheers from the first Brigade infantrymen they passed on the way to the rear.

Back home in New Jersey, the feverish pace of recruiting picked up once more as the state attempted to fill the federal government's second request for troops that summer. On the authority of the Militia Act of July 17, 1862, in August New Jersey was assessed an allocation of 10,478 men to be drafted from the militia for nine-months service as part of another nationwide quota of 300,000 soldiers. The draft was scheduled for early September, but state officials were advised that it could be avoided if enough volunteers were raised prior to that date to fill the troop requisition.[26]

Adjutant General Stockton established a quota for each town in the state and then appointed county draft commis-

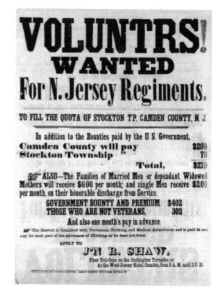

An 1863 recruiting poster.

sioners who hired enrollment officers to create a list of eligible potential draftees as towns moved quickly to raise bounty money to entice volunteers before the September draft date. In Bergen County, seat of much antiwar sentiment, bounties ran to $200 and higher, more than those offered to three-year volunteers. Regimental commanders and staff officers for these new regiments, in line with their classification as militia units, seem to have mostly been appointed through political influence, with company grade officers elected by their men; both processes produced leadership of varying abilities.[27]

The state would later claim that all the men who served in the nine-months regiments were volunteers and that there had been no draft. This was not, however, true. Although the state raised volunteers beyond its quota, Warren Township in Somerset County failed to offer a recruiting bounty and did not enlist anyone. Stockton ordered a draft in the township and forty-eight men were conscripted. Of these, twenty-five provided substitutes, seven reported for duty, and sixteen did not report at all. The substitutes were hardly fit material for soldiers. One was rejected as "totally unfit being deaf and imbecile" and another as a "habitual drunkard."[28]

In the end the state formed eleven nine-months regiments, the 21st through the 31st New Jersey Infantry. Newspaper articles intended to stimulate recruiting assured potential volunteers that they would serve their term of service engaged in safe duty in comfortable fort garrisons well behind the lines, and that serving would provide "an agreeable episode in their lives," but the Jersey regiments ended up in the field. The first major engagement of their service was the Battle of Fredericksburg.[29]

### THE BATTLE OF FREDERICKS-BURG

Major General Burnside, who had succeeded in the coastal war in North Carolina, with help from the 9th New Jersey, replaced General McClellan, relieved by Lincoln due to his excessive caution, in command of the Army of the Potomac. Burnside tried to steal a march on General Lee in late November, 1862, rapidly moving his army to the Rappahannock River, across from the town of Fredericksburg, in hopes of crossing the river and advancing towards Richmond before the Army of Northern Virginia could arrive to block his passage. Although Burnside did beat Lee to the crossing, a delay in the arrival of pontoon bridges negated his initial advantage, and the Confederates were able to assume a strong position on the high ground beyond the town.

Burnside began his river crossing on December 11, and, with the town secured, attacked the virtually impregnable Rebel lines beyond in a frontal assault the following day. New Jersey units were in action all along the line, and many of the nine-months soldiers ended up in the thick of the fighting. The 24th New Jersey, assigned to the First Division of the II Corps, went from encountering Rebel pickets who traded "tobacco for drawers, shirts, stockings." on December 9 to charging over fences and across a canal into a maelstrom of enemy fire from Marye's Heights three days later. Some of the Jerseymen got within twenty-five yards of the Confederate lines, but to no avail, as the regiment, which shot away all its ammunition only to be shot to pieces itself, fell back down the hill. The 24th lost sixteen men killed, 115 wounded, and twenty-nine missing.[30]

The 28th New Jersey also charged the enemy line and officers and its men went down in heaps—one sergeant was decapitated by a cannon ball. Captain Joseph Crowell of Company I was hit in the face by a shell fragment that took off part of his nose, and Colonel Moses Wisewell was hit in the neck by a bullet that exited through his mouth. Despite these losses, the regiment pushed on towards the enemy, getting as close to the Rebel line as any Union army unit that day, until stopped cold by the volume of fire. The Jerseymen hit the ground and returned fire, laying there all night amidst the dead from successive assault waves, until withdrawn the following morning. The 28th lost fourteen men killed, 147 wounded, and twenty-nine missing in action, thirty percent of the force the regiment brought to the field.[31]

Four of the nine-months regiments, the 22nd, 29th, 30th, and 31st New Jersey, were formed into a single brigade

The stone wall that protected the Confederate line at Fredericksburg

and were fortunate enough to escape the disastrous battle at Fredericksburg. They were assigned to rear area provost guard duty and unloading supplies at the army's Aquia Creek Landing base. Following the battle, these Jerseymen also assisted in loading the wounded onto ships that would take them back to Washington. Although closer to the front, the 26th and 27th New Jersey were held in reserve, although the 27th patrolled the town during the battle. The 21st, assigned to the VI Corps, was also spared the worst of the fighting. The regiment was deployed in support of a Maryland artillery battery, and lost seven men wounded.[32]

The state's longer service soldiers were, for the most part, not engaged at Fredericksburg. The 11th New Jersey, assigned to the III Army Corps, was held in reserve with the rest of the corps, which included the regiments of the Second New Jersey Brigade. The 12th did not arrive at its assigned II Corps brigade until after the battle, and the already battered 13th and its XII Corps did not rejoin the army until after Fredericksburg. The 14th continued on duty guarding the railroad bridge at Frederick.

The units of the First Brigade, including the newly enlisted 15th and 23rd Regiments, crossed the river on December 12 with the VI Corps and, after encountering a strong enemy force, deployed in a defensive position on the Union left. The 15th manned the brigade picket line and skirmished with the enemy all morning. Later in the day the brigade was ordered to advance to "straighten the lines." Elements of the 4th and 15th moved out, supported by the 23rd. Colonel Henry Ryerson of the 2nd New Jersey, who assumed command of the 23rd after its initial commander, Colonel John S. Cox, was dismissed for attacking several officers with his sword in a drunken rage, ordered his regiment to wheel to the right and attack the Rebel picket line on its flank, but the inexperienced nine-months soldiers, some of whom did not hear the command, faltered. As they fell back, Ryerson rallied his men and restored order.

As the disastrous day came to a close, the 25th New Jersey tentatively advanced with its division of the IX Corps, but the division halted under heavy fire and several of the regiment's companies began

Soldiers of the 1st New Jersey Brigade's 2nd Regiment in reserve in May 1863 at Fredericksburg. This photo was mislabeled as a Petersburg photo until recently.

to panic. Colonel Andrew Derrom, a Paterson architect in civilian life, personally rallied his men, noting that "some few of the officers seem to be wanting in promptness," but the attack was abandoned. The regiment lost six men killed, sixty-one wounded, and eighteen missing in its first engagement. As the army withdrew after the battle, the 21st and 25th New Jersey, assigned to help the engineers take up the pontoon bridges, were among the last units to cross the Rappahannock.[33]

In all, the seven New Jersey nine-months regiments that fought at Fredericksburg lost forty-four men killed, 365 wounded, and eighty-five missing in action, for a total of 494 casualties. The 28th suffered the most casualties, with the 24th a close second. The 4th, one of the few New Jersey three-year infantry

regiments engaged in offensive action at Fredericksburg, lost seven men killed and three wounded. The 15th, in its first battle, suffered three men killed and six wounded. Among that regiment's dead was Sergeant Major John P. Fowler, the colonel's cousin.[34]

Battery A deployed with the First Brigade and was engaged in covering and counter-battery fire against Rebel artillery. Brigadier General William T. H. "Bully" Brooks, commanding the VI Corps' 1st Division, commented that the battery's fire "appeared to be very effective." Battery B, under Captain Judson Clark, was posted with the VI Corps' Vermont Brigade, which also included the 26th New Jersey, and engaged in extensive counter-battery fire, dismounting five enemy guns. Division commander General Albion Howe praised "Capt.

Clark's New Jersey Battery for continued and good effect in firing. I have never seen them equaled."[35]

In the wake of the Fredericksburg disaster, the Army of the Potomac occupied dismal winter quarters at Falmouth, Virginia, where First Lieutenant Oscar Westlake of the Third New Jersey complained of "devilish poor dinner" and, worse yet, the fact that he could "get no whiskey." There would be one more Burnside-inflicted trial on the army, a winter offensive. The campaign plan was to feint to the north of Fredericksburg along the Rappahannock and then launch a crossing south of the town, coupled with a large cavalry raid. The movement began on January 20 in mild weather that quickly turned horrible, with heavy rain bringing the maneuver to a virtual halt. It took 400 men from the 23rd New Jersey, well primed with whiskey, an entire hour to drag a pontoon 100 yards. His army hopelessly bogged down in what became known as the "Mud March," Burnside gave up. On January 26 President Lincoln relieved the luckless commander, replacing him with the brash, self-assured, Major General Joseph Hooker.[36]

The Army of the Potomac's morale, which had plumbed the depths, soared over the next few months as Hooker improved mail distribution and rations and allowed soldiers limited home leave, although his introduction of distinctive corps badges proved his most lasting contribution to the army. Each army corps was assigned an insignia, with the corps' First, Second, and Third Divisions wearing, respectively, red, white, and blue versions of it. As members of the VI Corps' First Division, the men of the First New Jersey Brigade were issued red Greek Cross cloth badges. The Second Brigade, assigned to the III Corps' Second Division, received white diamond shaped badges. New Jerseyans would wear their corps badges with pride for the rest of the war—and as veterans in the long twilight that followed.

## THE BATTLE OF CHANCELLORSVILLE

The Jerseymen of the First Brigade got a significant morale boost when newly inaugurated Governor Joel Parker visited their camp on April 26, 1863. Parker presented the 1st, 2nd, and 3rd Regiments with new state colors similar to one issued previously to the 4th Regiment. The flags were inscribed with a tribute to the brigade's victory at Crampton's Gap and a state crest on one side, while the other side bore "the American eagle in a halo, and the same inscription."[37]

The flags would soon be carried into battle. General Hooker was supremely confident in his rebuilt army, as well as his own abilities, and deciding to take a page from Burnside's book, he launched a diversionary cavalry raid on April 27, then marched much of his army north, leaving some troops, including General John Sedgwick's VI Corps, which crossed the Rappahannock on April 30 near Fredericksburg, to distract the enemy. Hooker's main force crossed the Rappahannock and then the Rapidan Rivers into the Confederate rear upstream. Once General Lee realized his situation, he divided his own army, moving the bulk of it north to face Hooker and leaving a lesser force deployed in the old Marye's Heights line to oppose the Federals at Fredericksburg.

Hooker established his field headquarters at Chancellorsville, where fighting began on May 1. On May 2, Stonewall Jackson's corps launched a devastating flank attack on Hooker's XI Corps. The

Confederate prisoners and captured battle flags being escorted to the rear at Chancellorsville.

Second New Jersey Brigade, which now included the 115th Pennsylvania Infantry, was originally deployed to protect the Rapidan bridgehead, but was rushed forward, along with the 11th New Jersey Infantry, to support the stressed Union line. When the troops in front of them were driven back on May 3, the Second Brigade men rose to the occasion, with rapid fire musketry and an advance with fixed bayonets, while the 11th, led by Colonel Robert McAllister, attacked alongside. The Jerseymen swept over the Rebels, capturing hundreds of prisoners and eight battle flags. Brigade commander General Gershom Mott went down wounded, and was replaced by Colonel William Sewell of the 5th New Jersey. Sewell continued the advance until he realized that his flanks were unsupported, and then fell back gradually, with the prisoners and enemy colors.

The 8th New Jersey saved some abandoned artillery pieces and rolled them back to safety. Former brigade commander General Joseph Revere, now leading New York's Excelsior Brigade, ordered a retreat when his men ran low on ammunition. His brigade's withdrawal opened a hole that threatened the whole Union line, and Revere was subsequently court-martialed and dismissed from the service, although the court's decision was later revoked due to his previous good conduct. The Second New Jersey Brigade finally withdrew north of the Rappahannock on May 6, having suffered losses of 378 men killed and wounded.[38]

Along with the 11th, the 12th New Jersey had its baptism by fire at Chancellorsville, holding a segment of the Union line against Rebel attacks on May 3. The regiment fought hard but was outflanked and routed, then rallied behind a new line of battle to the rear. The 13th New Jersey, which led the initial federal advance at Chancellorsville, engaged in heavy skirmishing and then dug in to await developments as a number of retreating XI Corps soldiers passed through the regiment's position. Some of the 13th's men were captured during a night reconnaissance, and the unit was withdrawn after exhausting its ammunition. The 13th New Jersey gained praise from senior commanders, one of whom noted that the regiment "behaved handsomely and fought bravely."[39]

The nine-months service Jerseymen of the 24th and 28th Regiments, already battered at Fredericksburg, were in the thick of the struggle again at Chancellorsville, fighting alongside each other at one point. The 28th was overrun and Colonel John A. Wildrick was captured. In the end the 24th suffered seven casualties and the 28th thirty.

As the fighting accelerated, Hooker ordered the VI Corps commander, Major General John Sedgwick, to advance in hopes of relieving the pressure at Chancellorsville. The VI Corps charged the formerly impregnable line on Marye's heights, more thinly held than in December, and overran it. The First New Jersey Brigade was held in reserve during the attack, but the 26th New Jersey, attached to the famed Vermont Brigade, was one of the units chosen for the assault. Shouting incoherently, the regiment's erratic colonel, Andrew Jackson Morrison, led his men off in the wrong direction. The regiment fell into chaos but was reorganized by Lieutenant Colonel Edward Martindale and completed its mission. Morrison was relieved from command, placed under arrest for drunkenness, and cashiered from the army. He would be heard from again.[40]

The Heights secured, Sedgwick ordered General Brooks to push his 1st Division, including the First New Jersey Brigade, commanded by Colonel Henry W. Brown of the 3rd New Jersey in General Torbert's absence, down the Orange Turnpike. Confederate brigadier general Cadmus Wilcox withdrew slowly, contesting the federal advance, until the 1st Division troops entered the woods around Salem Church, where Wilcox had deployed several regiments in ambush. The 23rd New Jersey, which had been presented with a new flag from the people of Burlington County in April, was hit especially hard. The regiment fought valiantly, but took heavy fire from the front and then its left flank as the brigade to its left collapsed. Battered, the 23rd retreated in disorder for 500 yards until rallied by Colonel E. Burd Grubb.[41]

The 2nd New Jersey's skirmishers were driven in and the 1st New Jersey, on the other side of Salem Church, was rolled up by the enemy as well (the 4th New Jersey was on detached duty). The 3rd New Jersey had entered the woods farther to the right, but was driven out by two Georgia regiments and replaced by the 15th, which held on until dark, finally retreating in order, the last 1st Division regiment to leave the field. The VI Corps consolidated and established a defensive perimeter as General Lee appeared on the scene with reinforcements. At 5:00 p.m. on May 4, Lee attacked Sedgwick's perimeter, with the main thrust directed at a section of the line held by the 21st New Jersey. When the regiments to the Jerseymen's right and left broke, they came under fire from three directions, suffering 211 casualties, including 141 men lost as prisoners. Colonel Gilliam Van Houten was mortally wounded and died in Confederate hands. The VI Corps held on, however, and crossed the Rappahannock later that evening.[42]

The remaining New Jersey nine-months regiments had varying experiences during the Chancellorsville Campaign, which was notable in having a larger number of New Jersey units present on the field than any other battle of the war. The men of the 22nd New Jersey, reluctant warriors from Bergen County, were brigaded with the 29th, 30th, and 31st New Jersey and a Pennsylvania regiment and assigned to the I Corps. The brigade crossed the Rappahannock as a reserve force but did not engage in combat. While recrossing under enemy artillery fire, the 22nd lost six men wounded and the 29th had four men wounded, one mortally, while the 30th and 31st suffered no losses.

The 25th and 27th New Jersey, dispatched to the Union's coastal enclave in southern Virginia prior to the campaign, escaped Chancellorsville, but the 25th, stationed at Suffolk, Virginia, was engaged in a stiff fight along the Nansemond River. The Jerseyans captured a line of Rebel defenses, but had to fall back from a stronger second line, dragging one prisoner along with them. During the attack the regiment's popular chaplain, Francis E. Butler, was killed while bringing water to the wounded. Butler was the only New Jersey chaplain killed in action during the Civil War. In addition to Butler, the regiment suffered one enlisted man killed.[43]

After an easy duty stint in the Newport News garrison, where its camp gained praise as a show place, the 27th, commanded by Colonel George W. Mindil, along with the rest of the IX Corps under Major General Burnside, shipped out to the West, arriving in Cincinnati, Ohio, on March 27. The Jerseymen pursued retreating Confederates across Kentucky without engaging in combat, but an accident involving an overturned flatboat while crossing the Cumberland River resulted in a loss of thirty-three men drowned, most of them from Rockaway Township. Alerted to march to Vicksburg, the 27th, its term of service about to expire, boarded a train east instead. The regiment halted briefly to bolster the defenses of Harrisburg during the Gettysburg Campaign, and then returned to New Jersey, arriving at Newark's Camp Frelinghuysen for muster-out on June 28.[44]

The 1st New Jersey Cavalry, after dueling with Major John Singleton Mosby's guerillas for the first months of 1863,

went off on Major General George Stoneman's generally unproductive cavalry raid, capturing a trainload of Rebel shoes as its contribution to the Chancellorsville Campaign. Battery A performed extremely well once more, halting the Confederate attack in the wake of the First Brigade's repulse at Salem Church, while Battery B served with the III Corps during the battle, moving to several critical positions and helping hold the line to facilitate Hooker's withdrawal.

Over the next two months, all of the New Jersey nine-months regiments left the army, while the state's longer service units marched north to engage in the most famous of all Civil War battles— Gettysburg.

## THE BATTLE OF GETTYSBURG

The Gettysburg Campaign began in the wake of Lee's "perfect battle" triumph over Hooker at Chancellorsville. As with Second Bull Run the previous year, Chancellorsville provided Lee with a springboard for an invasion of the North. The Confederate commander intended to take the war out of ravaged Virginia, supply his army off the enemy's land, encourage antiwar elements in the Union states, and perhaps capitalize on unforeseen events. Hooker followed, too tentatively for President Abraham Lincoln, who, given an opportunity, replaced him with Major General George G. Meade.

As the armies began to shift in Virginia, the Union cavalry, united under Brigadier General Alfred Pleasanton, marched out to find its Rebel opponents, and encountered them at Brandy Station, Virginia, on June 9. In the ensuing fight, the largest cavalry action of the war, the 1st New Jersey Cavalry was involved in a saber slashing, handgun shooting melee, routing two Virginia mounted regiments. The fighting disorganized the Jersey boys, however, and when hit by a counterattacking enemy regiment they reeled, but were successfully relieved by the 1st Pennsylvania Cavalry. Although the regiment suffered a number of casualties, including a major and lieutenant colonel killed, morale was high, as the Jersey cavalrymen had mostly held their own against the vaunted Confederate horsemen.[45]

Both New Jersey infantry brigades in the Army of the Potomac, along with the 11th, 12th, and 13th Infantry Regiments, Batteries A and B, and the 1st Cavalry, marched north with Meade's army, as the nine-months regiments marched home. With the enemy roaming the adjacent state of Pennsylvania, Adjutant General Stockton called for militiamen to bolster the state's defenses and perhaps entrain for Harrisburg if necessary. He appointed his father, Mexican War hero and one-time peace advocate, Robert Stockton, as commander of what turned out to be a token force that never left Trenton.[46]

As battle drew nigh, both armies began to concentrate near Gettysburg, where General John Buford's Union cavalry division traded fire with Confederate infantry skirmishers on July 1. The horse soldiers managed a gradual fighting withdrawal, delaying the enemy while federal foot soldiers marched to the rescue. Union infantry, the I, and then the XI Army Corps, arrived in the nick of time, halting the Rebel advance. As the day wore on, however, more Confederates poured into the fight and the advantage swayed back and forth until the Union line broke and defeated Yankees streamed back through Gettysburg to the high ground beyond on Cemetery Ridge, where they rallied and set up a defensive position.

During the night and into the morning hours reinforcements arrived for both sides and July 2 found the Army of the Potomac deployed in a "fishhook" line, anchored on its barb end at Culp's Hill. That afternoon Major General Daniel Sickles advanced his III Army Corps from its position on the shank along Cemetery Ridge forward to the Emmitsburg Road, his left flank hanging in the air at an ancient glacial rock formation known as Devil's Den.[47]

The units in Sickles's advance included the Second New Jersey Brigade, acting as the Third Brigade of the III Corps' 2nd Division and including, along with the four New Jersey regiments, the 2nd New Hampshire and the 115th Pennsylvania, under the command of Colonel George C. Burling, which arrived on the field around 9:00 a.m. The 2nd Division's First Brigade included the 11th New Jersey. The 11th was deployed along the Emmitsburg Road, while Burling's Brigade was positioned slightly to the rear in a reserve formation. Captain Clark's Battery B, part of the III Corps' Artillery Brigade, was deployed at the Peach Orchard.

Sickles, who thought he was improving his tactical situation by advancing, was unaware that Lee had ordered General Longstreet to conduct an attack on the Union left. The assault, delayed by organizational difficulties, was launched late that day, and in heavy fighting at sites that would forever after be part of the American military iconography—Devil's Den, Little Round Top, and the Wheatfield—the stubborn federals were driven back to Cemetery Ridge, from where an exhausted Confederate force could push them no further. An evening strike at Culp's Hill failed as well.

New Jersey units were busy across the field on July 2. When Longstreet's attack

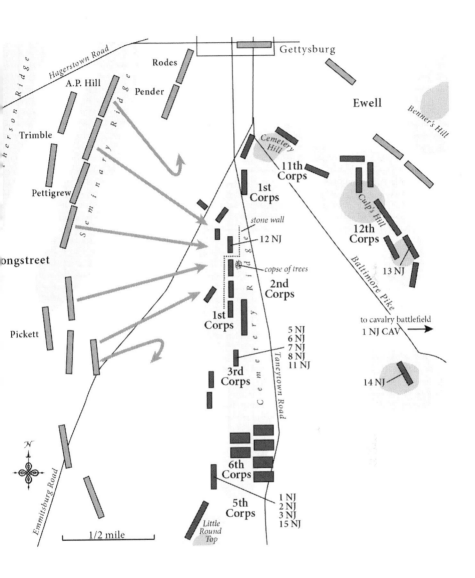

New Jersey troop positions at Gettysburg on July 3, 1863.

began to roll out around 4:00 p.m., Colonel Burling's brigade was split up to plug holes in the Union line. The 7th New Jersey and 2nd New Hampshire were deployed near the Peach Orchard, the 5th New Jersey across the Emmitsburg Road, and Burling personally led the 6th New Jersey down the valley that separated Devil's Den and Little Round Top. When he returned he found that the 8th New Jersey had been ordered to join the troops in the Wheatfield, leaving him only the 115th Pennsylvania, a very small regiment. Burling, with no effective command remaining, went to the rear. He later complained that his brigade was "dismembered."

The 5th New Jersey, deployed in a loose skirmish line, fell back before an Alabama brigade's advance but managed to hold back the Rebels long enough to allow an artillery battery to escape to the rear. The regiment lost thirteen men killed, sixty-five wounded, and sixteen missing, almost half the number it brought to the field.

The 6th New Jersey, under Lieutenant Colonel Stephen R. Gilkyson, marched through some woods to Plum Run, the little valley between Houck's Ridge and Devil's Den and Little Round Top. Seeing some Confederates advancing into the valley, Gilkyson had his men open fire at 400 yards' distance, then advanced to a position where his regiment was protected by boulders, and continued to fire in the direction of the enemy, although gun smoke prevented aiming at specific targets. The 6th held that position until Devil's Den fell to the Confederates around 7:00 p.m.; they then withdrew to Cemetery Ridge. The regiment lost one man killed, thirty-two wounded, and eight missing.

The 7th New Jersey, the first unit detached from Burling's command, was deployed in support of Battery B along the Wheatfield Road near the Peach Orchard. The regiment, commanded by Colonel Louis R. Francine, laid down in a depression in the ground, but still suffered a number of casualties from enemy artillery fire late in the afternoon. As the Union line at the Peach Orchard disintegrated, the artillery along the Wheatfield Road began to withdraw, protected by the 7th. The regiment, divided into two components by stampeding artillery horses, engaged advancing Confederate infantry and fell back towards Cemetery Ridge. Colonel Francine was badly wounded where the regiment's monument stands today. The 7th lost fifteen men killed, eighty-six wounded, and thirteen missing. Francine died of his wound in a Philadelphia hospital on July 16, the only New Jersey regimental commander who lost his life as a result of the battle.

The 8th New Jersey was detached from Burling's brigade at the same time the 7th was, and marched across the Wheatfield to support the Union troops holding that position. The exact location and movements of the regiment are difficult to track, since its commander, Colonel John Ramsey, was wounded and neither he nor his successor in command, Captain John Livingston, filed an after action report on the battle. The 8th apparently ended up somewhat north of where its monument now stands and, with little cover, fell back under heavy fire. The regiment did manage to make it back to Cemetery Ridge by nightfall, with a loss for the day of seven men killed, thirty-eight wounded, and two missing.

The last New Jersey infantry regiment engaged in fighting along the Third Corps line on July 2 was the 11th New Jersey, commanded by Colonel Robert McAllister. Initially deployed along the Emmitsburg Road, the regiment came under heavy artillery fire as the enemy prepared for the late afternoon assault, and was then hit by Confederate brigadier general Cadmus Wilcox's Alabama brigade, which had swept away the 5th New Jersey skirmishers to its front around 6:00 p.m. Major Philip J. Kearny, nephew of the general, was shot in the knee almost immediately and Colonel McAllister was wounded shortly afterward. As the Yankee line began to crumble, the 11th began a fighting withdrawal towards Cemetery Ridge. As other officers assumed command they were killed or wounded in quick succession. Three went down within ten minutes. In thirty minutes the regiment lost almost half its men, but still rallied for a counterattack that swept back across the field, before falling back again.

At the end of the day, the 11th was under the command of Captain Samuel Sleeper of Shrewsbury, the unit's sixth commander that day. The regiment lost seventeen soldiers killed, 124 wounded, and twelve missing—fifty-six percent of the men it brought to the field, and the greatest loss of any New Jersey regiment that fought at Gettysburg.

Farther north, along Cemetery Ridge, The 12th New Jersey was engaged in severe fighting on July 2, when it attacked the Bliss barn, a large structure to its front, to clear out Confederate sharpshooters. Although suffering considerable loss, the attack was successful, and netted the regiment one hundred prisoners.

July 3 opened without major combat, but an afternoon artillery duel preceded the disastrous Confederate infantry assault known forever afterward as "Pickett's Charge," after Major General George Pickett, who commanded one of the three divisions. The attack hit the II Corps portion of the Union line, held in

part by the 12th New Jersey Infantry. The Jerseymen, armed with obsolete smoothbore muskets, which fired a combination round of a round ball and three buckshot, known as "buck and ball," reserved their fire until the enemy was within fifty yards and then delivered a devastating volley into the 26th North Carolina regiment, shattering that unit and capturing its battle flag. The flag was sent as a trophy to Trenton, where it remained until returned to North Carolina in the early twentieth century. It is currently at the Museum of the Confederacy in Richmond. Over several days of heavy fighting, the 12th lost twenty-three men killed, eighty-three wounded, and nine missing.

The 1st New Jersey Cavalry was engaged in a cavalry action that occurred some three miles behind the Union lines as Major General J. E. B. Stuart, maneuvering his cavalry division to exploit any advantages gained by Pickett's infantry attack on the Union center, engaged Brigadier General David M. Gregg's Union Cavalry division in a series of dismounted firefights and conventional saber charges. Although the 1st was, at times, in the thick of the fight, casualties were light, amounting to nine men wounded.

The 13th New Jersey reached Gettysburg late in the day on July 1, and was deployed in reserve behind Culp's Hill, the barb end of the "fishhook" Union line. The 13th's brigade was sent to reinforce the Federal center late on July 2, but returned to occupy a position by Spangler's Spring. Engaged in skirmishing and repulsing a Rebel attack, the regiment lost one man killed and twenty wounded.

The regiments of the First Brigade arrived at Gettysburg after a forced march late in the afternoon of July 2. The brigade was detailed to occupy a section of the Union line a short distance to the north of Little Round Top and did not engage in any serious combat, but had eleven men wounded by shellfire on July 3, several of whom subsequently died of their wounds.

In the months after the climactic battle at Gettysburg, the New Jersey units in the Army of the Potomac were involved in the fruitless Mine Run Campaign in November and December 1863. The 14th New Jersey joined the Army of the Potomac after Gettysburg and fought in its first engagement on November 27 at Locust Grove, Virginia, suffering a loss of sixteen men killed and fifty-eight wounded—its first losses in battle. As the year waned, the 13th New Jersey, along with the rest of the XII Corps, was consolidated with the XI Corps to form the XX Corps, which was then shipped to Chattanooga, Tennessee, to reinforce a Union army that had been besieged there since the Battle of Chickamauga.[48]

Over the winter, soldiers who had enlisted for three year terms in 1861 were given the option to be discharged in January and then reenlist, with considerable bounties from both federal and state levels, as "veteran volunteers." Many Jerseymen took advantage of the offer, but perhaps more did not. Even those who had declined to reenlist, though, would still have to fight well into the summer, when their three-year terms of service would officially end.

## THE ENROLLMENT ACT OF 1863

The Enrollment Act of 1863, which established a federally supervised draft, gave rise to riots in New York City and minor disturbances in Newark. Governor Parker managed to get conscription postponed in the state by promising to raise new regiments and recruits to meet New Jersey's assigned manpower quota. In response to Parker's promise, spurred by large bounties offered by counties and municipalities, three new infantry regiments, the 33rd, 34th, and 35th, along with two cavalry regiments, the 2nd and 3rd, and three artillery batteries, the 3rd, 4th, and 5th, were recruited in the state in late 1863 and early 1864.[49]

The 33rd and the 35th Infantry Regiments received colorful French North African style Zouave uniforms as an extra incentive to join. Unfortunately, many of the original recruits in these units were "bounty jumpers," who intended to collect their bounties and desert at the earliest opportunity. One drunken soldier from the 35th attacked an officer in the streets of Flemington with a bayonet. The officer shot and killed him on the spot and a local newspaper charged that the 35th's men were "scoundrels from New York and Philadelphia." A number of the 33rd's recruits tried to desert by jumping the fence at Newark's Camp Frelinghuysen and were shot by members of a Vermont regiment assigned to guard them.[50]

The older regiments in the field also sent recruiting parties back to New Jersey in an attempt to fill their depleted ranks. Sergeant Samuel Cavileer of the 4th New Jersey, home on recruiting duty in Freehold, wasn't particularly eager to enlist new men, however. He preferred that the draft take the "stay at homes," many of whom he suspected of Confederate sympathies. Acting Surgeon Levi D. Miller of the 1st New Jersey complained that replacements arriving at the First Brigade camp in the winter of 1863–64 were "men over 50 . . . boys under 18, men recently discharged on account of disease or disability from wounds." These "recruits" expected to be discharged immediately, having scammed an enlistment bounty and, at the same time, filled a municipality's manpower quota. It was a win-win for everyone but the army.[51]

The three new infantry regiments were assigned to the Western Theater of the war. The 2nd Cavalry Regiment was also sent west, and the 3rd, dressed in fancy European-style uniforms, also known as the "First US Hussars" and nicknamed the "Butterflies," was assigned to the Eastern Theater, as were the new artillery batteries. Joseph Karge, a solid veteran officer, was promoted to colonel and assigned to command the 2nd Cavalry, but the 3rd was unfortunate enough to be led by Colonel Andrew J. Morrison, who had returned from disgrace—for a while.

## THE WAR IN 1864

The campaign season of 1864 would prove to be particularly bloody, with the First and Second Brigades heavily engaged in the Wilderness and at Spotsylvania and Cold Harbor as Lieutenant General Ulysses S. Grant accompanied Major General George Gordon Meade's Army of the Potomac, which fought its way overland toward Richmond. The First New Jersey Brigade, reinforced by the 10th New Jersey Infantry, which had been on easy duty chasing draft dodgers and rebellious miners in the Pennsylvania coal fields, crossed the Rapidan River with the VI Corps of the Army of the Potomac on May 4, 1864. The following day the brigade was engaged in heavy combat with Confederate forces in the Wilderness. On May 6, Captain Ellis Hamilton of the 15th New Jersey, who, as a sixteen-year-old lieutenant, had been the youngest commissioned officer in the Union army in 1862, was mortally wounded.[52]

Ellis Hamilton of Camden and the 15th New Jersey Infantry. When he was commissioned a lieutenant in 1862, Hamilton was the youngest officer in the Union Army. He was mortally wounded in the Battle of the Wilderness in 1864.

The battered brigade lurched on to Spotsylvania, and, after a hard march and preliminary fighting on May 8, was ordered on May 12 to support the II Army Corps, which had penetrated the enemy line but had been pushed back to its breakthrough point. After a wild hundred-yard charge into a blizzard of bullets, the Jerseymen slugged it out at point blank range with a brigade of Mississippians. The 15th New Jersey, which led the attack, lost over half its men in the charge, but helped halt the Rebel counterattack at a point forever after known as the "Bloody Angle." In the aftermath, a brigade staff officer surveying the body-strewn scene said he hoped he "would never again witness such a sight."[53]

Officers of the 15th New Jersey Infantry pose for a group photograph in March, 1864. By the end of the year, many of them would be killed or wounded.

The Second New Jersey Brigade, now including the 11th New Jersey, and commanded by the 11th's Colonel McAllister, who had recovered from his Gettysburg wound, was also heavily engaged in the Wilderness and at Spotsylvania. The basic load of ammunition for a soldier going into combat was sixty rounds, but the Jerseymen of the brigade fired an average of 150 rounds per man in two days of fighting in the Wilderness. The brigade was in the first wave of the May 12 attack and was pushed back but hung on. The fast shooting Jerseyans had to be resupplied with ammunition several times during the battle.[54]

Sergeant John W. Mitchell of the 12th New Jersey, which also participated in the assault, recalled that he "never saw such firing in my life. There wasn't a tree the thickness of your finger hardly, but what was all cut to pieces with balls." The regiment's commander, twenty-eight-year-old Lieutenant Colonel Thomas Davis of Camden, was killed in the assault.[55]

After Spotsylvania, both armies tumbled south, as General Grant sought a way around General Lee's right flank, clashing intermittently and bleeding casualties all the way. The next big fight for the Jerseymen of the First Brigade was Cold Harbor, where they arrived on June 1. The men in the 1st through 4th Regiments who had declined to reenlist and had survived thus far were discharged, and the reenlisted "Veteran Volunteers," were reassigned to the 15th New Jersey. The brigade attacked the Confederate line on June 3 with three regiments, the 10th, the 15th, and the 4th—the latter having reenlisted enough men to retain its regimental designation. The enemy fire was so heavy that the Jerseymen dropped to the ground after a short distance and began digging trenches with bayonets, tin plates, and cups. Trench warfare had begun. Captain Dayton Flint of the 15th reflected that from then on "spades will be trump." He was correct.[56]

The Second Brigade was deployed in reserve during the Cold Harbor assault and avoided the carnage, but the 14th New Jersey, which had escaped with relatively low casualties in the Wilderness and at Spotsylvania, was not spared. The 14th actually penetrated the Confederate lines, something few Union regiments were able to do that day. Captain John C. Patterson and a fourteen-man detachment succeeded in flanking a Rebel regiment and capturing over one hundred Confederate soldiers. The 14th paid a heavy price, however, losing twenty-nine men killed, 110 wounded, and fifteen missing.

The 1st New Jersey Cavalry, riding with Major General Philip Sheridan's cavalry division, engaged in several fights with its Confederate counterparts, as did the 3rd New Jersey Cavalry, which was equipped with Spencer repeating carbines after Colonel Morrison, was, once again, dismissed due to drunkenness. Batteries A and B were held in reserve for the most part, occasionally exchanging fire with enemy artillery. The Third Battery did not arrive at the front until after Cold Harbor. The Fourth Battery, assigned to Major General Benjamin Butler's Army of the James, was slightly engaged at the battle of Drewry's Bluff on May 15 during that army's failed advance on Richmond and lost several men wounded. The Fifth Battery, also assigned to the Army of the James, was also minimally involved at Drewry's Bluff.

In a dramatic contrast, the 9th New Jersey Infantry, shipped up from North Carolina to reinforce Butler's army, also fought at Drewry's Bluff and was outflanked and almost surrounded in a dense fog. During a chaotic withdrawal, the 9th's commander, Colonel Abram Zabriskie of Hackensack, was mortally wounded. The regiment lost more men at Drewry's Bluff than in any other engagement it was in during the war, with over 200 killed, wounded, or missing. The 9th's heroic rear guard action against heavy odds, however, managed to delay the enemy advance and avoid a complete Union disaster. Butler's army withdrew to the Bermuda Hundred, where it entrenched.[57]

The Army of the Potomac moved on once more, to Petersburg, a vital rail junction south of Richmond, where an attempt to seize the town by Butler's army had failed earlier, although the African American Jerseymen of the 22nd U. S. Colored Infantry had captured two enemy forts. By June 9 the armies were deadlocked. Siege trench lines were dug from Petersburg towards Richmond, and the stalemate would last until the spring of 1865.

## THE SHENANDOAH VALLEY CAMPAIGN

In an attempt to divert troops and attention from the Union lines at Petersburg, General Lee ordered General Jubal Early to take his army corps from the siege lines and launch an attack in the Shenandoah Valley to ultimately threaten Washington. Early's initial efforts were successful, and he brushed aside Union forces in the Valley, moving into Maryland. Grant's response was to detach the VI Army Corps, which had more New Jersey soldiers than any other corps in his army, to block Early's advance. The corps' 3rd Division arrived at the Monocacy River, across from Frederick, Maryland, as Early approached. The division, along with some other scratch Union forces in the area, deployed on the heights overlooking the river. The 14th

New Jersey played a significant role in the ensuing battle on July 9, which delayed the Confederate advance on Washington, and, although the Union forces had to retreat, became known as "the battle than saved the capital." Early advanced to the outskirts of Washington and, finding the garrison reinforced by the entire VI Corps, retreated back to the Shenandoah. Shortly afterward Grant authorized the creation of the "Army of the Shenandoah," including the VI Corps and other troops in the area, put Major General Phil Sheridan in command and gave him orders to attack Early.

Sheridan's army, including the First New Jersey Brigade, the 14th New Jersey Infantry, and the 3rd New Jersey Cavalry, advanced on Early, and, from September through October, decisively defeated the Confederates at Winchester, Fisher's Hill, and Cedar Creek. Jerseymen played a critical role in all of these battles, and suffered heavy casualties, including Major Peter Vredenburgh, commanding the 14th at Winchester, who turned to his men as they began to advance and said "I'll do all I can for you boys" just before he was hit in the throat by an artillery shell and killed instantly. In the wake of the victory at Cedar Creek in October, the Jerseymen returned to the siege lines at Petersburg.[58]

### THE CAMPAIGN IN THE WEST

Meanwhile, in the West, the New Jersey regiments of Sherman's Army Group, which began its campaign on May 4, 1864, had their baptism of fire. The 33rd was the first to see combat, engaging the enemy at Rocky Face Ridge. The other Jersey Zouave regiment, the 35th, saw its first combat at Resaca, Georgia, as Sherman neared Atlanta.[59]

Soldiers of the 22nd United States Colored Infantry at Petersburg, where the predominately New Jersey African American unit broke through Confederate lines on several occasions.

Near Ruff's Mills, Georgia, Captain Augustus Angel of the 35th, considered one of the best small unit tacticians in Sherman's army, was shot through the heart and killed on the skirmish line. On the late afternoon of July 20, as the Union forces tightened their stranglehold on Atlanta, the 33rd was overrun by a surprise Confederate attack while digging trenches 500 yards in advance of the main Union lines. Lieutenant Colonel Enos Fouratt managed to rally his men and most escaped, but the regiment lost its battle flag. On September 2, led by Colonel Mindil, the 33rd marched into Atlanta. Both regiments had suffered severely over the course of the campaign, but received replacements while encamped at Atlanta over the next several months.[60]

The 13th New Jersey moved towards Atlanta as well, skirmishing with Confederates as Sherman feinted at General Joseph Johnston's Army of Tennessee. The regiment was fortunate to be held in reserve at Kennesaw Mountain, Sherman's only serious tactical mistake, losing only one man wounded. After closing in on Atlanta, the 13th dug trenches and spent most of the time dodging sharpshooter bullets. Following the Confederate abandonment of the city on September 2, the regiment also marched in, flags flying, and spent two months on garrison duty, during which it received replacements from New Jersey.[61]

The 34th New Jersey spent the summer and fall of 1864 on guard and counter-guerilla activity in the federal rear, as did the 2nd Cavalry. The 2nd, armed with Spencer repeating carbines, provided the rear guard for the Union retreat following the disastrous battle of Brice's Crossroads, Mississippi, on June 10, 1864. Colonel Karge of the 2nd gained credit for being the only Union cavalry leader to best legendary Nathan Bedford Forrest on another occasion, and even led his regiment into Arkansas, the furthest west of any New Jersey unit in the war.[62]

General Sherman realized that merely holding Atlanta would not end the war, and on November 15 marched a streamlined force out of the city heading for Savannah and the coast. All three New Jersey infantry regiments marched with him, living largely off the land. One soldier in the 13th recalled that "on the way through Georgia we feasted on sweet potatoes, fresh pork, chickens, turkeys, geese." Sergeant William Lloyd of the 33rd managed to "dig up out of the ground" a "silver chalice" some fleeing Georgia clergyman had buried. None of the Jerseymen were involved in combat until early December, when the 35th met

scattered resistance and had a corporal killed and several men wounded by a buried "torpedo" or land mine. To avoid future incidents, the Jersey boys made Rebel prisoners clear the road ahead of them. On December 21, Savannah fell. And then General Sherman looked north. The end was in sight.[63]

## THE NEW JERSEY HOMEFRONT

On the home front, the federal draft had finally come to New Jersey, with the first drawing held on May 10, 1864, in Ocean County, followed by other counties during the month. Unlike the previous year, there were no civil disturbances, largely because counties and municipalities had agreed to pay the $300 commutation fee to exempt a draftee from service under a particular draft—several would be held through the spring of 1865—with taxpayer money. *Newark Journal* editor Edward N. Fuller, himself a draftee, was delighted that the Essex County freeholders decided "to represent him with a $300 greenback." The commutation exemption was eventually ended, leaving the only options for a draftee to either provide an increasingly expensive substitute or serve himself. Many substitutes, often supplied by "substitute brokers" were veterans of more than two years of service, but a number were Confederate deserters or, in the words of New Jersey's acting assistant provost marshal general, "pimps and vagabonds." In the end, of the 103,296 New Jersey men enrolled for the draft, only 951 ever entered the army as draftees.[64]

## RECRUITING AFRICAN AMERICAN SOLDIERS

Once New Jersey officials realized that African American recruits counted as part of the state's assigned quota of soldiers, and that out of state recruiters had been whisking them away to enlist in units like the famed 54th Massachusetts, the 29th Connecticut Infantry, and the 14th Rhode Island Heavy Artillery, local recruiting agents began to actively solicit black volunteers. Most of these men were routed through Trenton to Camp William Penn, on the outskirts of Philadelphia. In the end more than 3,000 New Jersey African American soldiers served in the units of the United States Colored Troops (USCT), as well as in the Navy. The 22nd United States Colored Infantry, with seventy-five percent of its ranks composed of Jerseymen, would go on to achieve a distinguished combat record, breaking through Confederate defenses on a number of occasions. The regiment was also chosen to participate in the hunt for John Wilkes Booth and represent the entire United States Colored Troops in Abraham Lincoln's funeral procession.[65]

In response to President Lincoln's call for volunteers for 100 days of service to temporarily replace soldiers sent to the front under Grant and Sherman, New Jersey raised one regiment, the 37th Infantry. When it left Newark in June 1864, the regiment's personnel did not look too promising, and were described by one observer thusly: "There were many with only one eye; several with less fingers than the regulations allowed; a few, long since passed the age at which military service terminates; and scores of boys from fifteen years of age upwards." Despite this, the regiment did its job in the trenches of the Bermuda Hundred, and when the unit left service a general attested that the Jersey boys "had gained the esteem of the veterans of this corps."[66]

While the draft proceeded Adjutant General Stockton was reforming the

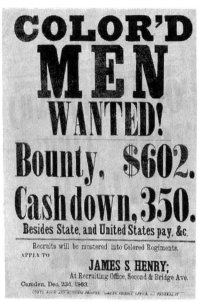

By 1864, African-American Jerseymen were sought after as recruits.

militia, creating the New Jersey Rifle Corps in 1863. Although units of the old militia still existed, recruits to the new organization were issued distinct uniforms. Initially, the Rifle Corps was less than a stunning success, with only six companies of the authorized fifty organized by the end of the year, but was deployed to control a riot that broke out between employees of two rival railroads in November.[67]

ARMAMENT MANUFACTURING IN NEW JERSEY

In 1863 and 1864, in order to properly arm the state's rifle corps, New Jersey purchased several thousand rifle-muskets to replace the obsolete smoothbore muskets carried by the militia. These guns were marked "NJ" on the barrel and stock opposite the lock to indicate state ownership. The first two orders, in July,

1863, were to New York arms merchants Schuyler, Hartley and Graham, for 2,500 and 1,500 Colt "Special Model" 1861s, paid for with federal promissory notes.[68] After delivery of the initial Colt order in January 1864, however, the state's quartermaster general cancelled the second one. It appeared that Colt, or Schuyler, Hartley and Graham, was trying to dispose of guns that had failed federal inspection by selling them off to unsuspecting customers. Unfortunately for them, New Jersey had a very sharp quartermaster general in Lewis Perrine, who saw to it that each weapon was taken apart and carefully inspected by "a competent person" at the state arsenal in Trenton. Perrine reported that "the inspector rejected a great number of parts." He added that he had "allowed the contractors in every instance to replace the parts rejected for defects with perfect parts." He did not provide details on why the second Colt contract was cancelled, although one would assume that there was a lack of "perfect parts" to replace the inferior ones.[69]

None of the other contracts, for standard Springfield pattern Model 1861 rifle muskets, to J. T. Hodge and A. M. Burton of the Trenton Locomotive and Machine Co. in Trenton, or Middletown Manufacturing of Connecticut, were cancelled, so it is safe to assume that those contractors either supplied satisfactory arms or had a ready supply of functional parts.[70]

## THE WAR WINDS DOWN

Three more regiments, the 38th, 39th, and 40th New Jersey Infantry, were raised for one year's service between July 1864 and March 1865. Bounties for recruits were higher than ever, with Newark adding $100 on top of Essex

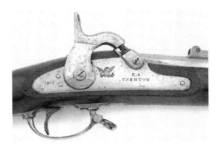

New Jersey contributed to the industrial war effort in many ways, including this Model 1861 rifle-musket, manufactured in Trenton. Trenton rifle muskets were issued to the Union army as well as the New Jersey Rifle Corps, a state based force.

County's $500 payment. These bounties drew a number of out of state residents to the ranks. A survey of two companies of the 40th revealed that more than half the enlisted men were born out of state. The 40th also had a fifty percent desertion rate. Overall, these regiments, commanded by veteran officers, did a reasonably good job in the Petersburg and Bermuda Hundred trenches in the last six months of the war. The 39th actually distinguished itself in an attack on Fort Mahone on April 2, 1865.[71]

The rest of the Union Army on the Petersburg lines attacked on April 2, 1865, as well, breaking through in a number of places, with the tried and true First and Second Brigades cracking the Confederate lines and pursuing the retreating enemy. In the days ahead, the 1st New Jersey Cavalry continually attacked the Confederate rear guard, and regimental commander colonel Hugh Janeway was killed in a wild charge on the enemy. At Sailor's Creek, during what was later referred to as "the grandest cavalry charge of the war," during which several thousand Rebels, including General Richard

E. Ewell, were captured, four Jersey cavalrymen were awarded the Medal of Honor. On April 9, 1865, General Robert E. Lee surrendered his army at Appomattox, Virginia, ending the war for the Jerseymen of the Army of the Potomac.[72]

In the spring of 1865 the 34th New Jersey ended its rear area security duties in Tennessee and moved south to New Orleans, where it joined the XVI Corps and moved on to the siege of Mobile, Alabama. The siege was brief. On April 5, the regiment engaged in a successful attack on Fort Blakely, and Mobile surrendered shortly afterward. Colonel William H. Lawrence of the 34th reported his regiment's losses as "2 killed, 1 wounded and 1 missing . . . Blakely having been gloriously captured."[73]

When Spring came north Sherman came with it, accompanied by erratic New Jersey cavalry general Judson Kilpatrick, who had to flee a Rebel raid with his girlfriend in their underwear, in command of his cavalry. Sherman's army, including the three regiments of New Jersey infantrymen, slogged through South and North Carolina, finally cornering General Joseph E. Johnston's ragged remains of an army at Bentonville.

The 13th New Jersey was the only Garden State regiment in the firing line on March 20, 1865, and ended what was probably the last Confederate charge of the war in a blaze of musketry. The Jerseymen captured a number of prisoners from the defeated Confederates, including Hiram S. Williams, a Montclair, New Jersey, carriage maker who had been working in Georgia when the war broke out and was drafted into the Confederate army. Williams was delighted to surrender to his fellow New Jerseyans. Sherman continued the pursuit, and Johnston surrendered his army on April 26, 1865.[74]

The 13th pushed on, meeting their fellow New Jerseyans of the 9th New Jersey, who had pushed inland from the coast, at Goldsborough, and then advanced to Raleigh, where the regiment camped on the grounds of the North Carolina Lunatic Asylum. Private Samuel Toombs heard one of the inmates shouting from a window that he was "perfectly sane and unlawfully imprisoned." The man, who was from New York but had moved to North Carolina shortly before the war began, claimed that he was committed to the asylum when he refused to join the Confederate army. He was examined by army doctors and released to march north with a New York regiment.[75]

It was all over but the parading—and there were victory parades in Washington by both the Army of the Potomac and Sherman's army, although the celebrations were diminished by the assassination of President Lincoln. The war over, New Jerseyans began to be discharged and sent home, all save the men of the 34th, who did not get home for another year, and the Jerseymen in the USCT units, who were sent to Texas on occupation duty, and did not return home until October.

## NEW JERSEY WOMEN IN THE CIVIL WAR

Men were not the only New Jerseyans who contributed to a Union victory. Many of the state's women served as nurses, both at the front and at hospitals established in Newark and Beverly. They wore no uniform, just subdued civilian dresses, usually with an apron. Most notable was Cornelia Hancock, a young Quaker woman from Hancock's Bridge, Salem County, who went to work following the Battle of Gettysburg in July 1863. Hancock, who had friends serving in the

"Welcome Home." Citizens in Trenton greeted returning soldiers in 1865.

12th New Jersey Infantry, closely followed the Army of the Potomac's Second Army Corps in the bloody Virginia Overland Campaign of 1864, and worked in the large depot hospital established at City Point, Virginia, during the long siege of Petersburg. After the war she taught freed slaves to read and write and went on to be one of the first social workers in Philadelphia.[76]

Clara Barton, who brought medical supplies and food to wounded soldiers at Antietam and Fredericksburg and founded the "Missing Soldiers Office" after the war to trace men missing in action, certainly qualifies as an honorary Jerseywoman, as she taught at, and then administered, a highly regarded public school in Bordentown before leaving for Washington.[77]

Somerville's Arabella Wharton Griffith married Francis Barlow of New York in April 1861. Barlow rose to be a general in the Union army and was seriously wounded at Antietam and Gettysburg. On both occasions, Arabella went to the battlefields and brought her husband back to Somerville, where she nursed

him back to health. She continued working as a nurse until she fell ill with typhus while nursing soldiers at Petersburg in 1864. She died of the disease in July 1864 and is buried in Somerville.[78]

Georgiana Willets of Jersey City began her nursing career in May 1864, during the Battle of Spotsylvania, at the II Army Corps hospital, and helped transfer 800 wounded men back to Washington. She returned to the front to manage several wards of a hospital at City Point, Virginia, during the Petersburg Campaign. After returning home in the fall of 1864, Willets returned to Washington, where she worked as a teacher and a nurse at Camp Barker, providing shelter, medical services, and educational opportunities for freed slaves.[79]

Women in the arts made their contributions as well. Poet Ellen Clementine Howarth of Trenton penned "My Jersey Blue," a tribute to the state's soldiers, and nationally known artist Lilly Martin Spencer of Newark produced several paintings, most notably "War News at Home," in support of the war effort. There were many other, less famous,

Left: The 12th New Jersey monument was the first New Jersey monument erected at Gettysburg. It bears the words "buck and ball," commemorating the ammunition used in the regiment's .69 caliber smoothbore muskets. Right: Veterans of the 14th New Jersey Infantry gathered in 1907 to dedicate a monument to their regiment and its valorous stand at Monocacy, Maryland, on July 9, 1864, the "battle that saved Washington."

New Jersey women who supported the troops in the field, directly and indirectly, as nurses or workers for the United States Sanitary Commission, a private organization dedicated to assisting soldiers.[80]

## NEW JERSEY'S CONTRIBUTION TO THE CIVIL WAR

New Jersey industry, initially the subject of fearful predictions of people like Rodman Price that the elimination of Southern markets would cause a total crash of manufacturing in the state, actually boomed during the war, as the growing importance of New Jersey, located between two of the largest cities in the country and with an excellent railroad and canal infrastructure, made it a source of readily transportable military goods. New Jersey produced rifle-muskets, revolvers, swords, uniforms, cartridge boxes, harness and other leather products, railroad steam engines, and ships for state and federal military needs, as well as serving a growing consumer market.[81]

By the end of the Civil War New Jersey had raised thirty-seven regiments of infantry, three of cavalry, and five batteries of artillery. The state claimed that 88,500 Jerseyans served in New Jersey's name during the war, although considering administrative errors and reenlistments, the actual number seems to be closer to 73,000. Included in the total were the more than 3,000 African American Jerseymen who served in United States Colored Troops regiments and in the United States Navy. Almost 6,000 New Jerseyans died in combat or from disease during the conflict. Jerseymen also served in the regular US Army, Navy, and Marine Corps as well as in the regiments of neighboring Pennsylvania and New York. Those men were a diverse lot, representing a state in the process of change from a rural, parochial past into an industrial, cosmopolitan future. Their motives for going to war were varied and many—patriotism, anger at the firing on Fort Sumter, a desire to abolish slavery, the excitement and change of going to war, or the fact that they were unemployed and soldiering was a job. No matter what brought them to the war, once there they did their job, and they did it well.

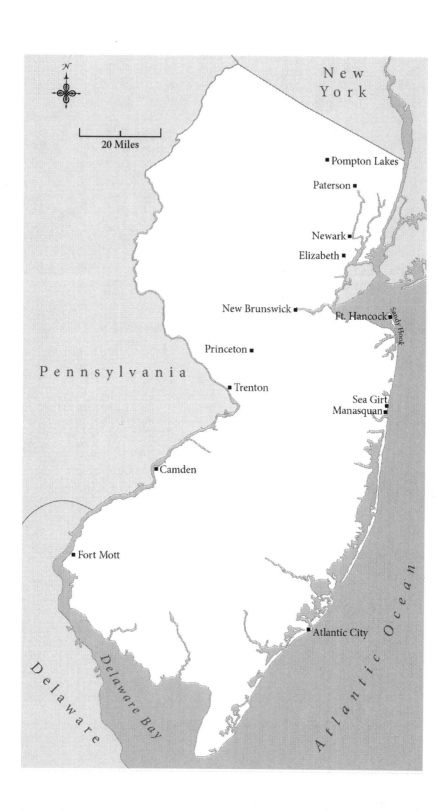

N e w
York

20 Miles

■ Pompton Lakes

Paterson ■

Newark ■
Elizabeth ■

New Brunswick ■          ■ Ft. Hancock    Sandy Hook

Princeton ■

P e n n s y l v a n i a

■ Trenton

Sea Girt
Manasquan ■

■ Camden

■ Fort Mott

■ Atlantic City

A t l a n t i c   O c e a n

D e l a w a r e   B a y

D e l a w a r e

# 8. New Jersey's Military, 1866–1914

In the aftermath of the Civil War, New Jersey adjutant general Robert Stockton reported to Governor Marcus Ward that the end of the conflict had "materially reduced the labors of this office," and that, compared with recent years, 1866 had "not proved eventful," and so he had reduced his staff and no longer collected the additional pay he received for wartime service. Most of the tasks of the adjutant general's office that year amounted to clerical housekeeping, including making sure that the last of the state's soldiers, including the men of the 34th New Jersey Infantry, home from occupation duty in Alabama, were formally mustered out of service. The adjutant general also issued state certificates of service to discharged veterans and facilitated the transfer of more men from the regular militia into the New Jersey Rifle Corps before leaving office early in 1867.[1]

Ward, a Republican and a Newark businessman and philanthropist, owed his election to his well-earned reputation as "the soldier's friend" during the war. Soldiers who encountered problems, including support for their families, wrote directly to Ward, who assisted them. He also oversaw the establishment of a military hospital in Newark for the recuperation of wounded and ill New Jersey soldiers, which was named Ward General Hospital in his honor. At the close of the war the hospital was converted to a "Soldiers' Home" for disabled veterans, establishing a precedent in the state which endures to the present day. In the postwar years the Soldiers' Home was moved to Kearny and then to Menlo Park. There are presently several such institutions run by the New Jersey Department of Military and Veterans' Affairs. The state also established a Soldiers Children's Home in Trenton to care for war orphans in the immediate post-Civil War era.[2]

On April 12, 1867, Governor Ward commissioned twenty-nine-year-old Civil War veteran William Scudder Stryker a brigadier general and appointed him as New Jersey's adjutant general. The Trenton-born Stryker had graduated from Princeton in 1858 and, in April 1861, enlisted as a private in A Company, New Jersey National Guard Infantry, a militia organization called up by Governor Charles Olden to protect the state arsenal. He was mustered out

Marcus Ward (1812–1884), the twenty-first governor of New Jersey.

William Stryker, the adjutant general of New Jersey from 1867 to 1900, in a photo taken in the 1890s.

after three months and in the summer of 1862 was appointed a major by Governor Joel Parker and assigned as disbursing and quartermaster officer at Freehold's Camp Vredenburgh, where he helped organize the 14th New Jersey Infantry Regiment.[3]

In February 1863, Stryker was commissioned a major and paymaster of U. S. Volunteers and assigned to Hilton Head, South Carolina. As a member of General Quincy Gillmore's staff, he participated in the siege of Charleston and was later transferred to the Columbus, Ohio, Parole Camp, where he served as senior paymaster until June 30, 1866, when he resigned as a brevet lieutenant colonel, an honorary rank he received for meritorious service.

Stryker held the position of New Jersey adjutant general for the rest of his life, and was brevetted major general during Governor Joel Parker's second term in 1874. His thirty-three years in office under both Republican and Democratic governors made Stryker the longest serving adjutant general in New Jersey history, but he is best known for his work as a historian. Stryker's assidu-

ous attention to detail in compiling lists of Jerseymen who served in the nation's wars resulted in publications that remain standard historical and genealogical references today, and no one can write a complete New Jersey military history without consulting his numerous books and articles, rich with primary source material, on the state's role in the American Revolution. As a member and officer of many American and European historical societies, including a term as president of the New Jersey Historical Society, William Stryker's contributions to New Jersey historiography were enormous.[4]

## NEW JERSEY NATIONAL GUARD

In 1869, General Stryker presided over the overhaul of the Militia and the Rifle Corps and their consolidation into the New Jersey National Guard. The new 4th regiment of the National Guard, for example, resulted from merging a number of companies of the 4th Regiment, New Jersey Rifle Corps and the 2nd Regiment, Hudson Brigade, New Jersey militia, that April.[5]

The post-Civil War New Jersey National Guard was a significant improvement over the state's "shreds and
patches" 1860 militia. There were Civil
War veterans at all levels of command,
organized units on the regimental and
brigade level, annual reviews and inspections, and even a "Competitive Trial of
Skill in Musketry," held at various places
around the state. In 1870 the competi-
tion was held in New Brunswick. It was
literally a "Skill in Musketry" exercise, as
the state's military was still armed with
Civil War era rifle-muskets, even though
the regular army and some other state
militia organizations had moved on to
breech-loading metallic cartridge small
arms. New Jersey, unlike other states, including neighboring New York, had
elected to await official federal issue of
breechloaders, rather than purchase its
own.[6]

Although there was no war on the
horizon, and there would not be for
many years, National Guard units were
occasionally called out for local domestic
duty, including answering the call of the
Camden County sheriff to control a November 8, 1870, election riot at Centre-
ville, where the Guard "restored the
authority of the law" to the sheriff's sat-
isfaction.[7]

Other less than glorious National
Guard assignments included playing the
opposition force for Civil War veteran
battle reenactments. Although there had
been some small local mock battles
staged even while the war was going on,
the first large demonstration, sponsored
by former general Judson Kilpatrick,
who was running for election to Congress, was held on Kilpatrick's property
in Sussex County's Deckertown. Never
one to miss a chance at self-promotion,
Kilpatrick dubbed his show "The First
Reunion." It featured parades, theatrical

A New Jersey National Guardsman of
the 1880s in full dress uniform.

performances, food, gambling, and beer
tents, celebrity appearances by Kilpatrick
and Congressman/General Dan Sickles
and, reportedly, "loose women." The
party was fueled by a trainload of beer
shipped to Deckertown from New York
City, and drew some 40,000 spectators,
4,000 veterans, and a National Guard detachment. As theater, it was a magnifi-
cent event, but Kilpatrick did not get to
Congress.[8]

In September 1883, the New Jersey
chapter of the Grand Army of the Re-

public veterans' organization invited the 4th and 6th New Jersey National Guard Regiments to attend its Fourth Annual Encampment at Princeton Junction. The encampment involved meetings, speeches, drills—and drinking. The event was capped off by a battle reenactment with the veterans versus the National Guard. The "battle" between 250 veterans and a like number of guardsmen, staged before over 4,000 spectators, took place on the last day of the encampment. To the horror of the local press, the mock combat resulted in a number of casualties, with thirteen men considered seriously wounded, three of whom needed additional care in the weeks afterward.[9]

Although it was a better organized force than the old militia, the National Guard's training schedule did not feature tactical field exercises, save the occasional mock combat with inebriated veterans. In 1875, for example, when the force was composed of "sixty–five companies of Infantry, two companies of Cavalry and two batteries of Artillery," organized into several regiments and two brigades, the only combined training exercises were a parade and review in Newark for the First Brigade and a parade and review in Beverly for the Second Brigade. Adjutant General Stryker was concerned that the Guardsmen had no permanent practice range to shoot their newly issued Springfield breech loading .45-70 caliber rifles the state had finally received from the federal government. He reported that "it would be of great advantage . . . if some plan could be devised, whereby all the force could have some regular season and a suitable place to gain a more perfect use of the weapon." It would be a decade before this problem was resolved.[10]

Beginning in March 1878, National Guardsmen had occasional access to the range of the New Jersey Rifle Association at Brinton, near Elizabeth, for marksmanship training, which evidently proved effective for at least some shooters, as a New Jersey team won a prize at the interstate rifle match at Creedmoor rifle range on Long Island in the fall of 1878.[11]

Marksmanship, following national trends, continued to be stressed through the next two decades, and in 1879 the state arsenal created special reduced power cartridges for the .45-70 caliber rifles so they could be used for practice on limited distance indoor ranges in armories around the state. National Guardsmen continued to shoot full power cartridges at the Brinton range of the New Jersey State Rifle Association near Elizabeth and also at the Stockton range outside Camden and at Creedmoor.[12]

Routine bureaucratic tasks increased for the adjutant general's office as the years passed. Stryker noted that he was receiving requests for "searches of records" for veterans who had apparently lost their initial discharges and other proof of service and were beginning to apply for pensions. Stryker was also completing his two-volume record of the Civil War service of New Jerseyans, in state units as well as the United States Colored Troops, for publication. The indexed result, published in 1876, is probably the best such printed record of a state's servicemen of the era.

In the post-Civil War years, New Jersey African American men, some no doubt veterans, became actively involved as soldiers in the peacetime military for the first time in the state's history. The Adjutant General's report for 1872 notes that the legislature authorized "companies of colored infantry" to serve in the National Guard. The number of African American companies was legislatively restricted to no more than ten, and the companies were consolidated into the 8th Regiment, National Guard of New Jersey. The 8th was an all-black unit, which, like the wartime USCT, was commanded by white officers. During its existence the 8th mustered a maximum of nine companies. A regimental headquarters and "field and staff" detachment was located in Camden, along with Companies C, D, E, and I. Company A was stationed in Elizabeth, Company B in Trenton, Company F in New Brunswick, Company G in Jersey City, and Company H in Newark. The 8th Regiment was not attached to either of the two National Guard Brigades composed of white soldiers, and declining enrollments led to the unit's disbandment in 1877.[13]

Stryker continued his work to record the service of Jerseymen in all the country's conflicts to date as well as paying out pensions to surviving War of 1812 veterans and making preparations for the forthcoming United States Centennial Commemoration, in which selected units would participate in parades in Philadelphia in 1876, as well as other commemorations. In 1881 a handpicked New Jersey detachment attended the 100th anniversary ceremonies of the battle of Yorktown, Virginia, and won a trophy for "presenting the best military appearance during the entire encampment." At the end of 1876, the New Jersey National Guard mustered a strength of 3,862 officers and men. Throughout the post-Civil War era, yearly strength totals were similar, but varied somewhat as companies that did not meet the strength requirements were occasionally disbanded or consolidated with other units.[14]

In July 1877, as the nation remained mired in the depression produced by the Panic of 1873, layoffs and wage cuts affected more and more workers, and a railroad strike that began in West Virginia spread across the country. National Guard troops in West Virginia refused to fire on the strikers, while Maryland Guardsmen engaged in pitched battles with them in Baltimore. Pennsylvania's state military killed more than forty demonstrators in Pittsburgh, and federal troops were sent in to restore order. The conflict spread to the border of New Jersey, and Governor Joseph D. Bedle called up the National Guard in anticipation of violence, but none materialized, and he and other state political leaders did not view the Guard as being a strikebreaking organization. Although there were a few minor disturbances, most New Jersey railroad workmen were apparently content with having their grievances heard by management and the public. The fact that the legislature had passed laws criminalizing railroad strikes may also have had an effect.[15]

Annual inspections of National Guard units were conducted throughout the post-Civil War era, with mixed results. Some companies, and even regiments, were found to be lacking basic records and failed to meet expectations in other areas. Artillery Battery A, located in Hoboken, was the sole remaining artillery unit in the New Jersey Guard after Battery B was replaced by Camden's Gatling Gun Company A in 1878. In an 1880 inspection the battery displayed, according to inspecting officer Lieutenant Colonel G. E. P. Howard, "a lack of proper discipline among both officers and enlisted men." The unit was subsequently disbanded and a new Gatling gun battery was created in Elizabeth. While inspecting officers praised the

Gatling Gun Company B in the Camden armory.

record keeping and bearing of many units, one infantry company inspected in 1880 "seemed to know but little about the manual of arms or company movements." Many units were still equipped with obsolete Civil War era cartridge boxes, with tin inserts designed for use with packets of shorter rifle-musket paper cartridges, and the inspector declared they were "unfit for the present fixed ammunition in general use." To correct this problem, New Jersey acquired McKeever cartridge boxes from the federal government. The state had brass "NJ" plates made and shipped them to a federal arsenal to be affixed to the new boxes, which were specifically made for the .45-70 cartridge.

The new Gatling gun battery in Elizabeth, commanded by Civil War Medal of Honor recipient J. Madison Drake, quickly became a headache to state officials. Drake, a genuine war hero who mustered out of the 9th New Jersey Infantry as a first lieutenant in 1865, was also active in the postwar New Jersey National Guard. He was elected colonel of the 3rd Regiment, and served for five

years before resigning after convincing the state legislature to make him a brevet (honorary) brigadier general. When Drake, an influential newspaperman and author in civilian life, returned to the Guard as a captain commanding the Elizabeth company, he wore his brevet rank star and preferred being addressed as "general." The company, which Captain/General Drake ran without regard for state or federal regulations, served as a home for his nationally known "Veteran Zouaves" drill team and marching society, much to the dismay of senior National Guard officials. The unit was finally ejected from the National Guard in 1892 for consisting of overage and overweight soldiers and failure to wear regulation uniforms—Drake would only allow Civil War veterans to join the company and they wore the Zouave uniform in service, while every other unit in the New Jersey National Guard wore the standard uniform. A new Gatling gun company was created in East Orange to replace Drake's Zouaves.[17]

After leaving the National Guard, the Veteran Zouaves continued to tour the

James Madison Drake's Veteran Zouaves returned to Sea Girt after being forced out of the National Guard. This photo, with Drake on the extreme left, dates from 1908.

country for years afterward. They also appeared at a GAR veterans' organization conventions and encampments, including one at Sea Girt in 1908. James Madison Drake, one of nineteenth century New Jersey's most colorful characters, died at his home in Elizabeth on November 28, 1913, and was buried in Evergreen Cemetery in Hillside.[18]

With the artillery batteries gone, in 1885 the legislature provided funding for the formation of a "gun detachment" in each regiment and separate battalion of infantry. Each detachment consisted of one first lieutenant (assigned to the regimental staff), one sergeant, one corporal, and twelve privates. Selected enlisted men were detached from infantry companies and assigned to the gun detachment by regimental order. Each detachment was armed with one small 3.2-inch "hand drawn" naval boat howitzer and the men were issued .45 caliber Colt revolvers and sabers.[19]

By the time the new artillery pieces were issued, General Stryker's long-term wish for a permanent state-owned training site with a rifle range had been ful-

filled. In his annual report for 1882, Stryker reinforced his earlier requests by commenting that "No better plan can now be devised than for the State to select some permanent summer camping ground for her troops," and urged legislative action on the subject.[20]

## CAMP ABBETT AND SEA GIRT

The search to meet Stryker's requirements led to coastal southern Monmouth County, centrally located and readily accessible by rail from north and south, yet still relatively undeveloped. The New Jersey National Guard first came "down the shore" in August 1884, to hold a five-day summer encampment at Manasquan at a leased site named "Camp Abbett" in honor of then Governor Leon Abbett, a practice that set a precedent for naming future camps after sitting governors. The encampment was commanded by Irish-born Brevet Major General William J. Sewell, a Civil War hero, Pennsylvania Railroad executive, Republican Party boss of Camden, and United States senator. Sewell strongly supported buying land for a permanent camp in the area, which, he believed, would "keep our National Guard up to that state of efficiency that we can point to it with pride."[21]

The adjutant general chose a section of Sea Girt, a Monmouth County shore town slightly north of the 1884 campsite, to lease for National Guard use in the summer of 1885. The New Jersey Assembly subsequently authorized R. S. Jenkins of Camden and W. T. Hoffman of Jersey City to act as state agents to purchase 120 acres in Sea Girt, which the legislators proposed to condemn for government use at a compensation rate of $425 an acre. The ground, formerly owned by Commodore Robert Stockton and part of a parcel developers had acquired at an 1868 sheriff's sale, was intended to serve a dual purpose—as a summer training camp for the National Guard and as an encampment site for the New Jersey posts of the Grand Army of the Republic. Governor Abbett was convinced that "the amount saved by the State in using the camp for a rifle range will in ten years be sufficient to pay for the land, improve the same and erect necessary buildings." Despite the governor's enthusiasm, the purchase bill faced rougher sledding in the state senate, where a number of senators opposed the condemnation proceedings, postponing state acquisition of the property.

Leon Abbett, who had personally approved the Sea Girt site, was one of New Jersey's first "hands on" chief executives, and perhaps the greatest of its nineteenth century governors. A Jersey City Democrat who helped integrate immigrants into the political system, Abbett advocated fair taxation of railroads and promoted early civil rights legislation. After consultation on acquisition of the Sea Girt property with the "principal officers of the National Guard interested in the

Governor Abbett (seated, second from left), who approved the original purchase of the Sea Girt land, with his military staff at the camp in 1890.

subject," General Stryker agreed, that "it would be difficult . . . to find another site as suitable, combining the natural advantages for a Brigade or even Division camp, with ample parade ground, singularly adequate facilities for rifle range purposes and the advantages of safe surf bathing under proper restrictions."[23]

New Jersey continued to lease the land for the Sea Girt encampment from the Sea Girt Land Improvement Company for an annual rental fee of $3,000 until purchase legislation could be passed. Although locals complained of Guardsmen prone to "merrymaking," at nearby resorts when off duty, the state would have its way, as Abbett's successor Governor Robert S. Green pushed ahead on the sale, which was concluded during Green's administration for a sum of $51,000, by appointed commissioners James Smith Jr., of Newark and William L. Dayton of Trenton. Following the initial acquisition, the state subsequently added a small parcel in 1907, but there is no formal record of the original sale extant today.[24]

The Manasquan encampment in 1884 was the first time a National Guard annual training camp featured rifle shooting as well as marching.

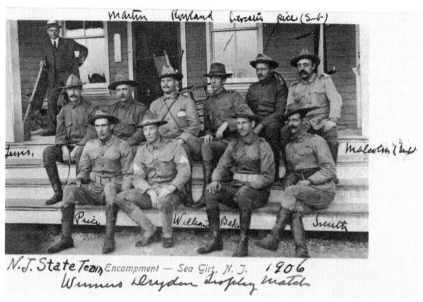

The New Jersey National Guard rifle team in 1906. Sea Girt was a nationally known marksmanship venue, and the Guard was very involved in target shooting.

The Sea Girt site proved adaptable to practice with Gatling guns and the small artillery pieces issued to regimental gun detachments, which fired at targets anchored on rafts 400 to 800 yards offshore. In 1889, travel writer Gustav Kobbe noted that "the State camp, where the N.G.S.N.J. holds its annual field exercises during one week in August, is a beautiful tract of land whose entrance is near the [railroad] station. The glamour and bustle of military life and the ball given at the Beach House [a hotel in town] to the Governor and his staff make the encampment a welcome episode of the summer season."[25]

Over succeeding decades, the rifle range at Sea Girt attained a national and international reputation in an era when target shooting was a popular sport for both soldiers and civilians. Inspector

General of Rifle Practice general Bird W. Spencer contributed lengthy detailed accounts of the state's marksmanship training to the annual adjutant general reports and was also an officer in both the state and national rifle associations as well as a long-time mayor of Passaic. It was said that Sea Girt and its range were Spencer's "passion." When Spencer died in 1931, a special remembrance ceremony was held in his honor on the Sea Girt rifle range.[26]

In the last years of the nineteenth century and the first decade of the twentieth, the New Jersey National Guard began to transition from a military-themed social and political club occasionally called out by the governor in civil disturbances into a more professional force. This trend, part of a national one, was fueled by national guard officers who wanted to gain respect from their regular army counterparts as well as federal officials seeking a reliable organized backup force for the regular army in an era of growing national responsibilities. The first tentative steps in this direction began in the 1890s, with the assignment of regular army officers to advise and train state forces. In 1895, the first of these officers, Lieutenant Melvin W. Rowell of the 10th United States Cavalry, was assigned to the New Jersey National Guard.[27]

## NEW JERSEY NATIONAL GUARD CAVALRY

The presence of cavalry in the New Jersey National Guard had been erratic at best, at least partially due to the expense to the state of maintaining horses. In the last decade of the nineteenth century this situation would change, however. The Essex Troop had its origins in a civilian riding organization created in 1890 to act as a private honor guard for local dignitaries in Essex County. Colonel James E. Fleming, a former Civil War officer who had served in the 11th Pennsylvania Cavalry and was a member of the socially exclusive Essex Club, which gave the unit its name, was the troop's commander. The members either owned their own steeds or rented them, bought their own saddles, and were loaned revolvers and sabers by the state. On May 17, 1893, the Essex Troop joined the New Jersey National Guard as Cavalry Company A.[28]

The troop was decidedly an elite organization, and when it attended its first training session at Sea Girt, a newspaper that described it as "the crack mounted organization from Orange and Newark known as the Essex Troop" also noted that "the regular train on the Long

The first regular army adviser assigned the New Jersey National Guard, Lieutenant Melvin W. Rowell of the 10th US Cavalry.

Branch road had three special coaches attached to it, one containing the men and officers and the others the horses and servants." The National Guard of the 1890s allowed units to design and privately purchase full dress garb beyond the regulations, and the Essex Troopers purchased uniforms based on a British "Hussar" style and custom tailored by Brooks Brothers in New York City. With the addition of the Essex Troop, the cavalry was back in the New Jersey National Guard to stay. A second troop, headquartered at Red Bank, joined the Guard in 1895.[29]

Although the Essex Troop could be viewed as a unit of locally prominent dandies, the New Jersey National Guard as a whole was a relatively socially and economically diverse organization. In 1896 four out of ten of the state's part-time soldiers were factory workers and mechanics and another three were clerks or bookkeepers.[30]

## NEW JERSEY NAVAL MILITIA

The New Jersey Naval Militia was founded in 1894 and, organized into two detachments, the Battalion of the East and the Battalion of the West, began active operations the following year. The organization, activated in many but not all states, was intended to act as a naval reserve to be integrated into regular navy ship crews in time of war. An attempt to cut state spending by disbanding the Naval Militia failed in the New Jersey legislature in 1897, and a contemporary newspaper account of that year flatteringly described the unit as "composed principally of young business and professional men." The active duty navy provided advising officers and training ships to the militia.[31]

## ORDNANCE MATTERS

Along with supporting the National Guard, the state Quartermaster Department also loaned weapons and equipment to private paramilitary organizations like the Essex Troop before it joined the Guard, the Atlantic City Morris Guards, and the Sons of Union Veterans, as well as Grand Army of the Republic veterans' posts throughout the state. These allocations were reflected on the department's annual report.[32]

In addition to state efforts, New Jersey was also the scene of federal military activity in the post-Civil War era. In 1874, Sandy Hook, the location of forts defending New York harbor off and on for many years, became the site of the U.S. Ordnance Department proving grounds, charged with testing the rapidly changing weaponry of the late nineteenth century. Some areas of the proving ground were shifted when Fort Hancock, a modern coastal defense fortification with "disappearing guns," was commissioned in 1895, but the grounds remained active until 1919, when even longer range artillery necessitated a move to Aberdeen, Maryland.

Tests of everything from new small arms ammunition to armor piercing shells took place on a 3,000-yard range at the proving ground, and longer range weapons were fired out into the ocean. Unfortunately, on July 9, 1892, A five-hundred-pound shell fired from the testing range at Sandy Hook accidentally hit the schooner *Henry R. Tilton* and sank it. There were near misses as well, including an incident in 1900 when a shell fired from shore hit the water 150 yards from the liner *City of Birmingham* and then ricocheted over the ship's deck.[33]

With the impending construction of Fort Hancock and other fortifications, including Fort Mott along Delaware Bay in Pennsville, intended to protect New York and Philadelphia, General Stryker requested the army to deliver coast artillery pieces to Sea Girt, not to defend the base, but so National Guardsmen could train on the weapons, because he believed that should the state's National Guard be called to duty in time of war, their most likely deployment would be to coastal forts. The guard actually formed a coast artillery unit in Atlantic City, which had nothing to train on and was eventually disbanded. The guns finally delivered in 1896 were actually obsolete muzzleloaders, two Civil War era Rodman cannons, and several small seacoast mortars. They remained at Sea Girt, mostly as decoration, along the beach for a number of years, until buried

Sandy Hook Proving Ground, circa 1900.

in the sand at some undetermined date. In 1938 a hurricane blew away the sand and revealed the buried guns. They do not appear on a detailed 1948 map of the camp. What happened to them is unknown, although it has been hypothesized that they were scrapped during World War II.[34]

## THE SPANISH-AMERICAN WAR

At the outbreak of the Spanish-American War in 1898, the governor of New Jersey received a request from the federal government to supply three regiments of volunteer infantry for two years' service, as there was no legal way at the time to compel such service. In early May, National Guard regiments reported to the state's training camp at Sea Girt, where they were requested to provide volunteers and organize war-service units. There was no trouble recruiting, for memories of the horrors of the Civil War

were dimming, and guardsmen looked on the war as a great adventure.

The 1st Regiment was assigned to Camp Alger, Virginia, to guard supplies and the 2nd Regiment was sent to Jacksonville and then Pablo Beach, Florida. One battalion of the 3rd Regiment was stationed at Pompton Lakes, New Jersey, to guard the gunpowder factory there, and the other two battalions of the 3rd garrisoned Fort Hancock as part of the New York harbor defenses. With no Spanish fleet on the horizon, the soldiers of the 3rd enjoyed the outdoor life, especially Corporal James Gladden "who, every time he goes fishing, returns with flounders, fluke and sometimes bluefish to burn, as the boys express it." In November, the entire 3rd Regiment moved to Athens, Georgia.[35]

A second call for troops produced a 4th Regiment, which was ordered to Camp Meade, Pennsylvania, and then Greenville, South Carolina. The 4th was

The obsolete coast artillery delivered to Sea Girt in the 1890s was covered with sand until a 1938 hurricane revealed the location by blowing the sand away.

unique in that it contained the paramilitary Atlantic City Morris Guards. No New Jersey regiment ever left the country, and all were discharged by February 1899.

The New Jersey Naval Militia was called to active duty during the Spanish American War and its men were assigned as individuals to the regular navy fleet. Some of the state's sailors served on the blockading squadron off Cuba. Two Paterson African American men serving in the regular army's 10th United States Cavalry, William H. Thompkins and George Wanton, were awarded the Medal of Honor for their courageous actions in rescuing members of a stranded reconnaissance party in Cuba. In 1921, Wanton served as an honorary pallbearer at the burial of the Unknown Soldier.[36]

Although not awarded a medal, New Jerseyan Clara Louise Maas proved to be a real heroine of the Spanish-American War era. Newark-born Maas, an early graduate of the Newark German Hospital School of Nursing, became an army contract nurse during the war. While she was serving in Cuba in 1900, Maas vol-unteered to be bitten by a mosquito in an experiment in the effort to find a cure for yellow fever. She contracted the disease and died as a result. Maas's body was returned to Newark. where she was buried with military honors. In 1952, the Newark German Hospital, which had been renamed Newark Memorial Hospital and then Lutheran Memorial Hospital, was renamed Clara Maas Hospital in her memory.[37]

Overall, National Guard performance in the Spanish-American War varied considerably from regular army standards, and in the wake of the conflict, Secretary of War Elihu Root was determined to reform and modernize the relationship between state and federal military forces, a goal many National Guard officers had been seeking since the 1880s. Root's ideas were codified in the Militia Act of 1903, also known as the "Dick Act" after its chief sponsor, Ohio congressman and National Guard officer Charles Dick. Dick considered the National Guard to be "in the service of the United States" as well as the state, and one commentator on the legislation noted that: "The organized militia is no longer considered by the government a kind of state police force. It is the secondary force of the United States Army for national defense."[38]

## REORGANIZATION: THE RESERVE MILITIA AND THE NATIONAL GUARD

The federal government had supplied firearms to state governments for militia use since the Militia Act of 1792, but the Dick Act and subsequent legislation expanded funding to include other equipment, pay for expenses incurred in annual training and professional education for officers. In return, National Guard units were required to be structured according to regular army organizational standards and meet a federally specified schedule of training days, and those requirements were steadily tightened in the ensuing decade. National Guard units that did not meet minimum strength specifications were to be disbanded, a practice that had been haphazardly followed in the late nineteenth century, and the New Jersey adjutant general complained that the new standards "have tended to greatly retard recruiting." The War Department also extended direct federal control over the reorganized state military organizations, which were now liable to be called directly into service by presidential order for periods of up to nine months of domestic service. Many Guardsmen who had initially supported the law began to change their minds due to what they saw as interference in and unnecessary control of state military affairs and protested many War Department actions, maintaining that the increased aid was not worth the trade-off. J. Madison Drake's Zouave Gatling gunners would not have

William H. Byrne, Jr., 3rd New Jersey Infantry, 1898.

been allowed anywhere near an armory under the new regimen.[39]

The law established two official classes of militia: The reserve militia, which included all able-bodied male citizens between the ages of eighteen and forty-five, making them subject to a potential draft in time of war, although they had no obligation in time of peace, and the organized militia, or National Guard units. This classification system was not uncommon in the states, and New Jersey had paid attention to it in preceding years, estimating the number of men theoretically available for military service in the annual adjutant general's report, but the Dick Act formalized and standardized the practice. In 1908, the law was amended to remove the time restriction of a maximum of nine months of federal service in the United States, specifying that the president could determine the length of service for federalized National Guard troops and deploy them "either within or without the territory of the United States."[40]

Adjutant General Stryker died in Trenton on October 29, 1900, and was buried in Trenton's Riverview Cemetery. Stryker was remembered as "modest and unassuming beyond most men." His accomplishments certainly spoke for him. Stryker and his former assistant and successor Alexander C. Oliphant, an 1881 Naval Academy graduate, spent the turn of the century year working on preserving and protecting records of the states' soldiers' military service back to colonial days and making sure they were stored in fireproof safes. One unusual task was clearing the records of Civil War veterans who, once the war ended, simply went home before their units were formally mustered out and hence were classified as deserters. In the early twentieth century more of these men were applying for pensions, and discovering that their classification as deserters forbid them from collecting.[41]

Newark's elite Essex Troop used a riding academy as an armory until the state built them this new one, between 7th Avenue and Orange Street, in 1908.

## THE PATERSON FIRE

The early twentieth century post-Spanish-American War New Jersey National Guard had missions other than maintaining order during civil disturbances and providing a potential reserve of volunteers for the army in time of war. Shortly after midnight on February 8, 1902, an overheated stove in the trolley "car barns" of the Jersey City, Hoboken and Paterson Railway Company, located on Broadway and Mulberry Streets in Paterson, set the building afire. Exacerbated by winds of up to sixty miles an hour, the fire swept over twenty-six city blocks in the city's business district, destroying 459 structures, including four banks, four churches, department stores, the Paterson Evening News building and city hall, as well as numerous private residences, before it burned out twelve hours later. Miraculously, only two people died in the disaster, which is generally considered to be the worst fire in New Jersey history.[42]

Paterson mayor John Hinchliffe called on the state for assistance. The response was rapid. Adjutant General Oliphant telephoned Governor Franklin Murphy at his home in Newark to tell him he had alerted a battalion of National Guard soldiers to proceed to Paterson. The order was revoked shortly afterward when Hinchliffe advised Murphy that the three companies of the 5th Regiment stationed in the city would be able to handle the situation. Quartermaster General Richard A. Donnelly sent a trainload of "tents, blankets, camp equipments and anything else available which might prove useful" from Trenton to Paterson the following day to provide shelter and aid for those made homeless by the disaster.[43]

The Paterson fire of 1902 was the greatest fire disaster in New Jersey history. The photo shows a New Jersey National Guard soldier on guard duty at the trolley "car barns" where it began.

## GOVERNOR'S COTTAGE AT SEA GIRT

The early twentieth century also brought big changes to the Sea Girt Camp. Teddy Roosevelt's visit to Sea Girt to see his friend Governor Murphy in 1902 graphically demonstrated the fact that camp facilities for entertaining and housing the governor, his entourage, and distinguished guests were severely limited, and the quartermaster general suggested that "a new headquarters house for the accommodation of the governor and staff is urgently recommended." The rambling two story farmhouse used by the governors as a summer residence was clearly inadequate. Something grander for receiving dignitaries was needed, and state officials found it in the New Jersey Exhibit Hall at the 1904 Louisiana Purchase Exposition, popularly known as the "Saint Louis World's Fair." At the end of the Exposition the New Jersey hall,

modeled on the Ford Mansion, General George Washington's Morristown headquarters during the winter of 1779–1780, was disassembled and brought to Sea Girt, where it was reassembled as the new governor's summer quarters in 1906.[44]

Described by the press as "a Colonial cottage, a century and a half old in design," the fifteen room house was actually quite luxurious and modern on the inside, with three bathrooms, electric lighting, and fancy furniture. It immediately inherited the "Little White House" nickname of its humble predecessor, which still stood alongside it. Republican governor Edward C. Stokes, the first summer occupant of the "cottage," moved in on July 7, 1906, for a month's stay, signaling the beginning of a new era for Sea Girt. In succeeding years, the state's governors would stretch their Sea Girt season to an entire summer, full of political and personal entertaining and deal making.

Theodore Roosevelt's appearance at the National Guard Camp proved to be the first of many Sea Girt political celebrity sightings. Over the next three decades a parade of state and national leaders and presidential candidates made Sea Girt, and the governor's "cottage" a must stop on the campaign trail, and for forty years after the Roosevelt visit, the loyal and curious among the general public would flock to the little Monmouth County town by the sea in incredible numbers to see them.

### SEA GIRT RIFLE RANGE

By the early twentieth century the New Jersey National Guard rifle range at Sea Girt was a nationally known target shooting venue, hosting a number of important matches. On September 5, 1906, exhibition shooters Adolph and Eliza-

The governor's new "summer cottage" was the New Jersey exhibit hall at the St. Louis World's Fair of 1904, which was disassembled and brought to Sea Girt by rail and re-erected at the camp, so that the governors could entertain in style.

beth "Plinky" Topperwein, who traveled the country as "The Wonderful Topperweins" performing eye-popping marksmanship tricks, including hitting tossed targets in midair with .22 caliber rifles, visited the Sea Girt range. Plinky took to the firing line with a nine-pound .30 caliber Krag Jorgensen army rifle and became the first woman to complete a military course of fire—dressed in her skirt. While "eyebrows were arched and cigars chewed" in initial consternation at the sight, the male shooters eventually cheered her on, and she was awarded a marksman's medal in the first step in the long march towards military equality for women.[45]

## THE NEW JERSEY NATIONAL GUARD IN THE EARLY TWENTIETH CENTURY

In 1905 the New Jersey National Guard replaced its Gatling Gun batteries with two artillery batteries, which served alongside five regiments of infantry con-

sisting of twelve companies each, two troops of cavalry, and one company-sized "signal and telegraph corps." This force was organized into a two brigade division with a total strength of 4,568 officers and men. Division headquarters was in Jersey City, First Brigade headquarters in Newark, and Second Brigade headquarters in Trenton. The Naval Militia, now classified by the adjutant general as the "Naval Reserve" was divided into two battalions. The first battalion, with a strength of 150 officers and men, well below its authorized strength of 273, was stationed in Hoboken, with a headquarters ship, the USS *Portsmouth*, on the Hudson River. The second battalion, with headquarters on the USS *Huntress* on the Delaware River in Camden, mustered 162 officers and men.[46]

The year 1905 also signaled an effort to honor surviving New Jersey Civil War veterans, with medals authorized for the "First Defenders"—the 90 day militiamen who responded to the call of

1861—as well as others for those who served longer enlistments afterward. In a spirit of reconciliation, the state returned captured Confederate flags to the southern states and invited the North Carolina governor to both the dedication of the 9th New Jersey Infantry's monument at the National Cemetery in New Bern, North Carolina, and to the governor's summer home at the Sea Girt camp. At the dedication of the 9th's monument the state returned the flag of the "Beaufort Plow Boys" captured by the "Jersey Muskrats" in 1862.[47]

On February 27, 1905, Sixty-four-year-old Quartermaster General Richard Donnelly passed away. As a sergeant, Donnelly had been carried wounded off the battlefield of Gaines' Mill in 1862 by Charles Hopkins, who subsequently received the Medal of Honor for his courage. Described by the *New York Times* as "one of the most prominent characters in New Jersey's present generation of old men," Donnelly was the last Civil War veteran on active duty with the state's National Guard, and the last vestiges of an era passed with him.[48]

In the coming decade, prompted by the Dick Act and subsequent increased federal aid, New Jersey's citizen soldiers would continue to evolve from a fraternity-like organization occasionally called on for serious work into a legitimate backup force for the regular army. And then, on June 28, 1914, a Serbian nationalist shot and killed Hapsburg Archduke Franz Ferdinand in Sarajevo, a long way from New Jersey, but the first act in a drama that would eventually draw the state's fighting men into what was the greatest conflict in history.

N
↑
W ⊕ E
S

**20 Miles**

N e w
Y o r k

1: Lyndhurst
2: Kearny

Haskell ■

Camp Merritt ■

Paterson ■

Teaneck ■

Morristown
■

West Orange ■

Orange ■ 1 Hoboken
2

Newark Jersey City
Elizabeth ■
Bayonne ■

Perth Amboy ■
Ft. Hancock ■
Sayreville ■ South
Amboy

Princeton ■

Ft. Monmouth ■

P e n n s y l v a n i a

Trenton ■

Asbury Park ■

Sea Girt ■
Manasquan ■

Burlington ■
Camp/Fort Dix ■

■ Camden

■ Fort Mott

A t l a n t i c   O c e a n

■ Atlantic City

D e l a w a r e

D e l a w a r e   B a y

A t l a n t i c

■ Cape May

# 9. New Jersey in World War I and the Interwar Years, 1914–1940

Woodrow Wilson, the governor of New Jersey, was notified of his selection as the Democratic candidate for president at the Sea Girt National Guard Camp in August 1912, and thousands of his supporters descended on the little town by the sea. Wilson went on to win the presidency, and the Essex Troop, garbed in Brooks Brothers finery, rode in his inauguration parade in March 1913. The future seemed bright.

On September 30, 1914, a little over two months after World War I broke out in Europe, the New Jersey National Guard, infantry, cavalry, artillery, and support services, including the Naval Militia, totaled 5,219 officers and enlisted men, which was about 1,000 men under the Guard's authorized strength. An inspecting officer criticized inadequate property and personnel records, and noted that many enlisted men did not meet Federal government physical standards and that some of the "drill halls lacked facilities for storage, lockers, gun cases, space in which to clean rifles and properly care for Federal property." Despite these failings, and although the Guard was still far from a professional military organization, the descendent of

the old militia was better equipped, trained, and prepared for conflict than it had ever been. New Jersey was one of only four states that funded 75 percent of the expenses of its National Guard. Many, like Arkansas, provided no state funding to their Guardsmen.[1]

Training, conducted for the infantry at Sea Girt, was more thorough than in previous years. It involved rifle target shooting on the post's excellent range and route marches and tactical exercises in the surrounding countryside on property leased for the purpose from local farmers. After use, the land was "restored as much as possible to its original condition by careful policing, burning of litter and garbage and filling of sinks and ditches." Cavalry and signal corps soldiers conducted mounted marches throughout the state and the revived artillery branch received live fire training at Tobyhanna, Pennsylvania. In 1903 the New Jersey National Guard had finally received an issue of the Krag-Jorgensen bolt action repeating rifles that had been the regular army standard since 1892. These guns were replaced in 1905 by Springfield Model 1903 rifles, making the Guard infantry as well armed as the regular army.[2]

In 1909 the Naval Militia had mustered a total of 350 officers and men and two training vessels, the USS *Portsmouth*, located at the Eastern, or First, Battalion headquarters in Hoboken and the USS *Vixen*, stationed with the Western, or Second, Battalion in Camden. The navy transferred the USS *Adams* to New Jersey to serve as a stationary training vessel for the First Battalion's men in 1915 and the Garden State sailors were commended by the navy for their successful effort to put the ship into "cruising condition" during the year.[3]

New Jersey governor Woodrow Wilson, his wife, and three daughters at Sea Girt in August 1912, when he was advised that he had received the Democratic Party's presidential nomination.

At the advent of the conflict in Europe, sympathies divided along domestic lines in New Jersey's large first and second generation immigrant communities. (According to the 1910 census, an estimated 25 percent of the state's population was foreign born.) New Jersey German-Americans were joined by many Irish-Americans, who expressed their opposition to everything British by supporting, at least tacitly, Germany and Austria-Hungary, especially after the failed 1916 Easter rising in Dublin, and many Russian Jews who had fled pogroms were not eager to help the tsar. In an exquisite example of historical irony, on August 12, 1914, as the conflict began to rage across Europe that would bring his deadly invention into its own as a weapon of modern war, New Jersey Irish-American submarine inventor John P. Holland died in Newark. Holland, who had launched his first prototype in the Passaic River at Paterson in 1878 and had sold his perfected design to the U.S. Navy in 1900 after tests in Raritan Bay, would not live to see the havoc it wrought, which would approach the shores of his adopted state.[4]

There was a degree of military reluctance in New Jersey as a whole. In March 1916, a commission established by the state legislature opposed a growing national trend to initiate military training for male high school students, maintaining that it "could have no beneficial effect at this stage of their lives." The commission report went on to declare that "military training and service, if they are necessary, are an obligation of citizenship, not of education." President Wilson successfully ran for reelection in 1916 on the campaign slogan "He kept us out of war."[5]

## MUNITIONS MANUFACTURING IN NEW JERSEY

In the years immediately following 1914, the United States had remained officially neutral. Despite that, the country supported Allied forces fighting the Central Powers through military hardware sales. Major American firearms manufacturing companies, including Winchester and Remington, made rifles for the British, French, and Russians, and other factories churned out ammunition and explosives from rifle cartridges to ar-

Black Tom pier in Jersey City after the July 30, 1916, explosion.

tillery shells and bombs. New Jersey was home to a significant number of those plants, and the Imperial Russian government established an ammunition testing facility in Lakehurst.

New Jersey had been a developing industrial state for many years, but according to one account, "the guns of Europe" were responsible for "the most intense industrialization in its history. The production of high explosives, textiles, steel, and ships rocketed to new heights. The Bureau of Statistics reported that expansion in manufacturing was 400 percent greater in 1916 than in any preceding year . . . The chemical industry in New Jersey sprang up almost overnight. Six factories for the production of aniline, formerly imported from Germany, were set up within the state, the most important at Kearny." Another source states that the state's overall industrial output "increased almost 300 percent between 1914 and 1919." By 1917, New Jersey was the largest ammunition producing state in the country. Unfortunately, all of this expansion also made New Jersey a target.[6]

On July 30, 1916, the "Black Tom" ammunition pier on the Hudson River in Jersey City exploded. The force of the explosion broke windows all over Jersey City and Manhattan and damaged the Statue of Liberty, as well as buildings on the nearby Ellis Island immigration station. Damage in Jersey City alone was estimated at one million dollars (twenty-three million dollars in today's money). Large amounts of ammunition manufactured in the United States were shipped to the allies in Europe through Jersey City and Hoboken, and it was believed German saboteurs had placed bombs on the pier.[7]

On January 11, 1917, the Kingsland ammunition plant in Lyndhurst, owned by the Canadian Car and Foundry Company, exploded. Switchboard operator Theresa "Tessie" McNamara was a heroine that day. She stayed at her post, calling every building on the site and telling the workers to evacuate, even though exploding shells hit the building she was calling from. All 1,700 workers escaped. An investigation into the disaster concluded that it was the result of sabotage.[8]

On the evening of January 12, 1917, 400,000 pounds of smokeless powder exploded at the Du Pont plant at Haskell, in Passaic County. Remarkably, only two employees were reported missing and twelve injured. The effects of the blast resonated for a 150-mile radius in New York and New Jersey. Shocks were reportedly felt as far away as Albany. Initially thought to be another case of sabotage, the Du Pont explosion was later determined to be the result of an accident. Other explosions would rock the state after American entry in the conflict, including a massive detonation on October 4, 1918, when the T. A. Gillespie Shell Loading Plant, located in the Morgan section of Sayreville, exploded, destroying the munitions manufacturing operation and setting off three days of intermittent blasts that destroyed more than 300 buildings and created chaos in Sayreville and South Amboy. The populations of Sayreville, South Amboy, and Perth Amboy were evacuated and over a hundred people are estimated to have perished. The Gillespie explosion was later determined to be an accident.[9]

Although postwar Germany contested the sabotage accusations regarding Black Tom and Kingsland, an international Claims Commission found that country guilty of sabotage in both explosions, and awarded $50 million in damages to claimants. World War II intervened, but in 1953, the West German government, without ever admitting responsibility, agreed to pay the compensation. It was finally paid in 1979.[10]

THE PUNITIVE EXPEDITION IN MEXICO

The first mobilization of National Guard units under the recent federal legislation occurred on June 19, 1916. The govern-

ment ordered Guardsmen across the country, including three infantry regiments, one squadron of cavalry, two batteries of field artillery, one signal corps company, one field hospital, and one ambulance company of the New Jersey National Guard, a total of 4,288 men, to report for duty on the Mexican border in the wake of the crisis caused by Mexican revolutionary leader Pancho Villa's raid into New Mexico. The selected units assembled at the National Guard camp at Sea Girt on June 21, and traveled from there to Douglas, Arizona, for border guard duty, where they remained for the rest of the year. The Jerseymen did not engage in combat and suffered no combat casualties during their tour on the border, but participated in some long grueling marches.[11]

Interestingly, the "elite" Essex Troop employed African Americans in a military role on the border. As was standard for the era, all of the troop's enlisted personnel and officers were white, but some African-American men filled slots normally held by white soldiers in a regular army unit. When the New Jersey cavalry, now a four troop strong squadron, was sent to the Mexican border, the Essex Troop carried a number of African American civilian cooks on its roster, as well as Robert D. Trott. Trott, the "armorer" or chief of maintenance and security at the Roseville Avenue armory in Newark, was reported on the squadron's rolls as a "saddler" for Troop C, and wore a uniform while performing his duties. On the long railroad trip to Arizona, Trott took charge of organizing the troop's "kitchen car," normally a job for a non-commissioned officer.[12]

ENTRY INTO WORLD WAR I

The possibility of entering the war in Europe seems to have created a surge in Na-

The New Jersey National Guard's "Essex Troop" on duty on the Mexican border in Arizona in 1916.

tional Guard enlistments in early 1917, which may have been due to the fact that many believed that in case of war the Guard would only be deployed on domestic duty. The subsequent revelation of the contents of the disconcerting Zimmermann Telegram, in which Germany encouraged Mexico into an alliance against the United States, pushed the country closer to intervening in the conflict, and the German resumption of unrestricted submarine warfare on the open seas proved the final straw. The United States Congress, fulfilling the request of President Wilson, declared war on Germany on April 6, 1917.

Immediately following the American declaration of war, Governor Walter Edge ordered some elements of the New Jersey National Guard mobilized to guard bridges, railroads, and other critical sites and established a state militia to replace the Guardsmen he realized were going to soon be called to national service. Edge also established a "state militia reserve" to assist local law enforcement and act as guards for critical infrastructure, including power plants as well as war industries, and the state began to re-

cruit a new National Guard coast artillery unit.[13]

The National Guard's engineer battalion was detailed, under federal orders, to lay out Camp Dix, a massive new training center in the heart of the New Jersey Pinelands that would boast 1,600 buildings within a year. While the engineers worked at Dix, most of the remaining New Jersey Guardsmen were mobilized at Sea Girt on July 25 and formally inducted into United States service on August 5. The mobilization did not include the coast artillery units created earlier in the year, as they had not passed federal inspection and been formally admitted to the Guard. In order to avoid potential authorization problems for overseas duty in what was interpreted as a vaguely written section of the 1908 law, the federal government decided to classify the National Guardsmen as draftees.[14]

A total of 9,285 New Jersey Guardsmen left the state for Anniston, Alabama, where they were assigned to the 29th Division, organized at Camp McClellan in late August from New Jersey, Delaware, Maryland, and Virginia national guard units. The 29th became known as the

New Jersey National Guardsmen, among them some recent recruits who have not yet been issued uniforms, marching into camp at Sea Girt in August 1917.

"Blue and Gray Division" because it included National Guardsmen from states that had opposed each other during the Civil War. The name inspired the division's distinctive insignia patch, a yin and yang combination featuring blue and gray elements.

Camp Little Silver was established by the army's Signal Corps on the site of a former race track in Monmouth County. The 468-acre tract was leased with an option to buy by the government in May 1917, and the first soldiers arrived the following month. The post, formed on a more permanent basis in September, was renamed Camp Alfred Vail, after an early associate of Samuel F. B. Morse. It was used as a site for training Signal Corps army reservists for deployment overseas and as an officer candidate school location.[15]

Another major New Jersey World War I site was located in Bergen County. Selected in 1915 as a potential location for an embarkation camp in case of war, the area that would become Camp Merritt in 1917 spanned several municipalities. The majority of the soldiers who left America for Europe in World War I, well over a million men, spent several weeks at Camp Merritt before moving by train or down the Hudson River by boat from Alpine to Hoboken, where they boarded ships for France. The camp also served as a demobilization site in 1919, processing more than a million returning soldiers. It closed in 1920 and General John J. Pershing subsequently dedicated a still-standing, now lonely, monument in Cresskill to the memory of the 578 soldiers who died there—mostly from influenza.[16]

Hoboken, the point of departure and return for soldiers from Camp Merritt, is directly across the Hudson River from New York City (and thus considered part of the port of New York for army purposes), and was already a major transoceanic cargo and passenger transportation hub. Following the declaration of war, the federal government seized existing German shipping company piers, warehouses, and vessels in the port city, including the Hamburg-American line

The 4th New Jersey Infantry camp at Camp McClellan, Alabama, where the New Jersey National Guard was consolidated into the 29th Division.

luxury liner *Vaterland*, which was renamed *Leviathan* and turned into a troop transport.

Hoboken's culture was transformed by the advent of war. Long known as "Little Bremen" due to the large number of German immigrants who had settled there since the mid-nineteenth century, the city had continued to attract German immigrants into the twentieth century. Hoboken was distinguished by its German specialty shops, social clubs, and beer halls, reflecting an enduring Teutonic heritage. With the outbreak of war, many recently arrived Germans living in the city were classified as enemy aliens prohibited from residing close to military facilities and were transported to Ellis Island.

A nationwide general climate of mistrust toward German-Americans was deliberately created by George Creel's United States Committee on Public Information, a government agency founded to foment anti-German sentiment among the American people. Creel's propaganda work led to sauer-

kraut being relabeled as "liberty cabbage," dachshunds becoming "liberty pups," and German Valley, New Jersey, being renamed Long Valley, among other absurdities. The Paterson *Evening News* echoed the mass media of the day when it editorialized that anyone with doubts about the war should "obey the law, keep your mouth shut."[17]

Self-appointed patriots were encouraged to report "slackers" or "idlers" who failed to register for the draft or otherwise tried to evade service to the authorities. A New York City doctor turned in one of his patients by sending a letter directly to Governor Edge. The doctor wrote that "there is a young man in West Hoboken [today's Union City] in a family of mine who is able bodied, capable but his family are in medium circumstances or worse and the boy won't work. He's his mother's boy. Go and get him."[18]

Hoboken became a military town, with soldiers patrolling the streets on the lookout for enemy sympathizers among the German-American population. In addition, the army, setting the stage for postwar Prohibition, banned the sale of alcohol to soldiers and demanded that local saloons surrounding the embarkation piers be closed so that soldiers were not tempted to have a parting glass before boarding ships for the war. Federal authorities then upped the ante by insisting that taverns within a half-mile radius of the docks be shut down and that those beyond that distance close by 10:00 p.m. every night. The city fathers resisted these last demands, allowing bars to stay open well past the designated hour. Eventually, a compromise was reached, but by then, many of Hoboken's traditional watering holes had closed due to loss of business.

Agents of the Bureau of Investigation patrolled Hoboken, seeking imbibing soldiers as well as German sympathizers and draft evaders. The agents, and their vigilante assistants, also kept a watch on other military installations and their surrounding towns across the state, including Camps Dix, Merritt, and Alfred Vail. Not satisfied with investigating the drinking habits of soldiers in federal service, agents visited Camp Edge at Sea Girt in August 1917 as a result of "several complaints that the militia now encamped at Sea Girt were obtaining liquors and bringing them on the encampment." Two investigators patrolled the camp, saw no obvious drunks and spoke to several officers, who professed ignorance and suggested that if any alcohol did enter the camp gates, it was obtained in "Manasquan or Belmar."[19]

Local people in Hoboken quickly became aware that young soldiers were interested not only in alcohol but also in female companionship, and a wartime loosening of morals was on many minds. One newspaper reported that due to the rising population of transient military men in the city, six society women had

volunteered to serve without pay patrolling the Hoboken streets at night, intercepting young ladies seeking adventure and escorting them back to their parents. The army did not look upon this situation lightly either and made efforts to round up single women walking the streets after dark and have them charged with prostitution.

## NEW JERSEY SOLDIERS IN THE EUROPEAN WAR

Although most New Jersey National Guard units ended up in the 29th Division, the ambulance company from Red Bank was assigned to the 42nd "Rainbow" Division as the 165th Ambulance Company. Another Jerseyman in the 42nd was Joyce Kilmer, the New Brunswick poet, who crossed the Hudson to enlist in the famed Irish-American 69th New York National Guard Regiment, which was later federally redesignated the 165th U. S. Infantry. The divisional insignia patch was a rainbow, symbolizing that its table of organization included National Guard units from across the country. The Naval Militia Brigade, now some 401 men from Newark, Jersey City, and Camden, was ordered to the U. S. Navy Yard in Philadelphia and absorbed by the navy as individuals.[20]

At Camp McClellan, the New Jersey Guard units gained new federal designations. For example, the former 3rd and 5th New Jersey Infantry Regiments were merged to form the new 114th U.S. Infantry Regiment, while other state units were combined to create the 113th U. S. Infantry Regiment. Both regiments and other New Jersey outfits were assigned to the 29th Division's 57th Infantry Brigade. Jerseymen were also transferred to the brigade's machine gun companies and

A group of soldiers from Captain William Reddan's B Company of the 114th Infantry, most of whom became casualties.

the state's cavalry troops were reassigned to military police and artillery duties.[21]

The consolidation of units was not appreciated by many Guardsmen, and it rankled them even more than two decades afterward, when one commented that: "Apparently pride in organization or esprit was not greatly valued or appreciated, or else was destroyed ruthlessly. In no division were there more famous old commands than in the 29th. These were merged and redesignated; personnel were transferred until no semblance of the old units remained."[22]

In June and July 1918, the 29th Division sailed for France out of Newport News, Virginia. After spending time training in relatively quiet areas of the western front, the division moved to a "Defensive Sector" in Alsace for more advanced training under enemy fire and then, in September, fought alongside the French 18th Division in the Meuse-Argonne offensive. Beginning on October

8, the division engaged in twenty-one straight days of combat, advanced over four miles, captured 2,500 prisoners, and lost one-third of its strength. It was relieved by the 79th Division on October 30.[23]

The story of Captain William J. Reddan, B Company, 114th Infantry, typifies the war time experience of the New Jersey National Guardsmen in the 29th Division. Reddan was born in England in 1883 of Irish parents who immigrated to the United States in 1894 and settled in New Jersey. In 1904 he joined the New Jersey National Guard as a private and became a naturalized American citizen in 1906. Reddan rose through the ranks to become a captain by 1914. In June 1916, Reddan's Company H of the 5th New Jersey Infantry Regiment, based in Orange, was mobilized, along with other New Jersey National Guard units, for duty in Arizona along the Mexican border. The men of the 5th returned home in November, but were activated again by

Governor Edge on March 25, 1917, as war with Germany became imminent, and deployed to guard bridges, railroads, and other critical sites in the state until transferred to Camp McClellan in early September, where Company H was consolidated with Montclair's Company K of the 5th to create Company B of the 114th Infantry Regiment in the 29th Division.[24]

Reddan was in command of Company B on October 12, 1918, when the unit was ordered to make a suicidal assault on a German position at Bois D'Ormont, France, where he was wounded but survived. Only thirteen men out of Reddan's company came out of the fight unscathed in the most savage battle New Jersey soldiers had been involved in since the First New Jersey Brigade stormed the Confederate line at Spotsylvania in 1864. The experience scarred Reddan forever, mentally and physically, and in 1936 he wrote and self-published a book titled *Other Men's Lives*, in which he described his service in the war and the battle. Reddan assigned blame for his company's horrendous casualties on the higher American command, which he believed was oblivious to the strength of the German position, something the French unit on his flank had realized and halted. After the battle a French officer, while praising the Jerseymen's courage, pointed to his head, and commented that they also must be "*beaucoup de malade ici*"—"very sick here!"[25]

Reddan rejoined the National Guard after the war, and was awarded the New Jersey Distinguished Service Medal in 1927 and the Silver Star in 1933 to accompany his Purple Heart, retiring as a major. His four sons fought in World War II. William J. Reddan died of a heart attack on the beach at Manasquan on July 7, 1944, and was buried in Immacu-

Captain William Reddan of the 114th Infantry in France in 1918.

late Conception Cemetery in Montclair.[26]

Following the end of hostilities on November 11, the 29th Division remained in France until receiving orders to return home on April 6, 1919. The division sailed for the United States between May 6 and 12. Separate units arrived in Newport News, Virginia, and Hoboken between May 14 and 25 and assembled at Fort Dix to be mustered out of service.[27]

Many New Jerseyans, draftees and volunteers from civilian life, served in other units during the war, particularly the 78th Division, organized at Camp Dix with draftees primarily from New York, Pennsylvania, and New Jersey in the summer of 1917. Two of the division's infantry regiments and one of its artillery regiments were primarily composed of Jerseymen.

The First Battalion of the 78th's 311th Infantry Regiment had men from Union,

NEW JERSEY IN WORLD WAR I AND THE INTERWAR YEARS, 1914–1940 ★ 187

Monmouth, and Ocean counties, Elizabeth, and Perth Amboy. The regiment's Second Battalion soldiers came from Hunterdon, Middlesex, Mercer, and Somerset counties and Trenton, and the Third Battalion came from Burlington, Gloucester, Camden, Atlantic, Cumberland, and Cape May counties and Camden and Atlantic cities.[28]

The 312th Infantry Regiment's First Battalion drew its men from Newark, the Second Battalion, from Jersey City and Bayonne, and the Third Battalion from Essex and Hudson counties, Orange, East Orange, Hoboken, and West Hoboken.[29]

The 308th Field Artillery's First Battalion was drafted from Bergen County, Passaic, and Paterson and its Second Battalion from Warren, Sussex, Passaic, and Morris counties.[30]

One unusual draftee who reported to Camp Dix for service with the 78th was thirty-year-old Kingdon Gould, scion of the wealthy Gould family, who resided at the family's Lakewood estate, Georgian Court. Although entitled to an exemption due to his recent marriage, Gould decided to waive it and entered service as a private in the 78th Division. Following a period as an enlisted man, he was given a direct promotion to first lieutenant in the Intelligence Corps, as he "could speak five languages and read and write in seven." Gould served with the division in France and was under fire as a "division observer" in the Battle of the Argonne Forest.[31]

The 78th Division left for France in May and June 1918 and was heavily engaged, as the "point of the wedge" in the Meuse-Argonne and St. Mihiel offensives later that year, losing 1,169 men killed and 5,975 wounded in action. Today the 78th Division is an Army Reserve training unit headquartered in New Jersey.

When rich guys went to war. Draftee George Gould of Lakewood, New Jersey.

An estimated 130,000 to 150,000 New Jerseyans served in all branches of the armed forces in World War I, and 3,836 died in combat or from accidents and disease, particularly influenza. This total included soldiers who were drafted into or voluntarily joined units other than the 29th or 78th Divisions, including the New York National Guard's 165th Infantry Regiment and the African-American 15th New York National Guard (later the 369th Infantry Regiment) known as the "men of bronze." Fifty Newark men crossed over the Hudson to enlist in the Fifteenth.[32]

One African American Jerseyman in the 369th, Trenton-born Needham Roberts, was manning an outpost with Sergeant Henry Johnson in the early hours of May 14, 1918, when a German patrol assaulted the position. Roberts told Johnson to run to the rear and sound the alarm. He began to run, but decided to not abandon his comrade and returned, only to be wounded. Although both men were wounded, they continued to fight, and Johnson, shot twenty-one times, fought off the Germans with his rifle, knife, and fists, killing a number of them. They both survived and, since the 369th—like most African-American units—had been assigned to the French army, received the *Croix de Guerre*.

New Jerseyans also served in the navy and Marine Corps. Philadelphia-born Reynold Thomas joined the Marines in Atlantic City, went through basic training at Parris Island and arrived in France in April 1918. He was assigned to the 55th Company, 2d Battalion, 5th Marine Regiment. His unit fought in the bloody battles of Belleau Woods in June and at Soissons in July, suffering heavy casualties.

78th division men in France in 1918.

Fortunately for Thomas, he escaped physically unharmed, although he showed signs of PTSD for years afterward. He returned to New Jersey after his discharge and after working at various jobs and locations around the country, married in 1931 and settled in Harvey Cedars, New Jersey, where he started a dredging company and was elected mayor in the 1940s. He remained mayor of Harvey Cedars until 1983, when he died in office.[33]

There were home front casualties as well. The "Radium Girls" were women who painted luminous dials on watches for the military at the United States Radium Corporation's factory in Orange, New Jersey. The work was delicate, and workers were advised by management to lick their brushes to create a fine point and so speed up production. On breaks, some painted their nails with the supposedly harmless luminous substance for entertainment.

As the years went by, the watch face painters developed illnesses, including anemia, brittle bones, and "radium jaw," a grotesque deterioration of the jawbone. In 1925, some concluded that their condition was due to their work with radium, and hired a lawyer, who filed a complaint against the company in 1927. The case moved slowly, but got nationwide headlines and was arbitrated out of court. Five women received $10,000 cash, payment of all medical bills, and a $600 a month annuity for the rest of their lives. The last one died in the mid-1930s.

Although the Armistice was signed on November 11, ending formal fighting, most Jerseymen remained in France until returning to the state in the spring and summer of 1919. On their return the New Jersey-based units were welcomed home by the governor or his representative, and ceremonies and parades were also held in the units' hometowns, where possible. The state subsequently allocated funding to pay a bonus of $10 a month for each month served to the state's veterans, and ordered bronze Victory Medals for every soldier or sailor as well.[34]

### SUBMARINE WARFARE

With the notable exception of the Confederate commerce raider CSS *Tallahassee*, which captured and burned four merchant ships, the *A. Richards, Carrie Estelle, William Bell*, and *Sarah A. Boyce* off Sandy Hook on August 11, 1864, World War I brought serious hostilities to the New Jersey home front for the first time since the War of 1812, when British ships had hovered offshore and occasionally landed foraging parties.

By early 1918, Americans were well aware of the dangers of crossing the Atlantic, as submarine warfare had become a significant aspect of the German war effort. Assistant Secretary of the Navy Franklin D. Roosevelt tried to boost domestic morale with an address at Harvard University in January. Roosevelt posited that the answer to the submarine peril was the building of "more destroyers, chasers, patrol boats and a great merchant marine." In 1916, the prescient Roosevelt had been responsible for the development and manufacture of wooden hulled sub chaser boats. As with most things in the industrial age, there is a New Jersey connection. Elco Manufacturing, located at Avenue A and North Street in Bayonne, made 722 of these small craft during World War I, many for sale to Great Britain.[35]

In February 1918, the United States government, in conjunction with Henry Ford, announced the planned production of "submarine killer" vessels. These ships, larger than those of the "mosquito

German mine of the type sowed by German submarines in New Jersey waters.

fleet" sub chasers intended solely to protect the coast, were designed to escort convoys but also provide coastal defense. Ford proposed producing these ships by expanding his River Rouge plant near Detroit and also by adding a new plant to be built "on an eighty-acre tract of land on the Lincoln Highway between Newark, N. J. and New York City." The New Jersey factory, proposed as a "duplicate of the River Rouge shipbuilding plant now in course of erection," was apparently never completed, although Ford did establish an auto plant in Kearny, later closed when a more modern facility was constructed in Edgewater, New Jersey, in 1930. Unfortunately, none of Ford's "Eagle Boats" ever saw combat in World War I.[36]

The German submarine U-151, a special long range vessel, reached American waters in early May 1918. The sub's skipper laid mines off the North Carolina coast near Currituck Sound and then moved north to lay more off the Chesapeake Bay inlets at Cape Henry and Cape Charles and then Delaware Bay and Cape Henlopen. The German captain used American lighthouses and lightships to assist in determining his position, and was surprised at the lack of war preparation he witnessed.[37]

On June 2, 1918, a day locals later recalled as "Black Sunday," U-151 sank six ships, the *Isabel B. Wiley,* the *Winneconne,* the *Jacob M. Haskell,* the *Edward H. Cole,* the *Texel,* and the *Carolina,* off the New Jersey coast. The Germans did not use torpedoes to sink these merchant ships, but would surface, tell the passengers and crew to get in lifeboats and row for the beach, and then use their deck gun or planted explosives to finish the job. While there were other submarine incidents in New Jersey waters in World War I, none ever surpassed the cruise of U-151.[38]

In Asbury Park, the submarine threat was considered a tourist event. Under the headline "Asbury interested but in no way alarmed" the *Asbury Park Press* noted that local people and vacationers were "evincing considerable interest in the work of the navy to protect the shores from U-boat activities. Yesterday afternoon many persons flocked to the beach to witness the patrol work of the airplanes and a dirigible which flew low over the surface of the water keeping a watchful eye open for a submarine. Rather than having the effect of alarming the city, the possibility of a Hun raid appearing off the coast has aroused the keenest interest and is resulting in many going to the boardwalk in the hope of seeing a chance encounter between the naval airplane and sub."[39]

In the wake of the sinkings, coastal guardians got more jittery than the resi-

dents and tourists at Asbury Park. On the evening of August 1, 1918, a Captain Mollere of the 22nd Infantry Regiment, stationed on Sandy Hook, reported that "two small skiffs had been sent out from a submarine, presumably to make a landing off the Sandy Hook General Supply Depot." Major Fields, Officer of the Day at Fort Hancock, later confirmed that the invaders were actually New Jersey fishermen. Later that night the Supply Depot guards heard four shots, one of which struck the sand near them. After an additional six shots, which seemed to come from the ocean, they returned fire and asked Fort Hancock personnel to train a searchlight on the water. By the time the light appeared, the shooting had stopped, and its source was never determined, although the parallel with the "friendly fire" incident at Sandy Hook during the War of 1812 is interesting. U-117 would have passed by that section of the New Jersey shore out at sea in early August, but it is extremely unlikely that the firing came from a German submarine, as it was not within the mission of the U-Boats, ordered to sow mines and sink merchant ships, to fire rifle shots randomly at the shore.[40]

The raid of U-151 brought to light one of the more front line contributions of women to the war efforts. Following the sinking of the passenger liner *Carolina,* the passengers and crew headed for the New Jersey shore in lifeboats. The heroine of one of these boats was a young woman named Lillian Dickinson, who had served as an ambulance driver in France. Another passenger recalled that "although we tried to dissuade her, that gallant girl insisted on taking her regular turn at the oars. It was one hour on and one hour off. Just to look at this beautiful young woman keeping pace with whatever the men did was enough to buoy

Returning soldiers after leaving a troopship in Hoboken in 1919.

Newark veteran Nicholas Casale states his case that he was the shortest man to serve in the US Army in France on the steps of the capitol in Washington, D.C.

our spirits and keep us going. She set the pace and the example." Dickinson's lifeboat landed on the Atlantic City beach, much to the surprise of thousands of tourists.[41]

## THE RETURN TO "NORMALCY"

Following the end of actual hostilities on November 11, 1918, and the peace treaty negotiations at Versailles the following year, the United States Senate, adamantly opposed to participation in the League of Nations, refused to approve the Treaty of Versailles, extending America's official involvement in World War I for years after the fighting had ceased. The war actually officially ended for the United States in New Jersey, when President Warren Harding, returning from a golf outing at the Somerset Hills Country Club on July 2, 1921, signed the Knox-Porter Joint Congressional Resolution declaring hostilities at an end at the home of New Jersey US senator Joseph S. Frelinghuysen in Raritan Borough. The house is long gone, but a small monument marks the spot near the entrance to the Somerville Circle Shopping Center.

With the end of actual combat and a feeling among many that the results had not benefitted the United States, the general and political public yearned for a "return to normalcy" and the nation turned inward. In the postwar years, a curious footnote to the state's war story emerged. In 1929, Nicholas Casale, a Newark veteran, laid claim to being the smallest man to serve in the American army during the conflict. When he registered for the draft in June of 1917, Casale, who lived at 127 Ridge Street, was described as "short" and "slender."

This photo of the Marine Jazz Band dates from 1919 and was taken in Princeton, NJ. Reynold Thompson is on the left and his friend Richard Stout, a member of the band from Kingston, NJ, is leaning on the piano with his violin.

Drafted in April 1918, he served a year with the 148th Infantry Regiment, which fought in the Meuse-Argonne and Ypres-Lys offensives and was the first regiment to cross the Scheldt River in Belgium on November 2, 1918, suffering heavy casualties in the crossing.[42]

The problem was that Casale was apparently never meant to be there. After the war, the Veterans Administration certified that he was 4´ 10″ tall and weighed 106 pounds; the army's minimum draft standard was, according to one source, 5´ tall and 110 pounds in weight. Casale hired an attorney and initiated what would become a more than ten-year campaign to be officially recognized as the smallest man who had served in the AEF. Representative Fred Hartley of Kearny, New Jersey, at that time the youngest U.S. Congressman, provided the veteran with "an affidavit from the U.S. Veterans Bureau" which certified his actual height and weight when drafted. Casale never got the gold medal he was seeking, but was eventually awarded an official U.S. Senate certificate of acknowledgment attesting to his claim.[43]

Since the federal government had considered National Guard soldiers as draftees for legal purposes, they discharged all returning Guardsmen, creat-

ing some confusion for the state, which had to discharge the state-maintained militia in January 1920 and reorganize militiamen and willing war veterans into a viable new National Guard organization. The first such unit created was the 6th Regiment, which received federal recognition as an official National Guard unit on November 13, 1919.[44]

## THE POSTWAR NEW JERSEY NATIONAL GUARD

Under the 1920 Army Reorganization Bill, the federally authorized strength of the post-World War I New Jersey National Guard, based on the criteria of "800 enlisted men for each member of Congress," was now 11,200 men. The state made an active effort to recruit veterans and young men reaching military age to the new units, which were assigned the prewar state designation numbers. They would carry the lineage of the older units but eventually receive new federal numerical designations reflecting 29th Division service. Following World War I, the National Guard would be subjected to federal authority and organizational standards more stringent than ever before.[45]

The reorganization got a rocky start. Authorized pay for sixty drills and fifteen days of training a year was $75 for a private, $200 for a master sergeant and $770 for a captain, but payroll records were incomplete for many units, with others not meeting attendance standards. As the decade advanced, however, these problems were largely resolved.[46]

The summer encampment held at Sea Girt in 1920 was the first training period for the revived New Jersey National Guard, with the new 6th Regiment in its first training cycle. The regiment was commanded by former state militia regimental commander Colonel Howard S. Borden, a socialite and polo player from Rumson. As in the prewar era, the encampment, with its drills and reviews, not only served as a training venue but also provided entertainment for visiting politicians and summer shore tourists. Borden's subsequent elevation to the rank of general, coupled with the desire of combat veteran officers, who considered him a feckless political appointee, to rejoin and reorganize the National Guard, initiated a feud that eventually had to be resolved by Governor Edward I. Edwards, who eased Borden into an early retirement. Recruiting for lower ranks continued apace, however, with the Sea Girt annual training location serving as a big plus for attracting potential Guardsmen.[47]

Potential recruits were told, "Uncle Sam offers you two weeks at the Seashore. All expenses paid. All equipment free." They were also advised, "Sea Girt offers ample opportunity for recreation and sport while the Guardsman is not on duty. There is swimming, boating and fishing, the site being in close proximity to many shore resorts." Despite the attractions, it was reported that "very few [WWI veterans] had any desire for further service in the National Guard at that time." Many of the new soldiers were

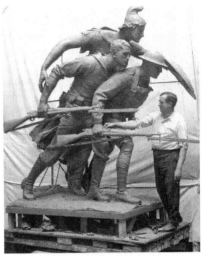

The sculpture at the base of Montclair's World War I monument by noted artist Charles Keck features the goddess of victory extending her shield to protect two soldiers. On the sides of the obelisk are etched the names of Montclair men killed in the war, and in front of the memorial there are plaques bearing the names of local soldiers who died in World War II, Korea, and Vietnam.

men too young to have served in the war, including at least one underage fifteen-year-old whose father came to the camp to retrieve him.[48]

Despite early problems, by the mid-1920s the New Jersey National Guard had evolved into an organization that was again considered an integral part of the nation's defense system. The Jersey Guard's infantry and artillery units were now the dominant part of the new 44th Division, which also included some New York organizations. As the decade progressed, the division added quartermaster, military police, and other support units. The New Jersey cavalry was reorganized and expanded as the 102nd Cavalry Regiment, but was a non-divisional unit. The 44th's divisional insignia was colored orange and blue, in commemoration of the colors of the Dutch colony of New Netherland, in which both New York and New Jersey had their origins.[49]

## NEW JERSEY MILITARY AVIATION

In September 1928, the United States War Department assigned two regular army soldiers to help organize the state's first aviation support unit. At the time the air arm was part of the army, and known as the "Army Air Corps." The regulars worked with New Jersey National Guard officers and enlisted men interested in flying, and had completed their training and organizational mission by the end of 1929, with the formal establishment of the 119th Observation Squadron.[50]

New Jersey airfields were scarce in the 1920s, but the new unit had a home waiting for it at Newark Airport. Under the direction of the city's Mayor Thomas Raymond, airport construction began on 68 acres of a 240-acre tract of marshland east of the city near U.S. Route 1 in late 1927. The airport site was also adjacent to Port Newark and major railroad lines, an ideal location for a military air unit as well as a commercial airline headquarters.

Newark Airport opened for business on October 1, 1928, and by 1932 it was the busiest airport in the world, handling more than a quarter of the country's air traffic. The 119th Observation Squadron became operational at the airport on January 30, 1930, when it received its first O-2H aircraft. The unit was assigned the numerical designation of the World War I-era 119th Aero Squadron, and the War Department considered it

O-17       NEWARK       1931

The first aircraft assigned to the New Jersey National Guard's 119th Observation Squadron arrived at Newark Airport in 1931.

the "reconstitution and consolidation" of that unit for lineage purposes, although the original organization had no formal connection with the state of New Jersey. Two hangers and an administrative office were built at the airport to accommodate the National Guard personnel and aircraft.[51]

An observation unit, the 119th was equipped with two seat biplanes, to accommodate a pilot and observer. The observer's job was to photograph and record information and intelligence of tactical use to the ground forces in combat or to patrol offshore waters looking for submarines.

## THE GREAT DEPRESSION

The 1930s were hard times in New Jersey and America, as the aftermath of the great stock market crash of 1929 plunged the nation into economic depression and domestic turmoil. Tensions were on the rise in Europe and Asia, and, coupled with the growing aggressiveness of the Axis Powers, seemed to indicate another war on the horizon, although many Americans, still unhappy with the results of World War I, became ever more isolationist. The New Jersey National Guard was considered a fully functional entity, with infantry, cavalry, artillery, and air-craft units. The Guard's maneuvers and training in the decade ahead would be far more complex than the old days of target shooting and marching at Sea Girt—and they would need to be.

Because weaponry was becoming more sophisticated and longer range, and military organizational structures more complex, summer training locations for the New Jersey National Guard continued to expand beyond the old Sea Girt camp. In the summer of 1928, soldiers from the 113th and 114th Infantry traveled from Sea Girt to Camp Dix to fire their machine guns and antitank guns, camping overnight at the larger base. In 1929, 44th Division Headquarters and supporting troops, along with other divisions from the northeast, spent their entire annual training period at Fort Dix planning division-sized operations. The soldiers of the 112th Artillery Regiment, from Camden, East Orange, Trenton, and Atlantic City, traveled to Pine Camp in upstate New York that year because the "artillery camp in northern New York permits firing of the 75-mm. field guns with which the 112th is equipped."[52]

Although Sea Girt declined somewhat as a training facility, the camp still served as the primary base of the New Jersey National Guard, as well as the center of the state's summer political universe. In 1932, Hudson County political boss and Jersey City mayor Frank Hague and his associate, Governor A. Harry Moore, staged the largest political event in American history at the camp. It was estimated that over 100,000 people attended Democratic presidential candidate Franklin D. Roosevelt's first stop after the nominating convention. Roosevelt reviewed Na-

Presidential candidate Franklin D. Roosevelt and Governor A. Harry Moore review the National Guard troops at Sea Girt in August 1932.

tional Guard soldiers at the camp at the conclusion of his well-received speech, which called for the end of Prohibition.

The New Jersey National Guard continued to expand through the decade of the 1930s, adding two new artillery regiments, a quartermaster regiment, a motorcycle company, and a tank company. The 102nd Cavalry was attached to the 59th Cavalry Brigade, along with Connecticut and Massachusetts mounted units, and in 1937 the brigade was made part of the 21st Cavalry Division. A detachment from the 102nd, the old Essex Troop, decked out in their Brooks Brothers full dress uniforms, represented the state at the Battle of Yorktown Sesquicentennial Commemoration in October 1931.[53]

As the Guard expanded, new armories were built, largely with Works Progress Administration funding, in Jersey City, Teaneck, Morristown, and West Orange, while Armories at Atlantic City,

New Jersey National Guardsmen at the opening of the Lincoln Tunnel in 1937.

Bridgeton, Burlington, Camden, Elizabeth, Newark, Paterson, and Trenton were upgraded. Unsurprisingly, considering Mayor Frank Hague's reputation of getting out the Democratic Party vote in New Jersey, the armory in Jersey City was the biggest of the new buildings. As in the past, the Guard provided color guards and ceremonial units for public civic events, including the opening of the Lincoln Tunnel in 1937.

## AFRICAN AMERICAN UNITS IN THE NEW JERSEY NATIONAL GUARD

In 1930 there were no African Americans in the New Jersey National Guard, and the segregated U. S. Army did not have plans to authorize a black unit in the state. Prominent New Jersey African American citizens, most notably William D. Nabors of Orange, petitioned their state legislators to create a state funded organization. In response, Assemblyman Frank S. Hargraves introduced a bill, and

on April 16, 1930, both houses of the New Jersey legislature passed Chapter 149, Laws of 1930, authorizing the "organization and equipment of a battalion of Negro infantry" at state expense. On July 14, 1931, committees were established to organize the first companies of what came to be called the First Separate Battalion, New Jersey State Militia. Companies were raised in Newark, Atlantic City, and Camden.[54]

Companies A and B were at Sea Girt for their annual field training on September 8, 1934, when the *Morro Castle*, a cruise ship returning to New York from Havana, caught fire offshore. As its control systems burned, the ship anchored two miles off Sea Girt in turbulent seas and desperate passengers and crew members tried to launch lifeboats and jumped overboard in efforts to save themselves from the flames. The disaster would prove to be the finest hour for many New Jersey shore residents, including Governor Moore, who was ending the season at his official summer residence in the National Guard camp. The governor boarded a Guard plane in the observer seat and flew out over the burning ship, dropping flares and smoke bombs and waving flags to guide rescue boats to survivors.[55]

Before he soared aloft over the surf, Moore ordered the black militia to the beach to bolster local rescue efforts. The men of Companies A and B braved almost hurricane conditions, rescuing survivors and recovering bodies drifting to shore. Some of the officers, morticians in civilian life, established an improvised morgue in the National Guard camp, which soon held seventy-eight bodies.[56]

Anxious relatives who appeared at Sea Girt to identify the dead were guided by the black soldiers, with nurses on hand for support. A reporter noted that when one man was overcome by grief on finding his younger brother among the dead "a Negro militiaman . . . left his post to comfort him, and to guide him to a secluded place where he might have an undisturbed rendezvous with grief." The men of Companies A and B were subsequently cited by Governor Moore and the State Legislature for their "courage, courtesy, and sympathetic handling of a very gruesome duty" and the city commissioners of Atlantic City presented Company B with a bronze plaque "in recognition of its heroic and devoted services to the community, state and nation."[57]

The battalion also distinguished itself in other venues, winning numerous athletic and marksmanship trophies. Company A boasted the largest percentage of men to qualify in rifle marksmanship in the state, won the Enoch L. ("Nucky") Johnson Trophy for shooting expertise six years out of nine, and took the battalion's Combat Trophy in 1932 and

The plaque awarded to Company B of the First Separate Battalion by Atlantic City for its work during the *Morro Castle* disaster.

1933. In the National Guard "small bore" (.22 rim fire caliber) rifle match of 1940, six out of the highest ten scores were posted by men from Company C.[58]

In 1936 the adjutant general persuaded the New Jersey state senate to redesignate the battalion as an adjunct unit of the New Jersey National Guard, and in May 1937 the "First Separate Battalion, New Jersey State Militia," was renamed the "First Battalion, New Jersey Guard." Although the battalion's "acting commander and instructor" was always a white officer, Major Samuel Brown in 1940, all company officers were African Americans, including former Essex Troop saddler Robert D. Trott, now a captain commanding Company A.[59]

## NAVY RESERVE, MARINE RESERVE, AVIATION, AND THE SIGNAL CORPS

In 1932 the Navy Department, constrained by a tight budget, ordered its reserve component units to seek training in facilities close to home. The state of New Jersey facilitated the request of the United States Marine Corps Reserve to

Officers and non-commissioned officers of Company C, 1st Separate Battalion, at Sea Girt in 1935.

use the Sea Girt facility for training. Marine Corps reservists from New York, New Jersey, and eastern Pennsylvania trained at Sea Girt six times during the decade. The Marines were especially happy with the firearms training facilities, which one officer characterized as "one of the best rifle ranges in the country." Sea Girt's location on the Jersey shore made it a very popular venue for the Marines, who enjoyed the attractions of the area on off-duty time, which drew some criticism from those not fortunate enough to train at Sea Girt. In response, one sergeant wrote in 1937: "We, of the Sixth Battalion, work hard during the various drill and maneuvers and we like to play just as hard during liberty."[60]

Although the 119th Observation Squadron was officially headquartered at Newark Airport, the unit's planes flew around the state, frequently landing on the parade ground at Sea Girt. Three-time governor Moore had his own private pilot from the squadron, Major Robert Copsey, assigned to fly him to of-ficial ceremonies at Fort Dix and other locations.

On November 6, 1933, a New Jersey National Guard airplane from the 119th, taking off from Red Bank Airport on a return flight to Newark Airport, crashed into a house on Peach Street in Shrewsbury and exploded. The pilot, Lieutenant George R. Johnson, his observer, and all five residents of the house, including two children, were killed in the accident. Johnson was a noted explorer of the era and considered "one of the best known aerial photographers in the world."[61]

The squadron had another aerial accident in 1940. Arthur F. Foran, New Jersey State Senate president, former mayor of Flemington, World War I veteran, and a National Guard colonel, was severely injured when the Guard plane in which he was a passenger crashed near New Orleans, Louisiana. Foran broke his leg in the crash and needed crutches or a cane to walk for the rest of his life.[62]

As the New Jersey National Guard expanded, federal military development

Governor A. Harry Moore (left) and his personal pilot Major Robert Copsey at Fort Dix in 1933. Above, the renaming of Camp Dix as Fort Dix.

continued apace in New Jersey as well. Camp Vail transitioned into Fort Monmouth, a permanent Signal Corps installation, in 1925. Fort Monmouth, named to honor those who had fought in the critical Revolutionary War battle in the county, had the best equipped radio laboratory of any post in the country and became an important site for research and development of communications equipment and techniques. It also served as a training camp for soldiers and Reserve Officer Training Corps (ROTC) cadets who were going to be commissioned in the Signal Corps. Along with Camp Dix, it was a major site for training cadets in the Citizens' Military Training Corps (CMTC), a program authorized in 1920 to provide an exposure to military life and training to young men.[63]

In the 1930s, Signal Corpsmen and civilian workers at Fort Monmouth worked on a "mystery ray" similar to one being developed in Great Britain. In July 1935, they tested the ray "for the first time . . . under actual working conditions." The "ray" was "said to be able to detect ships more than 50 miles off the coast, even though they are drifting without their motors running." The experiment, carried out at the Navesink lighthouse, was considered "a valuable adjunct to coastal protection." Additional experiments were carried out through 1941 on the site of the old Sandy Hook Proving Ground. Radar, the ultimate development of these experiments, would be needed in the near future.[64]

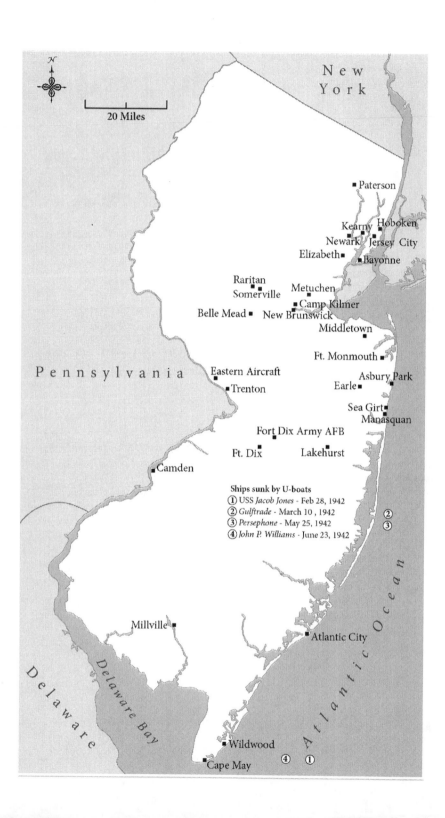

New
York

20 Miles

Paterson

Kearny  Hoboken
Newark  Jersey City
Elizabeth  Bayonne

Raritan
Somerville  Metuchen
Camp Kilmer
Belle Mead  New Brunswick
Middletown

Ft. Monmouth

Pennsylvania  Eastern Aircraft
Asbury Park
Trenton  Earle
Sea Girt
Manasquan

Fort Dix Army AFB
Ft. Dix  Lakehurst

Camden

Ships sunk by U-boats
① USS *Jacob Jones* - Feb 28, 1942
② *Gulftrade* - March 10 , 1942
③ *Persephone* - May 25, 1942
④ *John P. Williams* - June 23, 1942

②
③

Atlantic Ocean

Millville  Atlantic City

Delaware

Delaware Bay

Atlantic

Wildwood
Cape May  ④  ①

# 10. New Jersey in World War II

World War II erupted in Europe with the German invasion of Poland in September 1939, and during the following year, despite the reluctance of most Americans to go to war again, the government began to build up its military, including the National Guard. The New Jersey Guard participated in the massive maneuvers held around Plattsburgh, New York, which included 14,000 regular army troops and 38,000 Guardsmen. A 1940 report proudly claimed that "New Jersey's National Guard, numbering 7,187 officers and men, is trained and ready to take the field with the traditions of the 'Jersey Blues.'"[1]

On August 31, 1940, President Roosevelt issued Executive Order No. 8530, "ordering certain units and members of the National Guard of the United States into the active military service of the United States" for twelve months of service "for training." The 44th Division, which also included New York's 71st Infantry Regiment, was activated on September 16 and assigned to the former Camp Dix, renamed Fort Dix in 1939. The 104th Engineers, as did their predecessor unit in World War I, designed and constructed an expanded base for the en-

tire division as well as a reception center for draftees at Dix. The peacetime draft was enacted at the same time, and draftees and volunteer recruits from New Jersey and New York were soon assigned to bring the division up to full strength. Governor Moore had the adjutant general organize a "state guard," similar to Governor Edge's World War I militia, to replace the Guardsmen.

In September 1940, the African American soldiers of the First Battalion, New Jersey State Guard, Companies A of Newark, B of Atlantic City, C of Camden, and D of Trenton, were suddenly welcomed by the War Department into the National Guard, where they were re-designated as the "First Battalion, 372nd Infantry Regiment (Colored)." The 372nd was also composed of African American Guardsmen from the District of Columbia, Maryland, Massachusetts, and Ohio.[2]

The 372nd was ordered into United States federal service on March 10, 1941, and initially stationed at Fort Dix, assigned to the Eastern Defense Command's First Army as part of an internal defense force for the greater New York City area.[3]

Top, the 44th Division, largely composed of New Jersey soldiers, during the Carolina Maneuvers in 1941. Left, the 102nd Cavalry, still partially mounted, brought horses to Fort Jackson, South Carolina, after it was mobilized in January 1941.

The 102nd Cavalry, which, as a non-divisional unit, had not been activated with the 44th Division, was called to active duty on January 6, 1941, and assigned to Fort Jackson, South Carolina. The 102nd entered service as a mixed horseback and mechanized unit, and one squadron remained mounted through April 1942.

Most of the Guardsmen mobilized in 1940 and 1941 eagerly anticipated the end of their one year of federal service for training, and there was much grumbling when their tour of duty was extended for another eighteen months by Congress in August 1941. In September, after spending nearly a year at Fort Dix, the 44th Division traveled to South Car-

olina to participate in the massive "Carolina Maneuvers," which lasted through early December. The men of the division were on their way back to Fort Dix when they heard the news of Pearl Harbor and realized that their active duty would last until the end of the war.

Immediately after Pearl Harbor, New Jersey governor Charles Edison, son of the famed inventor, who had succeeded A. Harry Moore in the office, activated the State Guard. As in World War I, the State Guard soldiers were assigned to guard bridges, government offices, war industry factories, and other critical sites. Civilian volunteers were quick to respond as well, and Lieutenant Margaret Houlday and her fellow volunteers of the

Red Cross's South Amboy Women's Motor Corps brought hot coffee and doughnuts to the part time soldiers guarding the bridges over the Raritan River.[4]

## NEW JERSEY SOLDIERS OVERSEAS

The 102nd Cavalry was the first New Jersey National Guard unit to go overseas. By September 1942, when the regiment shipped out for England, it was completely mechanized, with its several squadrons equipped with "jeeps" produced by the Bantam Motor Car Company, armored cars, light tanks, and self-propelled 75 millimeter "assault guns." In December, the regiment's second squadron was transferred from England to North Africa, where it served as a guard force for dignitaries and the allied high command and subsequently campaigned in Italy and France as the 117th Cavalry Squadron. The second squadron was replaced by the 38th Cavalry Squadron, composed primarily of Iowa and Texas draftees, and the regiment was redesignated the 102nd Cavalry Group, now composed of the 38th and 102nd Squadrons. The 102nd's commander, Colonel Donald McGowan, reassigned a number of his New Jersey officers and enlisted men to the 38th, essentially "Jerseyfying" the new squadron. With this organization, McGowan, who had served as sergeant major of the 114th Infantry at the age of nineteen in World War I, led the 102nd ashore at Omaha Beach on June 8, 1944, D-Day plus two, and immediately pushed inland. The 102nd was the only New Jersey National Guard unit to land at Normandy during the invasion.[5]

One of the most significant displays of American wartime ingenuity can be

Margaret Houlday of the Red Cross Perth Amboy Women's Motor Corps.

traced to a New Jerseyan from the 102nd. As the Allies drove inland following D-Day, they became stalled in the bocage, a series of four- to six-foot-high earth berms topped with dense vegetation used to mark French farm boundaries in peacetime, but now occupied as defensive positions by German troops. Attempting to cross the hedgerows, American tanks were pushed upward at a forty-five-degree angle, exposing them to enemy infantrymen armed with anti-tank weapons firing from cover. The offensive stalled.

Sergeant Curtis Culin, a National Guardsman from Cranford in the 102nd, suggested that "something like a snow-plow" mounted on the front of a tank could carve a path through the hedgerows and that steel German beach obstructions would be the perfect material for crafting such an apparatus. Sergeant Culin, Lieutenant Steve Litton of his squadron maintenance shop, and Captain James DePew devised a device

Sgt. Curtis Culin of Cranford had the idea for the Rhino Plow, seen here mounted on a tank. The plow enabled tanks to break through the bocage the army encountered as it advanced into France.

to attach to the front of their tanks, and Chief Warrant Officer Frank Reilly put his maintenance men to work on the job. The result, the "Rhino Plow," cut through vegetation and dirt and General Omar Bradley pronounced the device "what we've been looking for." By July 24, every tank in the army was fitted with a Rhino Plow, and the Americans soon broke out of the bocage country.[6]

As the Allies closed in on Paris, the spearhead of the effort was the 102nd Cavalry Group. Captain William Buenzle of Roselle recalled that his men charged though rain, mist, and German gunfire toward the city on August 24, fighting through the suburbs until they saw the Eiffel Tower in the distance, then halted for the night. The following morning, French civilians rushed into the streets to disassemble German barricades. The Americans returned sniper fire with machine guns, to the cheers of civilians who, mindless of danger, poured out of their houses.[7]

Buenzle was ordered to "put the show on the road and get the hell into Paris." He urged his driver to speed up, and ran the cavalry column down the main road at 40 miles an hour towards the city center, reporting his position at 7:30 a.m. with the words, "I am at Notre Dame." The response from headquarters was, "How do you know?" Buenzle responded, "Damn it, I am looking right up at Notre Dame!"[8]

Captain Charles H. Peterson of Cliffside Park had actually arrived in the city the night before with his Troop B of the 102nd Squadron, but Buenzle's dramatic entry gained the Roselle captain and his men the credit and glory of being the first Americans into Paris. In the end, it was of no matter, for New Jersey's 102nd Cavalry Group could claim the honor either way. Meanwhile, in a double win for New Jersey, the 117th Squadron was entering Rome at about the same time. Following the fall of Paris, the 102nd continued its advance across Europe, accompanied by *Newark Evening News* war correspondent Warren Kennet, who had landed with the unit in Normandy.[9]

Warren Kennet was perhaps the most significant individual in New Jersey's World War II military history who was not a soldier. Although he had served in previous years in the 102nd Cavalry, Kennet was beyond military age at the time of the war. A *Newark Evening News* reporter who covered both military affairs and "equestrian" news, including polo matches, he made his way to England as a war correspondent for the paper. Kennet, who would eventually gain the nickname "Newark's Ernie Pyle," not only told the story of his old regiment, but tracked down New Jerseyans in a variety of units. His articles included accounts of the state's soldiers playing in an impromptu swing band, as members of bomber crews, and as military cameramen—they all fit into Warren Kennet's personalized account of the war, as long as they were Jerseymen—or women.[10]

The 44th Division would not see action until later in the conflict, but not with all of its constituent units. In February 1942, the 113th Infantry was permanently detached from the division and assigned to the Eastern Defense Command. The regiment was strung out from Long Island to Delaware in company-sized posts intended to defend the coastline from saboteurs landed from submarines. The 113th subsequently moved around the country, serving as a

Sgt. John Kunika of Spotswood, New Jersey, and the New Jersey National Guard's 695th Armored Artillery Battalion with two Red Cross "Donut Dollies" at Champey, France, in 1944.

local defense and training command until it was inactivated at Fort Rucker, Alabama, on September 25, 1945.

The 104th Engineer Regiment was also detached from the Division, with the first battalion sent to Camp Claiborne, Louisiana, as the 104th Engineer Battalion and the second battalion transferred to Camp Pickett, Virginia, where it became the first battalion of the 175th Engineer Regiment. The 104th Battalion went on to Fort Lewis, Washington, and then the Pacific Theater of War, from the Aleutian Islands to the Philippines, while the 175th participated in campaigns in North Africa and Italy.

Part of the 44th's artillery arm was separated from the division in 1939, and called up separately in January 1941. A battalion of the 112th was redesignated as the 695th Armored Artillery Battalion

The 114th Infantry on the march in Germany, 1945.

and after being transferred to several bases around the country, including Fort Sill, shipped out to England in February 1944 and landed on Utah Beach, Normandy, in July 1944. The battery fought its way across Europe with the 5th Armored Division.[11]

The 44th Division, less the detached units, was transferred from Fort Dix to Camp Claiborne, Louisiana, and then moved on to Fort Lewis, Washington, where it served as part of the United States' West Coast defenses throughout 1942. In early 1943, a number of men from the 71st and 114th Infantry, supplemented by draftees, were transferred to the 324th Infantry, a new regiment created within the division to replace the departed 113th. In early 1944, the 44th was shipped back to Louisiana for three months of field maneuvers and then on to Camp Phillips, Kansas, for final training before deployment overseas. When that task was accomplished, the division traveled by train to Camp Miles Standish in Massachusetts in August, its final stop before shipping out to Europe.

The 44th Division landed in Cherbourg, France, in mid-September 1944, trained intensively for a month, and was then assigned to the Seventh Army. The division relieved the 70th Division in the front lines and was first engaged in combat on October 18, near Luneville, France, as part of an offensive to secure the passes through the Vosges Mountains. Less than a week after the offensive began, the division was struck by an intense German counterattack, which it defeated, inflicting heavy losses on the enemy.

In November, the 44th fought alongside the French 2nd Armored Division in a drive to liberate Strasbourg, broke through the Maginot Line on December 19, and then assumed a defensive position near Sarreguemines, where it defeated several German counterattacks. In late March 1945, the division relieved the 3rd Division and crossed the Rhine River at Worms. The advance was rapid, as the German army collapsed. One soldier from the 114th Infantry Regiment recalled that: "The woods all around us

New Jersey African American soldiers of the 372nd Infantry in classroom training in 1941.

swarmed with German soldiers, but the fight was gone out of them, and they would flee in confusion or surrender meekly." The 44th crossed into Austria in early May, took the surrender of the German Nineteenth Army, and reached Imst and Landeck as the war in Europe ended.[12]

The 44th Division spent a short period of time on occupation duty in Austria and then returned to the United States in July 1945 for retraining prior to redeploying to the Pacific for the invasion of Japan. Fortunately, the Japanese surrendered before the division left the country again, and it was deactivated that November. The 44th Division was in combat for 190 days and earned three Distinguished Unit Citations.

The 119th Observation Squadron was detailed to coastal defense duty. Some members of the squadron transferred to other units and served overseas. Perhaps the best known of these men was Donald Strait of Verona. Strait served as an enlisted man with the 119th, but in early 1942 he qualified as an aviation cadet

and attended flight school at Maxwell Field, Alabama. Rising to the rank of captain, he became an ace, credited with aerial victories over German aircraft as a fighter pilot in the 356th Fighter Group. After the war, Strait served in the New Jersey Air National Guard, from which he retired as a major general in 1978.

The former First Separate Battalion officers and men, serving with the 372nd Infantry, were initially assigned to the Eastern Defense Command's First Army and stationed at Fort Dix as part of an internal defense force for the greater New York City area. Like the 113th, the 372nd later became a training regiment, and many of the original members were transferred out to different units. In April 1944, the 372nd became a "rotational regiment," moving about the country to posts in Kentucky, Arizona, and Washington, until arriving in Hawaii in April 1945 to prepare for the invasion of Japan. With the end of the war, the regiment returned to New Jersey and was inactivated at Fort Dix on January 31, 1946.

The torpedoed *R. P. Resor* burned for some time off Manasquan before sinking.

## WAR ALONG THE JERSEY SHORE

As in World War I, war came home to the Jersey Shore. In 1940, as the National Guard was called up and the peacetime draft initiated, Congress passed legislation funding the modernizing of coastal defenses. The result of this legislation in New Jersey was the establishment of a battery of two sixteen-inch guns in the Navesink Highlands overlooking the Atlantic Ocean as part of the harbor defenses of the Port of New York. The battery was completed in 1943 and supplemented by a sixteen-inch gun battery.[14] Unfortunately, the battery, although useful against an unlikely attack by battleships, had no effect on the real threat to the New Jersey coast—German submarines. U-Boat attacks along the coast in World War II were more deadly than they had been in 1918, due to the greater use of torpedoes and, initially, the navy's refusal to conduct coastal convoys. The first sinking in New Jersey waters,

the torpedoing of the oil tanker *Varanger* off Atlantic City in January 1942, heralded what the Germans would refer to as "the happy time" when they sank ships up and down the Atlantic Coast, in the Caribbean, and the Gulf of Mexico with no losses on their part.[15]

On the night of February 27, 1942, the Standard Oil Tanker *R.P. Resor* was torpedoed off Manasquan. There were only two survivors, crewman John K. Forsdal and navy coxswain Daniel Hey, a member of the eight-man Navy "Armed Guard" detailed to man the deck gun on the ship. Both men were brought into the Manasquan Coast Guard Station, where the oil was washed off them and they posed for a photo. Forty-one merchant seamen and eight navy personnel on board failed to survive the attack. The following day reporters took a boat out of Manasquan Inlet and photographed the still burning tanker. The carnage would last into the late summer, when

New Jersey governor Charles Edison (right) listens as Newark mayor Vincent J. Murphy shows him the sites for sirens and whistles to signal a "black-out" in the state's largest city.

the navy finally got a handle on proper antisubmarine warfare techniques, including coastal convoys, which Admiral Ernest J. King, commander of the United States fleet, had originally disdained.[16]

Around 5:00 a.m. on February 28, U-578, the same submarine that sank the *R. P. Resor*, fired two torpedoes at the destroyer *Jacob Jones*, patrolling off Cape May on a bright moonlight night. They hit the destroyer's port side almost simultaneously and the *Jones* split into three pieces. The *Jacob L. Jones* was the first navy warship sunk on the Eastern Sea Frontier. There were only eleven survivors.[17]

The anti-submarine campaign included a "dim-out" of lighting along the Jersey Shore, authorized in March 1942 and designed to deter enemy attack by eliminating possible silhouetting of passing ships by shore lighting reflecting off the ocean. The visual effect was sobering: "From the ocean the usually bright,

cheery boardwalks looked like ghost towns as blackout curtains cut off (or at least reduced) as much light as possible from the concession stands."[18]

Unfortunately, army and navy requirements were unclear and often contradictory as to which lighting—boardwalk, inland business, street and home, or automotive—they wanted "dimmed or eliminated." State officials disagreed with navy accusations of noncompliance. A June 1, 1942, survey of the shore from New York to Long Branch by state police superintendent colonel Charles H. Schoeffel and Civil Defense director Leonard Dreyfuss revealed that "the lighting in New Jersey did not in any way reflect a glare on the waters which would silhouette a ship." They added that a visit to Asbury Park found that city completely blacked out. The navy's contention that the dim-out was "not sufficient" at Wildwood Crest and Atlantic City was countered by state offi-

Workmen mounting a gun on a merchant ship in Hoboken in November 1941 as part of the navy's "armed guard" program.

cials' observation that the lights of the naval station at Cape May could be seen far out at sea. A dredge working at the base was described as being "lit up like a Christmas tree."[19]

Blackout requirements, ordered in inland areas as a defensive measure against potential, if unlikely, air attacks, and practiced in drills even before American entry into the war, clashed with war time industrial production goals as factories ran twenty-four hours a day. In April 1942, Harrison's Crucible Steel Company indicated it could not completely black out operations during a drill or actual air attack because "they have large furnaces where the light could not be extinguished or screened."[20]

While the propaganda-induced domestic renaming hysteria of World War I was not repeated in the international conflict's second act, in addition to blackouts and dim-outs, New Jersey officials acted to shut down the Nazi-

linked German American Bund Camp Norland, in Andover, as well as other Bund associated sites in the state.

WARTIME INDUSTRY

New Jersey again became a major supplier of war materiel as its industrial base shifted into high gear once more, producing everything from battleships and aircraft carriers to the B-25 bomber engines that powered Lieutenant Colonel James "Jimmy" Doolittle's raiders over Tokyo in 1942. The Depression was finally over and full employment came to New Jersey. State businesses received more than $12 billion worth of defense contracts and New Jersey's industrial workforce doubled to more than a million workers. Enormous contributions to the war effort flowed from factories throughout the state.[21]

The New York Shipbuilding Company in Camden and the Federal Shipbuilding and Drydock Company in Kearny built capital ships for the navy, and guns for the navy "armed guards" were mounted on merchant ships in Hoboken. The Curtiss-Wright Corporation of Paterson produced more than 139,000 airplane engines. In Trenton, the Switlik Parachute Company's productivity was so impressive that the War Department presented it with the first of five army-navy "E" awards in 1942. One of Switlik's contributions was five hundred paradummies—fireworks-armed rubber decoys, attached to parachutes and dropped behind enemy lines during the Allied D-Day invasion in 1944. The decoys, which exploded with a sound similar to gunfire when they made contact with the ground, were intended to distract German troops from the actual drop zones where live paratroopers were landing.[22]

During World War II New Jersey women faced opportunities and challenges as they were absorbed into the massive workforce the industrial state needed to fuel America's war machine. Women joined the ranks of employees on assembly lines and in manufacturing and even management jobs, filling the void left by departing husbands, brothers, sons, and boyfriends. By the end of 1942, seventy-six percent of Bell Telephone employees were women. "Rosie the Riveter" Jersey girls filled factories, and by 1943, most of the production workers on the Avenger torpedo bomber assembly line at the General Motors Eastern Aircraft Division in Ewing Township were women.

For many female defense workers, the prospect of a decent salary was dampened by overt hostility expressed by men who didn't believe women belonged in heavy industry. Elizabeth Hawes, a journalist who worked in the gear department at the Wright Aeronautical Plant in

New Jersey women, including 19-year-old Ruth Mae Moy of Paterson, stepped up to the plate during World War II. Moy, photographed on the job in 1942, worked at the Wright Aeronautical Corporation as a machine tool operator grinding rocker arms for Cyclone aircraft engines used in B-25 bombers.

Paterson with the intention of writing a book about her experience, recounted the resentment of her male co-workers. Their popular lament, she wrote, was: "Women, women, women: What's going to happen after the war? Will the men ever get their jobs back?" In addition to negative male attitudes, Hawes and many of her female co-workers on the third shift (midnight to 8:00 a.m.) also endured an exhausting regimen of domestic chores by day before reporting to work at night. Hawes, married with a five-year-old son, recalled her grueling schedule: "You come home about 8:30 a.m., eat some breakfast or dinner or whatever you call it. Then you know you'd better get to bed quick because if you want to get your child from school or want to have dinner with your hus-

New Jersey National Guard soldiers conduct training maneuvers on the Asbury Park beach in 1942.

band . . . you must be up around 5:00 p.m." Despite difficulties, however, women found factory war work empowering and meaningful and bonded over conversations that captured the pressing issues in their hectic lives. These topics of discussion, according to Hawes, included "the price of food; the sleep or the no sleep; the sick children or husbands; the hours it took to get to work . . . " As she reflected on the significance of her war work, Elizabeth Hawes pondered, "Can people be heroic without knowing it?"[23]

Existing military posts around the state were expanded and new ones established during the course of the conflict. After the departure of the 44th Division, Fort Dix continued as a major training base, and the navy and Coast Guard maintained installations at Cape May and other sites, as well as instituting beach patrols. In 1943, in an attempt to move resupply efforts from New York after the explosion of an ammunition ship in Bayonne, the navy established Naval Ammunition Depot Earle in Monmouth County, with a pier jutting into Sandy Hook Bay. Camp Kilmer, near New Brunswick, became a major transit camp, as Camp Merritt had been in World War I. Newark Airport became a military base, and, in 1944, members of the US Army Air Forces' WAAC (Women's Army Auxiliary Corps) force had communications training in the city.

Atlantic City was virtually taken over by the Army Air Forces, and became known as "Camp Boardwalk." Beginning in 1942, when Convention Hall became the Army Air Forces Technical Training Command Center, the resort city flooded with thousands of soldiers who stayed in forty-seven hotels and hostels occupied by the military. The navy trained pilots at nearby Wildwood and the Air Forces conducted pilot training at a base established in Millville. Lakehurst Naval Air Station served as a major antisubmarine airship base, and, in January 1943, Navy WAVES (Women Accepted for Volunteer Emergency Service) were assigned to Lakehurst, while an aerographer's school intended to train seventy-five WAVES a month was established in nearby Lakewood.[24]

In November 1943, Atlantic City's Chalfonte-Haddon Hall hotel complex (two hotels linked by a skyway), became an Army Air Force medical facility named "England General Hospital," after Colonel Thomas England, an army doctor who worked with Walter Reed in the campaign against yellow fever early in the century. England Hospital was a facility dedicated to rehabilitating casualties transferred from other hospitals, and while soldiers participated in training exercises on the beach, the boardwalk provided an even path for wounded men going through physical therapy, particularly those adjusting to prosthetic limbs.[25]

Asbury Park was also transformed by the invasion of military personnel. Before the war, the city had been regarded as "one of the best-known resorts in northern New Jersey," with a boardwalk lined with "eating places, a fishing pier, recreational attractions, solariums, and shops where everything from imported Oriental rugs to souvenirs of the *Morro Castle* disaster are sold." As with Atlantic City, the city's festive ambiance took on a distinctly martial tone once war was declared. Two of the city's signature hotels—the Berkeley Carteret and the Monterey—were set aside for rest and relaxation for Allied forces, including British sailors. Like its neighbor to the south, Asbury Park became a hub of military activity: "Sixth Avenue between the two hotels served as the parade ground for morning drills," and on most nights, "the Salvation Army canteen came to the main gate at the Berkeley to give out cocoa."[26]

With the National Guard off to war, the state's Sea Girt camp was leased from the state by the Army Signal Corps as a

During the war Lakehurst served as a major antisubmarine airship base. This photo, from January 1943, shows the first three WAVES assigned to Lakehurst to await an aerographer's school intended to train seventy-five WAVES a month in Lakewood.

substation of Fort Monmouth. The Sea Girt base—with mess hall space for 1,700 men, a post exchange, and other buildings as well as its outstanding rifle range—provided a ready-made training site. Recruits drilled on the parade ground, fired on the ranges and conducted route marches up and down nearby highways and out into what is now Allaire State Park. The routine of daily military exercises was enlivened by on-base USO dances, where a GI band belted out hit tunes while soldiers jitterbugged frenetically with local girls. In nearby Bradley Beach, local businessman Harry Whelan, whose son and son-in-law were serving in the armed forces, established the "Dad's Club" on the boardwalk as a place for the town's servicemen to relax when on leave.

Inland New Jersey also did its part. The United Seaman's Service and the War Shipping Administration teamed up to create a "rest center" at Gladstone for "convalescing seamen" whose ships had been torpedoed off the coast or on convoys to Europe. The center was located on the 500-acre estate of Charles and Mary Suydam Cutting, wealthy international celebrities. Charles was an explorer and the first Westerner to enter the "forbidden city" of Lhasa, Tibet. On May 31, 1943, the seamen in residence were visited by the Duke and Duchess of Windsor, who chatted with them and signed autographs. The newspaper story was accompanied by a photo caption that described the Duchess's "colorful" dress as "inscribed with gin rummy terms."[27]

German spy Carl Emil Ludwig Krepper after his arrest in Newark.

Scattered throughout the state were closely guarded POW camps that housed captured German and Italian soldiers, shipped to this country because the number of prisoners being held in Great Britain, close to the actual combat zone, was considered at capacity. From 1942 through 1945, more than 400,000 Axis prisoners were shipped to the United States and detained in camps across the country. In New Jersey, POW camps included sites at Belle Mead, Fort Dix, Jersey City Quartermaster Supply Depot, Camp Kilmer, Fort Monmouth, Raritan Arsenal, Metuchen, and the Somerville Quartermaster Supply Depot.

Due to the home front labor shortage, many POWs were put to work at canneries, mills, farms, and other businesses and transferred to small temporary camps close to their assigned work areas. The Parvin State Park camp housed an estimated 150 POWs who labored in three separate shifts at nearby Seabrook Farms. Like many such camps, the Parvin facility was situated in an isolated area of the state. It was enclosed by a single wire fence ten feet high, with guard towers at each corner of the square enclosure, which was illuminated at night by floodlights.

Given that the prisoners were well fed and treated humanely, few attempted to escape; the army recorded a little more than two thousand attempts, less than 1 percent of the total number of POWs, nationwide. Germans held at Fort Dix were comfortable enough to create costumes and put on a play for their fellow prisoners.

Interestingly, the response of some New Jerseyans toward German and Italian prisoners of war as workers was better than that accorded interred Japanese-American workers. On April 11, 1944, more than 500 residents of Great Meadows met at the local school to protest laborers assigned to a nearby farm by the War Relocation Authority (WRA). Although a march on the farm was averted, assembled residents voted to petition their state senator to find "legal means to remove the laborers." A sign

The Red Cross Perth Amboy Women's Motor Corps brought coffee and food to State Guard members guarding bridges and other strategic sites in Middlesex County in the days after Pearl Harbor. Members had to be able to drive, change tires, and make minor repairs on their vehicles.

posted on the road to the farm read "One Mile to Little Tokyo," some residents spoke of "running the Japanese out of the county with shotguns," and a shed was burned down on the farm. The WRA removed the workers the following day.[28]

New Jersey was also the scene of enemy espionage. The German saboteurs who were landed by submarine on Long Island in 1942 and captured shortly afterward, were actually on their way to Newark. Their contact man, who was to provide them with money and shelter, was Carl Emil Ludwig Krepper, a German immigrant and former Lutheran minister who lived in the city. The agents were captured before they got in touch with Krepper, but the FBI put him under surveillance and arrested him in a sting operation in 1944. Charged with a variety of espionage related crimes, he was housed in the Hudson County Jail in Jersey City until his trial in February 1945. Convicted, Krepper was sentenced to twelve years in prison. Attempts to ap-

peal his conviction were denied in 1947 and 1950, and after his release he faded into history. Carl Emil Ludwig Krepper died at a nursing home in Massachusetts in 1972 and his body was cremated. No one claimed his ashes.[29]

Around 560,500 New Jerseyans, 360,000 draftees among them, served in all branches of the armed forces in all theaters of the conflict during World War II. The total included 10,000 women, most notably Marine Corps Women Reserves commander Ruth Cheney Streeter of Morristown and Navy WAVE commander Joy Bright Hancock of Wildwood.[30]

New Jersey women were closer to the front lines than they had ever been before. Lieutenant Margaret Jennings, an army nurse from Spring Lake Heights, was assigned to the hospital ship *Seminole*, caring for wounded soldiers, including enemy prisoners, being returned to the United States. The *Seminole* was caught in the middle of a night bombing attack by German aircraft while docked

Virginia Farr of West Orange, one of twenty-five American women who served in the British ATA in World War II.

Medal of Honor recipient John Basilone, WWII hero from Raritan, at his award ceremony on June 25, 1943.

at Naples, Italy, and Jennings once witnessed a German submarine "at periscope depth" observing a burial at sea from her ship.[31]

Not every Jersey girl served in the American forces. Virginia Farr of West Orange was one of twenty-five women pilots recruited in 1942 for the British Air Transport Auxiliary (ATA) by Jackie Cochrane, president of the "Ninety-Nines," a women pilot's organization founded by Amelia Earhart. Farr, then twenty-four-years-old, had over 1,000 hours flying time and was a certified instructor and active member of the organization.[32] Farr and the other women pilots went to Great Britain via Canada by ship through submarine infested waters in March 1942 to serve in the ATA, which ferried Spitfire and Hurricane fighters from the factories where they were produced to RAF bases around the

British Isles. She served until June 1945.[33]

New Jersey soldiers, National Guardsmen, volunteers and draftees, officers and enlisted men, served all over the world. Samuel Bilby of Newark, an artilleryman, entered combat at the Battle of the Bulge and ended the war on the Elbe River, where his unit met the Soviets. Army Air Forces B-25 crewman John Ziegler of Paterson served in New Guinea and participated in the bombing campaign against Rabaul. Al Meserlin of East Orange, a combat cameraman who landed in Normandy, became General Dwight D. Eisenhower's personal photographer and was present at the German surrender in 1945. William Gill of Newark served in the navy as a member of the thirty-man "Armed Guard" assigned to merchant ships, and traveled all over the Pacific, from New Caledonia to Australia, India, Fiji, Pago-Pago, and

Top left, army photographer Al Meserlin of East Orange (left), who was General Eisenhower's personal photographer. Top right, Chaplain John Washington of Newark, who sacrificed his life that others might live. Lower left, PFC Samuel Bilby (middle) of Newark in England prior to his unit's movement to France. Lower right, Sergeant John Ziegler of Paterson (kneeling, center) in New Guinea.

the Philippines, to name a few locations where the ships he served aboard delivered supplies.[34]

An estimated total of 10,372 New Jerseyans, including ten of the state's seventeen Medal of Honor recipients, made the ultimate sacrifice and were killed in action or died of wounds or other causes. Perhaps the most famous New Jersey soldier was Marine Corps sergeant John Basilone of Raritan, awarded the

Medal of Honor for his heroic actions in defense of Henderson Field on Guadalcanal in 1942. After a stint selling war bonds, including a stop at the Duke estate in Somerville that drew 30,000 people, Basilone requested a return to combat duty and was killed in action on Iwo Jima in February 1945.

Another New Jersey hero of World War II was Father John Washington of Newark, an army chaplain traveling aboard the troop transport SS *Dorchester*. At around 1:00 a.m. on February 3, 1943, the *Dorchester* was torpedoed amidships by a German submarine off the coast of Newfoundland and began to sink. Soldiers, many still in their underwear and without life jackets, swarmed up to the deck, where Washington, along with his chaplain friends Reverend George L. Fox, a Methodist minister who had served in World War I as an enlisted man, Rabbi Alexander P. Goode, who counted Al Jolson among his relatives, and Reverend Clark V. Poling, son of a clergyman and a minister of the Reformed Church in America, had already stationed themselves. The chaplains guided panic-stricken soldiers to a life jacket storage area and then, when those jackets were all handed out, gave up their own to those who had none.[35]

The 44th Division's 157th Artillery comes home to New York City in the summer of 1945.

The four chaplains, calm and cool in the face of disaster, displayed outstanding leadership qualities, encouraging and assisting enlisted men to the few available lifeboats to get off the rapidly sinking *Dorchester*, which went down in twenty minutes. Numerous survivors recalled seeing the four men join hands and hearing them pray above the din in English, Latin, and Hebrew as the ship finally slipped beneath the North Atlantic waves. There is a monument to Father Washington at his home parish, Saint Rose of Lima, in Newark, and in 2013 Saint Stephen's parish in Kearny, where he spent his last days as a civilian, dedicated a memorial to him and his three comrades, ensuring that the public memory of their story, although it may flicker, will never truly die.[36]

The memories endured long after the shooting stopped. In 1949, journalist Warren Kennet returned to Normandy and stood on the beach where he had landed in 1944. He wrote of the experience: "The beaches and fields of Normandy are quiet today. Only the gentle ripple of the waves lapping the shore, the chatter of the birds and the humming of the bees can be heard. But the battered landing ships which lie rusting in the surf . . . and the bombed out buildings in nearby towns, brought back memories today to some 40 D-Day correspondents who landed with the American forces just five years ago in the greatest mass invasion in all history."[37]

The end of World War II in Europe found one squadron of the 102nd Cavalry, the first New Jersey-based unit in combat, in Czechoslovakia and the other on the Elbe River. In a 2001 oral history interview, Sergeant James Kane, who had joined the 102nd in 1936 because it was "a poor man's riding club" that he believed would "provide an opportunity to ride horses and impress girls," reflected on the long ago war. He expressed a still lingering sorrow about the men who did not make it home, but remarked that "the old 102nd Cavalry, New Jersey National Guard, was a good outfit to go to war with—if one had to go."[38]

And so, with the surrender of Germany in May and Japan in September 1945, World War II came to an end. But soon another long struggle began—the "Cold War," which sporadically heated up. After that fearsome era ended, new struggles and conflicts emerged. As in the past, New Jersey would play its part, and the sons and daughters and grandchildren of the state's World War II veterans would answer the call.

**N e w
Y o r k**

20 Miles

**Nike Missile Sites**
1: Middletown
2: Holmdel
3: Ft. Hancock
4: Old Bridge
5: Summit
6: Livingston
7: Wayne
8: Franklin Lakes
9: Lumberton
10: Marlton
11: Berlin
12: Pitman
13: Swedesboro

8

7    ■ Paterson

6  Kearny  Hoboken
5  Newark  Jersey City
Elizabeth ■
■ Bayonne

Raritan ■
Somerville  Metuchen
New Brunswick ■  Camp Kilmer
South Amboy  3
4 Middletown
1
2
Ft. Monmouth ■

**P e n n s y l v a n i a**

■ Trenton    Earle ■   Asbury Park
Camp Evans
Sea Girt ■
Manasquan

McGuire AFB

Ft. Dix    Lakehurst

■ Camden   9
10

11

13   12

Millville ■

Atlantic City ■

*A t l a n t i c   O c e a n*

*D e l a w a r e*   *D e l a w a r e   B a y*

Wildwood ■
Cape May ■

# 11. New Jersey's Military History after World War II

Following World War II, the 44th Division designation was reassigned to Illinois, and the New Jersey National Guard was reorganized into the new 50th Armored Division, which was officially activated in the state in July 1946. The component organizations of the new division, which were organized in 1946 and 1947, inherited the old 44th and 29th Division lineages of their predecessor units.[1]

The New Jersey National Guard made the newspapers in 1947 when the seven Weeks brothers—Robert, Edward, Albert, John, LeRoy, James, and Joseph of Jersey City—showed up to enlist in the 50th Armored Division's 309th Anti-Aircraft Artillery Battery. All but Joseph, an underage fifteen year old, were sworn into the organization, in the largest recorded group family military enlistment in New Jersey history.[2]

Although federal control of the National Guard was supposed to be stringent, lower level units were often more liberal in their interpretations of the regulations. Sixteen-year-old high school student Bill Paynton of Bloomfield, for example, was allowed to join the 102nd

Cavalry in Newark, in 1952, even though he was underage. Paynton was never sent to basic training (that requirement was not yet in effect for Guardsmen) and assigned as a medic, although he had no medical corps training. When Paynton was twenty-two-years old, a company first sergeant left the unit and no one else wanted the job, so Paynton ended up as first sergeant, a rank usually reserved for experienced soldiers. He left the National Guard after eight years of service, but returned to duty in an Army Reserve unit years later.[3]

Although many New Jersey World War II veterans had had enough of the military life, a number joined the National Guard in the postwar era. Colonel Donald McGowan of the 102nd Cavalry was one of those who returned to the colors, serving as the state's assistant adjutant general. Promoted to brigadier general in 1947 and major general in 1948, McGowan commanded the 50th Armored Division from 1948 to 1955, when he was appointed chief of the Army National Guard Bureau and then chief of the entire National Guard Bureau in Washington, a position from which he retired in 1963.

The Sea Girt camp returned to state control at the end of the war and once again became a National Guard training site, particularly for the Guard's Officer Candidate School, marksmanship training, and as a headquarters for several combat support units. Following an accelerating trend begun in the prewar years, field training for the 50th Armored Division, with its long range artillery and armored units, was conducted at larger military reservations, principally at Pine Camp, renamed Camp Drum in 1951, located in upstate New York.

As in the past, the New Jersey National Guard was called on to assist in local crises by the state's governors. At 7:26 p.m. on May 19, 1950, an explosion occurred at a pier in South Amboy where ammunition was being loaded on a barge for shipment to Pakistan. Fifty drums of phosphorus on the grounds of the nearby American Agricultural Company were ignited by flying land mines. Thirty-six workers, thirty-one of them from the James Healing Company, an explosives handling business, were killed, including a number of members of the Healing family, and another 350 injured, as windows were shattered all over South Amboy. Four barges were destroyed and fourteen others damaged, as were a number of buildings. Units of the National Guard were called out to assist in securing the area, and 50th Armored Division military policemen were soon in control of the situation.[4]

## MILITARY DESEGREGATION

The post-World War II era dawned with a new realization that the promises of the Civil War could no longer be denied, and the civil rights movement gained new strength based on the wartime sacrifices made by African-American men and

The Weeks brothers at the largest single family enlistment in New Jersey military history in 1947.

women in defense of the country. In 1947, New Jersey voters approved a new constitution, which went into effect in January 1948, replacing the previous Constitution of 1844, and specifically forbidding racial discrimination. With this in mind, and considering the fact that the state's National Guard, then engaged in a rebuilding effort, was actively recruiting men for the 50th Armored Division, Governor Alfred E. Driscoll advised Secretary of Defense James Forrestal that the New Jersey National Guard would be desegregated in compliance with the state's constitution and that men would be recruited into units regardless of race.

Driscoll issued an order to his National Guard officers to disregard an army regulation stating that "mixed units are not authorized and Negroes cannot be enlisted in white units." Secretary Forrestal passed the buck down to Army Secretary Kenneth C. Royall. Royall, in response to Driscoll, averred that although he considered regular army segregation to be "in the interest of national defense," he would make an exception for the New Jersey National Guard because the people of the state, in voting for their new constitution, had indicated that "no person shall . . . be segregated in

New Jersey Air National Guard P-47s flying over Newark.

the militia because of race, color." On February 12, 1948, the New Jersey adjutant general's office published General Order No. 4, stating that "no qualified person shall be denied any military rights, nor be discriminated against in exercise of any military rights, nor be segregated in the militia because of religious principles, race, color, ancestry or national origin."[5]

New Jersey's actions put the state decisively ahead of the federal government in eliminating discrimination within the military. In 1945, then Secretary of War Robert B. Patterson had appointed a board of general officers headed by General Alvan C. Gillem to review the U. S. military's racial policies. The Gillem Board concluded that it was necessary to "eliminate . . . any special consideration based on race" within the armed forces. Throughout 1947 and 1948 President Harry Truman's advisors and African-

American organizations and civil rights leaders pressed him to desegregate the military, and he essentially agreed to do so around the same time the New Jersey integration program was ordered. Truman did not, however, issue his military desegregation Executive Order 9981 until July 26, 1948.[6]

Foot dragging on the part of military officers, some of whom leaked to the press that the order did "not specifically forbid segregation in the army" delayed actual full implementation of Truman's order below the regimental level until mandated by necessity during the Korean War, when General Matthew Ridgeway requested that he be allowed to fully integrate all units in his command in April 1951. There would be a hard road ahead to full civil rights, but for once New Jersey, thanks to its voters and Governor Driscoll, was in the forefront; the dream of equality that New Jersey's

African-American soldiers fought so
hard for in 1865 finally began to be realized in 1948. It was a shame that New
Jersey's last surviving Civil War veteran,
First Sergeant George Ashby, Company
H, 45th United States Colored Infantry,
who died two years earlier, did not live
to see it.[7]

## THE KOREAN WAR

On June 25, 1950, North Korea invaded
South Korea, beginning the Korean War.
New Jersey National Guardsmen and Reservists, many of them World War II veterans, had every reason to believe that
they would, as in the previous conflict,
be called to active duty. On June 30,
1950, President Truman signed the Se-
lective Service Extension Act, extending
the draft, which had been discontinued
at the close of World War II and reinsti-
tuted in 1948 in order to counter what
was seen as a growing Soviet threat. During the Korean War, a number of National Guard and Reserve units were
called to active duty and several, including two full divisions, served in combat
in Korea. As Guardsmen rotated out of
the war zone, they were replaced with
draftees. New Jersey Army National
Guard units called up during the Korean
War included the 112th Artillery Group
Headquarters, 695th Armored Field Artillery Battalion, 30th Ordnance Battalion, 122nd Ordnance Company, 63rd
Army Band, and the 150th Engineer
Pontoon Bridge Company. None were,
however, deployed in Korea. The naval
militia, which was activated for the war,
reached its peak strength of 3,950 officers and enlisted personnel at the time.
Starting in the late 1950s, the naval militia was gradually absorbed by the federal
naval reserve, and it was officially disbanded in 1963.[8]

A Sherman tank from the 50th Armored Division rolls along a road at
Camp Drum, circa 1950.

In 1947 the US Air Force became a
separate armed force, and the New Jersey
Air National Guard became a separate
entity as well. The New Jersey Air National Guard's 108th Fighter Wing, 108th
Fighter Group, 141st Fighter Squadron,
108th Air Base Group, 108th Maintenance and Supply Group, 108th Medical
Group, 141st Weather Station, and 105th
Aircraft Control and Warning Squadron
were activated for the Korean War. As
with the army organizations, none of
these state units were deployed in Korea.[9]
More than 190,000 New Jerseyans in
all, including Guardsmen, Reservists,
draftees, and volunteers in the regular
armed forces, served in the U.S. military
at various locations during the Korean
conflict between 1950 and 1953, and 836
lost their lives. New Jerseyans Nelson V.
Brittin of Audubon, Hector A. Cafferata
of Montville, and Samuel F. Coursen of
Madison were awarded the Congressional Medal of Honor for their heroism
during the war.[10]

## THE COLD WAR

During the Cold War, the ominous threat of nuclear annihilation hung heavy over the nation and New Jersey in particular, considering its proximity to New York City, presumably a major target. As a result, air raid drills became a part of everyday life. NAD Earle continued as a major Atlantic fleet ammunition depot and Forts Dix and Monmouth remained as major military installations, the former as a basic training base for draftees and volunteers. Among these trainees in the early 1950s were members of the "Alien GI" program, introduced through legislation by Senator Henry Cabot Lodge, which involved accepting recruits from countries currently behind the Iron Curtain and trading them citizenship in return for five years of service. There were fifty of these men at Fort Dix in June 1953. Major New Jersey colleges and universities, including Rutgers, Seton Hall, Newark College of Engineering (today's NJIT), Princeton, and Saint Peter's, had robust ROTC programs.[11]

Fort Monmouth became a Signal Corps scientific post for research in communications and radar, and included Camp Evans, a former substation in Gugliemo Marconi's old wireless communications center in Wall Township. In November 1948, the Air Force formally opened McGuire Air Force Base, an expansion of the old Camp Dix Airfield. The base was named for Ridgewood, New Jersey, native, World War II ace, and Medal of Honor recipient Major Thomas B. McGuire, who died in a plane crash in the Philippines in 1945.

Another milestone for the state's military occurred in January 1957, when the first women to serve in the New Jersey National Guard, Captain Frances Roberta Comstock and First Lieutenant

Top, soldiers in the army's "Alien GI" program training at Fort Dix in 1953. Bottom, the first women to join the New Jersey National Guard, nurses Captain Frances Comstock (left) and First lieutenant Lucille Valentino, are sworn in in East Orange in January 1957.

Lucille Valentino, both nurses, were sworn into service in East Orange. That July, Comstock, Valentino, and two other nurses left Paterson for annual training with the Guard's 114th Surgical Hospital. They were the first women to ever deploy for training with a New Jersey National Guard unit. Comstock had served as a U. S. Navy Nurse during World War II. She went on to join the faculty of Paterson General Hospital School of Nursing and was subsequently

Top, a Nike Ajax antiaircraft missile on display at the Sandy Hook National Recreation Area. Bottom, the scene after the Middletown Ajax missile explosion in 1958.

appointed head of the school. In 1960 she married Marino Tedeschi and afterward was known as Frances Tedeschi.

In an increasingly more federalized armed forces, the old big gun forts of past defensive eras gave way to Nike antiaircraft missile bases, which were scattered throughout strategic areas of New Jersey from Franklin Lakes to Woolwich Township, part of a national defense network against the possibility of an air attack by long range Soviet bombers. New Jersey Nike locations in the northern part of the state were associated with the New York Defense Area. Sites in southern New Jersey were part of the Philadelphia Defense Area.

The Continental United States, or CONUS, Air Defense System, including the New Jersey sites, was under the overall control of the North American Air Defense Command, or NORAD, manned by a joint operations group from the U.S. and Canadian air forces and headquartered in Cheyenne Mountain at Colorado Springs, Colorado. The first successful firing of a Nike missile, the Nike Ajax, was achieved in 1951 and the weapon was deployed in 1954. Work on a more effective successor weapon was quickly underway, with the goal of producing a missile with improved speed, range, and altitude capabilities, and armed with a powerful nuclear warhead. The end result was the Nike Hercules, with a nuclear capability, able to destroy closely spaced formations of attacking aircraft. Nike sites, initially primarily manned by members of the regular army, were often staffed by members of the Army National Guard after 1959. By 1969, an estimated four thousand Army Guardsmen were on duty across the country to help protect the United States from a surprise enemy bomber attack.[13]

Although the Nike sites were never called into action to meet an external threat, a devastating accident at the Middletown, New Jersey, installation in 1958 ended the lives of ten men. Known at the time as "the world's worst missile disaster," the tragedy occurred on May 22, when eight Nike missiles exploded, killing six regular army soldiers and four civilian technicians.[14]

The subsequent investigation revealed that the explosion occurred while army personnel were installing safety and arming mechanisms on the missiles, although the exact cause has never been discovered. Two of the three warheads on one of the missiles had been removed to gain access, when the third one suddenly detonated. In addition to destroying the other six aboveground missiles in the vicinity, a flying red-hot pellet apparently ignited the booster of the nearest missile in an adjoining section, blasting

it into the side of a nearby hill. Fortunately, the Ajax warhead failed to detonate.[15]

In the wake of the disaster, newspaper and magazine editors mocked army claims that a Nike installation in a town was no more dangerous than a gas station. Today, the only evidence of the horrific accident is a memorial to the men who died, which stands at Fort Hancock, now a part of Gateway National Recreation Area at Sandy Hook. The monument, which is in the form of two rockets symbolizing the Nike Ajax and Nike Hercules missiles, overlooks Sandy Hook Bay. Sandy Hook was the site of another Nike base, one of the few that remain intact. It is open for guided tours by appointment.

The Nike program itself wasn't the only New Jersey-related air defense tragedy during the Cold War era. On January 15, 1961, twenty-eight men were killed after the collapse of Texas Tower #4, a massive radar installation in the Atlantic Ocean, some seventy-five miles off the New Jersey coast. The tower, one of three similar installations off the East Coast named "Texas Towers" for their resemblance to offshore Gulf of Mexico oil rigs, was designed to provide early warning in the event of an enemy air attack so that Nike missiles could respond. Dubbed "Old Shaky" by the men who worked aboard it because of its tendency to shift in the ever-moving ocean, the structure was built on three pilings in 185 feet of water.[16]

Two previous hurricanes had damaged the tower's underwater bracings, so the structure was particularly vulnerable when a vicious winter storm struck, battering the tower with forty-mile-per-hour winds and thirty-foot-high waves. Evacuation plans were formed to rescue the crew by helicopter but at 7:30 p.m.

the tower fell, plunging the men into the
frigid Atlantic waters. Following an in-
tensive air and sea search, the twenty-
eight men—fourteen air force personnel
and fourteen civilians—were presumed
dead. The disaster led to a reassessment
of the towers and the other two off the
Massachusetts coast were closed shortly
thereafter.[17]

New threats posed by intercontinental
ballistic missiles as opposed to long-
range strategic bombers, the expense associated with the Vietnam War, a general
desire to trim budgets, and changing national and military priorities led to the
end of the Nike program. In 1974, the
last remaining sites were closed, and the
New Jersey National Guard unit charged
with operating some of them, the First
Battalion, 254th Air Defense Artillery,
was inactivated that year.

When the Hungarian Revolution
against that country's communist government literally went down in flames
following a Soviet invasion in November
1956, some 200,000 Hungarians fled the
country, crossing over the border into
Austria. Many of these refugees ultimately ended up in the United States,
passing through New Jersey's McGuire
Air Force Base and on to Camp Kilmer,
near New Brunswick, "a gateway to freedom," which became a staging area for
their further movement throughout the
country.[18]

New Jersey Army and Air National
Guard units were periodically called into
federal service during Cold War crises.
One situation began simmering in 1959,
when Soviet premier Nikita Khrushchev
initially demanded that Britain, France,
and the United States leave their occupied zones in Berlin, which was located
in the middle of Communist East Germany. Khrushchev vowed that he would
sign a treaty with East Germany giving

Top, Hungarian refugees preparing to
land at McGuire Air Force Base. From
there they traveled to Camp Kilmer,
near New Brunswick, for final settlement in the United States. Bottom, a
New Jersey Air National Guard plane
deployed to Chaumont, France, during
the Berlin Crisis of 1961.

that government control over the surrounding countryside. This threat was,
of course, largely fabricated, since the Soviets actually controlled East Germany,
"treaty" or not.

In 1961, following the building of the
Berlin Wall, Khrushchev issued an ulti-
matum date of December 31 to President John F. Kennedy, stating he would
cut off all access to Berlin if the Western
powers did not leave the city. In August

Kennedy ordered the mobilization of 150,000 Reservists and National Guardsmen, including New Jersey's 108th Tactical Fighter Wing and its support squadrons, which were deployed to Chaumont, France.

The New Jersey Army National Guard's 112th Artillery Group Headquarters, 30th Ordnance Battalion, 122nd Ordnance Company, 114th Surgical Hospital, 141st and 253rd Transportation Companies were also mobilized for the crisis, but were assigned to posts within the United States. The situation was defused by a compromise and the New Jersey National Guard units were released from active duty between August and October 1962. Three New Jersey airmen from the 108th interviewed in 2011 "recalled that the mood at the Chaumont base was fairly relaxed, and that no one thought too much about the potential magnitude of the situation. It was not until after they were home and reflected on their experience that they realized the significance of the crisis and the danger of war at the time."[19]

### THE VIETNAM WAR

The deadliest conflict for the post-World War II American military was the Vietnam War. American involvement began with advisers assigned to the South Vietnamese army in the mid-1950s, and combat units were introduced as the situation deteriorated in 1965. Approximately 212,000 New Jerseyans served in Vietnam during the course of the conflict. Although several Reserve and National Guard units were mobilized for brief periods during the war, including the New Jersey Air National Guard's 117th Tactical Fighter Group and the 119th Tactical Fighter Squadron in 1969, no New Jersey Reserve or Guard organi-

zations served in Southeast Asia, although some individuals did volunteer for overseas service.

Many, if not most, New Jerseyans who served in the regular armed forces during the Vietnam War, especially in the early years of the conflict, as noted by Robert Hopkins of Bradley Beach, a 1967 ROTC graduate of Saint Peter's College who served in Vietnam as a lieutenant with the 25th Infantry Division artillery, believed they were simply fulfilling their duty, as their fathers and uncles had done before them in World War II. In sharp contrast with previous conflicts, during the Vietnam War National Guard or Reserve enlistment was widely regarded by active duty soldiers, including the author—a 1965 ROTC graduate of Seton Hall University who served as a lieutenant in the 1st Infantry Division's Military Police Company in Vietnam in 1966-1967—as a way to avoid war service. It was believed, with more than a bit of evidence, that political contacts were especially useful in jumping a growing line of applicants for the Guard and Reserves.[20]

In early 1967, Congressman F. Edward Hebert of Louisiana "pledged . . . an all-out battle to plug legal loopholes which permit draft dodgers to use the Reserves and National Guard as a safe haven from combat duty." This statement was of particular note because Hebert had a reputation of being the "staunchest defender of the Reserves and Guard in Congress." A National Guard spokesman from New York disagreed with the congressman, stating that there was no way of knowing why someone would join the Guard. Major General James Cantwell, president of the National Guard Association and chief of staff of the New Jersey Guard, seemed to agree with Hebert, however,

Members of the 1st MP Company 81mm mortar platoon at Di An, Vietnam, January 1967. Left to right, SPC4 Ferri, the author, SFC Fahey, CPT Anderson.

stating "I have no illusions about it," but adding that he "was in no position to test the patriotism of volunteers." At this late date, those who served in those components of the military should not be rashly judged, since, as General Cantwell correctly pointed out, we have no way of reading their minds, and so must give them the benefit of the doubt.[21]

As in all the other twentieth century conflicts in which the United States was engaged, New Jersey proved to be an industrial asset to the war effort. Unfortunately, this time one assumed asset turned into a disaster. The Diamond Alkali Company, located on the Passaic River in Newark, churned out almost a million gallons of the "Agent Orange" herbicide, intended to be sprayed on Vietnamese jungles to destroy the cover used by the Vietcong. Agent Orange, however, proved to be toxic to American

soldiers handling it or coming in contact with it by walking or driving through sprayed areas. The location of the factory is now a Superfund site.[22]

As in most states, New Jersey witnessed a number of antiwar protests during the Vietnam War. Protesters periodically approached the main gate of Fort Dix and picketed other military bases, including a crowd of several thousand on Armed Forces Day 1970, and some stopped traffic on the New Jersey Turnpike, but the antiwar action that gained New Jersey nationwide attention was a raid staged on the Camden draft board, with the intent to destroy draft records, on Sunday, August 22, 1971. Unbeknownst to the activists, the FBI had been tipped off and arrested them. The "Camden 28" were subsequently tried but were acquitted when probable FBI entrapment was uncovered.[23]

Standoff between Military Police and antiwar demonstrators at Fort Dix, 1969.

Far more serious than any antiwar protests were the civil disturbances that broke out in Newark on July 12, 1967. The trouble started when Newark police arrested John W. Smith, an African-American cab driver. The officers claimed that Smith resisted arrest and that they had to "subdue" him. He claimed they beat him for no apparent reason. Smith was hospitalized with broken ribs and a head wound, but rumor spread throughout the city's Central Ward that he had been killed. The result, a riot outside police headquarters, led to further violence, as smoldering resentments and frustrations regarding police racism and real estate redlining that led to ghettoization that in turn led to limited opportunities for the city's black citizens, boiled over.

As the troubles in New Jersey's largest city grew, the National Guard reverted to its nineteenth century role. Governor Richard Hughes called General Cantwell in the afternoon of July 14, ordering him to prepare to send National Guard soldiers into Newark to assist the state police, who had already been dispatched, in controlling the disturbances. In total, three brigade headquarters and headquarters companies, four infantry battalions, one reconnaissance battalion, one artillery battalion, and one military police company were mobilized at their home stations.[25]

Chief of Staff Cantwell and other officers, as well as police and state and local political leaders, including Governor Richard Hughes and Newark mayor Hugh Addonizio, set up headquarters at the Roseville Avenue Armory. A reconnaissance determined that the "greatest volume of disorder centered along three principal east-west through streets—

The 114th Infantry deployed in Newark during the July 1967 civil disturbances.

South Orange Avenue, Springfield Avenue, and Clinton Avenue." Over 4,000 activated Guardsmen, acting with state police, blocked off the area and were ordered to conduct joint patrols with the state police. A newspaper retrospective a decade later, however, reported that "there was almost no coordination among soldiers and police." The Guardsmen had had no significant training for the situation they encountered in Newark.[26]

Over the night of July 14–15, Guardsmen and state police officers reported "snipers" firing from "apartments and roof tops of high-rise public housing apartments." The fire was reportedly "brief in time length and deliberately or otherwise inaccurate." It has been suggested that most of this fire, often exaggerated in anecdotal retelling, was actually due to state police and National Guardsmen firing at suspected snipers on rooftops, with the bullets going over the roofs and randomly landing among Guardsmen and troopers on the other side, who, believing they were being shot at from the rooftops, returned fire. Twenty-six civilians were killed, many by random return fire from city and state police. One twenty-four-year-old man who stole a six-pack of beer from a liquor store with a shattered window was shot and killed by Newark police, who also accidentally wounded a nearby twelve-year-old boy. By Monday, July 17, the rioting had ended, and the National Guard and state police pulled out of Newark. National Guard casualties were light—one man got a hernia from lifting ammunition boxes.[27]

A decade later Richard Hughes, then chief justice of the New Jersey Supreme Court, was asked if he had any regrets about how the disturbances were handled. His response was: "The unfortunate thing about it was the National Guard were young people from nonurban areas. They are not trained to handle snipers in high rises. That's how the lives were lost. I never blamed anybody for it. It was just a tragedy." Although there were other civil disturbances in New Jersey during that troubling era, the National Guard was not deployed to contain them. Sergeant Daniel Moore was activated for a couple of days to drive a two-and-a-half-ton truck (aka "deuce and a half") to Asbury Park during disturbances there in July 1970 and told to wait for state police officers to conduct prisoners for him to bring to

The war is over—at least for America. George Vohden of Wall Township, New Jersey, points to a picture of his son, Raymond, a prisoner of war since 1965, now free and debarking from a plane at Clark Air Force base in the Philippines in February 1973.

another location. There were no prisoners and he drove back to the Long Branch Armory.[28]

In the real war, the one in Vietnam, New Jersey lost 1,562 men and one woman, Captain Eleanor Grace Alexander, a nurse. Of these, 1,046 were killed in action, and the remainder died of various causes, including accidents, disease, and suicide. The remains of three percent of those who died were never recovered. The average age of the New Jersey soldier who died in Southeast Asia was twenty-three. Six in ten were volunteers, three were draftees, and one a reservist. Sixty-two percent were in the army, twenty-nine percent were Marines and the remainder served with the air force and navy. Although half of all communities in New Jersey lost at least one resident to the conflict, the largest number of fatal casualties were from the state's largest cities, Newark, Jersey City, and Trenton. Ninety-six percent died in

South Vietnam, and the remainder in North Vietnam, Laos, and Thailand. While the first New Jersey death occurred in 1960, and the last in 1975, thirty percent of those who died did so in 1968, the most intense year of the war. The New Jersey Vietnam Memorial and Museum in Holmdel stands as a monument to their sense of duty, their sacrifice, and their valor.[29]

## DESERT SHIELD AND DESERT STORM

The end of the draft and the transition to all-volunteer armed forces in the wake of the Vietnam War increased the role and responsibility of both Reserve and National Guard units in the national defense structure; they would be essential in the conduct of future operations and called to active duty in combat zones as well as during state and national emergencies in the years ahead. The New Jersey Army National Guard was reorganized in 1988, when the 50th Armored Division was deactivated and the state's Guard became the 50th Armored Brigade of the 42nd Division. The Guard remained, as before, a state force as well, subject to call up by the governor for various internal duties as diverse as disaster relief and providing medical support at the 1976 Battle of Monmouth Court House reenactment at Monmouth Battlefield State Park in Manalapan Township.

Following the August 2, 1990, invasion of Kuwait by Saddam Hussein's Iraqi army, President George H. W. Bush crafted a coalition of unlikely allies to assist the United States in protecting Saudi Arabia in operation Desert Shield on August 7 and then ejecting the Iraqis from Kuwait in operation Desert Storm, a task completed on February 28, 1991. As was

The New Jersey Vietnam Memorial at Holmdel.

always the case, numerous New Jerseyans served in the regular armed forces in the short war.

Desert Shield/Desert Storm was the first major test of the new role of the Reserves and National Guard in large scale operations. The New Jersey Army and Air Guard, as well as Reserve units stationed in the state, responded to the challenge. The Air National Guard's 170th Air Refueling Group, 177th Fighter Interceptor Group, 108th Tactical Fighter Wing, the 328th Transportation Detachment, 253rd Transportation Company, and 144th Supply Company, were all activated, and the state authorized family support groups to assist families of deployed Guardsmen and women. In all, more than 700 New Jersey Guard soldiers and airmen participated in support of Operation Desert Shield/Desert Storm.[30]

New Jersey Reservists also served in Operation Desert Shield/Desert Storm. Former Essex Trooper sergeant first Class William Paynton of Lincoln Park was a Truck Master in the Seventy-eighth Division's 920th Transportation Company, a unit about 120 men strong headquartered at Caven Point, Jersey City. The company was notified in December 1990 that it would be mobilized for overseas service, and left for Saudi Arabia in January 1991, arriving several weeks later. The 920th was tasked with transporting fuel from Saudi refineries to units in the field during Desert Storm and returned to New Jersey in April 1991.[31]

In their role as the regular military's back-up force, National Guard units were also mobilized in the various peacekeeping efforts and interventions of the 1990s, including the war in the former Yugoslavia. In order to improve support to active duty organizations, the New Jersey Air National Guard's 170th Air Refueling Group and 108th Tactical Fighter Wing, stationed at McGuire Air Force Base, were combined to form the 108th Air Refueling Wing. The new unit was equipped with twenty KC-135E Stratotankers and has since provided worldwide refueling support for American and NATO aircraft, deploying frequently to Incirlik Air Base in Turkey. During the same reorganization, the 177th Fighter Interceptor Group, equipped with F-16 aircraft, transitioned into the 177th Fighter Wing, which was also called up during the 1999 fighting in the Balkans.[32]

## TWENTY-FIRST CENTURY CONFLICTS

In the aftermath of the September 11, 2001, terrorist attacks, the New Jersey Army and Air National Guard immedi-

Sergeant First Class Bill Paynton on the Saudi Arabia/Kuwait border in 1991.

ately rose to the occasion, under the overall command of the Emergency Operations Center at Fort Dix. The 177th Fighter Wing, based at Atlantic City Airport, soon had its F-16s in the air over New York City and the surrounding area in preassigned "air sovereignty missions." The state's Naval Militia, reconstituted by Governor Christine Whitman in 1999, also responded to the call, contributing valuable service. Other New Jersey Army and Air Force Guard units, part of the 57th Troop Command, established "Task Force Liberty" headquarters at Liberty State Park in Jersey City and deployed security forces at local bridges, airports, tunnels, and nuclear facilities. The New Jersey Guard subsequently created "Task Force Respect," at Staten Island's Fresh Kills landfill, where two million tons of debris from the World Trade Center was sifted and examined for the remains of victims, which were carefully collected, although few were identified.[33]

Following 9/11, Garden State units also served in peacekeeping operations in the Sinai Peninsula and Bosnia and assisted the Albanian army following a massive explosion in that country in 2008, a mission that established a relationship between the Albanian military and New Jersey. The Army Guard, now characterized as "truly a global force," was consequently restructured and modernized once again according to the "modular conversion" program, as the 50th Infantry Brigade Combat Team, to mirror regular army units and become more "flexible" so as to be able to fulfill a variety of missions, including detainee supervision, security, logistical support, and military police functions. In effect, the Guard's role as a backup force was ended and it was considered a fully deployable entity. And it was indeed deployed. More than 6,000 members of the New Jersey National Guard were activated for overseas service in the seven years following 9/11.[34]

The New Jersey Guard served around the world in support of operations Iraqi Freedom and Enduring Freedom. In March 2003, the 253rd Transportation Company, based in Cape May, became the first New Jersey National Guard unit to deploy to Iraq. Others followed in succeeding years. In January 2004, Battery B, Third Battalion, 112th Artillery, was sent to Fort Dix, where the artillerymen were retrained in military police duties. In March 2004, the Battery B soldiers arrived in Baghdad, where they were attached to the 89th Military Police Brigade and redesignated as Company C. The Jerseyans would engage in combat in Baghdad, Fallujah, and Sadr City, where the unit suffered the New Jersey Guard's first post-9/11 casualties when,

The 9/11 memorial at Fresh Kills.

on June 4–5, 2004, Staff Sergeants Steve Carvill and Humberto Timoteo, Sergeant Ryan Doltz, and Specialist Timothy Duffy were killed in IED attacks. Company C returned to New Jersey in February 2005. Adding to the state's casualty list, Staff Sergeant Jorge Oliveira of the 113th Infantry was killed in Paktika Province, Afghanistan, on October 19, 2011.[35]

In May of 2004, more than 1,400 members of the New Jersey National Guard were mobilized in the largest deployment of the state's military assets since 1940, and deployed in Iraq to pro-

The New Jersey National Guard 253rd Transportation Company "Battle Wagon" used for convoy escort duty in Iraq.

vide organizational support for regular army detachments. New Jersey National Guard soldiers from the 102nd Armor and 113th Infantry were deployed to Guantanamo Bay in 2002–2005 to provide security at the Detention Center at the base. First Lieutenant Amelia Thatcher served with an eight-person team from the New Jersey National Guard's 444th Mobile Public Affairs Detachment commanded by Major John Powers. The team was assigned to Guantanamo Bay in 2011–2012. She and her fellow New Jersey Guard soldiers handled media relations and escorted members of Congress and other VIPs visiting the site.[36]

In 2008 the 50th Brigade Combat Team was deployed to Iraq and served as a security force at Camp Cropper, Camp Bucca, Balad Air Base, Ashraf, and Baghdad. The duties were diverse and required flexibility. First Lieutenant Jarrett

Feldman of Neptune, a Transportation Corps officer, was a platoon leader in the 250th Brigade Support Battalion, Assistant S-4 for the 744th and 519th Military Police Battalions, and provided contract and logistical support for the Remembrance Two Detention Facility.[37]

New Jersey's soldiers were also called on, as they had been in the past, for domestic disaster duty. In 2005, the 177th Medical Group of the Air National Guard flew to New Orleans in the wake of Hurricane Katrina, and elements of the 102nd Armor and 114th Infantry provided security for FEMA operations during the disaster. National Guard units were mobilized for duty in New Jersey during Hurricane Irene in 2011 and Superstorm Sandy in 2013, in the latter disaster rescuing people stranded by flooding in Hoboken. It is safe to say that almost 100 percent of the men and women of the current New Jersey National Guard have been deployed on one mission or another since 9/11.[38]

New Jersey Army Reservists also served in Iraq. Pratik Mavani of Glen Ridge, the son of Indian immigrants, was a member of the 961st Movement Control Team, located on Staten Island. In the last week of April 2003, the 961st flew from New Jersey to Germany, and then on to Kuwait. The unit moved frequently, from Camp Arifjan in Kuwait to Tallil Air Base and Camp Cedar in Iraq, managing convoys, and then further north, riding in a night convoy to the city of Mosul, where the 961st would spend the rest of its tour managing humanitarian convoys carrying fuel, food, and other supplies.[39]

Mavani also served with the Civil Affairs Patrol in Mosul, walking the city's streets to assess which public works needed repair and maintenance. The 961st included female soldiers, and Mavani recalled that young Iraqi girls would swarm around the women, amazed to see them in such a role. The 961st returned to McGuire Air Force Base in April 2004 and Sergeant Mavani returned to his studies at Rutgers University, eventually becoming a physician.[40]

In March 2012, the New Jersey National Guard's 117th Combat Sustainment Support Battalion deployed to Fort Hood, Texas, for training, and departed for Afghanistan the following month. The unit, a battalion headquarters, was stationed at Kandahar Airfield to direct National Guard and regular army companies providing logistical support to Regional Command South. Captain Jarrett Feldman of Neptune, who had previously served in Iraq, was the battalion's operations officer. Captain John Bilby of Fair Lawn was the battalion transportation officer, involved in organizing available transportation assets for the support

Top, the New Jersey National Guard 102nd Cavalry at a detention center, Bucca, Iraq. Bottom, Sergeant Pratik Mavani (rear seat) in Mosul.

of ongoing combat operations and transporting military gear out of the country and back to the United States. The battalion, which was awarded a Meritorious Unit Citation for its work, moved over twelve million tons of equipment before returning to New Jersey in January 2013.[41]

Captain Vincent Solomeno of Hazlet was Future Operations Officer for a detachment of twenty-five officers and non-commissioned officers of the New Jersey National Guard's 50th Infantry Brigade Combat deployed to Kuwait and Jordan from December 2014 to September 2015 as a Military Engagement Team. The team had a twofold mission. In Jordan, working daily with key leaders of the Jordanian Armed Forces and Border Guard to improve security on the Syrian border, and traveling throughout U.S. Army Central Command (the Arabian Peninsula, Levant, and Central

Asia). In nine months, team members visited nine countries, conducted forty-three engagements, and traveled a total of 281,908 miles, meeting with soldiers from generals to privates from Afghanistan, Algeria, Canada, Egypt, Great Britain, Jordan, Kazakhstan, Kuwait, Kyrgyzstan, Lebanon, Nepal, New Zealand, Oman, Saudi Arabia, Tajikistan, Turkey, the United Arab Emirates, the United Kingdom, and Uzbekistan.[42]

Although the pace of deployments has declined precipitously with the winding down of American participation in the Iraq and Afghan Wars, the modern mission of the New Jersey National Guard, as well as the state's Army Reserve forces, makes it certain that New Jersey's soldiers and airmen, along with the state's citizens in the regular armed forces, will continue to serve their state and nation—as they always have.

New Jersey National Guard captains Jarret Feldman (a major as of this writing) and John Bilby of the New Jersey National Guard's 117th Combat Sustainment Support Battalion in Kandahar, Afghanistan, 2012.

# Appendix

## New Jersey's Military Monuments, Historic Sites, Museums, and Memorials

The Sandy Hook Peninsula, with the Atlantic Ocean on one side and Raritan Bay on the other, is rich with New Jersey history, dating from the time it was first rounded by Verrazano in 1524. The lighthouse at Sandy Hook, erected in 1764 on what is the gateway to New York harbor, is the oldest existing lighthouse in the United States. Loyalists established a fortified camp and raider base around the lighthouse during the Revolution, and New Jersey militiamen and federal Sea Fencibles garrisoned a fort and blockhouses on Sandy Hook during the War of 1812. A coast defense fort was partially constructed on Sandy Hook in the late 1850s, but was abandoned when the Civil War proved such forts vulnerable to artillery. **Sandy Hook** served as the US Army Ordnance Corps' first weapons and ammunition proving ground from 1874 to 1919 and **Fort Hancock**, named for Civil War major general Winfield Scott Hancock, was constructed in the 1890s. Fort Hancock's guns were fully manned during World Wars I and II. After the war, continental defense weaponry evolved from coastal guns to anti-aircraft artillery to Nike anti-aircraft missiles. It was the site of a prison for military offenders during the latter part of World War II. The fort was decommissioned in 1974 and subsequently became part of the Gateway National Recreation Area. Much of the fort remains and there is also a museum dedicated to its history on the site. Sandy Hook is also the site of a **Nike antiaircraft missile base** that was, along with a number of other such bases in New Jersey and elsewhere, part of America's Cold War defense system. The base is open for guided tours. Location: 128 South Hartshorne Drive, Highlands, NJ 07732.

**Fort Mott** was envisioned as part of a three-fort defense system designed for the defense of the Delaware River against enemy ships in the post-Civil War era and was originally planned to have eleven gun emplacements housing twenty heavy artillery pieces and a mortar battery with six massive mortars. The current fortifications were completed in 1896. The installation was named for Gershom Mott, a New Jersey native who served as an officer in the Mexican and Civil Wars and commanded the state's National Guard in the postwar period. Regular army soldiers were stationed at

Fort Mott from 1897 to 1922, and the federal government maintained a caretaker detachment at the fort between 1922 and 1943, during which time the fort's guns were dismantled. The fort was declared "surplus property" in 1943. New Jersey acquired the military reservation as a historic site and state park in 1947, and it was opened to the public on June 24, 1951. Although Fort Mott was disarmed long ago and the guns are gone, emplacements and magazines still line an impressive 750-foot long, thirty-five-foot-thick poured concrete parapet, which is buttressed by an additional thirty feet of sand and earth. The site, maintained by the New Jersey Department of Environmental Protection, provides a self-guided tour with interpretive signs. There are eleven stops on the tour and the Visitor Center features exhibits on the fort's history. It is also the southern anchor for the New Jersey Coastal Heritage Trail. Fort Mott State Park is located at 454 Fort Mott Road, Pennsville, NJ 08070.

Built in 1734, the **Hancock House** was the home of a prominent Salem County family and is an excellent example of English Quaker pattern brick houses associated with the lower Delaware Valley and southwestern New Jersey. Perhaps the most notorious British raid of the Revolution had this house as its focal point. On the night of March 20–21, 1778, Major John Simcoe's Loyalists conducted a surprise attack on the Hancock's Bridge garrison, killing everyone they could find in the vicinity, including men they encountered along the road, twenty to thirty militiamen sleeping in the Hancock house, and the house's owner Judge William Hancock and his brother, who happened to be noted local Loyalists. After the war Simcoe bragged about the massacre of the militiamen as

a stellar surprise operation, but expressed sorrow at the "unfortunate circumstances" of the bayoneting of the judge and his brother, stating that "events like these are the real miseries of war." Cornelia Hancock, the saintly New Jersey Civil War nurse known as "America's Florence Nightingale," was the great granddaughter of William Hancock. Hancock House is located at 3 Front Street, Hancock's Bridge, NJ 08038.

On January 3, 1777, in the second phase of George Washington's brilliant New Jersey counteroffensive, American militiamen and Continental soldiers personally led by Washington decisively defeated a British force at Princeton. It was the last encounter of the "Ten Crucial Days" which began with the crossing of the Delaware River for the attack on Trenton. The battlefield ranged over a considerable terrain, extending into the town itself. The present **Princeton Battlefield State Park** was expanded in 2016 by the acquisition of fourteen critical acres saved from development through the auspices of the Princeton Battlefield Area Preservation Society. The famous Mercer Oak, under which General Hugh Mercer was mortally wounded by British bayonets, once stood in the middle of the battlefield. The **Clarke House**, where General Mercer died, was built by Thomas Clarke in 1772, and was used as a field hospital in the battle's aftermath, contains period furniture and an exhibit of Revolutionary War artifacts. A memorial colonnade stands by the gravesite of twenty-one British and fifteen American soldiers killed during the battle. Princeton Battlefield State Park is located at 500 Mercer Road. Princeton NJ 08540-4810.

**New Bridge**, in Bergen County, was a strategic Hackensack River crossing throughout the American Revolution. Its homes served as headquarters for commanders of both sides and both armies camped on its hills and fields. Skirmishes between Loyalists and Patriots were commonplace at New Bridge throughout the conflict. Soldiers passed this gateway to New Jersey's hinterland so often that the still-standing "Steuben House," confiscated by the state from a loyalist and owned by Baron von Steuben for a time after the war, is said to have seen more of the Revolution pass by than any other house in America. American troops fleeing the victorious British from Fort Lee crossed the Hackensack at New Bridge, Thomas Paine reportedly penned the first draft of *The American Crisis* there, and most of the military notables of the Revolution, from George Washington on down, made a stop, at one time or another, at the little mill town. The site has been preserved and restored by adjoining towns, Bergen County, and the Bergen County Historical Society and hosts Revolutionary War living history encampments a number of times a year, as well as other events. Historic New Bridge Landing Park is located at 1201 Main Street, River Edge, New Jersey, 07661.

Located in Wall Township on the site of Camp Evans, a former adjunct facility to Fort Monmouth, the **InfoAge Museum** is dedicated to creating an "Information Age Learning Center" in historic buildings that once housed the staff of the Marconi trans-Atlantic wireless transmittal station. The site was also a World War I overseas communications station and a major World War II and Cold War era radar laboratory as a part of the larger Fort Monmouth complex. It was the site of a famous visit by Senator Joseph McCarthy during his investigation of alleged Communist infiltration of the Fort Monmouth Signal Corps installation. Exhibits display the evolution

of military radio and radar technology over those years. **Camp Evans** is listed on the National Register of Historic Sites, and the National Park Service has approved an application to use thirty-seven acres of the camp and all the buildings in the historic district to help improve the public understanding of science, technology, and science history, honoring the communication pioneers of wireless, World War I, World War II, space exploration, and the Cold War. InfoAge also has a large collection of military vehicles on display. InfoAge is located at 2201 Marconi Road, Wall Township, New Jersey 07719.

The Millville Airport was dedicated as "America's First Defense Airport" on August 2, 1941, by local, state, and federal officials. In less than a year, construction began, and in January 1943, the Millville Army Air Field opened as a gunnery school for fighter pilots. Training began with Curtiss P-40F Warhawks, but after a few weeks, the P-40s were replaced by Republic P-47 Thunderbolts. About 1,500 pilots received advanced fighter training in the Thunderbolt at Millville before it closed in 1946. Following the war, the airfield was declared excess federal property and returned to the city of Millville. Most of the buildings were converted to apartments for veterans' housing. The apartments were phased out by the early 1970s, and the airport soon became a southern New Jersey industrial and aviation hub. The **Millville Army Airfield Museum** originated with the collection of Michael T. Stowe, who, as a teenager in the 1970s, began exploring abandoned World War II bunkers and collecting artifacts and documents relating to the airport. In 1983, Stowe approached the city to request a permanent location at the airport to display his collection, which remains the cornerstone of the museum. The collection has grown through donations of time, effort, and artifacts from the local community and veterans who served at Millville, and the museum has gained recognition for its contributions to World War II aviation history. The Millville Army Airfield Museum is located at 1 Ledden Street, Millville Airport, Millville, NJ 08332.

The longest single day battle of the American Revolution took place in the fields and forests that now make up **Monmouth Battlefield State Park** on June 28, 1778. Although the configuration of the landscape has been somewhat modified by nineteenth century farming practices, the park preserves a splendid pre-industrial rural landscape of hilly farmland and hedgerows. There are miles of hiking and horseback riding trails, picnic areas, and a restored Revolutionary War farmhouse. Well marked trails with accompanying brochures enable the visitor to accurately follow the course of the battle across the field. A new visitor center dedicated on June 14, 2013, houses exhibits that deal with the battle, as well as the use of part of the park land as a Civil War rendezvous camp that processed and organized over 3,000 soldiers in the 14th, 28th, 29th, and part of the 35th New Jersey Infantry Regiments in 1862 and 1863. The annual Battle of Monmouth reenactment hosted by the Park is a significant event that draws a large number of Revolutionary War reenactors and spectators. The park is located at 16 Business Route 33, Manalapan, NJ 07726.

**Morristown National Historical Park**, established in 1933, is the oldest National Historic Park in the country. The park's mission is to commemorate the encampment of General George Washington's Continental army at Morristown over the winter of 1779–1780, the worst win-

ter of the eighteenth century. Morristown was a strong Patriot town and a perfect location for a base with the British occupying New York, and the Americans had spent the remainder of the winter there after their victories at Trenton and Princeton in 1776 and early 1777. Washington's outposts could observe British movements and were protected from surprise by the Watchung Mountains. Features of the park include the Ford Mansion, used by Washington for his headquarters in 1779–80, and reconstructed soldier huts at Jockey Hollow, as well as a research library and archive and a museum with an extensive display of equipment, artifacts, and art connected with the era. The park is located at 30 Washington Place, Morristown, NJ 07960.

The mission of the **National Guard Militia Museum of New Jersey** at Sea Girt is to preserve and explain the military heritage of New Jersey and enhance public understanding of how armed conflicts and military institutions have shaped our state and national experience. The museum collects, preserves, and displays artifacts, documents, and memorabilia that have specific historical significance to the Army National Guard, the Air National Guard, and the Naval Militia of New Jersey. The museum presents the role of the New Jersey Militia and National Guard within the context of the larger history of the state, using original and reproduction uniforms, weapons, photographs, artifacts, and art from the period of Dutch, Swedish, and British colonization through the War for Independence, Civil War, and World Wars I and II to the present day, paying particular attention to the diversity of the New Jersey citizen soldier and his or her experience. The museum is also the home of the Center for U.S. War Veterans' Oral History Project. It is the center's mission to collect and preserve the memories of veterans through recorded oral history interviews, and it does so in cooperation with the Library of Congress. The museum is located at the National Guard Training Center, Sea Girt Avenue & Camp Drive, Sea Girt, NJ 08750.

**Naval Air Station (NAS) Wildwood Aviation Museum** is a non-profit museum located at the Cape May Airport inside historic Hangar #1. Commissioned in April 1943, the original Naval Air station served as an active dive-bomber squadron training facility during World War II. Today, Hangar #1 has been restored and transformed into an aviation museum that houses a number of aircraft, engines, special exhibits, and educational interactive displays. The "Avenger" torpedo bomber on display was manufactured at the General Motors Eastern Aircraft Division in Ewing Township, outside Trenton, in 1943. The Ewing factory turned out 7,546 Avengers during the war. The museum invites visitors to explore aviation, New Jersey, military, and World War II history through "hands-on," fun and educational activities for the entire family in a 92,000 square foot sampling of New Jersey's war effort in the 1940s. Photography is encouraged. The museum is located at 500 Forrestal Rd., Cape May Airport, NJ 08242.

A joint project of the New Jersey Civil War Heritage Association and the New Jersey State Museum, with the assistance of the Sons of Union Veterans of the Civil War, the **New Jersey State Museum Civil War Flags Annex** displays five historic New Jersey Civil War flags from the museum's vast collection. Every six months the flags, displayed in acid-free exhibit cases, are rotated. The rotation event features a historical presentation by a New Jersey Civil War scholar. The flag display, originally located at the New Jersey State Archives building at 225 West State Street, was temporarily removed for property rehabilitation in 2017, and the flag display was moved to the **New Jersey State Museum**, 205 West State Street, Trenton, NJ 08625.

The **New Jersey Vietnam Veterans Memorial**, located in Holmdel on the grounds of the PNC Bank Arts Center located at Garden State Parkway exit 116, is intended to honor New Jerseyans who served in the Vietnam War, especially the 1,561 men and one woman from the state who lost their lives in the conflict. The design was created by Hien Nguyen in 1988, and the completed memorial officially dedicated on May 7, 1995. The memorial is open 24 hours a day, every day of the year, and admission is free. Guided tours by volunteer docent New Jersey Vietnam veterans are available for groups. The memorial is a circular pavilion, containing 366 8-foot-tall black granite panels, each one representing a day of the year, and casualties are listed by the day on which they lost their lives. The center of the pavilion features a red oak, the New Jersey state tree, and three statues; a dying soldier, a nurse tending to his wounds, and another soldier standing by their side, representing those who died, the women who served, and those who returned. The Vietnam Era Museum and Educational Center, which explains the war and the era and their effect on the state and country, provides a lens into history for the visitor. The New Jersey Vietnam Veterans' Memorial Foundation can be contacted at #1 Memorial Lane, PO Box 648, Holmdel, NJ, 07733.

The **Trenton Old Barracks Museum**, built in 1758, is the only French and Indian War era barracks still standing. It was also used during the Revolutionary War by both the Hessian occupiers of Trenton in 1776 and American forces thereafter. In the years after the Revolution it was used as housing and the central part of the building was torn down to allow a street to pass through. Purchased by the DAR and presented to the State in the early twentieth century, the Old Barracks was eventually restored to its original configuration and serves as a museum commemorating the role of New Jersey in both the Colonial Wars and the Revolution. The site hosts a number of events during the year, including summer day camps for students, living history encampments and permanent and changing exhibits on the era. The Trenton Old Barracks Museum is located at 101 Barrack Street, Trenton, NJ 08608.

# Notes

CHAPTER ONE: NEW JERSEY'S
NATIVE PEOPLE AND EARLY EU-
ROPEAN CONTACT

1. Kraft, *Lenape-Delaware Indian
Heritage*, 45, 361. Kraft offers evidence
of bison presence in today's Cumber-
land County, New Jersey, and in eastern
New York; MacKenzie, *The Fisheries of
Raritan Bay*, 14-15; Boyd, *Atlantic
Highlands*, 14-15.

2. Kraft, *Lenape-Delaware Indian
Heritage*, 1-8, 250. Kraft's book is the
definitive to date work on the Lenape.

3. *Ibid.*, 251-253.

4. *Ibid.*, 253.

5. Dowd, *The Indians of New Jersey*;
Boyd, *Atlantic Highlands*, 25-26; Moss,
*Monmouth—Our Indian Heritage*.

6. Moss, *Monmouth*, 32; Lender, *One
State in Arms*, 7; Kraft, *Lenape-
Delaware Indian Heritage*, 365.

7. Moss, *Monmouth*, 32; Alan and
Barbara Aimone, "New Netherland Defends Itself"; Lurie and Mappen, *Encyclopedia of New Jersey*, 581; Lender, *One
State in Arms*, 9.

8. Kraft, *Lenape-Delaware Indian
Heritage*, 404.

9. Schmidt, *Agriculture in New Jersey*,
25; Lurie and Mappen, *Encyclopedia of
New Jersey*, 622; Lovero, *Hudson
County*, 8-9.

10. Kraft, *Lenape-Delaware Indian
Heritage*, 412-413.

11. Kraft, *Lenape-Delaware Indian
Heritage*, 413-414; Shorto, *Island at the
Center of the World*, 126; Given, in *A
Most Pernicious Thing*, argues that trading of firearms to the Indians was not
as pervasive as often claimed, with each
colonial power blaming another, stating
that colonists did not have enough
first-rate arms for themselves for some
time after establishing the colonies, and
that the bow was a superior weapon for
forest warfare. His argument resonates
when the matchlock is considered, but
the flintlock was a far superior arm—
and the greed for furs pervasive, and
seeming irrationality often trumps
what would appear in retrospect to be
common sense. Still, his points bear
consideration.

12. Email Correspondence with Mark
van Hattem, curator of textiles, Royal
Netherlands Army and Arms Museum;
Jacobs, *The Colony of New Netherland*,
36-37, 182.

13. Alan and Barbara Aimone, "New
Netherland Defends Itself"; Email Cor-
respondence with Mark van Hattem,
curator of textiles, Royal Netherlands
Army and Arms Museum; Jacobs, *New
Netherland*, 38.

14. Peterson, *Arms and Armor in
Colonial America*, 20, 46-47.

15. Peterson, *Arms and Armor in
Colonial America*, 20, 46-47; Gale, *For
Trade and Treaty*, 9; Given, *A Most Per-*

*nicious Thing,* 46; Van Der Donck, *The Representation,* 271. Silverman, *Thundersticks,* 41.

16. Jacobs, *The Colony of New Netherland,* 195.

17. Alan and Barbara Aimone, "New Netherland Defends Itself"; Wacker, *Land and People,* 77; Volo & Volo, *Family Life in 17th and 18th Century America,* 140.

18. Pomfret, *The Province of East Jersey,* 42.

19. Lurie and Wacker, *Mapping New Jersey,* 48; Pomfret, *The Province of East Jersey,* 42.

20. Shorto, *Island at the Center of the World,* 160-161.

21. Kraft, *Lenape-Delaware Indian Heritage,* 414-415.

22. Alan and Barbara Aimone, "New Netherland Defends Itself."

23. Boyd, *Atlantic Highlands,* 30; Schmidt, *Agriculture in New Jersey,* 26-27.

24. Jacobs, *The Colony of New Netherland,* 196-198.

25. Pomfret, *Colonial New Jersey,* 42.

CHAPTER TWO: NEW JERSEY
UNDER ENGLISH RULE,
1664–1775

1. Salter, *A History of Monmouth and Ocean Counties,* 33-34; Dowd, *The Indians of New Jersey,* 47, 58-59; Wilson, *New Jersey Shore,* 3; Boyd, *Atlantic Highlands,* 24.

2. Pomfret, *Colonial New Jersey,* 24-29.

3. For a modern, understandable account of this political labyrinth, see Fleming, *New Jersey,* 6-20.

4. Studley, *Historic New Jersey Through Visitors' Eyes,* 7.

5. Wacker, *Land and People,* 58; Dowd, *The Indians of New Jersey,* 50-51;

Salter, *Monmouth and Ocean Counties,* 116-117; Kraft and Kraft, *The Indians of Lenapehoking,* 39.

6. Wallace, *King of the Delawares,* 2.

7. Pomfret, *Colonial New Jersey,* 57; Lender, *One State in Arms,* 15.

8. Lee, *New Jersey as a Colony and as a State,* 138-142; *National Guard Yearbook, 1940,* xvii-xviii; Lender, *One State in Arms,* 15.

9. *National Guard Yearbook, 1940,* xviii.

10. Fleming, *New Jersey,* 23.

11. Parker, "New Jersey in the Colonial Wars."

12. Lee, *New Jersey as a Colony and as a State,* 371; Parker, "New Jersey in the Colonial Wars."

13. Lee, *New Jersey as a Colony and as a State,* Vol. I, 373.

14. Lee, *New Jersey as a Colony and as a State,* Vol. I, 374-375; Folsom, "Colonel Peter Schuyler;" Parker, "New Jersey in the Colonial Wars."

15. Folsom, "Colonel Peter Schuyler."

16. Lee, *New Jersey as a Colony and as a State,* Vol. I, 376; Fleming, *New Jersey,* 29; Pomfret, *Colonial New Jersey,* 171.

17. Parker, "New Jersey in the Colonial Wars."

18. Pomfret, *Colonial New Jersey,* 171; Parker, "New Jersey in the Colonial Wars."

19. Lee, *New Jersey as a Colony and as a State,* Vol. I, 379-380; A copy of the Crosswicks treaty is available at http://gnadenhutten.tripod.com/bethe-lindiantown/id23.html; Kraft, *Lenape-Delaware Indian Heritage,* 24.

20. Veit, *Digging New Jersey's Past,* 58-62.

21. Lee, *New Jersey as a Colony and as a State,* Vol. I, 380-381; Pomfret, *Colonial New Jersey,* 172-173; Purvis, "The Aftermath of Fort William Henry's Fall."

22. Fowler, *Empires at War*, 120-128; Pomfret, *Colonial New Jersey*, 172-173; Parker, "New Jersey in the Colonial Wars;" Casterline, *Colonial Tribulations*, 135; Purvis, "The Aftermath of Fort William Henry's Fall." Although a nightmare for some, the post-surrender "massacre" was not as devastating as it has been popularly portrayed in the pages of *The Last of the Mohicans*. The garrison surrendered 2,308 men of whom approximately 69 were killed and 100 carried off as captives. Fowler, *Empires at War*, 129.

23. Lee, *New Jersey as a Colony and as a State*, Vol. I, 382-383; Pomfret, *Colonial New Jersey*, 173; Pierson, *History of the Oranges*, 77-78; Urquhart, *History of Newark*, 228. Johnson would later be killed in the campaign to capture Fort Niagara.

24. http://www.njrangingco.org/.

25. Casterline, *Colonial Tribulations*, 146; Purvis, "The Aftermath of Fort William Henry's Fall"; Lee, *New Jersey as a Colony and as a State*, Vol. I, 382.

26. Lee, *New Jersey as a Colony and as a State*, Vol. I, 383.

27. Wallace, *King of the Delawares*, 2; Salter, *A History of Monmouth and Ocean Counties*, 306; Kraft and Kraft, *The Indians of Lenapehoking*, 39.

28. Parker, "New Jersey in the Colonial Wars;" Purvis, "The Aftermath of Fort William Henry's Fall."

CHAPTER THREE: NEW JERSEY IN THE AMERICAN REVOLUTION, 1775–1777

1. Fleming, *New Jersey: A History*, 47-50; Maxine Lurie, "New Jersey: Radical or Conservative?" in Mitnick, *New Jersey in the Revolution*, 41; David Fowler, "These Were Troublesome Times Indeed," in Mitnick, *New Jersey in the Revolution*, 21.

2. Fleming, *New Jersey*, 59-60; Larry R. Gerlach, "William Franklin," in Stellhorn and Birkner, *The Governors of New Jersey, 1664-1974*, 75-76.

3. *National Guard Yearbook, 1940*, xix; Lundin, *Cockpit of the Revolution*, 114.

4. Irwin, ed., *A History of Randolph Township*, 38.

5. Stryker, *Official Register of the Officers and Men of New Jersey in the Revolutionary War*, 10.

6. Wright, *The Continental Army*, 255-256.

7. Stryker, *Official Register of the Officers and Men of New Jersey in the Revolutionary War*, Vol. 1, 23.

8. Stryker, *Official Register of the Officers and Men of New Jersey in the Revolutionary War*, Vol. 2, 321. Handwritten note, apparently by Adjutant General Stryker, on a copy of this publication in the collections of the NGMMNJ/Sea Girt.

9. Mark M. Boatner III, *Encyclopedia of the American Revolution*, 797-798. Boatner gives Washington a paper strength of 28,500 men, but notes that actual "fit for duty" strength was around 19,000, with little artillery and no cavalry; *National Guard Yearbook, 1940*, xix.

10. Lundin, *Cockpit of the Revolution*, 115, 123-127; Boatner gives Howe's paper strength as 32,625 with the number of "effectives fit for duty" at 24, 464. Boatner, *Encyclopedia*, p. 798.

11. Captain Francis Hutcheson to General Frederick Haldimand, July 10, 1776, British Library; Lundin, *Cockpit of the Revolution*, 115-121.

12. Lundin, *Cockpit of the Revolution*, 126-130; Kidder, *A People Harassed and Exhausted*, 127. Kidder's book is a detailed history of the New Jersey militia's First Hunterdon Regiment and its war.

13. Kidder, *A People Harassed and Exhausted*, 136-137.

14. Lundin, *Cockpit of the Revolution*, 135-136.

15. Braisted, *Bergen County Voices from the American Revolution*, 103-104; Lundin, *Cockpit of the Revolution*, 141-142.

16. Lundin, *Cockpit of the Revolution*, 145.

17. Lundin, *Cockpit of the Revolution*, 146-151.

18. *Ibid.*, 143-145; Stryker, *Official Register of the Officers and Men of New Jersey in the Revolutionary War*, 321-322.

19. Lundin, *Cockpit of the Revolution*, 160-161. Karels, ed., *The Revolutionary War in Bergen County*, 69-70; Braisted, *Bergen County Voices from the American Revolution*, 10, 97-98. Noble's military career was ended by the wound, and he became a commissary in New York, where he was murdered by highwaymen in 1779. For details on the course of the Loyalist counterrevolution in Monmouth County, the other most significant Loyalist county, see Chapter 2 of Bilby and Jenkins, *Monmouth Court House*.

20. Lundin, *Cockpit of the Revolution*, 189-193; Kidder, *A People Harassed and Exhausted*, 206.

21. Wood, *Battles of the Revolutionary War*, 61.

22. *Ibid.*, 74.

23. *Ibid.*, 77-78.

24. *Ibid.*, 81.

25. *Ibid.*, 84-85.

26. *Ibid.*, 89.

27. Lundin, *Cockpit of the Revolution*, 157; Cunningham, *The Uncertain Revolution*, 13; Hunter and Burrow, "The Historical Geography ..." in Mitnick, ed., *New Jersey in the American Revolution*, 175; Kidder, *A People Harassed and Exhausted*, 229.

28. Karels, *Revolutionary War in Bergen County*, 23; Hunter, *The Journal of Gen. Sir Martin Hunter and Some Letters of His Wife Lady Hunter ...*, 27.

29. "The Reverend Alexander MacWhorter on British Brutality," in Larry R. Gerlach, *New Jersey in the American Revolution, 1763-1783*, 296-297. Ironically, Nuttman was subsequently arrested by Patriot militia as a Loyalist and jailed in Morristown. Frey, *The British Soldier in America*, 75-76; Cunningham, *Uncertain Revolution*, 183; Rees, ed., "'We ... wheeled to the Right to form the Line Of Battle'"; Curtis, *The British Army in the American Revolution*, 32; Mark Edward Lender, "The Cockpit Reconsidered: Revolutionary New Jersey as a Military Theater," in Mitnick, *New Jersey in the American Revolution*, 49.

30. Discussion with Jason Wickersty and review of his notes, May 14, 2016.

31. *New York Gazette and Weekly Mercury*, February 24, 1777; Fischer, *Washington's Crossing*, 346-348; *Official Register ... Revolutionary War*, 324; Kidder, *A People Harassed and Exhausted*, 231.

32. Lender, *The New Jersey Soldier*, 23; Cunningham, *Uncertain Revolution*, 183-185; Braisted, "Refugees & Others."

33. William Livingston to Philemon Dickinson, January 14, 1777, Neilson family papers, copy at NGMMNJ; Ward, *General William Maxwell*, 1-51; Fischer, *Washington's Crossing*, 349.

34. Scheer and Rankin, *Rebels and Redcoats*, 222; Fischer, *Washington's Crossing*, 354-359.

35. Cited in Spring, *With Zeal and With Bayonets Only*, 278; *Pennsylvania Journal*, April 2, 1777.

36. Braisted, *Bergen County Voices*, 63-64.

37. Lundin, *Cockpit of the Revolution*, 307-310.

38. Lundin, *Cockpit of the Revolution*, 314; Martin, *Philadelphia Campaign*, 21.

39. Lundin, *Cockpit of the Revolution*, 307-310.

40. Martin, *Philadelphia Campaign*, 24-26; Bailey, *Small Arms of the British Forces in America*, 72, 181.

41. Ward, *General William Maxwell*, p. 65-66.

42. *Ibid.*, 66-67.

43. Jackson, *With the British Army in Philadelphia*, 7.

44. Ward, *General William Maxwell*, 67-69; Ewald, *Diary of the American War*, 76-79.

45. Wood, *Battles of the Revolutionary War: 1775-1781*, 94-97; Uhlendorf, ed., *Revolution in America*, 107; Ward, *General William Maxwell*, 70-71

46. Ewald, *Diary of the American War*, 81; Yee, *Sharpshooters*, 49-50; Bailey, *Small Arms of the British Forces*, 181. Bailey claims that Ferguson's company, originally 100 men strong, were probably not all armed with the captain's breechloader, as "33 [Ferguson] rifles and 40 bayonets did not leave England until 22 June 1777, and Ferguson's unit sailed . . . south from New York on 20 July." Considering its reduced strength at Brandywine, however, it is likely that the remains of the company were all equipped with breechloaders.

47. Wood, *Battles of the Revolutionary War*, 98-101. Ewald reports that the British loss was "nine hundred killed and wounded, among which were sixty-four officers," and that the American casualties were "fairly equal with ours," and included 400 prisoners. Ewald, *Diary of the American War*, p. 87.

48. Jackson, *British Army in Philadelphia*, pp. 11-12; http://www.chaddsfordhistory.org/exhibits/path/path08.htm.

49. Martin, *Philadelphia Campaign*, 146.

50. Martin, *Philadelphia Campaign*, 148-149.

51. Martin, *Philadelphia Campaign*, 149-151; Stryker, *The Battle of Monmouth* 2; Wright, *The Continental Army*, 118; Boatner, *Encyclopedia*, 426-430.

52. Martin, *Philadelphia Campaign*, 151.

53. Martin, *Philadelphia* Campaign, 152-155; Jackson, *With the British Army in Philadelphia*, 92-93; Boatner, *Encyclopedia*, pp. 861-862.

54. Martin, *Philadelphia Campaign*, 157-175; Stryker, *Monmouth*, 3; Risch, *Supplying Washington's Army*, 150.

55. Risch, *Supplying Washington's Army*, 23-24, 208; William Maxwell to Governor Livingston, October 4, 1777, *Selections from the Correspondence of the Executive of New Jersey*, 103; "The Reverend Nicholas Collin on the Ravages of War," in Gerlach, *New Jersey in the American Revolution*, 303; Ward, *General William Maxwell*, 89-92.

56. Risch, *Supplying Washington's Army*, 39, 221; Wright, *The Continental Army*, 140; Lockhart, *The Drillmaster of Valley Forge*, 42, 203-204. Lockhart is ambivalent on Steuben's homosexuality. Although stating that "there is circumstantial evidence to suggest it," offering a story by a friend of the baron's that he once dropped a "miniature portrait of a beautiful young woman" as a counterargument. The circumstantial evidence is more substantial.

57. Wright, *The Continental Army*, 141.

58. "Collin on the Ravages of War," in Gerlach, *New Jersey in the American Revolution*, 303-304.

59. Ewald, *Diary of the American War,* 121; Jackson, *Philadelphia,* 97-98; "Collin on the Ravages of War," in Gerlach, *New Jersey in the American Revolution,* 302-303; Lundin, *Cockpit of the Revolution,* 376.

60. Lundin, *Cockpit of the Revolution.* 388-389; "Colonel Elijah Hand to Colonel Charles Mawhood," in Gerlach, *New Jersey in the American Revolution,* 338; Ward, *General William Maxwell,* 93; Simcoe, *Simcoe's Military Journal,* 52.

61. *The Pennsylvania Evening Post,* April 3, 1778, in Francis B. Lee, ed., *Documents Relating to the Revolutionary History of the State of New Jersey, Extracts from American Newspapers, Vol. II, 1778,* 146; "Collin on the Ravages of War," in Gerlach, *New Jersey in the American Revolution,* 303-304; Braisted, *Bergen County Voices from the American Revolution,* 71-72.

62. "Collin on the Ravages of War," in Gerlach, *New Jersey in the American Revolution,* 304; Martin, *Philadelphia Campaign,* 179.

CHAPTER FOUR: NEW JERSEY AND THE AMERICAN REVOLUTION, 1778–1783

1. Martin, *Philadelphia Campaign,* 197-198.

2. Ward, *General William Maxwell,* 93-95.

3. Jackson, *With the British Army in Philadelphia,* 234-240.

4. New Jersey was often referred to as "the Jerseys," a reference to its former division into the colonies of East and West New Jersey.

5. Jackson, *With the British Army in Philadelphia,* 81-84, 89-90.

6. Ewald, *Diary of the American War,* 131.

7. Stryker, *Battle of Monmouth,* 31-32, 50; Ewald, *Diary of the American War,* 132-133; Kidder, *A People Harassed and Exhausted,* 295.

8. Stryker, *Battle of Monmouth,* 50; Simcoe, *Military Journal,* 6.

9. Stryker, *Battle of Monmouth,* 50; William Maxwell to Philemon Dickinson, 19 June 1778, cited in Rees, "New Jersey Brigade at the Battle of Monmouth"; Trevelyan, *The American Revolution,* Vol. 4, 371; Stryker, *Battle of Monmouth,* 51-52; Ewald, *Diary of the American War,* 133, cited in Rees, "New Jersey Brigade at the Battle of Monmouth."

10. Stryker, *Battle of Monmouth,* 53-54; Cited in Rees, "New Jersey Brigade at the Battle of Monmouth"; Uhlendorf, ed. *Revolution in America,* 185.

11. Simcoe, *Military Journal,* 67.

12. Lender and Martin, *Citizen Soldier,* 136.

13. Morris, "The Hessians at Monmouth;" Interview with Dr. Garry W. Stone, Monmouth Battlefield State Park Historian, January 15, 2010.

14. *Ibid.,* 77-78.

15. Dearborn, *Journals of Henry Dearborn,* 15; Stryker, *Battle of Monmouth,* 70-71; Trevelyan, *American Revolution,* 373; Morrissey, *Monmouth Courthouse,* 85-86. Morrissey attempts to sort out the organization of Washington's ad hoc units of "picked men" which some other authors have confused with formal organized regiments.

16. Stryker, *Battle of Monmouth,* 79-80; Higginbotham, *Daniel Morgan,* 88.

17. Boatner, *Encyclopedia,* 718.

18. Stone, Lender, Rees and Morrissey, "Lee's Advance Force," 115-116; William Maxwell testimony, *Proceedings of a General Court Martial, Held at Brunswick in the State of New Jersey;* Martin, *Philadelphia Campaign,* 211;

Ward, *General William Maxwell*, 103. The actual units composing Lee's force have also been confusing historians since the time of the battle. His command included the special "picked men" detachments Washington had been creating out of existing units and sending forward during the previous week, as well as certain regular regiments and brigades. Sometimes officers were in command of "picked troop" units rather than their usual regimental and brigade formations, which has added to the confusion. For a more detailed breakdown of the forces involved, see Bilby & Jenkins, *Monmouth Court House*.

19. Gordon, *History/Gazetteer of New Jersey*,145; Lossing, *The Pictorial Field Book of the Revolution*, Vol. 2, 358; Lynn, *Annals of the Buffalo Valley*, 72; http://files.usgwarchives.net/pa/union/history/lynn/l126166.txt; Stryker, *Battle of Monmouth*, 114; Martin, *Private Yankee Doodle*,116. The terms "morass" and "ravine," along with actual names, have often been used interchangeably to describe the various brooks and ancillary wetlands crossing the battlefield. For the purpose of clarity and consistency, this account uses the terms used by Dr. Garry W. Stone in his maps of the battlefield. Stone, et al. "Lee's Advance Force," Stryker, *Battle of Monmouth*, 118-119.

20. Lundin, *Cockpit of the Revolution*, 399; Fleming, *Washington's Secret War*, 313.

21. Stryker, *Battle of Monmouth*,122; Reprint of John Laurens letter of July 2, 1778, in "The Battle of Monmouth," *Monmouth Democrat* [n.d.], MCHA. *Military Journal*, 68-72; Lockhart, *Drillmaster of Valley Forge*, 154-155.

22. Martin, *Philadelphia Campaign*, 211.

23. Callahan, *Daniel Morgan: Ranger of the Revolution,* 164-165.

24. Martin, *Philadelphia Campaign*, 212.

25. Interview with Dr. Garry W. Stone, January 15, 2010. The hill on which Clinton established his headquarters was called Briar Hill in the nineteenth century, but not so known in the eighteenth century.

26. Anonymous officer, 1st Battalion British Grenadiers, to Lord Amherst, WO 34/111, The Amherst Papers, 71 (microfilm, David Library of the American Revolution, transcribed 1993 by Dr. Garry Wheeler Stone, Gilbert Riddle, and Mark Lender. Transcription provided by Gilbert Riddle.

27. John Laurens to Henry Laurens, July 2, 1778, *The Lee Papers, vol. II, 1776-1778*, NYHS; Maxwell and Lafayette testimony, *Lee Court Martial Proceedings*; Interview with Dr. Garry W. Stone, January 15, 2010.

28. Oswald testimony, *Lee Court Martial Proceedings*.

29. Wilkin, *Some British Soldiers*, 257.

30. Interview with Dr. Garry W. Stone, January 15, 2010; Pepe, *Freehold*, 42.

31. Testimony of Lieutenant Colonels Harrison and Tilghman, *Lee Court Martial Proceedings*.

32. Wilkin, *Some British Soldiers*, 258; Martin, *Private Yankee Doodle*,115.

33. Martin, *Private Yankee Doodle*,116; James Jordan pension deposition (W8225), *Revolutionary War Pension Applications*, NA, cited by John Rees, http://www.revwar75.com/library/rees/monmouth/MonmouthI.htm; Kidder, *A People Harassed and Exhausted*, 297; Testimony of Lieutenant-colonels Tilghman and Brooks, *Lee Court Martial Proceedings*.

34. Smith, *Monmouth*,19.

35. Anonymous officer, First Battalion British Grenadiers, to Lord Amherst, WO 34/111; Smith, *Monmouth*, 17, 19; Martin, *Philadelphia Campaign*, 222-223.

36. Stone, Sivilich, and Lender, "A Deadly Minuet; Henry B. Livingston to Robert Livingston, July 31, 1778, Rutgers University Special Collections and Archives, Alexander Library, Accession # 3097, copy in MCHA; Wilkin, *Some British Soldiers*, 258-259, 263; Testimony of Captain-lieutenant John Cumpston, 3rd Continental Artillery and Brigadier General Knox, *Lee Court Martial Proceedings;* Anonymous officer, 1st Battalion British Grenadiers, to Lord Amherst, WO 34/111, The Amherst Papers; Wilkin, *Some British Soldiers*, 258; Notes on the Battle of Monmouth [*London Chronicle* newspaper. It seems possible, but increasingly less likely, that Monckton was killed later in the battle. Morrissey, *Monmouth Court House*, 70, is ambivalent on the site and time of Monckton's death. It should be noted that Monmouth Battlefield State Park historian Dr. Garry Wheeler Stone, who is more familiar with the details of the battle than anyone else, is of the opinion that Monckton died at the time of the earlier hedgerow fight, as is Dr. David Martin; Interview with Dr. Garry W. Stone, January 15, 2010, email correspondence with Dr. David Martin, January 28, 2010.

37. Interview with Dr. Garry W. Stone, January 15, 2010.

38. Lockhart, *Drillmaster of Valley Forge*, 160-161.

39. Interview with Dr. Garry W. Stone, January 15, 2010; Stone, Sivilich, and Lender, "A Deadly Minuet."

40. Wilkin, *Some British Soldiers*, 260; Ironically, the British artillery was in

part manned by members of the Loyalist Second Battalion New Jersey Volunteers, detailed to artillery service in 1777. The battalion was originally raised by Lieutenant Colonel John Morris from among Monmouth County Loyalists, some no doubt from the Tory stronghold of Upper Freehold Township, in 1776. http://www.royalprovincial.com/military/rhist/njv/2njvhist.htm; North Callahan, "Henry Knox, American Artillerist" in Billias, ed., *George Washington's Generals and Opponents*, 252-253; Martin, *Private Yankee Doodle*, 96-97. For the full story of "Molly Pitcher," see Chapter 6.

41. Callahan, "Henry Knox, American Artillerist," 253; Interview with Dr. Garry W. Stone, January 15, 2010.

42. Stone, Sivilich and Lender, "A Deadly Minuet."

43. *Ibid.*

44. Barber and Howe, *Historical Collections of the State of New Jersey*, 341; Interview with Dr. Garry W. Stone, January 15, 2010.

45. In retrospect, much of the movement at Monmouth was probably at a slower pace than would usually be the case due to the heat. This fact may well have facilitated disengagements for both sides.

46. Andrew Bell, "Copy of a Journal."

47. State of New Jersey, *Documents Relating to the Revolutionary History of the State of New Jersey, Volume II, Extracts from American Newspapers*, 273-274; Andrew Bell, "Copy of a Journal."

48. Wilkin, *Some British Soldiers*, 260; Martin Hunter, *The Journal of Gen. Sir Martin Hunter and Some Letters . . .* , 42; Baurmeister, *Revolution in America*, 185-187; Cornelius Van Dyck, "A Report of the No. slain buried in the Field of Battle near Monmouth Court Ho. 29th. June 1778," George Washington

Papers, Presidential Papers Microfilm (Washington, DC, 1961), series 4, reel 50, cited by John U. Rees in *"What is this you have been about to day?"*; Montross, *Rag Tag and Bobtail*, 287; George Washington to John Washington, July 4, 1778, in Gerlach, ed., *New Jersey in the American Revolution*, 307-308; Martin, *Philadelphia Campaign*, 233; Ewald, *Diary of the American War*, 135-137; Interview with Dr. Garry W. Stone, January 15, 2010.

49. "General Orders Head Quarters Brunswick Landing July 3rd 1778," Washington Papers, Alderman Library, University of Virginia, MCHA; "Lt. Thomas Blake's Journal" in Kidder, *History of the First New Hampshire Regiment*, 43.

50. J. Huntington to father, June 30, 1778, John Rees Collection, copy in MCHA Battle of Monmouth Collection; Henry Knox to brother, July 3, 1778. Henry Knox Papers, Vol. 4, Item 117 (reel 4), Massachusetts Historical Society copy in MCHA Collection; Higginbotham, *The War of American Independence*, 247.

51. Lundin, *Cockpit of the Revolution*, 402.

52. Leiby, *Revolutionary War in the Hackensack Valley*, 22-23.

53. Rees, "The Enemy . . . Will Have no Mercey upon our loaded barns . . . ," in Karels, ed., *Bergen County*, 112-113.

54. For a detailed account of the Baylor Massacre, see Braisted, *Grand Forage 1778*, 100-112. The remains were discovered in an archeological dig in 1967 and the site dedicated as a public park and historic site. Historic walking tour signage was erected in 2004. http://www.co.bergen.nj.us/bcparks/Cs BaylorMemorial.aspx.

55. Rees, "The Enemy . . . Will Have no Mercey upon our loaded barns . . . ," 114.

56. Leiby, *Revolutionary War in the Hackensack Valley*, 180.

57. *Ibid*, 53-54.

58. War Office order dated "6th March, 1777," David Library of the American Revolution, Microfilm Collection P. R. O. W. O. 4/99 217. Transcription courtesy of Gilbert V. Riddle. For Juliat's curious full story, see Braisted, *Grand Forage 1778*, 151-152, 173.

59. Lender, *The New Jersey Soldier* 17-18; Walling, *Men of Color at the Battle of Monmouth*, 15-16; Dann, ed., *The Revolution Remembered*, 390-399; Quarles, *Negro in the Revolution*, 185.

60. Lender, *New Jersey Soldier*, 20; William Schleicher and Susan Winter, "Patriot and Slave: The Samuel Sutphen Story."

61. For a complete discussion of slavery in New Jersey during the Revolution see Gigantino, *The Ragged Road to Abolition*, 18-63.

62. Fleming, *Forgotten Victory*, 50-51.

63. *Ibid.*, 112-114.

64. *Ibid.*, 163-187.

65. *Ibid.*, 161-163.

66. *Ibid.*, 229-234.

67. *Ibid.*, 235-243.

68. *Ibid.*, 253-288.

69. Ward, *General William Maxwell*, 98; Kidder, *A People Harassed and Exhausted*, 326.

70. *Ibid.*

71. Adelberg, *The Razing of Tinton Falls*, 10-13.

72. Ward, *General William Maxwell*, 100.

73. *Ibid.*, 102. A survey of Monmouth County court records for 1780 by the author revealed that the most common offense was "trading with the enemy."

74. Hodges, *Slavery and Freedom*, 104; *New Jersey Gazette*, April 24, 1782; Adelberg, *The American Revolution in Monmouth County*, 75-76.

75. Adelberg, "'A Combination to Trample All Law Underfoot.'"

76. Ellis, *History of Monmouth County*, 206.

77. Petition to the Legislature, Monmouth County, NJHS.

78. Adelberg, "A Combination to Trample All Law Underfoot.'"

79. *Ibid*, pp. 25-26. The memorialization of extreme acts survived into the twentieth century. In 1927 the Daughters of the American Revolution and the descendants of Captain Samuel Allen placed a memorial plaque alongside New Jersey State Highway #70, just north of the Manasquan River, at "the spot where Capt. Allen executed six Tories and their chief," presumably on his own authority without benefit of trial. Allen served as a company commander in the Third Monmouth Militia Regiment from 1780 through 1783.

80. Ward, *William Maxwell*, 166-167.

81. Ward, *William Maxwell*, 168.

## CHAPTER FIVE: NEW JERSEY THROUGH THE WAR OF 1812

1. Kidder, *A People Harassed and Exhausted*, 329-330.

2. Mahon, *History of the Militia and the National Guard*, 46.

3. Mahon, *History of the Militia and the National Guard*, 47.

4. Sword, *President Washington's Indian War*, 91-94.

5. *Laws of the United States of America from the 4th of March 1789 to the 4th of March 1815*, 234-235.

6. Sword, *President Washington's Indian War*, 146-147.

7. Military Journal of Major Ebenezer Denny, 172-173; Sword, *President Washington's Indian War*, 148–149. Duer went bankrupt in the Panic of 1792 and spent the rest of his life in debtor's prison. He died in 1799.

8. Winkler, *Wabash 1791*, 29.

9. *Ibid.*

10. Sword, *President Washington's Indian War*, 177-178.

11. For a detailed account of the fight, see Sword, *President Washington's Indian War*, 178-189.

12. Sword, *President Washington's Indian War*, 195; State of New Jersey, Record of Officers and Men of New Jersey in the Expedition against the Indians in 1791.

13. Mahon, *History of the Militia and the National Guard*, 52.

14. *Ibid.*

15. *Ibid*, 53.

16. *Ibid.*

17. Rene Chartrand, *A Most Warlike Appearance*, 103.

18. 1940 National Guard History, xxii-xxiii.

19. *Record of Officers and Men of New Jersey in the Pennsylvania Insurrection of 1794*, 6.

20. Gigantino, *The Ragged Road to Abolition*, 126-127.

21. Stellhorn & Birkner, *The Governors of New Jersey*, 84-85.

22. Stellhorn & Birkner, *The Governors of New Jersey*, 85; *Officers and Enlisted Men in the United States Navy and Marine Corps from New Jersey in Commission and Enlistment during the War with France, 1798-1801*, 3-4; *Record of Officers and Enlisted Men in the United States Navy and Marine Corps from New Jersey in Commission and Enlistment during the War with Tripoli, Africa, June 10, 1801 to June 4, 1805*, 3-4.

23. "An Act to authorize a detachment from the militia of the United States," in *Record of Officers and Men in the War With Great Britain, 1812-1815*, 3; *Western Star*, June 27, 1812.

24. Lee, *New Jersey as a Colony and State*, Vol. III, 82; Pierce, *Iron in the Pines*, 90, 114; Mahon, *History of the Militia and National Guard*, 66.

25. Mahon, *History of the Militia and National Guard*, 64; Strum, "South Jersey and the War of 1812," 5.

26. Moller, *American Shoulder Arms*, 237

27. Prince, *New Jersey's Jeffersonian Republicans*, 240.

28. Strum, "South Jersey and the War of 1812," 6, 18; *New Jersey Journal*, July 7, 1812; *Poulson's American Daily Advertiser* [Philadelphia], November 14, September 25, 1812; *New Jersey Journal*, October 6, 1812.

29. *Record of Officers and Men in the War With Great Britain, 1812-1815*, 3; Hutchinson, "The 'Essex Patriot' of Elizabeth"; New York *Evening Post*, September 12, 1814.

30. Ogden to Jonathan Rhea, August 8, 1812, NJSA. A "stand of arms" included a musket, bayonet, cartridge box, and sling. Stellhorn & Birkner, *Governors of New Jersey*, 87-88; Luzky, *The Adjutants General of New Jersey*, 14; Mahon, *The War of 1812*, 100.

31. *Record of Officers and Men of New Jersey in the War With Great Britain, 1812-1815*, 13; http://www.njcu.edu/programs/jchistory/pages/d_pages/dickinson_high_school.htm; New York *City Gazette*, August 4, 1812; Guernsey, *New York City and Vicinity During the War of 1812*, 72; Trenton *Evening Times*, April 21, 1912; Lane, *From Indian Trail to Iron Horse*,183; Lee, *New Jersey as a Colony and as a State*, Vol. III, 103. The arsenal was used as a barracks by a New York regiment during the Civil War and reportedly torn down in 1879. In 1916, a bronze plaque commemorating the wartime use of the property was placed by the Daughters of the War of 1812.

32. Gardiner, *The Naval War of 1812*, 11-37.

33. Fleming, *New Jersey*, 98; Lockard, *The New Jersey Governor*, 48; Adjutant General John Beatty to Governor Aaron Ogden, January 21, 1813, NJA, DOD, AGO, War of 1812, Box 1; P. J. Stryker to New Jersey legislature, January, 1813, NJA, DOD, AGO, War of 1812, Box 1; Salem [Massachusetts] *Gazette*, November 24, 1812.

34. New York *Public Advertiser*, December 4, 1812.

35. Rene Chartrand, *A Most Warlike Appearance*. 58-59, 103-104.

36. Skelton, "High Army Leadership in the War of 1812"; Guernsey, *New York and Vicinity during the War of 1812-1815*, 343; Lender, *One State in Arms*, 37-39; Lender and Martin, *Citizen Soldier*, 26-27; Mahon, *The War of 1812*, 316.

37. 1940 NJNG Yearbook, XXIII; Salter, *A History of Monmouth and Ocean Counties*, 293; *The Putnam* (NY) *County Courier*, June 24, 1987; Strum, "South Jersey and the War of 1812," 7. Trenton *True American*, September 6, 1813.

38. Lee, *New Jersey as a Colony and as a State*, Vol. III, 96-97; Guernsey, *New York City and Vicinity During the War of 1812*, 180.

39. *Record of Officers and Men of New Jersey in the War With Great Britain, 1812-1815*, 138-146. There is a marker on the probable site of the Somers Point fort.

40. 1940 NJNG Yearbook, XIIII; "1813 receipt for militia supplies," John Hulick Collection, Princeton Library.

41. Lee, *New Jersey as a Colony and State*, Vol. III, 91.

42. 1940 NJNG Yearbook, XXIV; *Record of Officers and Men of New Jersey in NJHS Proceedings*, 19-23.

43. Lee, *New Jersey as a Colony and as a State*, Vol. III, 107, 110; Mahon, *The War of 1812*, 316.

44. Essex Brigade Orders of September 2 and 26, 1814, Caldwell, NJ Historical Society.

45. Dodd, ed., " Reminiscences of the War of 1812," 3-4; *Record of Officers and Men of New Jersey in the War With Great Britain, 1812-1815*, 52.

46. Dodd, ed., "Reminiscences of the War of 1812," 3-4; "Letters from Camp Liberty, 1814" NJHS1923; Harris and Hilton, *A History of the Second and Fifth Regiments*, 47; Salter, *A History of Monmouth and Ocean Counties*, 293.

47. "Letters from Camp Liberty, 1814" NJHS1923; Dodd, ed., "Reminiscences of the War of 1812," 3-4.

48. *Record of Officers and Men of New Jersey in the War With Great Britain, 1812-1815*, 140.

49. Salter, *A History of Monmouth and Ocean Counties*, 291; Edwin Salter and George C. Beekman, *Old Times in Old Monmouth*, 149.

50. Dorwart, *Cape May County*, 75-76.

51. Lee, *New Jersey as a Colony and as a State*, Vol. III, 99; Strum, "South Jersey and the War of 1812," 9-13.

52. Barber & Howe, *Historical Collections*, 70, 363.

53. Powell, *History of Camden County*, 77-78; Lee, *New Jersey as a Colony and as a State*, Vol. III, 101.

54. *Record of Officers and Men of New Jersey in the War With Great Britain, 1812-1815*, 149, 179.

55. Mahon, *The War of 1812*, 103, 141-142; Coates, Kochan, and Troiani, *Don Troiani's Soldiers in America*, 88-89; *Trenton True American*, May 24, 1813; Murphy, "Remembering Two Forgotten Soldiers."

56. Mahon, *The War of 1812*, 123-125.

57. *Ibid*, 41, 42, 128.

58. Unfortunately, the New Jersey census of 1810, which might have provided information on the exact number of slaves in the state, was destroyed in a long ago fire. Mahon, *The War of 1812*, 313, 352, 358. The note is affixed to page 9 in a copy of *Record of Officers and Men of New Jersey in the War With Great Britain, 1812-1815* in the library of the NGMMNJ.

59. Fleming, *New Jersey*, 99-100.

60. Mahon, *History of the Militia and National Guard*, 79-80.

61. *Harper's Magazine*, September 1878; Trenton *Evening Times*, April 18, 1894; Jersey City *Jersey Journal*, May 19, 1916.

## CHAPTER SIX: NEW JERSEY ON THE EVE OF THE CIVIL WAR, 1826–1860

1. Mahon, *History of the Militia and National Guard*, 83-86; Cunliffe, *Soldiers and Civilians*, 192-212.

2. Mahon, *History of the Militia and National Guard*, 87-90.

3. Cunliffe, *Soldiers and Civilians*, 78.

4. *NJAG Report for 1847*.

5. Frederick M. Herrmann, "Daniel Haines," in Stellhorn and Birkner, *The Governors of New Jersey*, 114–115.

6. *Encyclopedia of New Jersey*, 517; Lee, *New Jersey as a Colony and State*, Vol. III, 355; Trenton *State Gazette*, September 30, 1847.

7. Lender, *One State in Arms*, 46; Frederick M. Herrmann, "Charles Creighton Stratton" in Stellhorn and Birkner, *The Governors of New Jersey*, 117–118; Lee, *New Jersey as a Colony and State*, Vol. III, 353-355.

8. Herrmann, "Charles Creighton Stratton," 118.

9. Herrmann, "Charles Creighton Stratton," 118; *Record of Officers and Enlisted Men of New Jersey in the War With Mexico, 1846-1848*, 4-15.

10. *Record of Officers and Enlisted Men of New Jersey in the War With Mexico, 1846-1848*. 4-15, 16-21; Robert C. Davis, US Adjutant General, Washington DC to Frederick Gilkyson, Adjutant General, NJ, August 3, 1925, NGMMNJ.

11. Lane, *From Indian Trail to Iron Horse*, 332; *New York Times*, October 9, 1866.

12. Blackman, "Fatal Cruise of the Princeton."

13. Bauer, *The Mexican War*, 172-196, 369.

14. Kearny, "Gen. Stephen Watts Kearny."

15. *Ibid.*

16. Kearny, "Gen. Stephen Watts Kearny"; Faulk and Stout, Jr., *The Mexican War: Changing Interpretations*, 5-9.

17. http://www.bergencounty history.org/Pages/captzabriskie.html.

18. Lender, *One State at War*, 47; Mills, *Historic Houses of New Jersey*, 127-128.

19. Lee, *New Jersey as a Colony and State*, Vol. III, 358.

20. *NJAG Report for 1851, NJAG Report for 1852*; Duane Lockard, *The New Jersey Governor*, 62; Philip C. Davis, "George Franklin Fort," in Stellhorn and Birkner, *The Governors of New Jersey*, 119-121.

21. *NJAG Report for 1852.*

22. Joel Schwartz, "Rodman McCamley Price," in Stellhorn and Birkner, *The Governors of New Jersey*, 121-124.

23. *NJAG Report for 1854*; Cunliffe, *Soldiers and Civilians*, 215, 223.

24. Joel Schwartz, "Rodman McCamley Price," in Stellhorn and Birkner, *The Governors of New Jersey*, 124-125.

25. *NJAG Report for 1854*; Joel Schwartz, "Rodman McCamley Price," in Stellhorn and Birkner, *The Governors of New Jersey*, 124.

26. Gillette, *Jersey Blue*, 33; Joel Schwartz, "Rodman McCamley Price," in Stellhorn and Birkner, *The Governors of New Jersey*, 124; *NJAG Report for 1856.*

27. *NJAG Report for 1856.*

28. *Ibid.*

29. *Ibid.*

30. *Ibid.*

31. *Ibid.*

32. Douglas V. Shaw, "William Augustus Newell," in Stellhorn and Birkner, *The Governors of New Jersey*, 127; Gillette, *Jersey Blue*, 42-43, 45.

33. Douglas V. Shaw, "William Augustus Newell," in Stellhorn and Birkner, *The Governors of New Jersey*, 127; *NJQM Report for 1856*; New York *Irish American*, March 28, 1858.

34. Jersey City *Jersey Journal*, February 5, 1858.

35. *NJAG Report for 1857.*

36. Luzky, *The Adjutants General*, 20.

37. *NJAG Report for 1858.*

38. *NJAG Report for 1859*; New York *Irish American*, January 28, 1871.

39. *Combined NJAG and NJQMG Report for 1860.*

40. Foster, *New Jersey and the Rebellion*, 16-17; William C. Wright, "Charles Smith Olden," in Stellhorn and Birkner, *The Governors of New Jersey*, 129-130.

CHAPTER SEVEN: NEW JERSEY AND THE CIVIL WAR, 1861–1865

1. Howard L. Green, *Words that Made New Jersey History*, 138-139; Cited in Gilette, *Jersey Blue*, 115.

2. New Jersey passed a gradual abolition law in 1804, freeing all born into slavery after July 4 of that year at the

age of 21 for females or 25 for males. Persons enslaved prior to that date remained so, although the 1844 Constitution reclassified them as "apprentices for life" with certain rights.

3. Paterson *Daily Guardian*, September 7, 1861.

4. Bilby, ed., *New Jersey Goes to War*, 144.

5. *NJAG Report for 1860.*

6. John Donaldson Diary, May 1, 1761, NJHS.

7. McAllister to wife, May 3, 1861, *McAllister Letters*, 30. For a complete and detailed history of all New Jersey's Civil War units, see Joseph G. Bilby and William C. Goble, *Remember You Are Jerseymen.*

8. Oscar Westlake to Mother, July 4, 1861, Kuhl Collection.

9. *Ibid.*

10. Bellard, *Gone for a Soldier*, 7.

11. Newark *Daily Mercury*, August 20, 1861; NJQM Report, 1861.

12. Newton *Sussex Register*, September 21, November 1, 1861.

13. Foster, *New Jersey and the Rebellion*, 267.

14. *OR, Ser. III, Vol. 1*, 109, 120, 121.

15. William H. Clairville Journal, RU.

16. Symmes Stillwell to mother, Stillwell Papers, Princeton University Library.

17. *Gone for a Soldier*, 51.

18. Merritt Bruen to Mr. Emmell, May 9, 1862, MHS; Joseph Trawin to Charles S. Olden, May 19, 1862, NJA.

19. Newark *Daily Mercury*, June 10, 1862.

20. For a brief biography of Hopkins, see Bilby, ed., *New Jersey Goes to War*, 68.

21. Bellard, *Gone For a Soldier*, 128-130.

22. *OR, Ser. I, Vol. 12, Pt. 2*, 644; Brown Memoir, NJHS.

23. Elizabeth *New Jersey Journal*, September 23, 1862; Eugene Forbes to [?] September 16, 1862, RU.

24. *NJAG Report for 1862.*

25. *OR*, Ser. I, Vol. 19, Pt. 1, 198.

26. Bilby and Goble, *Remember You Are Jerseymen*, 17.

27. *Ibid*, 17-18.

28. NJAG Correspondence, 1862, NJA.

29. Newark *Advertiser*, August 15, 1862.

30. Borton, *On the Parallels*, 90; *OR*, Ser. I, Vol. 21, 33.

31. Bilby, "Sunshine Soldiers."

32. *Ibid.*

33. *OR*, Ser. I, Vol. 21, 53, 133; Paterson *Guardian*, December 22, 1862.

34. Bilby, "Sunshine Soldiers."

35. *OR*, Ser. 1, Vol. 21, 627, 529.

36. Oscar Westlake to brother, December 26, 1862, Kuhl.

37. Newton *Sussex Register*, May 8, 1863.

38. Bilby and Goble, *Remember You Are Jerseymen*, 116-117.

39. *OR*, Ser. I Vol. 25, Pt. 1, 715.

40. Rosenblatt, ed. *Hard Marching Every Day*, 78.

41. Newton *Sussex Register*, May 8, 1863.

42. *Ibid*, May 15, 1863.

43. Paterson *Guardian*, April 24, 1863; *OR*, Ser. I, Vol. 18, 287.

44. Bilby and Goble, *Remember You Are Jerseymen*, 350-351.

45. *OR*, Ser. I Vol. 27, Pt. 1. 169.

46. *NJAG Report for 1863.*

47. Martin, *New Jersey at Gettysburg Guidebook*, 11. David Martin's book is the latest and most accurate account of New Jersey's soldiers at Gettysburg, and all following accounts of troop dispositions regarding the battle are taken from Dr. Martin's book.

48. Peter Vredenburgh to father, December 4, 1863, MCHA.

49. Bilby and Goble, *Remember You Are Jerseymen*, 26-27.

50. Trenton *State Gazette and Republican*, September 18, 1863.

51. Samuel Cavileer to S. H. Ashley, December 2, 1863, ACHA; Newton *Sussex Register*, March 25, 1864.

52. Bilby, ed., *New Jersey Goes to War*, 59.

53. Bilby, *Three Rousing Cheers*, 134-140.

54. Morristown *Jerseyman*, May 28, 1864.

55. For the full story of Davis's family's attempts to recover his body, see John Bilby, "Death and Lieutenant Colonel Davis: A Jerseyman's Journey," in Bilby, ed., *New Jersey's Civil War Odyssey*.

56. Dayton Flint to father, June 6, 1864. Kuhl Collection.

57. Bilby, ed., *New Jersey Goes to War*, 150; Bilby and Goble, *Remember You Are Jerseymen*, 154-157.

58. Bilby, ed., *New Jersey Goes to War*, 143.

59. Joseph Bilby, "Jersey Zouaves," *New Jersey's Civil War Odyssey*, 66-71.

60. *Ibid.*

61. Bilby and Goble, *Remember You Are Jerseymen*, 235-240.

62. *Ibid*, 396-388, 470-477.

63. William H. Lloyd to Mary Lloyd, December 26, 1864; Newark *Daily Advertiser*, January 3, 1865; Bilby and Goble, *Remember You Are Jerseymen*, 412.

64. For a comprehensive account of New Jersey's recruiting efforts, see Bilby and Goble, *Remember You Are Jerseymen*, 3-51.

65. For the full story of New Jersey's African-American soldiers, see Bilby, *Freedom to All*.

66. Bilby and Goble, *Remember You Are Jerseymen*, 416, 418, 431.

67. *NJQM Reports for 1863.*

68. *NJQM Reports for 1863 and 1864.*

69. *Ibid.*

70. *Ibid.*

71. Bilby and Goble, *Remember You Are Jerseymen*, 48, 430.

72. *Ibid.*, 460.

73. *OR*, Ser. I Vol. 49, *Pt. 1*, 265.

74. Bilby and Goble, *Remember You Are Jerseymen*, 245.

75. Toombs, *Reminiscences of the Thirteenth Regiment*, 217.

76. Bilby, ed., *New Jersey Goes to War*, 60.

77. *Ibid.*, 7.

78. Bilby, ed., *New Jersey Goes to War*, 5.

79. Silvia Mogerman, "Georgiana Willets," in Bilby, ed., *New Jersey's Civil War Odyssey*.

80. Bilby, ed., *New Jersey Goes to War*, 5, 69, 124.

81. John Kuhl, "Trains, Ships and Guns: New Jersey's Civil War Production Line," in Bilby, ed., *New Jersey's Civil War Odyssey*.

CHAPTER EIGHT: NEW JERSEY'S MILITARY, 1866–1914

1. *NJAG Report for 1866.*

2. Dr. David G. Martin, "Marcus Ward" in Bilby, ed., *New Jersey Goes to War*, 145; John Zinn, "His Widow and His Orphan," http://amanlypastime. blogspot.com/2016/05/his-widow-and-his-orphan.html?spref=fb

3. Luzky, *The Adjutants General*, 21.

4. *Ibid*, 22.

5. 113th Infantry Lineage papers, Sheet number 4, NGMMNJ.

6. NJ Adjutant General report for 1871.

7. *Ibid.*

8. Joseph Truglio, "The First Reunion," in Bilby, ed., *New Jersey's Civil War Odyssey*.

9. John Kuhl, "The Battle of Princeton Junction," in Bilby, ed., *New Jersey's Civil War Odyssey*.

10. *NJAG Report for 1875*.

11. *NJAG Report for 1879*.

12. *Ibid.*

13. *NJAG Report for 1872*.

14. *NJAG Reports for 1876 and 1881*.

15. *NJAG Report for 1877*; *Cincinnati Enquirer*, July 22, 1877; Cooper, *The Rise of the National Guard*, 45–46.

16. *NJAG Report for 1880*.

17. Bilby, ed., *New Jersey Goes to War*; *NJAG Report for 1892*.

18. *New York Times*, November 29, 1913.

19. 113th Infantry Lineage papers, NGMMNJ, supplement to sheet # 7.

20. *NJAG Report for 1883*.

21. Manasquan Chamber of Commerce, *Manasquan*; *NJAG Report for 1884*.

22. *Sea Girt Camp*, undated monograph in NGMMNJ collection.

23. *NJAG Report for 1885*. For a detailed study of Leon Abbett's rise from hatter's son to corporate attorney and governor of New Jersey, see Hogarty, *Leon Abbett's New Jersey*.

24. Manasquan Chamber of Commerce, *Manasquan*; Ingham & Anspach, *Map of Sea Girt Situated in Monmouth County*; Lewis, *History of Monmouth County*, 479-480; Parsons, ed., *New Jersey: Life, Industries and Resources of a Great State*, 47; *New York Times*, September 3, 1887; *Camden Daily Courier*, April 23, 1891.

25. Kobbe, *Jersey Coast and Pines*, 56.

26. *American Rifleman Magazine*, September 1931.

27. *NJAG Report for 1895*; *New York Times*, July 22, 1896.

28. *History of the Essex Troop*, 12-13; *National Guard of the State of New Jersey*, 1940, 331.

29. *Ibid.*, 14.

30. Cooper, *The Rise of the National Guard*, 73.

31. *Trenton Evening Times*, March 27, 1897; Nofi, "The Naval Militia: A Neglected Asset?"

32. *NJQM Report for 1895*.

33. New Orleans *Times-Democrat*, July 22, 1900.

34. New Jersey Adjutant General Report for 1896.

35. New Brunswick, NJ, *Daily Times*, June 20, 1898.

36. http://www.arlington cemetery.net/ghwanton.htm.

37. Lurie and Mappen, *Encyclopedia of New Jersey*, 489.

38. Cooper, *The Rise of the National Guard*, 122.

39. *Ibid.*, 123-127.

40. *Ibid.*, 109.

41. Luzky, *The Adjutants General*, 24; *NJAG Report for 1905*.

42. *New York Times*, February 2, 2002.

43. *Chicago Daily Tribune*, February 10, 1902.

44. *NJQM Report for 1902*.

45. Price, *Shooting for the Record*, 91-92.

46. *NJAG Report for 1905*.

47. *Ibid.*

48. *New York Times*, February 28, 1905.

## CHAPTER NINE: NEW JERSEY IN WORLD WAR I AND THE INTER-WAR YEARS, 1914–1940

1. *NJAG Report for 1914*; Cooper, *The Rise of the National Guard*, 132.

2. *NJAG Report for 1914*.

3. *NJAG Report for 1909*.

4. Lender, *One State in Arms*, 75.

5. Shenk, *Work or Fight*, 83.

6. Federal Writers Project. *New Jersey: A Guide to its Present and Past*, 73-74; Lender, *One State in Arms*, 76, 78.

7. Bilby, Madden and Ziegler, *Hidden History of New Jersey at War*, 69-74; Federal Writers Project, *New Jersey: A Guide to its Present and Past*, 275; New Jersey Adjutant General report for 1918-1920.

8. Lender, *One State in Arms*, 75-76.

9. *Ibid.*, 76.

10. *Ibid.*, 76-78.

11. *NJAG Report for 1916*.

12. *History of the Essex Troop: 1890-1925*, 3-4, 257, 84.

13. *NJAG Report for 1918-1920*.

14. *Ibid.*

15. Rejan, *History of Army Communications*, 1-4.

16. Marsena, "Report of Camp Merritt Memorial Committee."

17. Lender, *One State in Arms*, 79; Shenk, *Work or Fight*, 91.

18. Shenk, *Work or Fight*, 103.

19. BI Report of F. A. Gaborino, August 20,1917, Old German Files 1909-1921, #33658 NA [Accessed through Fold3.com.]

20. *NJAG Report for 1918-1920*.

21. *NJAG Report for 1918-1920*; *National Guard Yearbook*, 1940, 331.

22. *National Guard Yearbook*, 1940, xxxi.

23. *Ibid.*

24. Reddan, *Other Men's Lives*, 18-19.

25. *Ibid.*, 190-192, 207.

26. *New York Times*, August 28, 1927, July 14, 1937, July 3, 1944.

27. *NJAG Report for 1918-1920*.

28. *NJAG Report for 1918-1920*.

29. *Ibid.*

30. *Ibid.*

31. *New York Times*, September 6, 1917.

32. A complete list of New Jersey men who died in the war is available, along with casualty cards, correspondence, and photos, at the NJ State Archives on line searchable data base: https://wwwnet1.state.nj.us/DOS/Admin/ArchivesDBPortal/WWICards.aspx.

33. Email correspondence with Margaret Thomas Buchholz, April 23, 2017.

34. *NJAG Report for 1918-1920*.

35. *Ibid*, January 15, 1918; Federal Writers Project, *New Jersey: A Guide to its Present and Past*, 206.

36. *Ibid.*, March 12, 1918.

37. Edwyn Gray, *The U-Boat War, 1914-1918*, 232.

38. US Navy, *German Submarine Activities on the Atlantic Coast*, 26-27, 127.

39. *Ibid.*

40. Report from "CO, Co. F, 22nd Infantry, RG 156, entry 5958, box 1, file 052, NA.

41. Buchholz, *New Jersey Shipwrecks*, 146.

42. *New York Times*, October 30, 1929; Casale Draft Card, Ancestry.com.

43. United States Senate Record of Proceedings held before the Committee on Military Affairs, S.J. Resolution 161, May 16, 1940.

44. *NJAG Report for 1918-1920*.

45. *NJAG Report for 1918-1920*; Cooper, *The Rise of the National Guard*, 172,

46. *NJAG Report for 1918-1920*.

47. *New York Times*, January 19, 1921; copy of recruiting flier in NGMMNJ collection; unidentified newspaper clipping dated May 29, 1921, in NGMMNJ collection.

48. *Elizabeth Daily Journal*, July 13, 19, 1921.

49. *National Guard of the State of New Jersey*, 1940, 331.

50. *National Guard of the State of New Jersey*, 1940, 315.

51. *Ibid.*

52. *Asbury Park Press*, April 19, 1929.

53. *National Guard of the State of New Jersey*, 1940, 324; 102nd Cavalry lineage, NGMMNJ.

54. Luzky, "History, 1st Battalion"

55. *Ibid.*

56. *Ibid.*

57. *New York Times*, September 10, 1934.

58. *Ibid.*

59. Luzky, "History, 1st Battalion;" *Historical and Pictorial Review.*

60. Dickerson, "Marine Reservists at National Guard Training Base Sea Girt."

61. *New York Times*, November 6, 1933.

62. *New York Times*, December 16, 1961.

63. Rejan, *History of Army Communications*, 7-10.

64. *New York Times*, July 30, 1935; Eberhardt, "Historical Account of Radar Testing"; Interview with Robert Perricelli, InfoAge Museum.

CHAPTER TEN: NEW JERSEY IN WORLD WAR II

1. *Ibid.*, 324-325.

2. *National Guard Yearbook*, 1940, 325; Luzky, "History, 1st Battalion."

3. Luzky, "History, 1st Battalion."

4. Oral history interview with Margaret Houlday Askew, NGMMNJ, http://www.nj.gov/military/museum/su mmaries/wwii/margaret-askew/.

5. Russen, "Combat History of the 102nd Cavalry Reconnaissance Squadron"; *Newark Evening News* clipping, n.d., NGMMNJ Archives.

6. Russen, "Combat History of the 102nd Cavalry Reconnaissance Squadron."

7. Jacobs, "In the Dash to Paris."

8. *Ibid.*

9. *Ibid.*

10. *Newark Evening News*, November 3, 1943, November 16, 1943, March 3, 1944.

11. Pringle, *Tally Ho!*, 3-10.

12. *Combat History, Forty-fourth Infantry Division, 1944-1945.* (no page numbers in book)

13. Haworth, ed., "Air National Guard Oral History of Donald Strait," 2012.

14. Ziobro, "The Navesink Military Reservation."

15. For the complete history of U-Boat attacks on the New Jersey coast, see Bilby & Ziegler, *Submarine Warfare on the New Jersey Shore.*

16. *New York Times*, February 28, 1942.

17. *Wilkes-Barre [PA] Record*, March 4, 1942; Homer H. Hickam Jr., *Torpedo Junction*, 60.

18. Russell and Youmans, *Down the Jersey Shore*, 192-193.

19. New Jersey Governor's War Cabinet Notes, June 2, 1942.

20. New Jersey Governor's War Cabinet Notes, April 28, May 4, 1942.

21. G. Kurt Piehler, "Depression and War," in Lurie and Veit, *New Jersey, a History*, 256-257.

22. *Bristol [PA] Daily Courrier*, November 27, 1942; Lurie and Mappen, *Encyclopedia of New Jersey*, 792; http://web.archive.org/web/2010032605 2243/http://home.att.net/~1.elliott/par atrooperdummyhistorysite.html.

23. Elizabeth Hawes, in Green, *Words That Make New Jersey History.*

24. G. Kurt Piehler, "Depression and War," in Lurie and Veit, *New Jersey, a History*, 254.

25. *New York Times*, April 29, 1944.

26. Helen C. Pike, *Asbury Park's Glory Days*, p. 126; Federal Writers' Project, *New Jersey: A Guide to its Present and Past*, 682.

27. *New York Times*, June 1, 1943.

28. *New York Times,* April 12, 1944.
29. *New York Times,* June 1, 1943.
30. G. Kurt Piehler, "Depression and War," in Lurie and Veit, *New Jersey, a History,* 254-255; Lurie and Mappen, *Encyclopedia of New Jersey,* 786, 348.
31. Summary of Margaret Jennings-Manzi's oral history interview. http://www.nj.gov/military/museum/summaries/wwii/Manzi.html. The NG-MMNJ Oral History site holds over 100 summaries of oral history stories, from World War II through Korea and Vietnam to current operations.
32. *New York Times,* June 1, 1942.
33. *Ibid.*
34. Family interviews, various dates; interview with Al Meserlin, 2005; narrative of William Gill, courtesy Daniel Moore.
35. Kurzman, *No Greater Glory,* 119-120, 137-145.
36. *Ibid.,* 173-174.
37. *Newark Evening News,* June 6, 1949.
38. Summary of James Kane's oral history interview: http://www.nj.gov/military/museum/summaries/wwii/kane.html.

CHAPTER ELEVEN: NEW JERSEY'S MILITARY HISTORY AFTER WORLD WAR II

1. *50th Armored Division, 1946-1956.*
2. Undated newspaper clipping and photo in NGMMNJ Archives.
3. Interview with William Paynton, April 12, 2016.
4. *Asbury Park Press,* May 21, 1950.
5. *New York Times,* February 5 and 9, 1948; Luzky, "History, 1st Battalion."
6. http://www.trumanlibrary.org/9981.htm.
7. "Desegregation of the Armed Forces," Harry S. Truman Library,

http://www.trumanlibrary.org/whistlestop/study_collections/desegregation/large/index.php?action=chronology; Luzky, "History, 1st Battalion."
8. NJDMAVA Factsheet, http://www.nj.gov/military/korea/factsheets.pdf.
9. *Ibid.*
10. *Ibid.*
11. *Shamokin* (PA) *News-Dispatch,* June 25, 1953.
12. NJNG Information office release, January 29, 1957; unidentified newspaper clipping, NGMMNJ collection; unidentified newspaper (Probably the *Star Ledger*) obituary dated August 28, 2000, courtesy Dan Moore.
13. *National Guardsman,* August 1970.
14. *Asbury Park Press,* May 28, 1958.
15. *Ibid.*
16. *Asbury Park Press,* January 16, 1961.
17. *Ibid.*
18. *New York Times,* January 2, 1957.
19. http://www.nj.gov/military/museum/summaries/cold_war/kuczmarski.html.
20. Interview with Robert Hopkins, April 23, 2016; *New York Times,* August 20, 1988.
21. *New York Daily News,* February 23, 1967; *Newark News,* February 24, 1967.
22. *New York Times,* November 8, 1998.
23. *Asbury Park Press,* May 22, 1973.
24. *Hackensack Record,* July 12, 1977.
25. Operational Report, Newark, N.J., Period 14 through 17 July 1967, NGMMNJ Archives.
26. *Ibid; Hackensack Record,* July 12, 1977.
27. Operational Report, Newark, N.J., Period 14 through 17 July 1967; http://blog.nj.com/ledgernewark/2007/

07/crossroads_part_1.html; Wittner,
"The killing of Billy Furr . . ."

28. Newton *New Jersey Herald,* July
11, 1977; Interview with Daniel Moore,
May 23, 2016.

29. http://www.njspotlight.com/sto-
ries/15/05/20/vietnam-veteran-deaths/;
*Desert Storm/Shield: Footprints in the
Sand,* 33, 45, 53, 77, 117, 145.

30. Ibid.

31. Interview with William Paynton,
April 12, 2016.

32. Schofield, "The New Jersey Army
and Air National Guard."

33. *Ibid.* The Naval Militia was ordered to stand down by the NJ adjutant
general in 2002.

34. *Ibid.*

35. *Ibid.*

36. *Ibid;* Interview with Captain
Amelia Thatcher, May 3, 2016.

37. Interview with Jarrett Feldman,
April 23, 2016.

38. NJNG, *Operation Iraqi Freedom.*

39. Oral history summary, Pratik Mavani, NJNGMM, http://www.nj.gov/
military/museum/summaries/opera-
tion-iraqi-freedom/pratik-mavani/.

40. *Ibid.*

41. Interviews with Jarrett Feldman
and John Bilby, April 23, 2016.

42. Interview with Captain Vincent
Solomeno, July 15, 2016.

# Further Reading

New Jersey: Overview and Regional

Barber, John Warner and Henry Howe, *Historical Collections of the State of New Jersey*. New Haven, CT: John Barber, 1868.

Bartholf, Howard E. *Images of America: Camp Merritt*. Charleston, SC: Arcadia Publishing, 2017.

Bilby, Joseph G. *Sea Girt: A Brief History*. Charleston, SC: History Press, 2008.

_____, and Harry Ziegler. *Asbury Park: A Brief History*. Charleston, SC: History Press, 2009.

_____, James M. Madden and Harry Ziegler. *Hidden History of New Jersey*. Charleston, SC: The History Press, 2011.

Boyd, Paul D. *Atlantic Highlands: From Lenape Camps to Bayside Town (NJ)* Charleston, SC: Arcadia, 2004.

Buchholz, Margaret Thomas. *New Jersey Shipwrecks: 350 Years in the Graveyard of the Atlantic*. Harvey Cedars, NJ: Down the Shore Publishing, 2004.

Cunningham, John T. *Made in New Jersey: The Industrial Story of a State*. New Brunswick: Rutgers University Press, 1954.

_____. *New Jersey: America's Main Road*. Garden City, NY: Doubleday, 1966.

Dowd, Gregory E. *The Indians of New Jersey*. Trenton, NJ: NJ Historical Commission, 1992.

Ellis, Franklin. *History of Monmouth County*. Philadelphia: J.B. Lippincott, 1886.

Federal Writers' Project. *Stories of New Jersey: Its Significant Places, People and Activities*. New York: M. Barrows and Company, 1938.

Federal Writers' Project. *New Jersey: A Guide to its Present and Past*. New York: Viking Press, 1939.

Fleming, Thomas. *New Jersey: A Bicentennial History*. New York, W. W. Norton, 1977.

Gabrielan, Randy. *Hoboken, History and Architecture at a Glance*. Atglen PA: Schiffer Publishing, 2010.

Hodges, Graham Russell. *Slavery and Freedom in the Rural North: African-Americans in Monmouth County, New Jersey, 1665-1865*. Madison, WI: Madison House, 1997.

Hodges, Graham Russell. *Root and Branch: African Americans in New York and East Jersey, 1613-1863*. Chapel Hill: UNC Press, 1999.

Irwin, Richard T., ed. *A History of Randolph Township: Morris County's First Bicentennial Community*. Randolph, NJ: Randolph Township Landmarks Commission, 2002.

Johnson, Ray Neil. *Heaven, Hell or Hoboken*. Cleveland OH: O. S. Hubbell Printing, 1919.

Karnoutsos, Carmela Ascolese. *New Jersey Women: A History of Their Status, Roles and Images*. Trenton: New Jersey Historical Commission, 1997.

Kull, Irving S. *New Jersey: A History* (4 vols.). New York: American Historical Society, 1930.

Lane, Wheaton J. *From Indian Trail to Iron Horse: Travel and Transportation in New Jersey, 1620-1860*. Princeton: Princeton University Press, 1939.

Lender, Mark Edward. *One State in Arms: A Short Military History of New Jersey*. Trenton: New Jersey Historical Commission, 1991.

Lovero, Joan Doherty. *Hudson County—The Left Bank*. Staunton, VA: American History Press, 1999.

Lurie, Maxine and Marc Mappen, eds. *Encyclopedia of New Jersey*. New Brunswick: Rutgers University Press, 2004.

Lurie, Maxine and Richard Veit, eds. *New Jersey: A History of the Garden State*. New Brunswick: Rutgers University Press, 2012.

Luzky, Colonel (ret.) Len. *The Adjutants General of New Jersey, 1776 to 2002*. Trenton: NJ Department of Military and Veterans Affairs, 2003.

Manasquan, NJ Chamber of Commerce. *Manasquan*. Lewiston, ME: Geiger Brothers, 1962.

Mappen, Mark. *Jerseyana: The Underside of New Jersey History*. New Brunswick: Rutgers University Press, 1992.

Moss, George H. *Monmouth—Our Indian Heritage*. Freehold, NJ: Monmouth County Board of Chosen Freeholders, 1974.

Prowell, George R. *The History of Camden County, New Jersey*. Philadelphia: R. J. Richards & Co., 1886.

Salter, Edwin. *A History of Monmouth and Ocean Counties*. Bayonne, NJ: E. Gardner & Sons, 1890.

Veit, Richard. *Digging New Jersey's Past: Historical Archeology in the Garden State*. New Brunswick: Rutgers University Press, 2002.

## COLONIAL PERIOD TO 1800

Adelberg, Michael S. *The American Revolution in Monmouth County: The Theatre of Spoil and Destruction*. Charleston, SC: History Press, 2010.

_____. *The Razing of Tinton Falls: Voices from the American Revolution*. Charleston, SC: History Press, 2012.

Alden, John Richard. *General Charles Lee: Traitor or Patriot?* Baton Rouge: LSU Press, 1951.

Beekman, George C. *Early Dutch Settlers of Monmouth County, New Jersey.* Freehold, NJ: Moreau Brothers, second edition, 1915.

Bilby, Joseph G. and Katherine Bilby Jenkins. *Monmouth Court House: The Battle that Made the American Army.* Yardley, PA: Westholme Publishing, 2010.

Bill, Alfred Hoyt. *New Jersey and the Revolutionary War.* Princeton, NJ: D. Van Nostrand, 1964.

Braisted, Todd W. *Bergen County Voices from the American Revolution: Soldiers and Residents in Their Own Words.* Charleston, SC: History Press, 2012.

_____. *Grand Forage 1778: The Battleground around New York City.* Yardley, PA: Westholme, 2016.

Casterline, Greg. *Colonial Tribulations: The Survival Story of William Casterline and His Comrades of the New Jersey Blues Regiment, French and Indian War, 1755-1757.* Author: 2007.

Cunningham, John T. *The Uncertain Revolution: Washington and the Continental Army at Morristown.* West Creek, NJ: Down the Shore Publishing, 2007.

Dearborn, Henry. *Journals of Henry Dearborn, 1776-1783, Reprinted from the Journals of the Massachusetts Historical Society, 1886.* Cambridge, MA: John Wilson and Son University Press, 1887.

Denny, Ebenezer. *Military Journal of Major Ebenezer Denny, an Officer in the Revolutionary and Indian Wars.* Philadelphia: Historical Society of Pennsylvania, 1859.

Di Ionno, Mark. *A Guide to New Jersey's Revolutionary War Trail for Families and History Buffs.* New Brunswick: Rutgers University Press, 2000.

Fabend, Firth Haring. *New Netherland in a Nutshell: A Concise History of the Dutch Colony in North America.* Albany, NY: New Netherland Institute, 2012.

Fischer, David Hackett. *Washington's Crossing.* New York: Oxford University Press, 2004.

Fleming, Thomas. *Forgotten Victory: The Battle for New Jersey, 1780.* Pleasantville, NY: Reader's Digest Press, 1973.

Gerlach, Larry R., ed. *New Jersey in the American Revolution: A Documentary History.* Trenton: New Jersey Historical Commission, 1975.

Given, Brian. *A Most Pernicious Thing: Gun Trading and Native Culture in the Early Contact Period.* Ottawa, Canada: Carleton University Press, 1994.

Jacobs, Jaap. *The Colony of New Netherland: A Dutch Settlement in Seventeenth Century America.* Ithaca, NY: Cornell University Press, 2009.

Karels, Carol. *The Revolutionary War in Bergen County: The Times that Tried Men's Souls.* Charleston, SC: History Press, 2007.

Kidder, Larry. *A People Harassed and Exhausted: The Story of a New Jersey Militia Regiment in the American Revolution.* Hopewell, NJ: Author, 2013.

Kraft, Herbert C. *Lenape-Delaware Indian Heritage, 10,000 BC to AD 2000.* Lenapebooks, 2001.

Kraft, Herbert C. and John T. Kraft. *The Indians of Lenapehoking.* South Orange, NJ: Seton Hall University Museum, 1988.

Lee, Francis Bazley. *New Jersey as a Colony and as a State, One of the Original Thirteen,* Vol. III, New York: Publishing Society of New Jersey, 1903.

_____, ed. *Documents Relating to the Revolutionary History of the State of New Jersey, Extracts from American Newspapers,* Vol. II, 1778. Trenton: John L. Murphy, 1903.

Leiby, Adrian C. *The Revolutionary War in the Hackensack Valley: The Jersey Dutch and the Neutral Ground, 1775-1783.* New Brunswick: Rutgers University Press, 1962.

Lender, Mark Edward. *The New Jersey Soldier.* Trenton, New Jersey Historical Commission, 1975.

Lender, Mark Edward and James Kirby Martin, eds. *Citizen Soldier: The Revolutionary War Journal of Joseph Bloomfield.* Newark: NJ Historical Society, 1982.

Lundin, Leonard. *Cockpit of the Revolution: The War for Independence in New Jersey.* Princeton: Princeton University Press, 1940.

*Minutes of the Council of Safety of the State of New Jersey.* Jersey City, NJ: John H. Lyon, 1872.

*Minutes of the Provincial Congress and Council of Safety of New Jersey.* Trenton: Naar, Day & Naar, 1879.

Mitnick, Barbara, ed. *New Jersey in the American Revolution.* New Brunswick: Rivergate Press, 2005.

Morrissey, Brendan. *Monmouth Courthouse 1778: The Last Great Battle in the North.* Cambridge, UK: Osprey Publishing, 2004.

Pingeon, Francis D. *Blacks in the Revolutionary Era.* Trenton: NJ Historical Commission, 1975.

Pomfret, John E. *The Province of East Jersey, 1609-1702.* Princeton: Princeton University Press, 1962.

_____. *Colonial New Jersey: A History.* New York: Charles Scribner's Sons, 1973.

Silverman, David J. *Thunderstics: Firearms and the Violent Transformation of Native America.* Cambridge, MA: Harvard University Press, 2016.

Tantillo, L. F., Charles T. Gehring and Peter A. Douglas. *The Edge of New Netherland.* Albany, NY: New Netherland Institute, 2011.

Van Der Donck, Adrian. *The Representation of New Netherland Concerning Its Location, Productiveness and Poor Condition, Presented to the States General of the United Netherlands, and Printed at the Hague, in 1650. (Classic Reprint)* Mineola, NY: Forgotten Books, 2015.

Walling, Richard. *Men of Color at the Battle of Monmouth June 28, 1778.* Hightstown, NJ: Longstreet House, 1994.

Ward, Harry M. *General William Maxwell and the New Jersey Continentals.* Westport, CT: Greenwood Press, 1997.

Weiss, Harry B. and Grace M. Weiss. *The Revolutionary Saltworks of the New Jersey Coast.* Trenton: Past Times Press, 1959.

## WAR OF 1812

Chartrand, Rene. *A Most Warlike Appearance: Uniforms, Flags and Equipment of the United States Forces in the War of 1812*, Ottawa, Canada: Service Publications,

Gardiner, Robert. *The Naval War of 1812*. Annapolis, MD: Naval Institute Press, 1998.

Guernsey, R. S. *New York City and Vicinity During the War of 1812, Being a Military, Civic and Financial Local History of that Period . . .* New York: Charles L. Woodward, 1889.

State of New Jersey. *Record of Officers and Men of New Jersey in Wars 1791-1815.* Trenton: State Gazette Publishing, 1909.

## U.S.-MEXICAN WAR

Bauer, K. Jack. *The Mexican War, 1846-1848* (New York: Macmillan, 1974).

Faulk, Odie B. and Joseph A. Stout, Jr. *The Mexican War: Changing Interpretations*. Chicago: Swallow Press, 1973.

State of New Jersey. *Record of Officers and Enlisted Men of New Jersey in the War with Mexico, 1846-1848*. Trenton, n.d.

## AMERICAN CIVIL WAR

Baquet, Camille. *History of the First Brigade, New Jersey Volunteers, from 1861 to 1865*. Trenton: MacCrellish & Quigley, 1910.

Bellard, Alfred. (David Herbert Donald, ed.) *Gone for a Soldier: The Civil War Memoirs of Private Alfred Bellard*. Boston: Little, Brown & Company, 1975.

Bilby, Joseph G. *Three Rousing Cheers: A History of the Fifteenth New Jersey from Flemington to Appomattox*. Hightstown, NJ: Longstreet House. 1993.

_____, ed. *New Jersey Goes to War: Biographies of 150 New Jerseyans Caught up in the Struggle of the Civil War, including Soldiers, Civilians, Men, Women, Heroes, Scoundrels—and a Heroic Horse*. Hightstown, NJ: Longstreet House, 2010.

_____. *"Freedom to All:" New Jersey's African-American Civil War Soldiers*. Hightstown, NJ: Longstreet House, 2011.

_____. and William C. Goble. *Remember You are Jerseymen! A Military History of New Jersey Troops in the Civil War*. Hightstown, NJ; Longstreet House, 1998.

Eckhardt, Charles and Robert MacAvoy. *Our Brothers Gone Before: An Inventory of Graves and Cenotaphs in New Jersey Cemeteries for Union and Confederate Civil War Soldiers, Sailors, Marines, Surgeons and Nurses*. Hightstown, NJ: Longstreet House, 2008.

Foster, John Y. *New Jersey and the Rebellion: History of the Services of the Troops and People of New Jersey in Aid of the Union Cause*. Newark: Martin R. Dennis & Company, 1868.

Gigantino, James J. *The Ragged Road to Abolition: Slavery and Freedom in New Jersey, 1775-1865*. Philadelphia: University of Pennsylvania Press, 2015.

Gillette, William. *Jersey Blue: Civil War Politics in New Jersey, 1854–1865.* New Brunswick: Rutgers University Press, 1995.

Gottfried, Bradley M. *Kearny's Own: The History of the First New Jersey Brigade in the Civil War.* New BrunswickJ: Rutgers University Press, 2005.

Hanifen, Michael. *History of Battery B, First New Jersey Artillery.* Ottawa, IL, 1905. Longstreet House reprint: Hightstown, NJ, 1991.

Hayward, John. *Give It to Them Jersey Blues!: A History of the 7th Regiment, New Jersey Veteran Volunteers in the Civil War.* Longstreet House, Hightstown, NJ 1998.

Hunter, Martin. *The Journal of Gen. Sir Martin Hunter and Some Letters of His Wife Lady Hunter . . .* Edinburgh: Edinburgh Press, 1894.

Longacre, Edward. *To Gettysburg and Beyond: The Twelfth New Jersey Volunteer Infantry, II Corps, Army of the Potomac, 1862-1865.* Hightstown, NJ: Longstreet House, 1988.

_____. *Jersey Cavaliers: A History of the First New Jersey Volunteer Cavalry, 1861-1865.* Hightstown, NJ: Longstreet House, 1992.

Marbaker, Thomas B. *History of the Eleventh New Jersey Volunteers.* Trenton, NJ, 1898. Longstreet House reprint, Hightstown, NJ, 1990.

Martin, David G. *Hexamer's First New Jersey Battery in the Civil War.* Hightstown, NJ: Longstreet House, 1992.

_____. *New Jersey at Gettysburg Guidebook.* Hightstown, NJ: Longstreet House, 2012.

Mitros, David. *Gone to Wear the Victor's Crown: Morris County, New Jersey and the Civil War, A Documentary Account.* Morristown: Morris County Heritage Commission, 1998.

Pyne, Henry R. *The History of the First New Jersey Cavalry.* Trenton: J. A. Beecher, 1871.

Stryker, William S. *Record of Officers and Men of New Jersey in the Civil War, 1861-1865.* (2 vols.) Trenton: John L. Murphy, 1876.

Toombs, Samuel. *Reminiscences of the War, Comprising a Detailed Account of the Experiences of the Thirteenth Regiment New Jersey Volunteers in Camp, on the March and in Battle.* Orange, NJ: Evening Hall Publishing House, 1878.

_____. *New Jersey Troops in the Gettysburg Campaign from June 5 to July 31, 1863.* Orange, NJ: Evening Hall Publishing House, 1888.

## SPANISH-AMERICAN WAR

Harris, Harry Lawrence and John Hilton, *A History of the Second Regiment, N.J.N.G. Second N.J. Volunteers, Spanish War, Fifth New Jersey Infantry.* Paterson, NJ: Call Printing and Publishing Co., 1905.

## WORLD WAR I

Connors, Richard J. *New Jersey and the Great War, 1914-1919.* Pittsburgh, PA: Dorrance Publishing, 2017.

Cutchins, John A. *History of the 29th Division, "Blue and Gray: 1917-1919.* Philadelphia: 29th Division Committee, 1919.
Essex Troop. *History of the Essex Troop, 1890-1925.* Newark, NJ: Essex Troop, 1926.
Gabrielan, Randy. *Explosion at Morgan: The World War I Middlesex Munitions Disaster.* Charleston, SC: History Press, 2012.
Reddan, William J. *Other Men's Lives.* Privately Printed 1934. Reprint: Yardley, PA: Westholme Publishing, 2017.
United States Navy. *German Submarine Activities on the Atlantic Coast and Canada.* Washington, DC: US Navy, 1920.
Witcover, Jules. *Sabotage at Black Tom: Imperial Germany's Secret War in America, 1914-1917.* Chapel Hill, NC: Algonquin Press of Chapel Hill, 1989.

## World War II

Bilby, Joseph G. and Harry Ziegler, *Submarine Warfare on the New Jersey Shore.* Charleston, SC: History Press, 2016.
Bishop, David H., et al. *Combat History: 44th Infantry Division, 1944-1945.* N.P. 1945.
Hickam, Homer H. Jr. *Torpedo Junction: U-Boat War off America's East Coast, 1942.* Annapolis, MD: Naval Institute Press, 1989.
Kurzman, Dan. *No Greater Glory: The Four Immortal Chaplains and the Sinking of the Dorchester in World War II.* New York: Random House, 2004.
Pringle, William B. *Tally Ho! A Record of the 695th Armored Field Artillery Battalion in Europe During the Course of World War II.* Lawrenceville, NJ: Author, n.d.
Rejan, Wendy, et al. *A History of Army Communications and Electronics at Fort Monmouth, New Jersey, 1917-2007.* Washington, DC: US Government Printing Office, 2008.
State of New Jersey. *Historical and Pictorial Review: National Guard of the State of New Jersey, 1940.* Baton Rouge, LA: Army and Navy Publishing Company, 1940.

## The Cold War, Korean War, and Vietnam War

Malz, Leora, ed. *The Cold War Period, 1945-1992.* New York: Greenhaven Press, 1993.
New Jersey National Guard. *50th Armored Division, 1946-1956: A Decade of Service.* Trenton: State of New Jersey, 1957.

## Recent Wars

New Jersey National Guard. *50th Infantry Brigade Combat Team, "Jersey Blues," Operation Iraqi Freedom, June 2008-June 2009.* Trenton: State of New Jersey, 2011.

# Acknowledgments

Any work like this necessarily requires considerable assistance, and I am happy to acknowledge the contributions of Adam Azzalino, John Beekman, John Bilby, Todd Braisted, Margaret Thomas Buchholz, Peter Culos, Ronald DaSilva, Jarrett Feldman, Carol Fowler, George Franks III, Susan Kaufmann, Duncan MacQueen, James Madden, Kevin Marshall, Dan Moore, Brian Murphy, Bill Paynton, Robert Perricelli, Janet Strom, Amelia Thatcher, Jason Wickersty and Harry Ziegler. Without that assistance, and in some cases inspiration, this book would not have been possible. If I have forgotten anyone, please forgive me, and, of course, any errors are my own.

# Index

# About the Author

Joseph G. Bilby is Assistant Curator of the National Guard Militia Museum of New Jersey. A graduate of Seton Hall University, he served as a lieutenant in the 1st Infantry Division in Vietnam. He is the author of a number of books including *New Jersey Goes to War* and *A Revolution in Arms: A History of the First Repeating Rifles*. He has received the Jane Clayton Award for contributions to Monmouth County (NJ) history and an Award of Merit from the New Jersey Historical Commission for his contributions to the state's military history.